The Rise of Big Business in India

The Rise of Big Business in India

The Rise of Big Business in India

Kamal Aron Mitra Chenoy

THE RISE OF BIG BUSINESS IN INDIA
Kamal Aron Mitra Chenoy

First Published 2015

ISBN 978-93-5002-324-2 (Pb)

Published by
AAKAR BOOKS
28 E Pocket IV, Mayur Vihar Phase I, Delhi 110 091
Phone : 011 2279 5505 Telefax : 011 2279 5641
aakarbooks@gmail.com; www.aakarbooks.com

Printed at
Sapra Brothers, Delhi 110 092

Contents

List of Tables

Chapter 8

Acknowledgements

I owe many people a debt for the finalisation of this book. Professor Rasheeduddin Khan guided this work with great patience, and ensured that it was not too filled with endnotes and data. I cannot forget how much I owe him. Professor C.P. Bhambhri who strongly suggested that I take up these issues. Professor S.K. Goyal who is remarkably well-informed on various aspects of economic policy, particularly industrial policy, taught me how to analyse policy statements, demands from industrial lobbies and the impact of all this on the economic regime. A lot of what has gone into this book I owe to Professor Goyal. I would also like to thank my erstwhile colleagues in the Institute for Studies in Industrial Development (ISID), especially K.S. Chalapati Rao, K.V.K. Ranganathan and founding members Nagesh Kumar and Anil Nauriya, with all of whom I had the good fortune to have detailed discussions. I owe a great debt to my friends whose insights helped me articulate the central arguments. These include Rajeev and Tani Bhargava, Mushirul and Zoya Hasan, Aijaz Ahmed, Utsa and Prabhat Patnaik, Jayati Ghosh and Abhijit Sen, C.P. Chandrashekhar, Pamela Philipose and Achin Vanaik, Praful Bidwai, Arati and Ajoy, Ritoo and Anjali, Mohan Rao, Muchkund Dubey, Manoranjan Mohanty, B.S. Chimni, Seema Mustafa, Prabir Purkayastha, Deepak Nayyar and S.P. Shukla, Aruna Roy, Nikhil De, Medha Patkar, Reetika Khera and Jean Dreze. I am also indebted to friends in the Aam Admi Party like Prashant Bhushan, Yogendra Yadav, Sundeep Narwani, Lalita and Ramu Ramdas, Aloke Aggarwal and Sylvy, and old friend and stalwart Professor Anand Kumar. Nivedita Menon, Aditya Nigam and Rajan Kumar have been consistent in their support. Nivedita cheerfully took over administrative responsibilities during stages in the drafting of this book. Special thanks to Khush-Hal Lagdhyan who prepared drafts of the book, and generally contributed to this effort. I am grateful to my office staff, especially Gurpreet Singh, who provided indispensable support.

Unfortunately a number of my mentors like H.K. Paranjape, who was closely involved with official enquiries into economic, especially industrial policy, died before he could see this book I had promised. Similarly, I am grateful to Mohit Sen, who suggested that this was a necessary area for research. I remember our debates on Indian and foreign issues, on which our disagreements were sorted out at great length. Unfortunately, he too has passed away.

I am of course indebted to my family. Anu kept the pressure on for me to finish this book and helped in innumerable ways. Ayesha, Ishaan, Archit and little Aari were a great support always. I hope if they read this book they will think it was worth it.

I have always had great affection and support from the JNU student community. One student leader who I was especially close to, Chandrashekhar Prasad, former president of the JNU Students' Union, took up the challenge of raising people's consciousness in Siwan, Bihar where he was later gunned down, in broad daylight.

Given the challenge that big business gives to pro-people policies and self-reliant development, I hope that this book will provide some clarity of explanation and possible alternatives.

Introduction

The devolution of authority to the representatives of the Indian National Congress (INC) by the withdrawing British power as envisaged in the Indian Independence Act, 1947, passed by the British Parliament transformed one of the biggest national movements for independence into a legitimised power-structure. Congress, the major forum for mobilising the people of India for national independence, suddenly found itself in the position of a government called upon to run a continental polity.

At the time of the transfer of power, the country was faced with various challenges. On the one hand the partition of India, the widespread communal riots, the massive migration of population and the consequent problems of settlement of refugees, had to be dealt with speed and firmness; and on the other, in addition to the post-World War II programmes of reconstruction, the political leadership had to take immediate steps for deciding on the nature, form and character of state intervention in the economy of independent India. Mere reaffirmation of the objectives of ending "poverty, and ignorance, disease and inequality of opportunity" was not sufficient[1]; the government was required to announce specific policy measures and programmes in order to fulfil the hopes and aspirations aroused among the masses during the freedom struggle. The content and the thrust of the new policies had to be such as would correct the distortions in the economy that the colonial government had created in order to protect and promote British interests in India. The Congress Party and its leadership had been actively engaged in discussions on the need to adopt a number of socio-economic policies. There were alternative policy frameworks which were under debate during the immediate preceding years, i.e. from 1944 to 1947. Thereafter the government announced a number of economic policies. In the area of industrial policy, the Industrial Policy Statement was placed before the Constituent Assembly (Legislative) on 6 April 1948. The Statement also announced the setting up of the Planning Commission. The approach towards foreign capital was articulated in the Statement on Foreign Investments exactly a year later, on 6 April 1949. The same day the Industries (Development and Control) Bill, 1949, was placed before the Constituent Assembly (Legislative). The sum total of the various economic policies adopted in the years immediately following independence became the basis for the determination of the precise role and character of state intervention in the economy. One of the more controversial areas of public policy is the industrial policy followed after independence. As a part of the effort to locate the roots of current problems[2], this study seeks to examine the development of Indian industrial policy in the light of the interaction between the government and Indian big business represented by its apex lobbying body, the Federation of Indian Chambers of Commerce and Industry (FICCI), particularly in the period from 1947 to 1966.

The FICCI is generally considered the representative apex body of Indian big business. There are probably historical reasons for this, as also the belief that FICCI has been able to maintain very close contacts with the government and the leadership of the Congress Party.[3] The modus operandi of FICCI whereby it has acquired such influence on the party and government needs close analysis to enable us to see if and why one group of industrialists succeeded more than others.

In this study of the interaction between the business and political leadership in India and the resulting effect on the formulation and implementation of Indian industrial policy I seek to examine the party and government responses to group strategies, and to evaluate the change in business stances. I pay special attention to the statements and policies in the broad area of economic policy during the pre-independence period and to industrial policy in the years immediately following independence.

This study encompasses an examination of the developments immediately following independence which laid down the foundation for and determined the general orientation of government policies towards most of the basic issues relating to industrialisation. These include the role of the state; the reservation of particular areas of industrial activity for specified sectors; the state, private, small-scale cooperative and cottage industries sectors; the scope and content of the planning of industrial activities, including the fixing of priorities; the licensing of industrial units; and the broad regulation of foreign investment and collaboration. The 1948 Statement of Industrial Policy, the 1949 Statement on Foreign Investment, and the 1956 Industrial Policy Resolution were a consequence of these developments.

Major changes, modifications and developments in these policies, particularly relating to industry are scrutinised within the background of the Congress Party's resolutions as well as the positions taken by FICCI. I discern if there was a particular pattern in these developments, either on the part of the Congress, or the government or FICCI. The lobbying techniques employed by FICCI both formal and informal, direct and indirect lobbying are focused on. The efficacy of business strategies and lobbying techniques are measured in terms of developments in the formulation and implementation of the industrial policy in India. Changes in the direction of industrial policy as lobbied for FICCI will be taken as indices of the success of the particular strategy and of the lobbying effort.

An examination of the interface between the Congress Party leadership and its government on the one side and FICCI on the other may provide some explanation for the changes in attitudes on both sides. It will then be possible to locate and assign relative weights to various factors responsible for the modification in policy and the changes in attitudes and overall approaches.

On the basis of these analyses, certain evaluations of the character of the Congress Party and Indian big business become clear. Some controversial questions relating to the purported pro-business or anti-business nature of Congress policy are therefore examined. Similarly, assessments of the character of Indian big business and FICCI are evaluated.

As a result of the study, therefore, some major aspects and dimensions of the path of industrialisation followed in India from 1947 to 1966 can be classified. This in turn may be of utility in an overall assessment of the political and economic forces that shaped the destiny of free India.

This book is about the process of interaction between Indian big business and the government during the period, 1947 to 1966. It argues:

First, while FICCI was organised to promote and protect the interests of trade and industry in general, in its actual working it has become the representative body of Indian big business; and it has consistently sought to promote and defend the interests of Indian big business and not that of the industry or trade at large.

Second, the main reasons for FICCI's influence with the Congress government were: (a) the ties that the FICCI leadership had been able to establish with the Congress leadership of the nationalist movement in the pre-independence period; and (b) FICCI's general policy of seeking to avoid confrontations with the Congress by working with and within the ruling party as far as possible.

Third, FICCI's relationships with the Congress government's leadership enabled this constituent of the Indian big business to influence the formulation and implementation of industrial policy.

Fourth, in the 1947 to 1966 period there were significant modifications of government industrial policy to the advantage of Indian big business.

Fifth, the processes of interaction between FICCI and the government contributed to the dilution over time of those elements of industrial policy which restricted the growth of Indian big business.

Primary Sources

This work is based on government and the business chambers records, as well as those of some political parties. Private papers of the influential FICCI leader Purshotamdas Thakurdas available in the Nehru Memorial Museum Library have been used. A number of government-appointed committee reports, including some unpublished studies dealing with pertinent areas, have been referred to.

The printed FICCI material includes three volumes of documents printed every year. Volume I is the "Report of the Proceedings of the Executive Committee for the Year", which contains a summary report of the proceeding of the Executive Committee and its meetings with representatives of government. The more important Volume II which is the "Correspondence and Relevant Documents Relating to Important Questions Dealt with by the Federation during the Year", reproduces all FICCI circulars to its constituents, and records all FICCI-government correspondence including some confidential communications, and also includes FICCI memoranda and published studies for the year. This volume also contains reports of meetings between FICCI representatives and government, as well as reports of the discussions in various advisory committees, e.g. the Central Advisory Council of Industries; which are usually prepared by FICCI representatives present. This volume is of special importance for a study such as ours, since it provides extensive documentation of the government-business relationship. I have substantially relied on data provided in this volume.[4] The annual FICCI Volume III is the "Proceedings of the Annual Session". From 1958, the verbatim report of the proceedings was replaced by a summary report prepared by the FICCI Secretariat. Since FICCI Annual Sessions were generally inaugurated by the Prime Minister, and many of the Central Ministers and important government functionaries also attended, the speeches made at the Sessions had important policy implications.

I have extensively used all three annual volumes of FICCI, particularly Volumes II and III, for the entire period under study, i.e. from 1927 to 1966. Most of the other FICCI publications and memoranda, e.g. on the Five Year Plans, are reproduced in Volume II for the year, and have been cited from there.

Limitations

Industrial policy, taken in a broad sense, encompasses a large number of separate policies for the regulation and development and promotion of the industrial sector. I have however focussed attention on the overall industrial policy framework, i.e. on the broad industrial policy statements and resolutions[5] as well as the changes over time in this framework as revealed by modifications in industrial licensing policy. In order not to spread the enquiry too thinly I have not attempted to analyse all aspects of industrial policy but concentrated more rigorously on 'given' aspects. Therefore, despite being conscious of the interlinked aspects of the totality of the industrial policy, I have deliberately avoided extensive discussion on issues like import and export policies, capital issues control, taxation and budgetary policies, policies regarding foreign capital, and the policies regulating government purchases from the private sector. An examination of these policies was not necessary for my purposes to arrive at overall assessment of the general direction of industrial policy in relation to Indian big business.

Similarly, I do not examine the effects of the external environment and foreign inputs on the developments in industrial policy, because this clearly constitutes a different dimension, regarding intensive enquiry as a significant 'microcosm' of the industrialisation process. The role of international financial institutions like the World Bank and International Monetary Fund (IMF), or of the governments of creditor nations is not therefore, dealt with. Consequently, the role of foreign private capital and of its apex body in India, ASSOCHAM, has not been analysed in any detail. Although the World Bank, for example was believed to have played a decisive part in the devaluation of the rupee in May-June 1966, and to have influenced post-1966 changes in industrial policy, I have deliberately restricted my focus to domestic factors.

Moreover, this study is limited to an examination of the role and relationships with government of only one apex body of Indian business, FICCI. This analysis seeks to bring out the divergences between the officially stated industrial policy objectives and the actual trends in the industrial sector. The policy shifts made by the government are scrutinised in the context of big business demands as enunciated by FICCI. The period of this study encompasses the long formative Nehru period, and the short interregnum of Prime Ministership of Lal Bahadur Shastri from 1947-1966. These years witnessed the formulation as well as the development of the basic framework of the industrial policy of free India. The following years were apparently marked by the accentuation of already existing trends in industrial development, established in this earlier period. It appears to me, therefore, that the period 1947-1966 provides sufficient evidence of the nature of linkages between Indian big business and government, together with the actual degree of influence enjoyed by the large private corporate sector in the formulation and implementation of industrial policy. These relationships determined, at least in some measure, the foundations and characteristic features of Indian industrial development in later years.

REFERENCES

1. Jawaharlal Nehru in his now famous "A Tryst with Destiny" speech delivered in the Constituent Assembly on 14 August 1947 had considered this a part of the service to the suffering millions to which the members of the Assembly (as well as the rest of the political leadership) should be, and were pledged of. Independence and After, *Speeches of Jawaharlal Nehru, (1946-1949)*, (Delhi: Director, Publications Division, 1949), pp. 3-4.
2. For instance, Bhagwati and Desai, in their study have sought to locate the causes of India's current economic problems, by an analysis of the policies of industrialisation followed in India after 1951. They however have not examined the role of pressure groups in influencing these policies. There is only one reference to FICCI and to ASSOCHAM in their book. Bhagwati, Jagdish N. and Padma Desai, *India: Planning for Industrialization and Trade Policies Since 1951* (London: Oxford University Press), pp. 1-9, 29.

3. See for example, Kochanek, Stanley A. (1974), *Business and Politics in India* (Berkeley: University of California Press).
4. Since then access to this volume has been severely restricted, and these records are not generally available to researchers.
5. That is the 6th April 1948 Industrial Policy Statement, the 6th April 1949 Statement on Foreign Investments and the 30th April 1956 Industrial Policy Resolution.

1

FICCI: Organisation of Indian Big Business: Its Origins, Development and Role

Origins of FICCI

The first European Chamber of Commerce was established at Calcutta in 1834; and this was followed by similar chambers being established at Bombay and Madras in 1836 (Buchanan, 1966: 174-175; Desai, 1976: 200). These chambers came into existence only after the Charter Act of 1833 had thrown overseas trade open to private trade (Bagchi, 1975: 170-171). These chambers were, as Amiya Bagchi has noted, efficient means for promoting the unity of European business interests on the one hand and of eliminating native competition, on the other (Bagchi, 1975: 170-171). The establishment of European chambers also reflected the high level of British control over the development of Indian trade and industry. In India British capital was primarily operating through a few of the managing agency houses. Thus while there were a fairly large number of European companies which were members of the European chambers of commerce; operationally, these were dominated by a handful of the large managing agency houses (Kochanek, 1974: 109).

In took more than five decades before the conflict of interests between the European and Indian commercial classes led to the establishment of the first native chamber: the Bengal National Chamber of Commerce which was organised in Calcutta in 1887. The Marwaris Chamber of Commerce was started in Calcutta only in 1900; but due to the fact that even at that stage the Marwaris and not the Bengalis, were the dominant native commercial force in Calcutta, the Marwari Chamber came to enjoy more influence than the BNCC in a short period (Kochanek, 1974: 133). The Indian Merchants Chamber and the South Indian Chamber of Commerce were founded in Bombay and Madras in 1907 and 1909, respectively (Desai, 1976: 200). The pattern of these Indian trade and industrial associations followed that of the earlier British associations. Because of the predominant economic role of the managing agencies which played such a prominent part in both trade and industry, these associations took a form unique only to India. The chambers and associations combined both commercial and industrial interests, a pattern which like the managing agency houses, is distinctive to India (FICCI, 1951: 2). These chambers, particularly, the British controlled ones, also performed an important political role. They sent representatives to the provincial legislative councils and to the Central Council of State (Buchanan, 1966: 172-175). Inevitably the clash of economic interests had political repercussions.

Many of the early Indian nationalist leaders who reacted to the colonial economic policies in India were those who themselves happened to be in trade and industry. Dadabhai Naoroji in 1869 had started Dadabhai Naroji & Co., M.G. Ranade played an important part in the setting up of a number of business concerns in Poona. Similarly K.T. Telang, Pherozeshah Mehta, D.E. Wacha, R.N. Mudholkar, Pandit Madan Mohan Malaviya, A.M. Bose, Durga Mohan Das and Bhoobun Mohan Das were actively engaged in setting up enterprises in the 1870's and the 1880s (Chandra, 1965: 85-86). Even Bal Gangadhar Tilak ventured into the industrial field for a short while when in 1891 he opened, in partnership with friends, a cotton-ginning factory at Latur (Chandra, 1965: 85). Hence many of these leaders had intimate connections with the emerging native chambers.

Surendranath Banerjee, A.M .Bose and Narendra Nath Sen became honorary members of the Bengal National Chamber of Commerce, from its inception in 1887 (Chandra, 1965: 86). Ranade, G.V. Joshi, M.B. Namjoshi and others played a notable role in organising Industrial Conferences from 1890 onwards (Chandra, 1965: 87-88). As a result of such efforts, an Industrial

Exhibition was held in Calcutta in 1901 as an annexe to the Congress session (Chandra, 1965: 87-88). According to A.R. Desai this lead to the increasing influence of the bourgeois class in the national movement and the Congress, which "after 1919-1920, it increasingly dominated" (Desai, 1976: 203).

Thus the development of the Swadeshi movement had as one of its manifestations the creation of important relationships between the Indian industrial community and its political leadership.

The growth of Indian political and economic nationalism led to certain shifts in British colonial policy. An important change was the moving of the Capital from Calcutta to Delhi. Though we are unable to accept Kochanek's assertion that this signalled the "ending (of) European dominance in policy-making" (Kochanek, 1974: 116), as this dominance persisted throughout the Raj, it did make a public impact. While the Raj was seeking to accommodate the demands of the rising national movement, British business sought to defend its own dominance through a federation of chambers under its control.

In January 1905, a conference of British-dominated Chambers of Commerce in India and Ceylon was held in Calcutta. Despite the fact of the Swadeshi movement of that year, which should have lent urgency to unity efforts, the British chambers were unable to form a permanent organisation (ASSOCHAM: 15). Edwin Montague's statement of 20 August 1917, that the objective of British policy in India was the development of self-government, spurred British business to further efforts at federation. In 1920, the British dominated chambers in Cochin, Karachi, Cocanada, Upper India, Punjab, Tuticorin, Chittagong, Calcutta, Bombay and Madras federated to form the Associated Chambers of Commerce (ASSOCHAM: 16).

In the meantime, Indian business associations were also making attempts to form an all-India body. In 1915, the first Indian Commercial Congress was held in the Town Hall, Bombay. In his Presidential speech, Sir Fazulbhoy Currimbhoy stressed the need for a federated Indian chamber and later an organising committee including Currimbhoy, Munmohandas

Ramji, Dinshaw E. Wacha, Purshotamdas Thakurdas et al. was set up (FICCI, 1951: 11). Later in 1920, the Indian Industrial Conference and the Indian Commercial Congress were amalgamated to form the Indian Industrial and Commercial Congress (IICC) (FICCI, 1951: 11).

The formation of ASSOCHAM gave further impetus to attempts to form an Indian federation. At the third session of the IICC in Delhi, Lala Harikishan Lal who presided, moved a resolution appointing an organising committee including one representative of each association and chamber affiliated to the IICC, with Lal himself as president and with J.K. Mehta as Secretary, to draft a constitution which was to be considered at a special session (FICCI, 1951: 11).

In the meanwhile, G.D. Birla wrote to Purshotamdas Thakurdas, recommending that the latter take the lead in the formation of an Indian chamber. Birla warned that ASSOCHAM's,

> strong organisation will be very detrimental to Indian interests if steps are not taken immediately to organise a similar institution of the Indian... You will, perhaps, agree with me that if we do not check their activities in time, their influence with the government will increase to an extent which (the) government will find it most difficult to resist...If you take up the lead, I am sure, you will have whole-hearted support from Calcutta, and it would be a great glory to see merchants from all parts of India standing on the platform and putting their well-considered and combined views before the government with a force which will carry greater weight than those of the combined European institutions.[6]

At the fourth session of the IICC held in Calcutta from 31 December 1926 to 2 January 1927, G.D. Birla in his welcoming address, repeated these sentiments and stressed the advantages of united business action:

> Personally I have got only the solution to offer and that is unity amongst businessmen. If you want to live, just unite... It was only at the end of the last year that after an agitation of nearly thirty years we could secure an abolition of the Cotton Excise Duty... due chiefly to the concerted action which we took.

Referring to ASSOCHAM he added,

> If we wish that in the interest of India the Indian community should wield an influence equal to, if not more than, that of the European community, on the administration of this country, I think we ought to unite (IICC, 1927: 4).

He further referred to a statement by a former President of the British-controlled Bengal Chamber of Commerce which dominated ASSOCHAM, who has remarked "a few years back that it was not the Government of India but the Bengal Chamber of Commerce which ruled the country" (IICC, 1927: 4).

At that session, presided over by Dinshaw Petit, a resolution formally launching the Federation of Indian Chambers of Commerce was passed, in which Petit was named as the President, Purshotamdas Thakurdas, MLA as Vice President, with G.D. Birla, MLA, Shri Ram, Kasturbhai Lalbhai, W.C. Bannerji amongst others, as members on the provisional committee. Two years later the word "industry" was added to the name of the Federation to make it the Federation of Indian Chambers of Commerce and Industry (FICCI, 1951: 11). This emphasis enlarged its functions as representative of both commerce and industry.

At the IICC session, Pandit Madan Mohan Malaviya while supporting the resolution for the formation of the FICCI stated,

> you can influence the course of events commercial, industrial, and agricultural and even political in a larger way and to a much greater extent by making this Federation a living institution then probably many people at present imagine (IICC, 1927: 31).

In the formation of FICCI, Purshotamdas Thakurdas and G.D. Birla played a dominant role. In fact, according to Thakurdas, the idea of forming a federation originated during talks between G.D. Birla and himself to counter the influence of ASSOCHAM[7] (FICCI, 1951: 183). Shri Ram considered Thakurdas "My guru in public life" and referred to him as "that uncrowned king of the business community in India..." (FICCI, 1951: 192; 189-199). Whereas Thakurdas, a cotton trader was a leading figure in the Bombay business community, G.D. Birla represented the Marwari business interests in Calcutta. Shri Ram, Kasturbhai

Lalbhai, Fakirji Cowasji and Devi Prasad Khaitan also played important roles. Khaitan, a chief lieutenant of Birla, handled the organisational and constitutional problems (FICCI, 1951: 183-184). His role was lauded by Shri Ram who stated: "If Purshotamdas Thakurdas and Mr. Birla are parents of this body, there is no doubt that Mr. Khaitan has been the wet nurse of the federation" (FICCI, Vol. III, 1937: 136).

The Nature of Business Representation in FICCI

In the late 1920s, the Indian business community was extremely heterogeneous. This heterogeneity of Indian business was bound to affect the formation of any chamber that sought to represent it. As Kochanek remarked, "The federation from the very beginning came to reflect the family, caste, regional, and political differences that divided the Indian business community as a whole" (Kochanek, 1974: 160).

An extremely important segment of the Indian business community was the Bombay industrialists who had substantial interests in the cotton textile industry. The Bombay industrialists were a very heterogeneous group, a mixture of Parsis, Gujaratis, Hindus and Muslims, with diversified interests in the cotton textile industry. A common feature however, was that because of their considerable interests in the cotton textile industry, in which the Bombay industrialists coexisted with the British, as the latter had retained substantial investments in the Bombay cotton textile industry: the premier industrial association in Bombay, the Bombay Millowners Association, therefore included both Indian as well as European, mainly British, millowners (Markovits, 1978).

The Bombay industrialists also differed in an important way from the Ahmedabad-based cotton textile industrialists led by Kasturbhai Lalbhai, a founder-member of FICCI. The Ahmedabad millowners had begun to specialise in the production of better quality products, in whose market they had to fight the supremacy of the Lancashire interests. The Bombay millowners on the other hand, did not produce the superior quality textiles, and feared Japanese competition more than that from Lancashire. Unlike the Ahmedabad millowners therefore, the Bombay millowners did not have an immediate major clash of economic interests with the British textile industry (Markovits, 1978). Moreover, Bagchi (1970: 215) has noted, "The most notable collaborators with British businessmen were the Parsis...", some of whom including the Tatas, the Wadias, Petit, etc., were leading Bombay millowners.

This factor was evidently crucial in the decision of the bulk of the Bombay-based Indian industrialists, organised in the Bombay Millowners Association to stay out of FICCI (Markovits, 1978). Although Purshotamdas Thakurdas succeeded in persuading Dinshaw M. Petit, the famous Bombay Parsi millowner to become the first President of FICCI, he never succeeded in getting other prominent Bombay millowners to join (Kochanek, 1974: 160). The other Bombay millowners must have been further alienated by the presence of known pro-Congress businessmen like G.D. Birla, Padampat Singhania, Kasturbhai Lalbhai and Shri Ram, in the leadership of FICCI. Thus, major Bombay-based industrial houses like the Tatas (then by far the biggest of the Indian industrial houses) (Markovits, 1978; Ray, 1979: 260-261), the Khataus, the Mafatlals, and the Wadias, kept out of FICCI.

However, by the mid-1930s in view of the increasing crisis of the colonial economy in the post-Depression period, and the withdrawal of mass agitational activity like the Civil Disobedience movement, the perceived interests of Bombay businessmen and the Congress increasingly converged. Hence the Tatas and the Mafatlals were briefly associated with FICCI. In response to an appeal by Shri Ram, a Tata representative served on the FICCI E.C. (FICCI, Vol. III, 1938: 86). He dropped out, however, on the eve of the 1939 crisis between the Congress and the government.

Moreover by this period, the Indian business elite was no longer a 'cotton' elite. Of the top twenty groups, only seven were based mainly on cotton textiles. In the 1930, the Parsis and the Gujaratis were in relative rise of the Calcutta-based business community vis-a-vis the Bombay-based industrialists (Markovits, 1978).

All these factors contributed to the considerable development of FICCI, whose membership increased from twenty-four chambers and associations in 1927, to sixty in 1937-38. Of these sixty, the fifty-five which submitted returns had a combined membership of 8,490 companies and individuals, a figure Markovits compiled from FICCI internal circulars (Markovits, 1978).

The absence of the number of the larger Bombay industrialists weakened both FICCI's representative character and its ability to pressurise the government. Furthermore, as these industrialists, in the main, affiliated themselves with ASSOCHAM, the very purpose of the formation of the Federation was in that measure defeated. Kochanek argues that the Bombay representatives in FICCI, in the absence of major millowners, "represented traders predominantly," whereas "the Calcutta contingent had a primary interest in industry. This division continues even today" (Kochanek, 1974: 161).

Kochanek's formulation does not appear to stand the test of empirical evidence. In the Bombay contingent, there were important industrial interests represented by the Kirloskars, the Walchands, the Kilachands, the Podars and the Scindias, among others. Furthermore, the demands that were articulated by the dominant sections of the Bombay representatives, and which corresponded to those put forward by the Calcutta industrialists, furthered the interests of industrialists rather than that of the traders. Traders from both Bombay as well as Calcutta, were, and are, representatives in FICCI. But neither in the early period of FICCI's existence, nor today, do they dominate the representation from any major region. However in India, even the larger industrial houses have trading interests. In some cases, as that of the Birlas, these are extensive. But these business groups are primarily interested in industrial activities, and are thereby treated as industrialists rather than traders or even industrialists-cum-traders. As we shall see below, FICCI was, and remains, primarily an industrialists' lobby.

Organisational Changes within FICCI

During FICCI's relatively brief history, there have been a succession of organisational changes. By and large, the effect of these changes, if not the intention behind them, has been to strengthen the Birla-led industrial elite's control over the chamber.

An important factor apparently behind some major changes in the FICCI constitution, which were passed at the 1933 Annual Session, just six years after the chamber's formation, was the sharp conflict that had taken place between the FICCI leadership and a pro-Congress dissident group led by A.D. Shroff and J.C. Setalvad, at the 1932 Annual Session. The amendments that were pushed through at the 1933 Annual Session were of two types: the first, procedural; and the second, structural, (inasmuch as these restructured the constituencies for election to the Executive Committee (E.C.) of the FICCI). The most important procedural change made was a restriction put on the moving of amendments to resolutions placed before the Annual Session. As a consequence of the constitutional changes, all amendments sought to be moved required the prior permission of the chair (the President). Additionally, the E.C. was empowered to disallow a resolution from being placed before the Session if prior notice had not been given.

The amendments put forward by the dominant Birla-led group within FICCI, were evidently an attempt to restrict the activities of the pro-Congress dissidents, who had succeeded in modifying an E.C. resolution the previous year, without any prior notice. These amendments, as A.D. Shroff, J.C. Setalvad and others argued, made it very difficult for members to alter FICCI policy resolutions which had the sanction of the E.C. Though the dissidents heatedly opposed the procedural amendments, they were outvoted and the constitution was suitably amended (FICCI, Vol. III, 1933: 139-140; 142).

More significant amendments were passed in the period from 1937 to 1939. The discussions in 1937 were held *in camera* and the dimension of the conflict between the two groups was highlighted by the fact that no less than 104 amendments were put forward in the Tenth Annual Session in 1937 (FICCI, Vol. III, 1937: 136). The elections to the E.C. were particularly affected. The old system of election to the E.C. by the total membership present at the annual meeting, was replaced by the representation of specific industries and trades. After the 1937 amendments, the functional representation on the E.C. was as follows: (1) textiles, two seats; (2) banking, insurance, plantations, sugar and transport, one seat each; (3) unspecified industries, three seats; (4) unspecified trade and commerce, eight seats; and (5) co-opted members, six (FICCI, Vol. III, 1938: 144). Except for the creation of the associate member constituency, this electoral system remained unchanged till 1962.

At the Twelfth Annual Session in 1939, the dissident group was outmanoeuvred by the leadership. At the time of the 1937 amendments, the dissidents were apparently promised that if they supported the amendments, the actual details of the voting methods, together with the votes allotted to chambers, would be discussed further at the later special sessions. At the special session in 1938, the old voting method was restored, and the postal ballot system rescinded (FICCI, Vol. III, 1938: 138-139). The leadership claimed that in return for this change the dissidents had agreed to accept the reduction of the voting strength of chambers from four to only one, whereas the latter denied this and wanted the two matters to be kept separate (FICCI, Vol. III, 1939: 62-65).

In the 1939 Annual Session when the dissidents out to restore the previous voting strength of the chambers, they, as Kochanek notes were, "completely routed" (Kochanek, 1974: 168). The dissidents were quite aware that the reduction in the voting strengths of the chambers would affect their own influence, as it was indeed intended. They argued that this would lead to a sharp drop in the attendance at the Annual Sessions, as chambers were unlikely to send delegates who were not entitled to vote (FICCI, Vol. III, 1939: 55-56). They criticised the leadership, who, somewhat ironically, defended the measure as one intended to reduce the power of the richer chambers, which because of their wealth had an unfair influence in deciding FICCI affairs, for they argued there were "at least a dozen 'members' (chambers) who are really pocket boroughs (of the large houses)" (FICCI, Vol. III, 1939: 68).

The voting on the amendment to restore the voting strength of the chambers, moved by the dissidents, clearly demonstrated the nature of the alignments in the business groups. Of the sixty-four chambers, forty-four were represented in the session. The dissidents' resolution was defeated by thirty-three votes to eleven. However it is manifestly incorrect to assert like Kochanek that: "This defeat ended Bombay's dominant role in the FICCI and initiated the ascendancy of Calcutta" (Kochanek, 1974: 169). In the first place, the various Bombay-based groups had never dominated FICCI, in which the pre-eminent influence, as we have seen earlier, was exerted by the Calcutta-based Birla house led by G.D. Birla, and its allies which included some industrialists from Bombay too. Notable amongst the latter were Thakurdas and Walchand Hirachand. The chambers controlled by the Bombay industrialists: the East India Cotton Association controlled by Thakurdas, the Maharashtra Chamber of Commerce and the Indian Steamship Owners Association, both controlled by Hirachand, voted against the amendment; as did the Marwari Chamber of Commerce, Bombay.

Those who supported the amendment included the rest of the Bombay chambers, including the Indian Merchants' Chamber (dominated by J.C. Setalvad and A.D. Shroff), the Grain Merchants Association and the Seed Traders Association (both led by Ratialal Gandhi), the Bombay Shroffs Association (led by Chunilal V. Mehta), the Indian Insurance Company Association and the Indian Life Assurance Officers Association, (in both of which Setalvad was very influential). The Karachi Chamber supported the dissidents, whereas the Calcutta chambers controlled by the Birlas and its allies and the Southern chambers in which the Chettiars and D.C. Kothari (the son-in-law of Thakurdas) were dominant influences, opposed it (Kochanek, 1974: 169).

Secondly, the division was largely between the larger industrialists aligned behind Birla, Thakurdas, Hirachand, Kasturbhai Lalbhai (Ahmedabad-based), Shri Ram (Delhi-based), the Chettiars (including both the Muthiah Chettiar and the Murugappa Chettiar families) and D.C. Kothari (Madras-based), who were opposed by the dissidents who largely represented smaller and mainly trading interests. A.D. Shroff, who was later a signatory to the Bombay Plan, was connected with the Tatas.

The nineteenth Annual Session of FICCI in March, 1946 was marked by a renewed challenge to the leadership. At this time, A.D. Shroff who together with Thakurdas, Birlas, J.R.D. Tata, Shri Ram, Ardeshir Dalal, Kasturbhai Lalbhai and Dr. John Matthai (later Finance Minister of India), was a signatory to the Bombay Plan, (also known as the Tata-Birla Plan), of 1944, was firmly aligned with the leadership. The contentious question, as before, was a proposed reorganisation of the Federation.

The resolution moved by D.P. Khaitan, a close associate of G.D. Birla, proposed: (a) appointment of a whole-time Chairman of the FICCI, and (b) further powers to the E.C. to organise "Sectional Committees or Councils by the issue of the Standing Order or Orders, or by such means as the Committee (E.C.) may be advised or deem proper" (FICCI, Vol. III, 1946: 56). Khaitan and Shroff (latter had seconded the resolution), defended the proposed reorganisation on the plea that it was necessary in view of the increased size and work of the Federation (FICCI, Vol. III, 1946: 56-58). It was sharply opposed by many, particularly by representatives of the trading community. This group was led by J.J. Kapadia (representing the Native Share and Stockbrokers Association, Bombay), Guruprasad Kapoor (of the Cawnpore Kapra Committee, Cawnpore) and Sardar Bachittar Singh (of the United Chamber of Trade Associations, Delhi).

In his very critical speech, Kapoor accused the Federation leadership of just putting forward the views of "big capitalists and industrialists", while ignoring the commercial interests. If this was to continue, suggested Kapoor rhetorically, the FICCI should drop "commerce" from its name and only claim to represent industrialists (FICCI, Vol. III, 1946: 179-180). Kapoor, unlike the others, did not oppose the proposal to appoint a whole-time Chairman provided, he also represented commercial interests (FICCI, Vol. III, 1946: 179-181).

Kapadia however criticised the leadership for the very short notice given for such an important matter, (the resolution was circulated just a few hours before the discussion), and suggested that it be taken up after three months or so, at a special session after member-bodies had sufficient time to discuss it (FICCI, Vol. III, 1946: 63).

Bachittar Singh, who echoed Kapoor's sentiments, claimed that his chamber which represented fifty to sixty associations was the biggest in India, but because it represented small traders, it was ignored both by the FICCI leadership and the government. He, like Kapoor, referred to the grievances of the small traders which had not been redressed. G.D. Birla, in defence of the resolution said, "that some of the previous speakers have tried to create a kind of division–completely artificial–between industrialists and non-industrialists" (FICCI, Vol. III, 1946: 68).

He stated that though,

> the old guards want to retire... unfortunately for the Committee it could not be expanded beyond a certain number... (although) every year an effort is made to introduce new blood, but... with the best wish in the world, it is not possible to give effect to that intention... (FICCI, Vol. III, 1946: 69).

He argued that the sectional councils would permit more representative discussion by the concerned interests, commercial or industrial. He suggested that an E.C. sub-committee be set up to prepare a complete scheme which could then be circulated to the member bodies. This statement was applauded by all. Birla went on to accept a special session. "if you want" but argued against it as he believed that the circulation method would allow more "constructive suggestions" to be sent. He urged,

> that the appointment of the Chairman ...be made as soon as possible. As you all know, political conditions are changing fast... (We) should have a man in Delhi with such a status that he can talk with the future national ministers on equal terms....

He reassured the critics that the Chairman's post would, "not ...subtract from the dignity... power or status for the permanent President or Vice-President. He is going to be a head of the organisation so far as the day-to-day work ... is concerned..." (FICCI, Vol. III, 1946: 70-71).

Despite Birla's advocacy, Ram Ratan Gupta (of the

Cawnpore Kapra Committee), who had discussed the matter with Birla earlier, reiterated the widespread reservations against the resolution, particularly regarding the proposed Chairman and asked for a day's postponement of the discussion (FICCI, Vol. III, 1946: 72). After some other members also voiced their objections, Kapadia who hesitated very much before differing from a gentlemen of the eminence of Mr. Birla in a matter like this..., rejected the latter's offer for circulation after provisional acceptance, arguing that once a Chairman was appointed, the FICCI "may find it very difficult to wriggle out ..." if the resolution was finally defeated (FICCI, Vol. III, 1946: 74).

Notwithstanding A.D. Shroff's seconding of Birla's offer of a special session "if the members consider it necessary... for the final adoption of the resolution...", (which was greeted with cheers) (FICCI, Vol. III, 1946: 75-76), the President Badridas Goenka called for voting. After noting that there were 51 votes for and 48 votes against, he declared the resolution carried. At that stage he was shown Rule 9, Clause 35 of the FICCI Constitution which stipulated that resolutions enacting "action... taken by the Federation in its collective capacity..." would require a majority of two thirds of the members voting. Goenka therefore, admitted that he was wrong in declaring the resolution having been carried (FICCI, Vol. III, 1946: 76).

Ramdeo A. Podar then argued that for the President to change his decision would diminish the "dignity of the House" and argued that the resolution be declared "carried but...inoperative until it is amended as suggested above..." (FICCI, Vol. III, 1946: 76-77). The President promptly accepted Podar's view only to resile when Kapadia citing the clause objected. Podar however persisted: "But it has been declared as carried and it will be on the Red Book (official records) of the Chamber". Despite the constitutional stipulation, Goenka accepted Podar's proposal and then adjourned the meeting (FICCI, Vol. III, 1946: 77).

This session highlighted some significant characteristics of the working of FICCI. In the first place, despite widespread dissent and a specific constitutional provision, the FICCI leadership insisted on ramming, through its resolution and having it declared carried, knowing fully well that it would be inoperative. Secondly, the industrialists including the Bombay-based group, notably Shroff and Podar, were more or less united behind Birla and Shri Ram. In this situation the dichotomy between the Calcutta and Bombay industrialists would appear to be only too simplistic and misleading. Thirdly, as indicated earlier, Birla realising the extent of opposition, was shrewd enough to claim in an attempt to refute the critics of FICCI's functioning, that the "old guard" wanted to retire, to make room for fresh blood. This of course, as events were to prove time and again, was untrue. The ruling elite in FICCI while it coopted some critics (especially in the later period after independence), continued to maintain its dominance over the Federation. Finally, this session demonstrated that there existed considerable opposition to the leadership, which recognised the "big capitalists" hold on the Federation but was able to do little but win Pyrrhic victories.

Despite the virtual rejection of the amendments in 1949, the E.C. placed a new resolution for the creation of a post of a Director-General who "shall be chief administrative head of the Central Secretariat of the Federation" and who would be delegated further powers by the E.C. (FICCI, Vol. III, 1949: 175-176). M.A. Master moving the resolution stated, that the amendments had been placed before the Annual Session: "After discussions with various member-bodies, and after holding consultations with various parties..." (FICCI, Vol. III, 1949: 176-177). The resolution was "strongly recommended" by Thakurdas and was passed by an overwhelming majority with only one dissenting vote (FICCI, Vol. III, 1949: 178). The nomenclature of the proposed Chairman's post had been changed to "Director-General", and since the amendment was brought forward after prior discussion, what could not be passed in 1946, was accepted quite readily in 1949. Of course, in 1949 the amendment did not seek to increase the E.C.'s powers as was sought under the earlier resolution. This was hardly necessary.

The Federation during this period was in considerable difficulty with its finances. Between 1947 and 1950, individual members of the E.C. drawn mainly from the large business houses, donated Rs. 42,5000, Rs. 47,500, Rs. 51,5000 and Rs. 40,5000 respectively during the four years.(FICCI Vol. I, 1943-1950). This necessitated the creation of a new type of membership: associate membership through constitutional amendment in 1951.

The resolution creating associate membership which permitted individual firms to join FICCI directly was moved by M.A. Master. Master justified the new category of membership as necessary to raise adequate finances for the Federation. So far, the FICCI had depended mainly on "voluntary contributions and donations" (FICCI, Vol. III, 1951: 204). J.J. Kapadia, who referred to his criticism since 1934, that more young people should be elected to the E.C., supported the reorganisation in the belief that this would help broad-base the Committee (FICCI, Vol. III, 1951: 205-206). Thus the amendment was passed without opposition.

Quite contrary to the expectation of Kapadia and others, the introduction of the new category of membership in FICCI actually strengthened the hold of the ruling elite over the Federation. The Birla house emerged at least as strongly as before, as the predominant group in the FICCI. Though 'associate members' had no voting rights at the Annual Sessions on the resolutions they elected nearly one-third members of the FICCI E.C. (FICCI, 1976: 21).

Table I: Character of Associate Members in FICCI and Estimates of Their Voting Power, 1965

Sr. No.	*Source of Membership*	*Number of Firms in the MIC and ILPIC*	*Percentage*	*Number of Voting Representation*	*Percentage*
1	42 of the top 73 houses	209	57.42	315	64.42
2	Others	155	42.58	174	35.58
3	Total	364	100.00	489	100.00

Source: The list of the Associate Members given in the FICCI, Vol. III, 1965, Appendix 'C' has been compared with the list of companies listed under specific houses in the MIC and ILPIC is the Reports.

As we can see from Table I below, the top 42 Industrial houses (identified the basis of the Reports of the Monopolies Inquiry Commission and the Industrial Licensing Policy Inquiry Commission), controlled almost 65 per cent of the votes in the associate members constituency.[8] Thus as stated above, the creation of the associate member constituency in 1951, instead of reducing the control of the ruling elite, as Kapadia and other small businessmen expected, actually strengthened it, though it simultaneously improved FICCI's financial position (See Table II).

Table II: FICCI Membership and Revenues, 1927-1966

Year	*Number of Ordinary Members*	*Number of Associate Members*	*Total Income in Rupees*	*Total Paid by the Associate Members in Rupees*	*Percentage Share of the Associate Members Individual*	*Made by Contribution E.C. Members in Rupees*
1927	24	–	13,050	–	–	8,100
1937	57	–	–	–	–	–
1947	102	–	1,31,423	–	–	42,500
1948	112	–	1,59,679	–	–	47,500
1949	121	–	1,63,973	–	–	51,500
1950	117	–	1,97,104	–	–	40,500
1951(a)	123	79	2,21,978	78,000	35.1	–
1952	115	115	2,55,869	89,000	34.8	–
1953	113	143	2,99,903	1,04,000	34.7	–
1954	113	117	3,10,690	1,60,333	51.5	43,502
1955	113	186	3,35,099	1,84,000	54.9	–
1956	117	207	3,68,825	1,97,000	53.4	–
1957	116	209	3,68,825	1,97,000	53.4	–
1958	116	221	4,88,473	2,24,000	45.9	–
1959	126	270	5,70,068	3,17,000	55.6	–
1960	137	285	5,61,228	3,27,000	58.3	–
1961	114	293	5,86,317	3,71,500	63.4	–
1962 (b)	170	336	10,01,817	7,51,086	75.0	–
1963	178	364	11,37,716	9,12,666	76.8	–
1964	177	369	11,76,036	8,93,750	76.0	–
1965	170	361	12,72,503	9,33,000	73.3	–
1966	179	384	13,95,270	10,13,250	72.6	–

Source: FICCI, Vol. I, 1927-1966

a: in 1951 Associate Membership was introduced.

b: upward reason of membership fees in 1962.

From 1962 onwards, the fees of the associate members totalled more than seventy per cent of the FICCI revenues (See Table II). Since generally he who pays the piper calls the tune, 'the financial dependence of FICCI on the associate members would, if anything, only have accentuated the dominance of the FICCI elite, i.e. of the big business houses threat controlled FICCI.

There were some relatively minor amendments of the FICCI Constitution in 1955 and in 1960 which further enhanced the powers of the E.C. In 1955, the term "Director-General" introduced in 1949 was replaced by "Secretary-General". Other amendments moved by Babubhai Chinai were "mostly of a minor nature", and increased the discretionary powers of the E.C. (FICCI, Vol. III, 1955: 40-44), and they were passed unanimously.

In 1960, Rule 14 of Appendix 'B' of the Articles of the Association was amended to allow the E.C. to co-opt upto 9 members of which four each should represent unrepresented interests and unrepresented states (FICCI, Vol. III, 1960: 29).

The reorganisation in 1961, was based on the recommendations of a sub-committee which included the FICCI President, Karam Chand Thapar, the Vice-President, Shriyans Prasad Jain, Babubhai Chinai, Ramnath A. Podar, Bharat Ram, C.H. Bhabha and Naval H. Tata. A special (Extraordinary) General Meeting of the Federation was held on 17 November, 1961, where the amendments were passed. The strength of the E.C. was expanded to 51 members including the President. Of these 30 were elected by the Member-Bodies, 14 by the Associate Members and 6 were to be co-opted (FICCI, Vol. I, 1961: 86-87). The membership subscription for the Associate Members was to be on a slab basis depending on the category of the firm and its turnover and deposits, ranging from a minimum of Rs. 1,500 per annum to a maximum of Rs. 10,000 per annum. Depending on their size, associate member firms could nominate upto 5 delegates, all of whom would have the right to vote for the E.C. representatives from the Associate Member constituency. A Standing Advisory Committee with a strength not greater than 15 members including the President and Vice-President to advise the E.C., was also created (FICCI, Vol. I, 1961: 86-88).

The result of these changes, was to further strengthen the oligarchical tendencies within the FICCI. As Thakurdas, whose influence had already been eclipsed by then observed, in an interview with his biographer Frank Moraes, by raising subscription fees "you will be making the Federation a pocket borough of the more affluent interests who can afford to pay the price" (Moraes, 1957: 47).

As we shall see later, the continued dominance of the FICCI by a small group of big houses, what we have referred to earlier as the FICCI "ruling elite", did not go wholly unopposed. But the opposition, given the structure of the FICCI, was ineffective.[9]

The Birlas' house, as stated earlier, had the largest voting strength in the associate member constituency. Companies associated with just six houses controlled 44.35 per cent of the total votes in this constituency. The Birlas alone controlled as much as 29.65 per cent (see Table III).

Table III: Estimated Voting Power Controlled by the Six Top Houses in FICCI, 1965

House	*Region*	*No. of Companies*	*Per-cent*	*Estimated Voting Re-presentatives*	*Voting Strength Percentage*
Birla	Calcutta	84	23.07	145	29.65
Soorajmull Nagarmull	Calcutta	16	4.39	16	3.27
Thapar	Calcutta	10	2.75	19	3.88
Sahu Jain	Calcutta	9	2.47	19	3.88
Bangur	Calcutta	7	1.92	10	2.04
J.K. Singhania	Kanpur	6	1.65	8	1.63
Total		36.25		44.35	

* This is based on a total of 364 associate members, and 489 representatives.
Source: FICCI, Vol. III, 1965.

The evidence provided by Tables I and III demonstrates the extent of the large houses' control over FICCI, and the predominant role of the Birla house, in particular.

Table IV shows the affiliation of the FICCI Presidents who held office between 1927 and 1966. Of the total of 40 Presidents, as many as 27 were affiliated to only 19 business houses or groups. This is also an indication of the domination of FICCI by a few of the big business houses, especially the leading monopolists.[10]

Presidents hailing from Bombay or Calcutta were generally affiliated to the a large business houses.

Table IV: Distribution of FICCI Presidents by Business Houses, 1927-1966

No. of Presidents from House	*No. of Houses*	*Name of Houses with Years*
3	2	Birla (1929, 1936, 1954) Scindias (1932, 1942, 1947)
2	4	Thakurdar (1928, 1953) Dalmia-Jain (1952, 1962) Shri Ram (1930, 1963) Singhania (1935, 1956)
1	13	Lalbhai (1934); Muthiah Chettiar (1943); Soorajmull Nagarmull (1949); Kilachand (1950); Mangaldas Jaisinghbhai (1955); Chinai (1957); Ruia (1959); Thapar (1961); Goenka (1945); Kothari (Madras) (1951); Murugappa Chettiar (1960); Kirloskar (1965); Amin (1966)
27	19	

Source: FICCI, Vol. I, 1927-1966. The method of house identification is the same as for Tables I and III.

Table V: Regional Origins of FICCI Presidents, 1927-1966

Bombay	13
Calcutta	14
Madras	4
New Delhi	2
Ahmedabad	3
Karachi	1
Kanpur	1
Poona	1
Coimbatore	1
Total	40

Source: FICCI, Vol. I, 1927-1966.

Intra-Elite Conflicts

The FICCI elite is not a monolithic bloc. There have been periodic differences, and even attempts to diminish the Birlas' hold on the Federation. There have been differences within the elite based on considerations of strategy, interests and perception of the government's role vis-a-vis big business. These cannot be reduced to any one single factor—for example, the difference between that of a Bombay group supposedly controlled by traders (in the absence of the Tatas, Mafatlals, Khataus et al.) and that of a Calcutta group dominated by industrialists (Kochanek, 1974: 161, 169, 188). Prominent Bombay industrialists affiliated to FICCI include the Scindias, the Walchands, the Kilachands, the Bajajs, the Mahindras, the Kirloskars and the Podars. These groups in fact dominate the overall 'Bombay group'. Kirloskar house is one of the top six controlling groups in the associate members' constituency (See Table III).

Nor are strategic agreements identical with regional origins. For instance, among the Bombay-based industrialists, not all houses espoused the Kirloskars' tactic of supporting the 'Right' opposition to the Congress. Among the Calcutta Marwaris, the Birlas and Goenkas had long-standing differences. Moreover, as an analysis of the debates within FICCI has revealed, much less important than the regional origins of FICCI members, was their affiliation to particular houses. The bigger Bombay-based industrialists, for instance, differed on a number of occasions with the Bombay-based traders.

However, given the very nature of the interests organised in FICCI, intra-elite conflicts were inevitable. Most of Indian big business, (with 42 out of the top 73 industrial houses listed in the ILPIC Report having associate membership), were participants in the FICCI (See Table VI). The large houses, represented therein would have a conflict of interests on many occasions. Firstly, they were often competing against each other, as they attempted to corner markets and sought industrial licenses, in the same industries. Secondly, it is claimed that there was a feeling that since the:

> Older Marwari houses... (have) large investments in coal, sugar and jute, these industries tended to get special consideration, even when their needs conflict with the more modern industrial sectors represented in the Committee (Kochanek, 1974: 141n).

This may well be an overstatement. The Birlas, for instance, have substantial investments in companies like Electric Construction Equipment, Central India Machinery, Indian Tool Manufacture, Indian Rayon Corporation, Gwalior Rayon, Zuari Agro Chemicals, Hind Motors and India Steamship Company (Goyal, 1979: 16-29), all of which are in "the more modern industrial sectors" earlier referred to. The growth, in fact, of a large number of the 73 houses, is due to the spread of their investments over both traditional and modern industries (Goyal, 1979: 64-103).

The resolution of intra-elite conflicts within FICCI tended to strengthen dominance of the Birla-led group. This, in a sense, was only to be expected, since in the absence of the Tatas and the Mafatlals, the Birlas were by far the largest industrial house[11], and the other houses, even if they occasionally resented the extent of Birla domination, could not afford to really fight the Birlas.

The composition of the industrial groups that formed the FICCI elite underwent certain changes. The major change was the eclipse of Purshotamdas Thakurdas, who in 1950 was dropped from the FICCI E.C. (FICCI, Vol. I, 1950: 1). Thakurdas, despite his eminence as one of the founder -statesmen of FICCI, was, more or less eased out of the FICCI leadership once he crossed swords with the dominant Birla-led groups.

In early 1956, the Forward Markets Commission had proposed certain changes in the bye-laws and procedures of the East India Cotton Association (EICA), of which Thakurdas was the Chairman and Director.

Table VI: Representation of Large Houses in FICCI, 1965

Sl. No.	*Name of House (ILPIC)*	*No. of Firms*	*No. of Representatives*
1	Bangur	7	10
2	Birla	84	145
3	K.P. Goenka	4	7
4	J.K. Singhania	6	8
5	Tulsidas Kilachand	4	5
6	Sahu Jain	9	19
7	J. Dalmia	2	3
8	Scindia	4	4
9	Shri Ram	3	7
10	Soorajmull Nagarmull	16	16
11	Thapar	10	19
12	Walchand	4	9
13	R.K. Amin	4	5
14	Bajaj	2	3
15	Jaipuria	1	1
16	J.D. Jatia	1	1
17	Kamani	1	2
18	B. Kanoria	4	4
19	R.K. Kanoria	1	1
20	Kasturbhai Lalbhai	3	3
21	Kirloskar	3	3
22	D.C. Kothari	3	3
23	Mangaldas Jeysinghbhai	1	1
24	Mangal Das Parekh	2	2
25	Modi	2	4
26	Murugappa Chettiar	3	4
27	Muthiah Chettiar	1	1
28	G.V. Naidu	2	3
29	Podar	2	2
30	Ruia	1	1
31	Simpson	2	2
32	Talukdar Law	1	1
33	Ramakrishna	2	2
34	Mafatlal	2	2
35	Sarabhai	1	1
36	Tata	2	2
37	T.V.S.	4	4
38	Andrew Yule	1	1

39	A.F. Harvey	1	1
40	V.R. Naidu	1	1
41	Seshasayee	1	1
42	K. Kapadia	1	1
43	Others	–	–
Total Voting Strength of the Large Houses (64.42%)			315 Votes
Total Voting Strength of Associate Members			489 Votes

Source: the list of Associate Members given in FICCI, Vol. III, 1965, Appendix 'C' have been compared with the firms listed under the 73 Houses in the ILPIC Reports.

In protest against these changes which were to take effect from 10 April 1956, and which he considered were an unwarranted interference in the affairs of the EICA, Thakurdas resigned from his posts in the Association (Moraes, 1967: 278-280).

As Thakurdas's biographer Moraes (1967: 281) notes, there was an "acrid controversy" over the matter. On its part, the Forward Markets Commission defended its act as necessary to protect the interests of cotton growers (Moraes, 1967: 282). When Thakurdas went to meet T.T. Krishnamachari (TTK), the then Finance Minister, to seek the latter's intervention, the two apparently had a sharp interchange.[12] Thakurdas then took his case to the E.C., but later this body who considered TTK a "very fine" Minister did not want to be hostile towards him over a relatively small matter. This led to Thakurdas's final withdrawal from the Federation, and must have been the basis for some unexpectedly trenchant criticism that he had made of FICCI functioning in his official biography. Moraes has quoted Thakurdas as deploring,

> (the) tendency on the part of some prominent members to create their own following or group in the organisation. Such a tendency he (Thakurdas) feels, cannot but in the end make for unfair representation at the cost of capacity and independence and tend ultimately to lower the quality of the Federation's chief office-bearers (Moraes, 1967: 47).

This criticism was a not very veiled attack on the Birlas. However, Thakurdas's differences with the rest of the FICCI elite, led to the former's own isolation in FICCI. An indication of this was his son-in-law R.G. Saraiya's defeat in the elections to the E.C., held the following year. Saraiya who had been elected President of FICCI in 1953-54, was unable to secure his own election to the E.C. in 1957 from the associate members' constituency, losing by a significant margin of 18 votes (FICCI, Vol. III, 1957: 100-101).

The exit of Thakurdas did not leave the Bombay chambers without representation. In the post-independence period, a new leader of Bombay business interests had emerged: Babubhai Chinai. Chinai, served as a member of the Bombay Legislative Council from 1952 to 1958, and thereafter was elected to the Rajya Sabha as a Congress candidate. Chinai was an influential Congressman and a "chief lieutenant of S.K. Patil, the Congress Party political boss of Bombay" (Kochanek, 1974: 150). Just as Thakurdas had been FICCI's spokesman in its relations with government, in the pre-independence period, so Chinai became its spokesman in the 'fifties and sixties'.[13] He therefore came to hold an influential position in FICCI similar to the one Thakurdas had held earlier.

In this particular case it is evident that the resolution of intra-elite differences, while it did lead to the departure of a founder member and respected business leader from the active ranks of FICCI, served the organisation's long-term interest. The FICCI, as it itself realised, could not have afforded to have alienated an otherwise sympathetic minister like TTK, just to appease Thakurdas over a relatively unimportant matter. Thus the resolution of this intra-elite conflict actually strengthened the FICCI's bargaining position vis-a-vis the government (TTK himself must have come to know the details of the incident, since Thakurdas's resentment as well as his withdrawal from FICCI affairs, were both quite evident).

A notable instance of intra-elite conflict, that also demonstrated the extent of control within FICCI by the Birla-led group of big business houses, was the struggle that occurred in the chamber over the demand for the resignation of Shriyans Prasad Jain, from the Presidentship of FICCI.

In the first half of the 1950s, the Tatas and the Mafatlals had joined FICCI. Naval Tata was nominated to the E.C., in the place of B.M. Birla, who became President (FICCI, Vol. I, 1954: 1-3). Companies associated with the Tatas and the Mafatlals joined as associate members of FICCI. However, in 1963 events occurred which virtually forced the Tatas and the Mafatlals to withdraw from FICCI.

In 1963, the Report of the Commission of Inquiry on the Administration of the Dalmia-Jain Companies, (generally known as the Vivian Bose Commission Report, after its Chairman), was published (Ministry of Commerce and Industry, Department of Company Law Administration, 1963). The Report of the Commission, which was appointed by the Government on 11 December 1956 under the Commission of Inquiry Act, 1952 (Ministry of Commerce and Industry, Department of Company Law Administration, 1963: 1), was a detailed indictment of the various illegal activities carried out in a number of Dalmia-Jain Companies. The Dalmia-Jain families were castigated by the Commission for their "very evident determination to thwart and obstruct inquiry" (Ministry of Commerce and Industry, Department of Company Law Administration, 1963: 8). Apart from various charges of misuse of public funds, the creation of "sick" companies by premeditated compliance with penalty clauses to facilitate the transfer of assets to other companies of the group, leading to an estimated loss of Rs. 1,72,80,000 (Ministry of Commerce and Industry, Department of Company Law Administration, 1963: 25-31), there were specific charges involving Shriyans Prasad Jain, the then FICCI President (for 1962-63).

According to the Report, Jain was appointed to a post in the Dalmia Cement and Paper Marketing Company Limited in 1943, with a gross salary estimated at Rs. 9,400 per month (including various benefits and allowances), even though he was only 36 years old at the time, for a term of 25 years. On 7 February 1950, Jain's appointment was terminated, allowing him to invoke a penalty clause, and secure a payment of Rs. 7 lakhs as compensation. The Vivian Bose Commission further noted that this firm had paid ordinary shareholders no dividends from 1941 (Ministry of Commerce and Industry, Department of Company Law Administration, 1963: 31-32).

At the FICCI Annual Session on 16 March 1963, speaking after Jain's Presidential Address, Nehru referred to the difficulties he had faced in accepting FICCI's invitation that year which "many people, my colleagues and friends..." didn't want him to accept for a "reason... (which was) obvious". In a further reference to the scandal created by the release of the Vivian Bose Commission Report, Nehru warned that though the defalcation and abuse of company funds cited "may not be representative of all...", if the private sector suffered "in public estimation" it would not be able to grow (FICCI, Vol. III, 1963: 10-14).

Concerned about the damage this scandal might cause the private sector in general and FICCI in particular, the Tatas and the Mafatlals insisted that Jain resign as President. According to Kochanek, "the top leadership (the FICCI elite centred around the Birlas) held that a hasty resignation would damage the prestige of the federation" (Kochanek, 1974: 182; see also Kochanek, 1978: 1291-1308). In protest the Tatas and the Mafatlals resigned from FICCI. Their firms including Mafatlal Gagalbhai, Tata Chemicals, Tata Industries, TISCO, Tata Oil Mills and Tata Power, amongst others, all resigned from associate membership in 1963 (FICCI, Vol. I, 1963: 9).

According to G.L. Bansal, this was a very delicate matter in which the E.C. could not interfere, to either ask Jain to resign or to ask the Tatas and the Mafatlals to withdraw their resignations. "It was for Shriyans Prasad Jain to decide"[14], and he decided to accept the Presidentship of FICCI, perhaps to avoid any action which could be construed as an admission of guilt. It is quite evident, in spite of Bansal's statement that the E.C. chose not to "interfere" because of the Dalmia-Jain group's position in the FICCI elite, as an ally of the Birlas. As the pressures from the Tatas and Mafatlals did not yield any result. The resignation by the latter was not only a protest, but it was equally motivated by their realisation that they could not budge the Birla-led elite even on an issue such as this. However, even during the short period of their involvement in FICCI, there is no evidence that the Tatas and the Mafatlals posed any real threat to the hold of the Birla group on the FICCI.

Another conflict within FICCI took place during the mid-1960s. At the time, the textile industry interests in particular, were opposed to the government-imposed price controls. The FICCI E.C. decided to send a delegation to the government to discuss the problems of the textile industry. Madanmohan Mangaldas, who was the then President of the Indian Cotton Mills Federation (ICMF) and a member of the E.C., objected strongly to FICCI's representing textile interests and threatened his resignation if the matter was pushed further (Sabade and Namjoshi, 1977; see also Venkatasubbiah, 1977: 39). Mangaldas argued that the ICMF being a specialised organisation of the cotton textile manufacturers was best suited to take up the matter. The rest of the E.C. however argued that the problems of the textile industry, were part of a larger pattern of controls over industry and that the FICCI therefore clearly had both the jurisdiction and the obligation to take up the matter. Although Mangaldas was prevailed upon to take back his resignation, when a resolution on the problems of the textile industry was moved at the 1968 Annual Session, he refused to support it (Kochanek, 1974: 191).

An instance of even greater divergences with the E.C., is the debate over the question of the abolition of controls. Following a decision by Prime Minister Shastri, Home Minister G.L. Nanda wrote to FICCI on 29 May 1965 that the government was reviewing controls and wanted FICCI's suggestions as to which ones should be abolished. The E.C. met on 28th June and on 16th August but was unable to arrive at a general agreement (FICCI, Vol. I, 1965: 98).

Thus without any concrete response from FICCI, Shastri announced in the Lok Sabha on 26th August, that controls over certain commodities would be removed in order to encourage increased production. Later, on 20th September, Nanda came to the Federation House, to discuss this and other matters with the E.C. (FICCI, Vol. II, 1965: 323-327). Once again the E.C. met on 1st December, to discuss the issue on the basis of a note prepared by the Secretariat, but the consensus was merely a general agreement on the need for the restoration of the market mechanism. Within the E.C., some members wanted a total abolition of controls, some wanted controls modified, and others opposed decontrol because the existing controls aided profitability in their industries. According to Kochanek, the "Textiles, coal and sugar interests... most strongly opposed decontrol", whereas "the newer industries, such as engineering, favoured a policy of total freedom from control" (Kochanek, 1974: 190).

Intra-elite differences, led to a majority within the elite imposing its will; to the E.C. actually taking no specific stand or to its taking an equivocal one; and to contradictory statements being issued or made by various FICCI representatives or members. This as we have indicated earlier, is due to the very character of FICCI, representing as it does a host of, sometimes divergent, interests. Thus a substantial portion of E.C. statements and resolutions, including those at Annual Sessions, represent the maximum possible agreement amongst differing groups. Nonetheless, these differences are resolved internally and the continuance of the elite's control over FICCI, much less the viability of the organisation itself, is never threatened.

Mechanisms of Elite Control

The above figure depicts the executive bodies of the FICCI. The most important is the Executive Committee (E.C.) which includes 20 representatives of the member-bodies (industry), 16 representatives of the member-bodies (trade), 17 representatives of the associate members and some 6 to 7 co-opted members. The last category of members are co-opted by the elected E.C. The E.C. also nominates a Standing Advisory Committee (SAC). This Committee includes some ex-presidents of FICCI and senior business leaders,

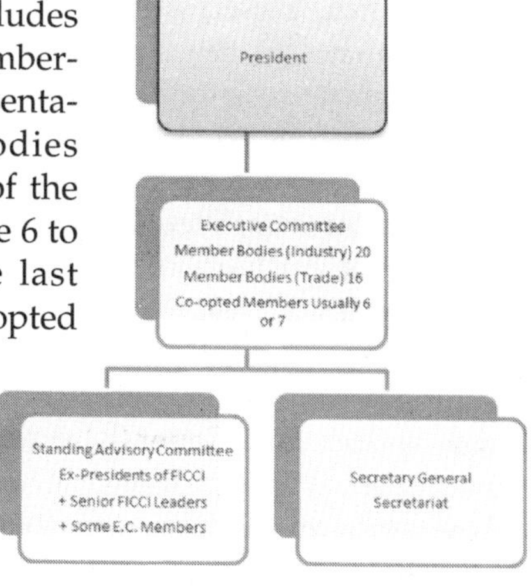

Fig: The Mechanism of Elite Control

most of whom are E.C. members. According to the FICCI constitution, the strength of the SAC cannot exceed 19, of which upto 17 can be members of the E.C. and upto 2 members who are not members of the E.C. and upto 2 members who are members of the E.C. and it will be appointed by the President. The SAC includes the President, Vice-President, immediate past President, Chairmen of the various E.C. sub-committees and others nominated by the President in consultation with the E.C., to ensure that no person who has lost in the election to the E.C. the same year is nominated. The tenure of office of SAC members is one year but they are eligible for re-nomination (FICCI, 1976: 26).

The Secretariat which is headed by a permanent official now designated the Secretary-General, not only advises the Committee and provides it information and background material for its discussions, but also exercises various powers delegated it by the E.C. (FICCI, 1976: 27). It is the E.C., which from among its own members elects the President and the Vice-President (the latter succeeding the former after their one-year term), that represents the real controlling powers centre of the Federation. The E.C. members retire as given in Table VII below:

All 17 associate members' representatives retire at the end of every two years (FICCI, 1976: 38-39). However, as we have noted earlier, based on our tabulations in Table VI the representatives of the associate members, in the main, are elected from representatives of monopoly houses dominant in FICCI, or are supported by them.

The E.C. besides electing the chief executives of the FICCI: the President and Vice-President, as per the constitution manages "the business of the Federation" (FICCI, 1976: 23). It has the power:

"(a) to perform all executive duties and to do all such acts and things as the Federation is authorised to exercise...(b) ... to appoint a Secretary-General, Secretary or Secretaries and such other officers as may be found necessary...(c) to establish a Trust or Trusts and appoint Trustees thereof and invest the funds or the surplus income or any property of the Federation... in such manner as the Committee may... think fit...(d) to make, issue, vary and repeal such Standing Orders for the furtherance of the purpose for which the Federation is established and for carrying on its business, as they may... consider necessary...(e) to appoint sub-committees, not exceeding eight in number and appoint the chairmen thereof who shall be members of the committee and other ad hoc committees, panels, working groups and persons, and to delegate them such functions on such terms and conditions as the committee may deem fit; and, (f) to present a report of their proceedings and a statement of accounts of the Federation at the Annual Meeting..." (FICCI, 1976: 23-24).

Table VII: Retirement Pattern of E.C. Members

Group	*Retiring at the End of the First Year*	*Retiring at the End of the Second Year*	*Retiring at the End of the Third Year*
Industry including Plantation and Mining	7	7	6
Trade including Banking/ Financial Institutions, Insurance and Transport	5	5	6

This extended quotation from the FICCI constitution should make the vast powers of the E.C. over the FICCI amply clear. Thus in Figure 1, where we have drawn a diagram of the major executive bodies of the FICCI, we have depicted the E.C. in the centre, with its advisory bodies (constituted by it): the SAC and the Secretariat on its sides. The President is as stated earlier, elected by the E.C. and functions in close contact with the E.C. members (especially the group of his supporters within that body).

The key to the control of FICCI, therefore is the control of the E.C. We have already examined the elite control over the associate member constituency. We shall now go on to examine the elite's control over the industry and trade constituencies. Whichever group controls these constituencies would obviously have the power to co-opt the members it pleases.

Here at the outset, it must be stressed that the distinction between the industry and trade constituencies is somewhat tenuous. There has been almost continuous criticism within FICCI, that nominees of the large houses have sought representation from both constituencies as the occasion demanded. In fact, as we shall see, that even amongst members elected from these two constituencies, those from the large houses or FICCI elite have dominated.

Table II shows the increases in FICCI membership and revenues, and focuses on the importance of the associate member's subscription as a source of revenue.

Yet another factor in the elite domination is the fact that E.C. meetings are held in various cities throughout India, usually on 10 or more occasions. Since E.C. members are unpaid, the less wealthy industrialists and traders cannot afford the cost of membership in the E.C.

Table VIII: Illustrative List of FICCI E.C. Members, 1944-1966, Showing House Affiliations

Name of House	*Name of EC Member*	*Year in EC*	*Constituencies Represented*
Birla (Calcutta)	*G.D. Birla	1944-48	Co-opted; Paper & Starch (Industries not specified)
	*D.P. Khaitan	1944-47	Paper & Starch (Industries not specified)
	*B.M. Birla	1949-1963	Industry
	*L.N. Birla	1952-	Associate Member; Industry
	*K.K. Birla	1964-	Associate Member; Co-opted Member
	*G.N. Khaitan	1964-	Industry; Associate Member; Industry
Bajaj (Bombay)	Kamalnayan Bajaj	1955-62	Trade; Industry; Co-opted
	Ramakrishan Bajaj	1963-	Industry; Associate Member; Co-opt
Bajoria-Jalan (or)Soorajmull Nagarmull (Calcutta)	*K.D. Jalan	1946-	Co-opted; Textile Mills; Insurance; Industry
	B.P. Bajoria	1962-63	Associate Member
	U.S. Bajoria	1962-64	Industry
Bangur (Calcutta)	R.N. Bangur	1964-	Industry; Associate Member; Co-opted

Dalmia-Jain (Calcutta)	*Shanti P. Jain	1944-63	Mining; Trade; Associate Member; Co-opted
	*Shriyans P. Jain	1954-63	Associate Member; Co-opted
	M.D. Dalmia	1958	Associate Member
Goenka (Calcutta)	*K.P. Goenka	1948-	Textile Mills; Petro-Chemicals, Industries; Co-opted
Tulsidas Kilachand (Bombay)	*Tulsidas Kilachand	1946-62	Trade; Co-opted
	*Ambalal Kilachand	1963-	Industry, Co-opted
Thapar (Calcutta)	*Karamchand Thapar	1945-61	Industry
	Lalit Mohan Thapar	1962	Co-opted
	I.M. Thapar	1963-	Industry; Co-opted
Singhania (Calcutta)	*Sir Padampat Singhania	1944-47	Textile Mills; Industry
	*Lakshmipat Singhania	1948-63	Co-opted; Trade
	Purshotamdas Singhania	1953-56	Associate Member
	Hari Shankar Singhania	1964-	Co-opted; Industry
Shri Ram (Delhi)	*Sir Shri Ram	1944-50	Textile Mills; Chemical & Ceramics (Industry)
	*Charat Ram	1951-53	Heavy Chemicals & Ceramics
		1954	Industry
Murugappa Chettiar (Madras)	*A.M.M. Murugappa Chettiar	1949	Associate Member
		1955-64	Insurance, Tube Manufacturing (Industry)
	*M.V. Arunachalam	1965-	Associate Member; Co-opted
Modi (Modinagar)	*G.M. Modi	1953-	Trade; Co-opted
Poddar (Bombay)	Ramdeo A. Podar	1944-49	Industry
	*Ramnath A. Podar	1953-	Co-opted; Industry; Associate Member
Mahindra (Bombay)	*Harish Mahindra	1965-	Industry; Co-opted

* They became FICCI Presidents

Source: FICCI, Vol. I, II and III, 1944-1966

Table VIII illustrates the hold of the large houses in the FICCI E.C. It reveals how influential members are able to change their constituencies for election to the E.C., often moving between the trade and industry constituencies. We have dealt only with the years 1944 to 1966. Some names that are cited in the table, e.g. G.D. Birla, D.P. Khaitan, Sir Padampat Singhania and Sir Shri Ram, were of industrialists who were also members of the E.C. before 1944. The table cites the instances of only fourteen houses, but that should be sufficient to indicate the continued control of the big business elite over the E.C., taken together with the other evidence already adduced.

In summation, because of their control over the delegates to the Annual Session including the associate members, and the ordinary members from both trade and industrial associations, the FICCI elite is able to retain its control over the organisation. Despite the continuing criticism by small business and trading interests, and the induction of some of their representatives into the E.C., e.g. Devji Rattansey, Hem Chand Jain and V.S. Aggarwal among others, these critics were unable to materially alter the prop-big business policies of FICCI. That is evident from the continued criticism of the leadership. However, in view of FICCI's very considerable influence, the small business and trading interests represented in FICCI prefer to retain their membership and seek to reform the organisation from within and secure all possible concessions.

FICCI: The Struggle Against Big Business Control

Within the Federation, almost throughout its history, a vocal minority, generally representing small traders and small industrialists have protested against the domination of FICCI by the elite. Sabade and Namjoshi (1977: 226) in their study commissioned by FICCI noted that, "The trade *versus* industry struggle takes place every year at the time of the annual general meeting". Almost every year's Annual Session provides evidence of such criticism.

In 1946, Guruprasad Kapoor (representing the Cawnpore Kapra Committee), warned that FICCI should not only propagate the views of "big capitalist(s) or industrialists"

(FICCI, Vol. III, 1946: 180). Devji Rattansey, speaking in 1950, charged "that this Federation has been made a pocket bought of certain groups" (FICCI, Vol. III, 1950: 129). J.J. Kapadia also alluded to this, when he urged in 1951 that "more young people" should be elected to the E.C. (FICCI, Vol. III, 1951: 206).

In the 1953 Session, M.G. Lakshminarasu (of the Hyderabad Chambers of Commerce and Industry), reacting to the domination of FICCI by the Bombay and Calcutta-based houses claimed that "the very constitution of this Federation remains very undemocratic...", and urged representation on the E.C. on a regional basis (FICCI, Vol. III, 1953: 178). In the 1955 Annual Session, there was sharp criticism of the manner in which the elite dominated FICCI. Sain Das Mahajan claimed that leading members "coming from Calcutta and Bombay... dominate the affairs of this institution" (FICCI, Vol. III, 1955: 130).

Gauri Shankar Goenka, and Bawa Bachittar Singh (the latter was to become an important representative of the traders in the E.C.) showed their awareness of how the elite controlled the E.C.. They referred to members of the large industrial houses who represented the traders' category on the E.C. (FICCI, Vol. III, 1955: 131-132). Bachittar Singh asked how the Singhanias, the Dalmia-Jains, Rai Bahadur G.M. Modi and Mohan Lal could be classified as traders. Referring to Mahajan's earlier comments, he stated that the overwhelming representation that the Bombay and Calcutta groups had over the FICCI Presidentship was because these groups had "forty to fifty votes each" (FICCI, Vol. III, 1955: 132). They thus dominated the E.C. and consequently nominated their men as President.

Shriram C. Chokhani (also an important E.C. member later), claimed that, "At present it (FICCI) is represented by Calcutta and Bombay" (FICCI, Vol. III, 1955: 134). In 1957, N.C. Mallik (of the Delhi Chamber of Commerce), referred to the "growing feeling among smaller and comparatively new associations that the Committee of the Federation is a sort of a family affair" (FICCI, Vol. III, 1957: 14-15).

N.S. Siamwala (representing the Tamil Chamber of Commerce) noted, "that some members are elected again and again (to the E.C.) without giving a chance to others, year after year and they monopolise the Federation" (FICCI, Vol. III, 1957: 20). In 1961 Hem Chand Jain (of the Delhi Hindustani Mercantile Association), a regular critic of the FICCI elite, claimed that the problems of small businessmen and traders did not receive adequate attention. He was supported by Shrikrishna Das Garg (a representative of the Madhya Pradesh Chambers of Commerce and Industry, Lashkar) (FICCI, Vol. III, 1961: 22).

Again in 1962, some members, demanded that the demarcation between trade and industry be properly maintained for elections to the E.C. (FICCI, Vol. III, 1962: 25). In 1964, Hem Chand Jain repeated his complaint that FICCI activities benefited big businessmen rather than small traders and small industrialists (FICCI, Vol. III, 1964: 20). The resentment felt by smaller businessmen often led to sharp and bitter criticism and on at least one occasion in 1965, "unparliamentary" language was apparently used (FICCI, Vol. III, 1965: 14-16).

The continued criticism of the functioning of FICCI by small traders and industrialists, may appear somewhat paradoxical. Observers may wonder why smaller businessmen dissatisfied with the state of affairs in FICCI choose to stay on. After all, associations of smaller businessmen exist. Fox example, there are All-India Manufacturers Organisation (AIMO) and the Federation of Associations of Small Industries of India (FASII). The latter organisation, which represents the small businessmen, was set up with the active participation of G.L. Bansal, then Secretary-General of FICCI, who chaired a committee which drafted the constitution and rules for the proposed federation (Sabade and Namjoshi, 1977: 235). The first President of FASII, A.R. Bhat, who served from 1959 to 1969, was formerly a member of FICCI.

There is an obvious reason why the smaller traders and industrialists do not leave FICCI despite the fact that, as a study commissioned by FICCI itself notes, the Federation does not "take up smaller regional or local issues like octroi, regional restrictions, sales tax, etc., about which the trading community is more worried" (Sabade and Namjoshi, 1977: 226-227). FICCI remains the most influential of all chambers, as its voice is heard in the offices where decisions regarding industry are made. This is a fact of which the smaller businessmen are well aware. They therefore choose to continue in the Federation and to fight the unequal battle against the domination of FICCI by a few industrial houses led by the Birlas.

FICCI: The Representative Organisation of Indian Big Business

FICCI has generally been viewed as the most representative organisation of Indian big business. The other contending apex body of big business, ASSOCHAM, has usually been identified with private foreign capital, at least till the end of the 'sixties' (Kochanek, 1974: 94n; see also Kidron, 1965: 59). However, writing in 1977, Sabade and Namjoshi in a work commissioned by FICCI have noted that,

> though the ASSOCHAM belonged to the British Chambers and British firms, now its character has been completely changed... Many Indian firms have joined British Chambers, foreign firms have been Indianised and there has been closer collaboration between Indian and foreign firms than before (Sabade and Namjoshi, 1977: 242).

The process of Indianisation of ASSOCHAM was a gradual one, and N.M. Wagle who was elected President in 1968, was elected President in 1968, was the first Indian to hold the post (Kochanek, 1974: 126). Hence during the period of our study, ASSOCHAM was more or less a foreign-dominated chamber.

The more representative character of FICCI as against that of ASSOCHAM, is brought out by a comparison of Tables IX and X. Table IX indicates the growth of 6 representative FICCI-affiliated chambers for the 1941 to 1961 period. Table X has similar data for ASSOCHAM affiliated chambers. The membership of the ASSOCHAM affiliated chambers has been relatively small, and their growth, apart from the case of the Bombay and Cochin Chambers, was not impressive. The Bengal Chamber, which for long dominated ASSOCHAM (Kochanek, 1974: 119-126), had a declining membership. However, as Table IX shows, FICCI-affiliated chambers had a larger membership base and generally registered an impressive growth in membership between 1941 and 1961.

Table IX: Growth of FICCI–Affiliated Chambers, 1941-1961

Name of Chamber	*1941*	*1951*	*1961*
Andhra Chamber of Commerce	115	586	774
Bharat Chamber of Commerce	–	532	739
Hindustan Chamber of Commerce	–	150	354
Indian Merchants' Chamber	753	2671	2173
Madura Ramnad Chamber	133	265	752
Southern Indian Chamber	421	883	879

Source: Sabade and Namjoshi (1977: 84-85, Table 5.1).

Table X: Growth of ASSOCHAM–Affiliated Chambers, 1941-1961

Name of Chamber	*1941*	*1951*	*1961*
Bengal Chamber of Commerce	285	306	258
Bombay Chamber of Commerce	–	356	335
Madras Chamber of Commerce	82	87	102
Upper India Chamber	77	128	139
Indian Chamber of Commerce, Cochin	–	100	209
Tutioorin Chamber	12	15	22

Source: Sabade and Namjoshi (1977: 84-85).

On the basis of the above data and our other findings above, it would appear that, for our period of study at any rate, FICCI should be considered the apex body most representative of Indian big business.

Lobbying

The term "lobbying" originated around the 1830s in the USA. At that time, representatives of certain interests groups loitered in the lobbies of the assembly halls of the American Congress in Washington, DC seeking to influence legislators (Milbraith, Vol. IX, 1968: 441-442). At that time, and in fact,

> throughout the nineteenth century, lobbying by interest groups

> inspired (in the USA) tales of corruption, bribery, and especially as seen in today's perspective, monumental conflicts of interest (Ornstein and Elder, 1978: 96).

Today the same pejorative connotation does not attach to the term "lobbying", at least in the USA (Milbraith, 1968: 442-443). A current deformation of the term "lobbying" is provided by Millbrath, who defines it broadly as:

> the stimulation and transmission of a communication, by someone other than a citizen acting on his own behalf, directed to a governmental decision-maker with the hope of influencing his decision (Milbraith, 1968: 442).

Lobbying involves two types of methods of communication. In the first, direct form, the lobbyist seeks to communicate his message through intermediaries; or by organising mass letter or telegram campaigns among particular constituents of the polity, or by promoting public relations campaigns through a judicious use of the mass media. As these methods, intended to indirectly influence the decision-makers and which are now commonly employed, are called "lobbying at the grass roots" (Milbraith, 1968: 443).

Business groups, as we have seen above have traditionally used both direct and indirect lobbying techniques. However, in India, unlike in the USA, lobbying activities, particularly by business interests, "were hampered by the low level of legitimacy attached by the political culture to such activity..." (Kochanek, 1974: 241). For instance, it is reported that when Nehru discovered that FICCI had arranged a tour of Indian industrial units for MPs elected in the 1952 General Elections, he reacted so adversely that the practice was stopped (Kochanek, 1974: 243-244).

FICCI only set up a liaison and lobbying office within its Secretariat in 1958, under the instructions of Babubhai Chinai, the outgoing FICCI President, and a Congress MP. The office was staffed by a former employee of the Lok Sabha Secretariat. The move was apparently a reaction to the sustained criticism of the private sector by the Left parties within Parliament (Kochanek, 1974: 243).

Apart from the efforts of FICCI Secretariat's office, set up in 1958, FICCI had its own representatives in Parliament. From the time of the constituent assembly, businessmen who were representatives of FICCI, or of its constituent bodies, had been members of the central legislature of independent India. An illustrative list is provided in Table XI below.

As Table XI reveals, a significant number of big business representatives were elected to the Indian Parliament in the 1947 to 1966 period, which is under study. They were elected from a variety of parties and from a number of regions. Of them, a sizeable number were elected with Congress support. These included important FICCI leaders like G.L. Bansal (the FICCI Secretary), G.D. Somani, Kamalnayan Bajaj, Shriyans Prasad Jain and Babubhai Chinai (See Table XI below). A number of FICCI leaders were elected to the respective Houses of Parliament, as Independents. These included Tulsidas Kilachand, Indubhai B. Amin, and Sitaram Jaipuria.

The presence of such senior leaders of FICCI in Parliament, was obviously of considerable benefit to the attempts by big business to influence MPs. Kilachand, Somani, Bajaj, Chinai and Shriyans Prasad Jain, and the other senior businessmen, were highly respected personages, who had access to Central Cabinet Ministers, not of proportion to their actual number in Parliament. Moreover the very fact that Bajaj, Somani, Shriyans Prasad Jain, Bansal and Chinai were elected to Parliament as Congress Candidates is itself indicative of the influence FICCI, as a representative of Indian big business, had on the ruling party.

In Table XI, only the cases of known FICCI leaders, or leaders of FICCI constituents, or of FICCI associations have been cited. Other eminent businessmen in Parliament, for instance, Mohan Singh Oberoi (a Rajya Sabha member from 1960, as well as a leading industrialist in his own right), who were not directly associated with FICCI, have not been included in the illustrative list. In any case, the list indicates only the representation of the better-known prominent business leaders in Parliament.

Apart from these leaders, there were a large number of MPs who were sympathetic to the private sector for a variety of

Table XI: FICCI Representatives in the Central Legislature, 1946-1966

Name	*Family/House*	*Chamber*	*Legislature*	*Period*	*Party*	*Constituency/ State*	*Membership of Other Bodies*
Tulsidas Kilachand	Kilachand	President FICCI, 1950-1951	Lok Sabha	1952-1957	Inde-pendent	Bombay	
Indubhai B. Amin	Amin	FICCI	Lok Sabha	1952-1957	Independent	Bombay	
G.L. Bansal		Secretary FICCI	Lok Sabha	1952-1957	Congress	Punjab	
G.D. Somani	Somani	E.C. FICCI	Lok Sabha	1952-1957	Independent	Rajasthan	Member, Public Accounts Committee, Lok Sabha, 1953-54
			Lok Sabha	1957-1962	Congress	Rajasthan	
Kamalnayan Bajaj	Bajaj	E.C. FICCI	Lok Sabha	1957-1962	Congress	Bombay	
		E.C. FICCI		1962-1967	Congress; Treasurer, Jaipur Session of Congress 1948; AICC Member	Maharashtra	
Bhawanji Arjan Khimji		President Indian Merchants Chamber 1949, (FICCI)	Lok Sabha	1952-1962	Congress; AICC Member since 1942	Bombay	Member, Constituent Assembly, 1946-50
P.R. Rana-krishan Naidu	V.R. Naidu	FICCI	Lok Sabha	1957-1962	Congress	Madras	

R. Ramanathan Chettiar		E.C. FICCI	Lok Sabha	1957-1962	Congress	Madras	Mayor of Madras, 1950-51; Councilor, Madras Corpn., 1948-1952
		E.C. FICCI		1962-	Congress	Madras	
G. Basu		President, Bengal National Chamber of Commerce and Industry, (FICCI)	Lok Sabha	1956-1962	Congress	West Bengal	
				1962-1967	Congress	West Bengal	
Sashi Rajan		Bihar Chamber of Commerce, (FICCI)	Lok Sabha	1962-1967	Congress	Bihar	
Ram Gopal		Vice-President, Bihar Chamber of Commerce, (FICC	Rajya Sabha	1952-1956	Congress	Bihar	
				1956-1962	Congress	Bihar	
Shriyans Prasad Jain	Dalmia-Jain	President FICCI, 1962-63	Rajya Sabha	1952-1956	Congress	Bombay	
				1956-1962	Congress		
Beni Prasad Aggarwal		Western India Chamber of Commerce E.C., Indian Merchants' Chamber, (FICCI)	Rajya Sabha	1952-1956	Congress	West Bengal	
Babubhai Chinai		President FICCI, 1957-58	Rajya Sabha	1958-	Congress	Maharashtra	
				1964-	Congress; AICC Member, Hony. Treasurer, AICC, 1964	Maharashtra	
Ram Gopal Gupta		UP Chamber of Commerce, FICCI	Rajya Sabha	1960-	Independent	Uttar Pradesh	
					Swatantra	Uttar Pradesh	

Dayabhai V. Patel	Son of Sardar Patel	E.C. Indian Merchants' Chamber, FICCI	Rajya Sabha	1958-	Mahagujarat Janta Parishad	Gujarat	Mayor of Bombay, 1954-55; Member Bombay Municipal Corporation, 1938-1956
				1964-	Swatantra, Leader of Swatantra in Rajya Sabha since 1962	Gujarat	Member Bombay P.C.C, 1946-56
Mriganka Mohan Sur		E.C. Bengal Chamber of Commerce and Industry, President, BNCCI, 1956-66 (FICCI)	Rajya Sabha	1954-	Congress	West Bengal	
				1960-	Congress	West Bengal	
				1966-	Congress	West Bengal	
Sitaram Jaipuria	Jaipuria	President, Merchants' Chamber of UP, Member Indian Cotton Milk Federation (FICCI)	Rajya Sabha	1962-	Independent	Uttar Pradesh	
Pannalal Saraogi		President, Chamber of Commerce, Bharat, Calcutta, (FICCI)	Rajya Sabha	1962-	Congress	West Bengal	West Bengal MLC, 1952-62
Ram Kumar Bhuwalka	Birla,	Associate Director of Birla Companies	Rajya Sabha	1963	Congress; Member West Bengal PCC·	West Bengal	West Bengal MLC, 1954-63

Suresh Desai	Secretary, Indian Chamber of Commerce, Calcutta, 1942-43 (FICCI)	Rajya Sabha	1961-	Congress; Member EC, CPP since 1963	Gujarat	Hony. Private Secretary to Sardar Patel, 1945-46
Sardar Santokh Singh	Member, FICCI	Rajya Sabha	1962-	Congress; Delhi Secretary, West Delhi, DCC	Delhi	Member, Delhi Municipal Committee, 1951-58; Member Municipal Corporation of Delhi, 1958-60
Salay Mohammad Sait	Member, Managing Committee, Indian Chamber of Commerce, Cochin since 1960 (FICCI)	Rajya Sabha	1964-	Independent	Kerala	
Sardar Ram Singh	Joint Secretary, UP Chamber of Commerce, Kanpur (FICCI)	Rajya Sabha	1964-	Swatantra	Uttar Pradesh	
Kuppuswan G.V. Naidu Sundaram	President, Indian Chamber of Commerce, Coimbatore (FICCI)	Rajya Sabha	1966-	Swatantra	Madras	Was with Congress, 1930-47

Abbreviations: AICC = All India Congress Committee; DCC = District Congress Committee; CPP = Congress Parliamentary Party; PCC = Pradesh Congress Committee; EC = Executive Committee; MLC = Member, Legislature Council

Source: Rajya Sabha, *Who's Who*, (For Respective Years).
Lok Sabha, *Who's Who*, (For Respective Years).
Times of India, *Who's Who*, (For Respective Years).

reasons. Some had had their election campaigns financed by industrialists. Others represented parties, regions or communities, where particular business groups were influential. Some MPs had been influenced by business lobbyists after coming to Parliament. This however, is a particularly murky area of politics and conclusive evidence is virtually impossible to obtain, as neither the MP who has been influenced, nor the lobbyist, would be willing to provide information.

The MPs favourable to the private sector evidently influenced the formulation of various legislative measures which impinged on the private sector, as we shall see below. Particularly at the select committee stage, when a draft Bill was referred for examination, lobbying by sympathetic MPs, could be vital, as cases cited below will indicate.[1] As clear from Table XI, these MPs belonged not only to the ruling Congress Party, but also to the Swatantra and to other opposition parties. Only the Communist Parties, for obvious reasons, did not have MPs sympathetic to big business.

Apart from direct lobbying by official liaison men and FICCI representatives elected to Parliament, other FICCI members or officers who represent the chamber in more than 100 advisory committees and councils, come into regular contact with MPs, administrators and ministers. These councils and committees include the Central Advisory Council of Industries, the Board of Trade, the Import Advisory Council, the Export Advisory Council, the Planning Commission Advisory Board, etc. The various industry-wise advisory committees, that recommend the plan targets for specific industries, during the Planning Commission's formulation of the Plan, also include business, especially FICCI, representatives. Members of these bodies almost invariably present evidence before all Parliamentary committees dealing with industrial legislation.

FICCI regularly organises seminars and discussions on matters of interest to its constituents. Some seminars and discussions are directly organised by FICCI, while others are conducted by the Diwan Chand Institute, which is controlled by the former. At these meetings, Ministers, Parliamentarians, administrators, journalists, scholars, and other opinion makers participate. The proceedings are generally given nation-wise coverage in the mass media, particularly when important personages participate, as is often the case.

The background material for these meetings is generally prepared by the Economic and Scientific Research Foundations (ESRF) staff. The ESRF also prepares a number of FICCI documents, including their representations to the government and to Parliament. Memoranda and notes are prepared on the Budget, the Plans, and on all important aspects of economic, especially industrial policy. These documents are generally circulated to MPs, senior administrators, sympathetic journalists, etc.

Lobbying efforts by FICCI representatives are considerably facilitated by the sympathy a large number of their subjects already have towards the private sector. The mass media, particularly the daily English-Language Press which is controlled by big business, is generally sympathetic to the private sector (See Chapter 1 above). Because of the sympathetic attitude of the large English-language daily newspapers, pro-big business attitudes are continually disseminated among the elite sections, particularly the decision-makers.

Similarly, informal lobbying by big business representatives, is made easier by the fact that many senior administrators, businessmen, and liaison officers come from the same social strata. They thus have opportunities to often meet informally. Very often informal discussions between FICCI representatives, and the decision-makers, provide the basis for more formal discussions. Informal lobbying efforts therefore, reinforce formal lobbying.

REFERENCES

1. G.D. Birla to Purshotamdas Thakurdas, 7 December 1923, *Purshotamdas Thakurdas Papers*, File No. 42, Part IV, NMML. At that time Thakurdas's reply was lukewarm as he feared that non-cooperation had alienated moderate businessmen (see Thakurdas to Birla 11 December 1923, *Purshotamdas Thakurdas Papers*, File No. 42, Part IV, NMML. This reply was not made in Thakurdas's letter to Birla on 7 January 1927, as claimed by Ray (1979: 304n).

It would have been extremely unusual for Thakurdas to have taken more than three years to reply to such an important letter from an influential personage like Birla.

2. G.D. Birla had suggested this in a letter to Thakurdas, 7 December 1923, *Purshotamdas Thakurdas Papers*, File No. 42, Part IV, NMML.
3. Kochanek has done a similar analysis for the 1966-67 period with similar results (see Kochanek, 1974: 174; Kochanek, July 1978: 1291-1308).
4. From 1958 onwards, the verbatim report of the proceedings of the FICCI Annual Sessions was replaced by a summary report prepared by the FICCI Secretariat. Only the speeches of the President, the Prime Minister (or whoever inaugurated the session), and some other important dignitaries who spoke at luncheon meetings, were reproduced in full. The main speeches, thanking the outgoing President and his reply were also reproduced (see FICCI, Vol. III: i, 1958, Prefatory note by G.L. Bansal, FICCI General-Secretary). This treatment of the proceedings undoubtedly led to some censorship of the criticism made within the organisation, as that inevitably, given the ruling FICCI elite's control over the Secretariat, led to the expungement of some of the more critical statements. Nonetheless, the fact that a certain amount of criticism, sometimes strident, continued is quite evident as we shall see below.
5. Here the term monopolist, as elsewhere in the manuscript, is not used in the strict economic sense, of a single seller controlling a market, but in a more general sense, as it is commonly used, to denote a large business group.
6. For instance, according to the Dutt Committee or ILPIC, Birla House assets amounted to Rs. 457.84 crores in 1966. The next largest house in FICCI, Bangur, had assets of only Rs. 104.30 crores at the time (cited in Goyal, 1979: 22).
7. Information from a confidential FICCI source.
8. In 1966, Chinai was awarded a Padma Bhushan.
9. Interview with G.L. Bansal, May 1980, New Delhi.
10. Kochanek (1974) has also examined several such cases.

3

FICCI and the Congress in the Pre-Independence Period

In the years prior to independence, during the course of the nationalist movement, the Congress emerged as the likely future ruling party. Business interests, like all others, had to endeavour to establish some sort of equation with the nationalist movement, particularly the Congress, while maintaining a cordial relationship with the colonial government. The relationships established during this period were a factor in the business-government understanding that developed in the post-independence era. This chapter aims to bring out the differing stances of Indian big business towards the colonial government and the nationalist movement. We also intend to examine various hypotheses regarding the reasons for these differences.

A number of scholars view Indian big business as having had a more or less common strategy towards the Congress Party during the pre-independence era. According to this hypothesis, the Indian capitalist class is represented by FICCI, which in turn is led by Purshotamdas Thakurdas and G.D. Birla, and ultimately by Birla himself (Chandra, 1979: 145-190; Ray, 1979; Mukherjee, 2 September 1978: 1516-1528). The Indian capitalist class or Birla strategy is hypothesised to be one of a class which is independent of imperialism. In this formulation, the strategy on the one hand, is to use nationalist agitations led by the Congress in order to put pressure on the imperialist rulers but on the other hand, the Indian capitalist class has no hesitation in compromising with the colonial rulers in order to extract concessions. The support to the Congress is seen only as a means to obtain further concessions. Thus in this hypothesis, as advanced by Bipan Chandra, for the operation of this strategy it was a prerequisite that not only the Congress but even other constituents of the nationalist movement, were controlled by Indian big business.

Other scholars like Amiya Bagchi and Claude Markovits identify particular groups of Indian big business as "compradore", i.e. as agents of imperialism, or as "collaborationist". Bagchi contends that Indian capitalists accepted the domination by foreign capitalists, and thus collaborated (Bagchi, 1973: 43-76; Markovits, 1978).

There are a number of hypotheses for differences in big business approaches towards imperialism and the Congress. Markovits and Gordon attribute it as largely due to the heterogeneity of the Indian business community, and consequently their diverse economic interests (Gordon, 1978). Bipan Chandra, Mukherjee, Bagchi and others view the class as more homogeneous, but attribute political differences as due to more ideological or subjective factors (Chandra, 1979: 145). The role of internal business contradictions is not given much importance.

In the hypotheses where Indian capitalists are seen as a nationalist force, the colonial government is assessed as generally unsympathetic to Indian business. It is not very often recognised that the differences could also be due to the colonial strategy of' 'divide and rule' towards Indian business. Bipan Chandra, Markovits, Mukherjee, Ray and others note the attempt by big business to mediate between imperialism and the nationalist movement. The manner, in which the actual balance is struck, differentiates various political strategies and approaches (Thus, the Tatas, Wadias and others were termed loyalists or moderates or conservatives, because they were more inclined to compromise with imperialism against the Congress). Distinctions are made between business's short-term and long-term interests, and the success of business strategies are assessed in these terms. Thus, various groups or leaders are judged politically mature or immature (Chandra, 1979: 190).

Attempts by big business to strike a balance between the

two major forces: imperialism and the nationalist movement, did not leave the capitalists themselves unaffected. The terms and manner in which they responded to various phenomena, was conditioned by the national, socio-economic environment, taken in a large sense. Most of these hypotheses however, concentrate more on the role of big business in influencing the nationalist movement, rather than the other way around. This is perhaps a consequence of treating the Congress, which led the nationalist movement, as an organisation dominated by the big business component of the Indian capitalist class.

An opposite approach is provided in hypotheses which consider the nationalist movement and the Congress to be essentially anti-business, or at any rate, to be somewhat hostile to big business. In these hypotheses, it is claimed that the Congress leadership of the national movement represented the urban middle class which had a fairly deep rooted hostility towards big business (Kochanek, 1974)). In some political circles, particularly in the Congress, there has been a consistent claim that the Party was a representative of the dumb millions. The Congress leadership has often spoken of its great tradition of sacrifice and struggle for the Congress leadership has pointedly disputed the party's dependence on, or even links with, Indian big business.

We have examined some major phases of the national struggle for independence. On each issue, the approach of the major business interest groups has been highlighted. The issues examined include: (a) the Swadeshi movement of 1905-1907; (b) the non-cooperation movement; (c) the first and second Civil Disobedience movements; (d) the Government of India Act, 1935; (e) the rise of the Congress Socialist Party and the 1936 Lucknow Congress session; (f) the 1937 elections and the Congress ministries, 1937-1939; and (g) the deliberations of the National Planning Committee, 1939-1940.

Business Dependence on the Government

The approach of the Indian business community towards the Government of India on the one hand, and the Congress-led nationalist movement on the other, depended on a number of factors. The Raj was the day-to-day administrative authority in the country, on which Indian business interests were dependent in innumerable ways. The government decided and implemented all economic policies. It was the agency that could provide some measure of protection, through tariffs and other means, for Indian industries from foreign, or at least non-British competitors. The government could not only permit the setting up of factories and enterprises but also provide the necessary facilities including land, electricity and raw materials. It had the authority to award mining concessions that were crucial for the coal, iron and steel industries. Since the government was the largest single purchaser, its patronage was a major outlet for sales. Similarly, its taxation policy had a decisive impact on the profitability of Indian companies. The Reserve Bank of India, which was the regulating body for the banking system, was yet another lever that government could deploy to affect the interests of trade and industry. The government was in full control of the major internal transport system (Railways) and the entire port organisation (Chandra, 1979: 154-156).

The government labour policy was another important instrument of leverage. As Bipan Chandra has noted,

> Above all, the capitalist class depended on the government for guaranteeing law and order and social peace in the period of intense social turmoil and political and labour unrest that followed the First World War (Chandra, 1979: 154-156).

The actual dependence of various sections of the Indian business class on the government, varied. This was because, as is now fairly well-accepted, the Indian business community was marked by considerable heterogeneity (Gordon (1978), Kochanek (1974), Markovits (1978), Ray (1979), and Bagchi (1975). The variegated business community not only had divergent interests but also diverse strategic perceptions. It was not possible for Indian capitalists, or even sections within FICCI, to have a uniform attitude towards the colonial government on the one hand, and the nationalist movement on the other. Gordon (1978), Markovits (1978), Kochanek (1974), Ray (1979), and Chandra (1979), all recognise the diversity in business attitudes towards the national movement. There are however, significant differences in their respective assessments of the role played by business in its relations with the Raj and the Congress. Bipan Chandra, unlike the others, believes that, "the (Indian capitalist) class as a whole...revealed a basic homogeneity in its economic and political relationship with imperialism. This homogeneity is revealed after 1927 in the pre-eminent position accorded by the class, as also the government, to the Federation of Indian Chambers of Commerce and Industry and to certain individuals such as Purshotamdas Thakurdas and G.D. Birla" (Chandra, 1979: 145).

Diversity in Indian Business

FICCI, however, has consistently portrayed itself as the economic arm of the national movement, claiming itself to be "wholly in conformity with the views of the Indian National Congress" (FICCI, 1951; Ram, 1963: 420). Senior Congress leaders such as Rajendra Prasad, the first President of India, praised FICCI for its purportedly consistent support to the Congress-led national movement (FICCI, 1951; Prasad, 1953). Not surprisingly therefore, some scholars accept that the role of the business community has been one of "always" aligning "itself with the national movement" (Fadia, 1980: 80). This quite manifestly is not true.

In the first place as we have already noted, the business community was a heterogeneous group, with divergent economic interests, and consequently with varying attitudes towards the Raj on the one hand, and the Congress on the other. This was a consequence of the differentiation within the Indian capitalist class, between industrialists on the one side and traders and merchants on the other. There are several characterisations of the various strata within the Indian capitalist class. Markovits (1978), distinguishes between the "industrialists" (or the national bourgeoisie), the "compradore traders" and the "non-compradore traders". For him the bulk of the Calcutta Marwaris led by G.D. Birla are non-compradore traders, becoming industrialists only in the 1930s. Gordon (1978), differentiates between the merchants who worked the markets, termed "marketeers" and the "industrialists". Ray

(1979: 310), finds Gordon's distinction "a useful one". And as a number of scholars have noted, and as we shall see below, Indian businessmen had a highly sophisticated awareness of the relationship between business and politics. Purshotamdas Thakurdas once remarked: "We (businessmen) can no more separate our politics from our economics than make the sun and the moon stand still".

Secondly, within the same category of businessmen important tactical, and even strategic differences existed. These as we have seen led to the Bombay millowners headed by the Tatas, Mafatlals and Khataus, staying out of FICCI when it was formed in 1927 (See Chapter II above).

Thirdly, there were differences within the leading members of FICCI itself, within what we have termed the FICCI 'elite'. All these differences will be briefly highlighted in the instances examined below.

Business and the Nationalist Movement: The Early Phase

At the beginning of the 20th century, not all sections of the Indian business community supported the national movement. Many millowners of Western India opposed the Swadeshi movement openly (Kannagara, 1968: 47-164). Kannagara has written of the 1905 Swadeshi movement:

> the millowners neither initiated nor gave much support to swadeshism;.. they gave none at all to the boycott... their interests as a class made them... remain absolutely loyal to the British Raj (Kannagara, 1968: 47-164; Gordon, 1978).

Similarly in Calcutta, the Marwari cloth importers opposed the Swadeshi movement as "compradore ties proved stronger then patriotism" (Sarkar, 1973: 143). During the agitations between 1918 and 1922, clear differences in the strategy of the business community emerged. Only three Bombay industrialists made substantial contributions to the Tilak Swaraj Fund, in 1920-1921. These were A.B. Godrej (3 lakhs), Jamnalal Bajaj and Anandilal Podar (2 lakhs) (Krishna, 1966: 426). All of them were well-known supporters of the Congress Party and Gandhi.[2] Bajaj expressed his views at the 1920 Nagpur session of the Congress thus:

> I have a special claim on my brothers of the business community on this occasion and I wish to make a special appeal to them... Fellow-businessmen, our trade, industry and commerce will flourish a hundredfold by our participation in the great national endeavour for Swaraj. We must give up our attitude of indifference and we must shed our fear complex (Quoted in Parvate, 1962: 29).

Bajaj's effort, despite some notable contributions referred to above, was not wholly successful. This led Gandhi in his July 1921 "Appeal to the Millowners", to state that,

> Many friends tell me that the nation is not to expect anything from you. They point out the fact that you have not, with one or two honourable exceptions, paid anything for the (Tilak) Swaraj Fund[3] (*Bombay Chronicle*, 6 July 1921; Quoted after Gordon, 1978: 158-159).

While some Bombay industrialists did not support the nationalist agitations, others were active appoints. In October 1920, at a meeting of the Liberals presided over by Dinshaw E. Wacha, a Parsi millowner, an "Anti-Non-Cooperation Committee" was elected, with Purshotamdas Thakurdas as an honorary secretary. J.R.D. Tata, of the Tata group, and another Parsi millowner, provided "anonymous" funds for the committee (Gordon, 1978: 159).

At the 1920 Nagpur session of the Congress, the party's general criticism of the colonial government's policy on the exchange question, pleased the business delegates present (Gordon, 1978: 159; Brown, 1972: 293). At this stage therefore, some industrialists, as well as a large number of smaller traders were united in their opposition to government economic policies, and consequently provided support to the Congress. It would therefore appear that Gordon's contention that, "While the industrialists were fairly consistently pro-government during the 1918-1922 period, so too were the Marwari and Gujarati marketeers fairly consistently pro-nationalist..." (Gordon, 1978: 159), is somewhat schematic and not wholly correct.

Apparently as a consequence of business dissatisfaction and Congress agitations, the Fiscal Commission in 1922, recommended a somewhat protectionist tariff policy. In 1924, the Government of India's representatives in the Legislative Assembly supported the Steel Protection Bill. But by 1926, the protectionist policy, limited as it was, "petered out" (Markovits, 1978). By the end of the 1920s, the position of Indian businessmen had only "marginally improved" over the previous decades (Markovits, 1978). Disillusionment with government policy led large sections of the industrialists to support the Congress.

Divergences in Business Strategy, 1928-1931

In this period, divisions arose once again among the industrialists. In 1928, many millowners who were members of the Bombay Millowners Association signed the Swadeshi pledge, as did members of the Indian Merchants Chamber and the Indian Chamber of Commerce, Calcutta (Markovits, 1978). Even Purshotamdas Thakurdas, a relatively moderate nationalist, wrote in October 1928 that,

> Should India have to be under a period of chaos in her struggle for self-government, I would prefer that to the present state of inanition and sloth which leads nowhere... (29 October 1928, *PT Papers*, File 71, NMML).

The next year, in 1929, the divergence between the FICCI strategy and that of the section of Bombay industrialists led by the Tatas, came sharply into the open. In the spring of 1929, the FICCI planned to spend about Rs. 50,000 on elections throughout the country in order to win strong representation in the Indian Legislative Assembly, to counter the European businessmen's plan to finance the Central Muslim group in the Assembly. They did not envisage the formation of a new party, but intended to work through the existing nationalist groups, and by maintaining an understanding with the Swarajist Congress. To avoid contests with the Congress, a committee was to be formed of P. Thakurdas, G.D. Birla, (who was then a member of the Nationalist Party), Motilal Nehru and Madan Mohan Malaviya. They were to decide how the proposed election fund was to be spent (Ray, 1979). Various leaders of Indian business had a very close relationship with Gandhi and other Congress leaders. The warm relationship Gandhi had with some leading Indian big businessmen was indicated in his letter to Birla in 1925, when among his "mentors" he mentioned only Birla and Jamnalal Bajaj by name (Letter dated 20 July 1925, reprinted in Birla, 1953: 7). Similar sentiments are exhibited in the Gandhi-Bajaj correspondence (cf. Kalelkar, 1951). Lala Lajpat Rai who together with Madan Mohan Malaviya formed the Nationalist Party in 1926, was also quite impressed by Birla's qualities. In a July 1927 letter to Birla, Lajpat Rai urged him to take to politics. He further confided in Birla about the inner-party differences between him, Malaviya, Vithalbhai Patel and Jayakar (cf. Birla, 1953: 21-22). Later in September the same year, Lajpat Rai stressed, "it is absolutely necessary for you (Birla) to become an All India Man" (letter from Lajpat Rai to G.D. Birla, dated 26 September 1927, in Birla, 1953: 26-27, emphasis in the original). There is substantial evidence of considerable contributions by Birla to Gandhi's activities and various funds (See Birla, 1953).This was an instance of the close ties between the rising big business, the FICCI leadership and that of the Congress.

At this stage, a reported move by a section of Bombay industrialists caused a furore. In reaction to the Bombay textile strike and the activities of the allegedly communist-led Girni Kamgar Union, Dorabji Tata, whose steel works factories in Jamshedpur and textile mills in Bombay had been affected by the strikes, joined together with two loyalist textile magnates, Ibrahim Rahimtoola and Cowasji Jahangir, to organise a political party of Bombay capitalists, both British and Indian. This party while opposing all political parties (especially the Congress) which had supported the textile strike, was to cooperate with European business interests in the Central Legislative Assembly against the 'Red Spectre' (Ray, 1979: 313-314).

Motilal Nehru and M.M. Malaviya reacted very strongly against the move for an anti-Congress political alliance of European and Indian business interests (Ray, 1979: 314). P. Thakurdas and G.D. Birla both wrote to the Tatas, arguing against the move as they realised that it would cost Indian industrialists the support of the Congress. Thakurdas pointed out that a capitalist party would not command the support of more than four members of the Legislative Assembly. Moreover, he argued, European business interests were opposed to the demands of Indian commerce and industry on issues like cotton cloth protection, the Coastal Reservation Bill, Indianisation of the services and preferential treatment to Indian industrial enterprises (P. Thakurdas letter to N. N. Mazumdar, 7 June 1929, *PT Papers*, File No. 42, Pt. II, NMML; Ray, 1979: 314). Birla also realised that Tata's project would be politically counter-productive. He put the matter succinctly in a letter to Thakurdas:

"The salvation of the capitalist does not lie in joining hands with the reactionary element... Men of... (this) type do not command confidence. The politicians feel that our capitalists are out for exploitation hand in hand with the foreign capitalists, and this new association can only confirm the suspicion".(G.D. Birla to P. Thakurdas, 30 July 1929, *PT Papers*, File No. 42, Pt. V, NMML.)

Dorabji Tata's abortive project for a United Capitalist Party highlighted the divergent strategies of the upper stratum of the Indian capitalist class. But its failure, as Ray has argued,

> was a significant event.. (as it) substantially proved that the logical strategy for big business in India was to work through the existing nationalist parties for the attainment of those national objectives which were also their own (Ray, 1979: 315).

Because a large segment of the Indian capitalist class understood that they required the support of the Congress to realise their aims, "henceforth there was a steady interpenetration of the Congress and big business" (Ray, 1979: 316).

Business attitudes towards the Raj and the nationalist movement respectively, varied according to the economic interests of specific sections. Thus various groups of businessmen reacted in diverse ways to the effects of the Depression in 1930, and the initiation of the Civil Disobedience Movement by the Congress leadership. For instance, the immediate economic interests of the Bombay and Ahmedabad millowners seemed to have divergence. The former did not produce better quality cotton textile products and thus feared Japanese competition more than that of Lancashire; whereas the latter had begun to specialise in better quality products and had to fight Lancashire's domination over the market (Markovits, 1978). The Calcutta-based businessmen led by G.D. Birla, had extensive interests in the export trade where they had to contend with British dominance, particularly in the external markets for jute textiles. Similarly, the mainly Gujarati cotton exporters of Bombay led by Purshotamdas Thakurdas, had to struggle against the British stranglehold. Apart from their trading interests, both groups, especially the Calcutta Marwaris, were increasingly investing in the industry, where also they came into conflict with British interests (Markovits, 1978).

Furthermore, both the Raj as well as the Congress sought to enlist the support of Indian businessmen. In 1930, the tariff on textile imports was raised to 25 per cent (Chandra, 1979: 157). On the other hand, in the Eleven Demands presented to the government in 1930, which purportedly represented the minimum national terms for a settlement,

> Gandhi included the capitalist demands for the restoration of the exchange rate to 1s.4d., a protective tariff against foreign cloth, and the reservation of coastal trade for Indian shipping (Chandra, 1979: 139). On the basis of this, Bipan Chandra believes that the Moderates, the Extremists as well as Gandhi and others, the Congress leadership were: "the ideological and political representatives of the industrial bourgeoisie... in the sense that they viewed national interest from the point of view of the industrial bourgeoisie... Moreover, the hegemony of the bourgeoisie over the national movement was, if anything, even more firmly clamped down in the Gandhian era than before" (Chandra, 1979: 139).

The differences among the business community cannot however, be wholly explained in terms of economic interests. For example, both Ambalal Sarabhai and Kasturbhai Lalbhai, were Ahmedabad millowners; but Sarabhai was a nationalist and a confidant of Gandhi and yet he kept out of FICCI. On the other hand, Kasturbhai Lalbhai while having been a founder-member of FICCI collaborated actively with the Bombay millowners in the negotiation with Lancashire ending in the Lees-Mody Pact 1933 (See below). The Civil Disobedience

Movement also brought out sharp divergences within the FICCI leadership. Even prior to the commencement of the movement in January 1930, Purshotamdas Thakurdas was prominent in organising together with Ibrahim Rahimtoola, Chimanlal Setalvad and Phiroze Sethna, (the last two being prominent Liberals), an attempt to offer an alternative to the Congress in the form of the All Parties Conference. Thakurdas et al. were unable to obtain sufficient support, and the attempt failed (Gordon, 1978: 228). Not surprisingly, in view of his distrust of mass agitational activity, Thakurdas opposed the civil disobedience almost from its inception. The more aggressive nationalist Sarabhai wrote to Thakurdas in November 1930 warning that economic distress is increasing and that the purchasing power of the people has gone down, which could lead to instability. Sarabhai concluded, that FICCI should therefore seek the Viceroy's intervention, failing which it should resort to a boycott. Thakurdas came to an opposite conclusion. He feared that civil disobedience might prove a dangerous weapon in the hands of the largely illiterate masses, even for a Swaraj government.[4] Thakurdas did not only oppose the boycott like the Tatas and the Wadias,[5] the leading Bombay millowners; he even wanted to attend the first Round Table Conference in his personal capacity, but in the end bowed to the FICCI mandate against it (Ray, 1979: 318).

G.D. Birla had adopted a policy quite different from that of Thakurdas. Under his guidance, FICCI in May 1930 passed a resolution withholding its cooperation from the first Round Table Conference and requested its member bodies to do likewise, unless Gandhi chose to attend or gave his approval for the same (FICCI, 1951: 62-64). Birla in his presidential reply at the Third Annual General Meeting of FICCI on 16 February 1930 neatly summed up his strategy:

> I am very sorry that we have not been able to influence the government or to convert them to our views, but we never anticipated that. It is impossible in the present circumstances and in the present political condition of our country to convert the government to our views; but I think the only solution to our present difficulties lies in every Indian businessman strengthening

> the hands of those fighting for the freedom of our country... Swaraj is not a question of sentiment. It is a question of bread. The prosperity of the country depends entirely on the amount of political freedom which we get and I think not only in the interests of the country but in the interests of the capitalists, the employers, and the industrialists we should try to fight and strengthen the hands of those who are fighting for Swaraj" (FICCI, Vol. III, 1930, pp. 264-265).At roughly the same time, Birla wrote to Motilal Nehru urging that the Congress relax the boycott (cited in Markovits, 1978).

Later in the year, the tactics of Birla and Thakurdas seemed to converge. While Vallabhbhai Patel was still in prison, Thakurdas threatened him that if the Congress leaders refused to call a truce, he (Thakurdas) and his friends (the Bombay industrialists and moderate politicians) would come into the open against the Congress. (cited in Gordon, 1978: 229). In January 1931, when Patel and Gandhi were released from prison, Lalji Naranji and Chimanlal Setalvad met them to urge peace. Thakurdas, who was informed of the discussions, disclosed the details to the Viceroy. He also informed the latter of the proposed meetings between the AICC Working Committee and some Bombay industrialists, where it was intended to arrive at a consensus for the new Constitution before Tej Bahadur Sapru and other moderates returned from the first Round Table Conference.[6] Thus as Markovits puts it, "One can safely assume that the pressure applied by (Indian) big business upon Gandhi played a part in the conclusion of the Gandhi-Irwin Pact of March 1931" (Markovits, 1978).

FICCI was quick to cash in on its warm relationship with the Congress leadership. Lala Shri Ram, the outgoing FICCI President, persuaded Gandhi to inaugurate the Fourth FICCI Annual Meeting on 7 April 1931. In his presidential address, Shri Ram observed:

> It has happened time and again that the Congress has committed itself to certain economic ideas of far-reaching effects... could we expect the Congress before committing itself to principles of such vital importance to consult the vital interests concerning them? (Quoted after Joshi, 1975: 226).

Gandhi in a very gracious reply welcomed the FICCI suggestion and stated that "the Congress would always be glad to avail of your (FICCI) advice and help... (as it stood) for the industrial propriety and progress of India". He went on to say:

> I cannot forget the services rendered by the commercial classes, but I want you to go a step further. I want you to make the Congress your own and we would willingly surrender the reins to you. The work can be better done by you. But if you decide to assume the reins, you can do so only on one condition. You should regard yourselves as trustees and servants of the poor. Your commerce must be regulated for the benefit of the toiling millions and you must be satisfied with earning an honest penny (Joshi, 1975: 226-227, emphasis added).

The close relationship between FICCI and the Congress is only too evident. Gandhi in his laudatory reference to the "services rendered" by FICCI to the nationalist movement, incidentally helped perpetuate the myth that the Indian business community, particularly as led by FICCI, had always supported the Congress.

The activities of G.D. Birla and Purshotamdas Thakurdas during the second Round Table Conference, reveal the duality of the strategies of nationalist big business towards both the Raj and the nationalist movement. While both Birla and Thakurdas publicly took an uncompromising stand on questions of control of Indian finance and economy, they were much more compromising in private conversations. In a private discussion with Edward Benthall, a leader of ASSOCHAM, Birla is reported to have stated that,

> for the last ten years of his life he (Birla) has been taking up an attitude of opposition, which was more often than not of a bitter nature because it was the only way he could bring pressure on the objects he had in mind, but that henceforward, he desired to work in collaboration and to drop all his hostility[7] (cited in Markovits, 1978).

Birla even seemed willing to accept that there should be no future discrimination against British capital in India (cited in Markovits, 1978). Even Birla therefore, a supposedly aggressive nationalistic businessmen, was prepared to compromise with the British, though probably not as much as he had apparently promised in his discussion with Benthall. The contradiction that sections of Indian big business had with the British is often overstated, e.g. Ray:"Indian big business, in its rationale and self-image, was consciously rooted in nationalism..." (Ray, 1978: 321). In the first place, as we have seen, Indian big business had no one strategy. Some sections like the Tatas and the Wadias, were the more loyalist among the nationalists. Moreover, among the 'nationalist' business sections, even the more pro-Congress elements like G.D. Birla compromised on a number of occasions with the British. Their nationalism therefore was of a different order than that of the Congress. We shall return to this point later.

Business and the Second Civil Disobedience Movement

Close cooperation between the Congress and FICCI, was disrupted by the former's decision to resume civil disobedience on 4 January 1932, after the failure of talks at the Second Round Table Conference. Initially, the Federation refused to participate in the Conference in protest against the imprisonment of Gandhi and police repression (Ray, 1979: 320). Later, he tried to temper its support because of the sharp reaction of the colonial government to the FICCI stand. In January 1932 P. Thakurdas was invited by the Viceroy to serve on a consultative committee of the Round Table Conference. The FICCI E.C. officially advised Thakurdas not to accept the invitation. The government interpreted this advice as an act of support to the nationalist agitation and therefore refused to permit any government members to attend FICCI's annual meeting.

G.D. Birla, who had also been offered a seat on the consultative committee, but had refused, undertook in correspondence with the government, "to persuade the Federation to officially offer its cooperation"[8] (Birla, 1953: 53). This, he clarified in a later letter to Sir Samuel Hoare he had done to,

> convince you that we were true friends who were very eager to see permanent friendly relations restored between the two countries and I had expected that once we could get your trust

> and confidence it would not be difficult for us later on to convince you of the wisdom of our advice[9] (Birla, 1953: 70).

Shri Ram who surveyed business opinion at the time found that "there was not the same enthusiasm in our (FICCI) members to give cooperation to the Congress as there was in 1930". The business community was divided. He therefore contacted G.D. Birla, and both agreed to work for a modification of the January resolution (Singh and Joshi, 1968: 204-205).

When Birla, Thakurdas and Shri Ram attempted to modify the January resolution, they faced stiff opposition from the member bodies. In Bombay, the Indian Merchants' Chamber's committee was controlled by pro-Congress businessmen, who had broken Thakurdas's and his allies grip over the chamber in 1931.[10] This group lead by J.C. Setalvad, A.D. Shroff and others, comprised mainly of traders, shroffs and insurance brokers. They threatened to revolt against the leadership at the FICCI annual meeting, if the earlier resolution was changed (Kochanek, 1974: 164).

The divergence between the nationalists sections of the industrialists and the smaller merchant traders was due, at least in part, to their respective economic interests. In the Finance Act of 1931, and later with the supplementary budget of 1931, the customs duties on sugar imports were substantially raised. This highly protective duty on imported sugar led to a drastic reduction of the sugar imports and to a phenomenal increase in imports of sugar machinery. The net imports of sugar fell from 933,000 tons in 1929-30, two 510,000 tons in 1931-32, and to 366,000 tons in 1932-33. On the other hand, the imports of sugar machinery rose from an average level of Rs. 1,160,000 per year during the 1925-26 to 1929-30, to the value of Rs. 15,311,000 in 1932-31 (Bagchi, 1975: 370-371). The phenomenal increase in machinery imports reflected the increasing investment during the sugar boom, from 1932 to 1936. Sugar factories increased from 32 in 1931 to 130 in 1934 (Chandra, 1979: 170). The vast majority of these new ventures were by Indian industrialists, which led to the share of British capital in the sugar industry to decline from 80 per cent before the boom, to only 20 per cent by 1935-36 (Markovits, 1978). According to

Bipin Chandra,

> Almost every major industrialist of the country took part in the sugar boom. Moreover, many a capitalist found that (the) profits of his sugar factory alone enabled him to keep up the old rate of dividends (Chandra, 1979: 170).

During this period, Indian industrialists also invested heavily in the cotton textile, paper and cement industries (Markovits, 1978; Ray, 1979 and; Bagchi, 1975). Therefore, by early 1932, the large Indian industrialists, despite the effects of the depression, had begun to invest substantially in new industrial undertakings. Consequently, they did not want to alienate the government whose support was necessary for their continued growth. The smaller traders, merchants and shroffs were not as susceptible to government pressures and did not require unofficial patronage in the same measure. Since the European business community dominated the export trade, there was a direct clash of interests between them and Indian traders in the export markets (Markovits, 1978). This led the traders, merchants and shroffs to support the civil disobedience in 1932.

The FICCI E.C. met before the annual session and passed a modified compromise resolution, changing the earlier January resolution to commit the Federation to a policy of cooperation. In the resolution, the first paragraph urged the government to change its policy of repression; the second paragraph rejected the government's interpretation of the January resolution; and the third paragraph offered limited cooperation, proposing the appointment of a committee to "examine and come to an agreed solution in our financial matters"[11] (Birla, 1953: 54). The E.C. was fully aware that they had "acted against the general opinion of their constituencies", but decided to pressurise their member bodies by threatening to resign *en bloc* if the modified resolution was rejected at the annual meeting (Birla, 1953: 55).

This major challenge to the industrialists dominating the E.C. came, as we have noted above, from the pro-Congress traders, shroffs and insurance brokers led by A.D. Shroff, Manu Subedar and J.C. Setalvad who controlled the Indian Merchants' Chamber. This group demanded an *in camera* session to discuss the revised resolution (see also, Kochanek, 1974: 165).

Apparently the session was stormy, because the resolution was "the most controversial that has ever come before the Federation" (FICCI, Vol. III, 1932: 62; 68). After a "very heated discussion", the pro-Congress group pushed through changes in the crucial third paragraph of the E.C.'s resolution[12] (Birla, 1953: 58). In the new third paragraph, the British "repressive policy" was condemned as "of no good to national interests". The FICCI agreed to participate in the consultative committee of the second Round Table Conference only if the government showed "a genuine desire" to change its earlier policies,

> and to discuss and come to an agreement with the progressive opinion of India on the question of financial autonomy, safeguards, reservations and trading rights; (and if)...towards this end, the consultative committee is at liberty to have a free and full discussion on the various questions...[13]

> although Birla, in his March 1932 letter to Sir Samuel Hoare claimed that the new paragraph was "in substance...the same" (Birla, 1953: 54), it was clearly more critical of the government and required more specific assurances from it before offering FICCI's cooperation. The FICCI elite headed by Birla, Thakurdas and Shri Ram had clearly not succeeded in having its own way because of the uncompromising stand of the pro-Congress group comprising mainly of smaller businessmen (Ray, 1979: 321-322).[14]

The re-modification of the E.C. resolution, led to an embarrassing situation for the FICCI elite later. Thakurdas, always more of a moderate than G.D. Birla attended the third Round Table Conference in his personal capacity. In October 1932 he was censured by the Indian Merchants' Chamber, and resigned from the membership of the chamber's committee[15] (see also, Gordon, 1978: 235).

Much greater embarrassment was caused to Indian big business by the activities of the leading Bombay millowners in the second half of 1933. The rapid depreciation of the yen after 1932, had created severe competition for both the Bombay and Lancashire textile interests (Gordon, 1978: 235). As we have seen above, since Bombay produced mainly coarser goods while Lancashire specialised in finer goods, it was now in the interests of both to come to some kind of agreement. In 1933, after prior consultation between Lord Derby, leader of the Lancashire textile interests, and Thakurdas, Homi P. Mody, the president of the Bombay Millowners Association, went to Manchester for discussions[16] (Gordon, 1978: 236). After these discussions, in October 1933, a Lancashire deputation led by Sir William Lees came to India for discussions both with Indian millowners and a non-official Japanese delegation. Initially it seemed that the Indian millowners would be able to reach a consensus on the bases of a quota agreement with Lancashire.[17] But, at this stage, the British government apparently intervened and insisted that the arrangement be on a preferential basis (Gordon, 1978: 236). At this point, the Ahmedabad millowners led by Kasturbhai Lalbhai who had so far participated in the discussions, and certain millowners influenced by him, withdrew their support (cited in Gordon, 1978). After further negotiations, Mody was able to convince the majority of the Bombay millowners, and a bilateral agreement was made between the Bombay and Lancashire interests[18] (cited in Gordon, 1978). In return for this trade agreement, the Lancashire interests were to offer no opposition to the 1935 Government of India Act. As it turned out, they kept their commitment at the time of the debate on Act in the House of Commons (Mankekar, 1968: 73; Gordon, 1978).

As could only be expected, there was a furore over the Lees-Mody Pact, as the agreement was called (Gordon, 1978). Nehru writing in his autobiography in 1934-35, noted that,

> From the point of view of the Congress, this was a gross betrayal, of the national cause, and it was characterised as such. The representative of the Bombay millowners in the Assembly also consistently ran down the Congress and 'extremists' while most of us were in jail (Nehru, 1962: 367).

FICCI, despite the earlier involvement of two of its founder members and leaders in the negotiations, condemned the pact as a "sectional" act, which did not have national approval[19] (FICCI, Vol. III, 1934: 9).

The business community continued its efforts to have the civil disobedience withdrawn so that it was enabled to take full advantage of the potentially favourable economic conditions. In September 1933, the Indian Merchants' Chambers, whose members were worried by the negative economic effects of the repeated closure of markets for political reasons, sent a deputation to persuade Gandhi to call off civil disobedience "in the interests of trade and commerce" (*Bombay Chronicle*, 2 September 1933; cited in Gordon, 1978: 234-235). When in April 1934, the civil disobedience was finally suspended, it would appear that business pressures also played a role in forcing the decision (Markovits, 1978).

Business Support to Conservative Congressmen, 1934-35

Thakurdas and Birla welcomed the withdrawal of the civil disobedience.[20] In an April 1934 letter to Birla, P. Thakurdas agreed, in a reference to the funds being collected by the Congress for the ensuing elections, about "money not being subscribed without making sure of the programme".[21] At this stage, within the Congress there were internal fights. The inter-party struggle was sharpened by the inauguration of the Congress Socialist Party (CSP) at Patna on 17 May 1934. The formation of the CSP was not a new step. Many of those who were later to become leaders of the party were imprisoned together in Nasik Jail in 1933. They included Jayaprakash Narayan, Asoka Mehta, Achyut Patwardhan, Yusuf Meherally and M.R. Masani (Tomlinson, 1979: 50). In the inner-party tussle between the CSP and the conservative members, the 'Gandhians', e.g. Vallabhbhai Patel, Rajendra Prasad, C. Rajagopalachari, Bhulabhai Desai, Jamnalal Bajaj, among others, both groups looked for allies. Inevitably, the latter looked towards business interests, as the capitalists also had the funds required for the reconstruction of the Congress into a parliamentary party (Markovits, 1978). On their part, during the April 1934 to August 1935 period, businessmen through the provision of necessary financial support sought to influence the Gandhian leaders, to make the latter opt for parliamentary struggle, rather than mass agitation (Markovits, 1978).

As the consequences of this business influence,[22] the Gandhians pushed through an anti-socialist resolution at the Congress Working Committee meeting of 17 and 18 June 1934, wherein it was stated "in view of loose talk about confiscation of property and the necessity of class war", that the 1931 Karachi Fundamental Rights resolution, which provided the Congress's economic programme,

> neither contemplates confiscation of private property without just cause or compensation, nor advocacy of class war. The Working Committee is further of the opinion that confiscation and class war are contrary to the Congress creed of non-violence (quoted after Nehru, 1962: 557).

This was clearly directed at the CSP, even though none of its members had spoken of confiscation of private property (Nehru, 1962: 557). As Nehru publicly observed,

> "The resolution had obviously been inspired by the new parliamentary wing of the Congress aiming at gaining the support of men of property in the coming election to the Legislative Assembly. At their instance the Congress was looking more and more to the Right and trying to win over the moderate and conservative elements in the country" (Nehru, 1962: 558). Nehru's autobiography, first published in 1936, was meant to be a public statement. For instance, referring to his sometimes severe criticism of some groups and individuals, Nehru justified it on the grounds "that those who meddle in public affairs must be frank with each other and with the public they claim to serve" (Nehru, 1962, Preface, xii).

In July, Patel sharply attacked the Congress socialists as a group of young men with brain fever who knew nothing about the real needs of the peasantry (Tomlinson, 1976: 52). He, in particular, was nervous that the rise of the CSP might damage the relationship between the Congress and the capitalists (Tomlinson, 1976: 52). Later, in mid-September, Gandhi made public his "fundamental differences" with the CSP programme, criticising the idea of the necessity of class war as "not sound" (Sinha, 1965: 371; Tomlinson, 1976). On their part, the Congress socialists tried to function as an 'official opposition' within the Congress as they realised that they could not take it over (Tomlinson, 1976: 52-53).

Industrialists responded to the anti-socialist tirade by funding the Congress. Dr. B.C. Roy in Calcutta, Bhulabhai Desai in Bombay, as well as Vallabhbhai Patel and Jamnalal Bajaj, collected election funds for the Congress from business circles.

However, business response does not appear to have been overwhelming. In early October, Patel in a letter to Birla, after mentioning the collection of Rs. 10,000 by Desai in Bombay stated that "I think the burden on you will be greater than the estimated when we met there"[23] (cited in Markovits, 1978). Despite this and other appeals, the Congress experienced a shortage of funds in several provinces, especially in Bihar and Uttar Pradesh (Tomlinson, 1976: 42). In March 1935, the Central Parliamentary Board still had a deficit of over Rs. 50,000 on account of the election campaign (Tomlinson, 1976: 42).

The Congress despite the financial constraints was still a nation-wide organisation with large resources of men and money, and did well in the Central Legislative Assembly election, securing 44 of the 88 elected seats (Tomlinson, 1976: 42). Shortly after the elections, the Bombay session of the Congress was held in mid-October 1934. Earlier, on the heels of the Congress victory, Patel issued a press statement expressing his hope that Gandhi would not even attend the Bombay session, since then the change to purge all indisciplined and insubordinate elements (the Congress Socialists) from the Congress might be lost, because of the Mahatma's obsession for compromise[24] (*Bombay Chronicle*, 29 September 1934; Tomlinson, 1976: 107). At the session itself, Patel made a strong anti-socialist speech, but no purge of the socialists could take place in Gandhi's presence (Markovits, 1978).

At the Bombay session, the Congress Constitution was radically amended, largely on the lines suggested by Gandhi. Attempts by the CSP to defeat certain amendments regarding the *Kahddar* qualification for membership of the Congress committee were defeated. The working committee was also given the right to bar from election to any committee, Congressmen who were also members of any other political organisation which it regarded as "anti-national and in conflict with the Congress"[25] (Tomlinson, 1976: 47-48). This however, was a far cry from what Patel had envisaged. Nonetheless, the CSP and other leftists in the Congress had been curbed. This must have reassured Birla and others about the efficacy of the Birla strategy.

The Government of India Act, 1935: Different Strategies for Big Business

After the promulgation of the Government of India Act in August 1935, differences in the political strategies of Indian big business again came out into the open. Homi Mody, the spokesman of the Tata-led Bombay industrialists, once again sought to mobilise for the earlier strategy of building a new political organisation which was openly an instrument of capitalist interests and would mobilise for a "limited but an unequivocal" acceptance of the Act (Mody's speech, *Times of India* 14 August 1935; Markovits, 1978). He warned business elements against the Congress coming into power at the provincial level because of "its flirtations with the extreme socialist elements..." (*Times of India*, 14 August 1935; Markovits, 1978). Mody was disappointed with the Liberals who are politically a weak force, and in any case were not openly supporting the new Constitution. He also feared that rural elements might engulf the businessmen and their supporters in the Congress (*Times of India*, 14 August 1935; Markovits, 1978). Thus, once again Mody representing the more loyalist *Bombay industrialists* mooted a proposal for a new, pro-capitalist party. Markovits (1978), following Kochanek (1974) uses the term Bombay line to refer to the strategy of the Tata-led Bombay industrialists. However, as we have already seen above, a substantial portion of the Bombay-based industrialists supported FICCI. To that extent the term 'Bombay line' is a misnomer.

This time Purshotamdas Thakurdas rejected Mody's proposal (cited in Markovits, 1978). The business leaders in FICCI sought to persuade the Congress to accept the Act. In line with the strategy G.D. Birla went to England in the summer of 1935 to obtain concessions to induce the Gandhian dominating the Congress to accept the Act (Birla, 1953: cited in Markovits, 1978). By October 1935, Mody was forced to change position. His group had failed to obtain the support of any major political party or the other sections of the Indian business community. Moreover, the Bombay millowners were dissatisfied with the advantages gained from the Lees-Mody

Pact. Japanese sale of piecegoods reached a recorded level in 1935-36, and in 1935 Ahmedabad had displaced Bombay as the top textile producer (cf. Markovits, 1978). Further, Lancashire purchases of raw cotton had not increased as expected (cf. Markovits, 1978).

In 1935-36, India's trade deficit had increased, to be slightly larger than that of 1931-32. Therefore, there was increased dissatisfaction in the Indian big business circles with the Government of India's commercial policy. The various segments of the Indian business community felt the need for Congress participation in the government, so that some representation of the Indian big business interests was possible. For this to be effective, some compromise was necessary between the British government and the Congress (cf. Markovits, 1978). By 1936 therefore, the strategies of the Tata group and that of the dominant group in FICCI again began to converge (cf. Markovits, 1978).

The FICCI group continued to strengthen its relations with the Congress. The Gandhian leadership was wished by the business interests, moved closer to a formal acceptance of the 1935 Act. By the end of 1935, Rajendra Prasad had *de facto* launched the Congress electoral campaign when he advocated that the Provincial Congress Committees should carry on propaganda amongst people to make them enrol as voters[26] (*Indian Annual Register*, Vol. II, 1935: 252; cf. Markovits, 1978). In February 1936, G.D. Birla held talks with leaders of the Congress Parliamentary Board, where he estimated the financial need of the Congress for the forthcoming Legislative Assembly Election to be a minimum of Rs. 5 lakhs, of which he proposed to raise a large amount from the business community (cited in Markovits, 1978).

Nehru's Leftism and Big Business, 1936

Nehru's actions after his assumption of the Congress Presidentship after his return to India, brought out into the open divergence in big business strategies towards perceived anti-business elements in the Congress. Before Nehru's becoming Congress President, the CSP had not been a major force in the national politics of the Congress. Nehru's presence and position made a very major difference. That a leader of Nehru's eminence and public standing should lead the left nationalists within the Congress, was a matter that alarmed many businessmen.

Within the Congress, there was considerable opposition to Gandhi's nomination of Nehru. Mahatma Gandhi however, felt that Nehru would serve as a link with the CSP integrating them into the Congress, and that his responsible post would temper his radicalism (Tomlinson, 1976: 56-57). Other Congress leaders were not so sure. Dr. Ansari, S. Satyamurthi and Bhulabhai Desai tried to convince C. Rajagopalachari to contest the presidentship against Nehru. Rajagopalachari, in the absence of support from other conservative Gandhian leaders of the Congress, refused. The majority of the Gandhians apparently believed that despite his radical statements, Nehru would fall in line with Gandhi's programme[27] (Tomlinson, 1976: 57).

Nehru's Presidential address at the April 1936 Lucknow Congress session dashed all such hopes. Speaking on 12 April, Nehru eloquently put forward his socialist principles. He categorically stated his conviction:

> that the only key to the solution of the world's problems and of India's problems lies in socialism... (defined) in the scientific economic sense... I see no way of ending poverty, the vast unemployment, the degradation and subjection of the Indian people except through socialism. That involves vast and revolutionary changes in our political and social structure, the ending of vested interests in land and industry, as well as the feudal and autocratic Indian states system. That means the ending of private property, except in a restricted sense, and the replacement of the present profit system by a higher ideal of cooperative service... In short, it means a new civilisation radically different from the present capitalist order (Gopal, 1975, Vol. 7: 180-181).

Nehru however, clarified that despite his earnest wish to advance the socialist cause he had "no desire to force the issue in the Congress and thereby create difficulties in the way of our struggle for independence". He further acknowledged that socialism did not fit in "the present ideology of the Congress"

(Gopal, 1975, Vol. 7: 181-182). Yet despite these qualifications, there was enough in the speech to alarm the business community, particularly its conservative sections.

On 20 May 1936, the manifesto signed by 21 Bombay businessmen was published. Starting from a quotation from Nehru's Lucknow speech, it sharply attacked socialist ideas. The signatories included: Naoroji Saklatwala (Tatas), Ardeshir Dalal (a director of Tata concerns), V.N. Chandervarker (acting president of the Bombay Millowners Association), Cowasji Jahangir (a loyalist textile magnate), Seth Iswardas Laxmidas (an ex-sheriff of Bombay connected with the Sassoons, the biggest foreign textile group in Bombay), Seth Mathuradas Vissonji (a loyalist connected with certain foreign houses), Dharamsey Khatau (a Bombay millowner's head of the Khatau group and an ally of the Tatas), A.D. Shroff (who had organised the campaign and acted as a link between small business and the Tatas in whose concerns he was a director), Phiroze Sethna (a representative of foreign insurance companies and chairman of Swedish match manufacturing interests in India, apart from being a liberal leader) and Chimanlal Setalvad (a leading lawyer and liberal). Two prominent FICCI leaders, Purshotamdas Thakurdas and Walchand Hirachand, also signed the manifesto[28] (Chandra, 1979: 189-190; Ray, 1979: 325-326; and, Markovits, 1978). Nehru got a biographical analysis of the signatories made and found that most of them were liberals or loyalists linked with the House of Tatas or with foreign capital (cf. Chandra, 1979). Furthermore, the political positions of these industrialists were not supported by large sections of the business community throughout the country. "Nehru", Bipan Chandra notes, "made full use of both these facts in his running polemic against the 'Bombay 21'" (cf. Chandra, 1979).

G.D. Birla's strategy in tackling Nehru was more one of containment rather than that of confrontation. He made his position quite clear in his fairly sharp letter to Walchand Hirachand, a few days after the manifesto was published:

"You have rendered no service to your castemen. It is curious how we businessmen are so short-sighted. We are all against socialism and yet nothing is being done to carry on augmentative propaganda and even people like Vallabhbhai (Patel) and Bhulabhai (Desai) who are fighting against socialism are not being helped. It looks very cruel for a man with property to say that he is opposed to expropriation in the wider interests of the country... Let those who have given up property say what you want to say. If we can only strengthen their hands, we can help everyone... I feel that your manifesto, far from helping has done positive harm to the capitalistic system".[29]

To Thakurdas, his elder, Birla expressed his pained surprise on finding a signature and reiterated that, "the manifesto has given impetus to the forces working against capitalism... I have not come across one (news)paper putting a favourable comment on the manifesto".[30]

From Thakurdas's and Birla's correspondence, it is evident that Gandhi had assured Birla that he would prevent Nehru from committing the Congress to rejection of office at the Lucknow session. In a reply to Thakurdas's query "whether you think that Mahatma's and your expectations have been fulfilled", Birla replied that he was, "perfectly satisfied with what has taken place..., Mahatmaji kept his promise and without his uttering a word, he saw that no new commitments were made".[31]

By this Birla was referring to the Congress acceptance of office and probably to the rejection of the controversial proposal for the direct affiliation of the trade unions and kisan sabhas to the Congress[32] (Chandra, 1979). He noted that "Jawaharlal's speech in a way was thrown into the waste paper basket because all the resolutions that were passed were against the spirit of his speech" (Birla, 1953: 140). Moreover, the new Congress Working Committee contained "an overwhelming majority of Mahatmaji's group... as 10 out of the 14 members were of the right-wing group" (Birla, 1953: 140). The Birla strategy therefore, of containing Nehru and the CSP by supporting the right-wing pro-business elements in the Congress leadership had been quite effective. The attitude of the 'Gandhians' including Gandhi himself, was in line with the strategy Nehru had perceived earlier, of moving the Congress to the Right to win over "moderate" and conservative elements" (Nehru, 1962: 106).

Nehru's biographer, S. Gopal has noted Nehru's reluctance to support the socialists within the Congress because of his desire to prevent a split. Thus he did not support the socialists' amendments committing the Congress to non-acceptance of office, even though he supported the leftist position. Even the appointment of three socialists: Narendra Dev, Jayaprakash Narayan and Achyut Patwardhan to the working committee was due to Gandhi who believed that their selection would help to reduce the support commanded by the terrorists among the younger generation (Gopal, 1976, Vol. I: 205-210).

Birla had also shrewdly assessed Nehru's character. He may well have arrived at this evaluation with the help of Gandhi, with whom he was very close. Birla considered Nehru "a typical English democrat who takes defeat in a sporting spirit". He also acutely observed that Nehru, "seems to be out for giving expression to his ideology, but he realised that action is impossible and so does not press for it" (Birla, 1953: 140).

Purshotamdas Thakurdas agreed with Birla's assessment of Nehru stating that he "never had any doubt about the bona fides of J (Jawaharlal)". But he felt "that a good deal of nursing will have to be done to keep J on the right trails all through"[33] (Chandra, 1979: 195). However, despite this agreement, Thakurdas and Birla evidently did not fully agree on how the "nursing" of Nehru was to be done. Thus, the formers alignment with the Bombay group.[34]

Between 18 and 22 May 1936, the large number of businessmen, mainly smaller traders and brokers, met Nehru to offer their support. These included the merchants and brokers of the Bombay Bullion Exchange; some 20 mercantile associations of Bombay including the Marwari Chamber of Commerce, the Bombay Cotton Brokers Association, the Bombay Grain Dealers Association, and so on. Leaders of these associations while expressing their disagreements with Nehru's socialistic views eulogised his services to the country (Chandra, 1979: 195-196). On 22 May, 15 members of the (Executive) Committee of the Indian Merchants' Chamber met and claimed that the mercantile community, as a whole, did not support the manifesto (Chandra, 1979: 196). However, as we have seen above, the mercantile community had, generally speaking, been much more sympathetic to the nationalist movement than the larger industrialists. Therefore, the support to Nehru from the Bombay mercantile associations was in keeping with their earlier political attitudes. Furthermore, they must have been fully aware like Birla, that despite Nehru's socialist call to arms, it was the conservative section in the Congress that had carried the day.

Indian Business and the Congress Ministries, 1937-1939

In consonance with the strategy of large sections of Indian business that the Congress should accept office after the elections, G.D. Birla worked as a mediator between the British and Gandhi (Chandra, 1979: 205-239). In this connection, he had discussions with Lord Halifax (formerly Lord Irwin) in London, and Lord Linlithgow, the new Viceroy. Both the British as well as Gandhi accepted him as a suitable representative of nationalist Indian opinion[35] (Birla, 1953: 214-218). Thus when Birla heard that, at the instance of Gandhi, the Congress had accepted office he "was simply overwhelmed with joy to hear this news" (Birla, 1953: 218).

Congress rule in the provinces coincided with the passing of the economic ill effects of the depression. There was investment in several new fields and new industrial enterprises. With the disappearance of the earlier tightness in the money market, both import and export trade showed signs of revival (Ray, 1979: 329). Moreover, as the President of the Indian Chambers of Commerce, Calcutta noted, the political stability that was a consequence of Congress rule created encouraging conditions for the growth of Indian capitalism[36] (cited in Ray, 1979: 329). Things were not wholly satisfactory though. There was some unhappiness with the provincial governments' labour and industrial policies. Between July 1937 and the spring of 1938, Indian capitalists hoped for a favourable trade agreement with the British. But when because of the intransigence of Lancashire interests, trade negotiations were deadlocked, big business moved towards a better understanding with the Congress (Markovits, 1978).

By 1939, Indian big business had begun to look towards Nehru and Vallabhbhai Patel to provide the necessary political leadership, rather than to Gandhi, as earlier. This was largely because of the Mahatma's ideological bias towards cottage and small-scale industries and his criticisms of large-scale modern industry. Thus during the 1939 strike of Tata Steel Mills in Jamshedpur, Nehru and Rajendra Prasad were called for the conciliation mission. J.R.D. Tata in an August 1939 letter thanked Nehru for his efforts and his "interest for the welfare of Indian industry"[37] (Markovits, 1978).

The National Planning Committee

In October 1938, Subhas Chandra Bose, the Congress President, convened a conference of ministers of industries from provinces where the Congress Party's economic programme was adopted. The conference appointed a National Planning Committee (NPC) under the chairmanship of Nehru. The non-government members included: Ambalal Sarabhai, A.D. Shroff, Purshotamdas Thakurdas and Walchand Hirachand—leading representatives of Indian big business[38] (Zaidi and Zaidi, 1979: 349). Significantly, while the last three were FICCI members they had been signatories to the Bombay Manifesto of 1936 which had attacked Nehru's socialism[39] (Zaidi and Zaidi, 1979: 357-358).

The participation of big business in the NPC was not an unprecedented or unexpected act. As early as the 1934 annual session of FICCI, its President Nalani Rajan Sarkar had elucidated the Federation's attitude towards state participation in the economy:

"There are certain industries, which by very nature of capital required, risks involved, and importance to national economy, will require direct state initiative, e.g. the construction of railways, big power plants, expensive housing schemes for labour; there are still other industries which may, in the main, be left to private enterprise, and would only be in need for some manner of state assistance. Such assistance may be either direct, e.g. provision of facilities for raising or securing capital required, or indirect, e.g. a sympathetic stores purchased policy and the grant of subsidies or imposition of tariffs against foreign competing products" (FICCI, Vol. III, 1934: 40-41).Hence for years prior to the NPC, FICCI had already accepted a substantial measure of state intervention in the economy.

The outbreak of the Second World War in September 1939 and the Congress resignation from office interrupted the NPC's activities. As K.T. Shah the Honorary General Secretary of the Committee put it: "...from 1940 to 1945, the National Planning Committee had a nominal existence, with the barest staff necessary to keep up that existence" (Planning Advisory Board, 1947; Shah, 1947: 175). Though the NPC never submitted a comprehensive report, some recommendations were made regarding planning in the relevant sub-committees that submitted reports. The left nationalists headed by Nehru contended that the principle of state ownership and control was to apply not only to key industries, public utilities and defence industries but also, "to other large-scale industries and enterprises which are likely to be monopolistic in character, or even to other large-scale industries" (cited in Mukherjee, 2 September 1978: 1519). Nehru insisted that defence industries had to be state-owned, but conceded, in the face of opposition from the conservative members, that in areas where state-ownership was not possible completely, strict state control was the minimum acceptable (cited in Mukherjee, 2 September 1978: 1519). K.T. Shah supported state control more strongly. He categorically stated that, "all key industries must be state-owned and state-managed. The profit motive must be summarily and completely excluded from... every such industry" (Shah, 1947: 61). Existing private enterprise in the key industries, he recommended, should be purchased by government with "just compensation" (Shah, 1947: 61). Shah in fact recommended state ownership of virtually all large-scale industry, particularly that which tended to become monopolistic:

> formal or virtual monopolies under private enterprise should be strictly prohibited... in the production and supply of materials needed for national defence, public utilities and social amenities. The moment any such enterprise evinces signs of getting under monopolistic organisations, the state should...acquire the same... (Shah, 1947: 66).

Moreover, "new industries suitable only for large-scale work by power-driven machinery and for standardised mass production...must be established and conducted as public enterprise" (Mukherjee, 2 September 1978: 1519-1520; see also Shah, 1947: 55).

However, in the important subcommittee on industrial finance which was carried by A.D. Shroff, the draft interim report stated that members could:

> not endorse the recommendation that the state should own and control all defence industries and public utilities and that key industries may be state-owned and state-controlled (Markovits, 1978; Mukherjee, 2 September 1978: 1520).

While Indian businessmen were willing to accept a certain measure of state enterprise and control, they could not accept the extent of state control and ownership, much less the anti-monopoly recommendations made by the left nationalists, particularly K.T. Shah[40] (Mukherjee, 2 September 1978: 1520-1521). Big business initiated a process to work towards their interests within the Congress Party and also pressurising the Party from outside.

The 1940s: Convergence between Big Business and Congress

During the Second World War period, particularly after the Quit India movement of 1942, it became clear to the various groups within the Indian business community that the days of the Raj were numbered. It was also apparent that the new ruling party would be none other than the Indian National Congress. In such a situation, the two major factions of Indian big business who held very different views on the question of support to the national struggle for freedom and the Congress Party, came together and sought to strengthen ties with the Congress. The most important outcome of the convergence between the moderate and 'aggressive' business groups, was the Bombay Plan of 1944. Among the signatories of this Plan were representatives of both the Tata-led as well as Birla-led groups. The need for national planning was advocated by various teams of the National Planning Committee. The NPC, however, because of a large number of its members having been imprisoned, could not complete an overall framework of the plan. In addition, it was also recognised even in colonial government circles, that the state would have to play a more important role by way of direct participation to meet the post-World War II situation. Since the question of planning is itself an important area, we propose to deal with it in detail in Chapter 6 below.

Conclusions

From the foregoing account a number of conclusions may be drawn:

(1) There was no uniformity in business attitudes towards the colonial raj and the Congress. The smaller traders and merchants were generally more strongly pro-Congress and anti-government, than even the 'nationalist' section of Indian big business, during the non-cooperation movement and civil disobedience movements. Beginning with the big business stratum itself, there were various divergent, and even conflicting strategies: as between some Bombay industrialists led by the Tatas and the FICCI group led by G.D. Birla. Even in the ranks of the FICCI leadership, there were substantial differences between the strategy adopted by Purshotamdas Thakurdas on the one hand, and G.D. Birla on the other. Therefore, the available evidence appears quite contrary to the hypothesis that the Indian capitalist class generally followed the strategy as laid down by G.D. Birla (Chandra, 1979; Ray, 1979).

(2) The differences among the different segments of Indian business in their approaches to political issues, were in some measure a consequence of diverging economic interests. Hence, the smaller traders and merchants, as well as the Calcutta Marwaris who were jute exporters and faced entrenched British interests, were more critical of the Raj and supported the Congress. Many of the Bombay millowners, who faced greater competition from the Japanese, rather than from the Lancashire interests, were less critical of the Raj and more hostile towards the Congress. On the other hand, the Ahmedabad millowners feared Lancashire dominance more than Japanese competition,

and were consequently more hostile to British interests and more favourable to the Congress.

(3) Notwithstanding the differences in big business approaches, there is no evidence to show that any group was collaborating with, or acting as an agent of, British imperialism. The diversities in the perception of these business groups reflected diverse strategies for the realisation of their attempts to obtain concessions necessary for the development of Indian capitalism.

(4) Differences in the political assessments of the big business groups cannot be reduced to their economic interests alone. A number of Bombay industrialists including Jamnalal Bajaj, the Podars, the Kilachands among others did not join with the Tata group, despite common economic interests.

(5) The divergent political strategies of the big business factions resulted in sometimes opposed political activities. While the Tata-led faction initially supported the Liberals, and later tried unsuccessfully to build up an alternative political party to the Congress, the FICCI leadership generally supported the conservative sections of the Congress leadership.

(6) There was a substantial amount of political vacillation. Purshotamdas Thakurdas, for instance, alternated between supporting the Tata-led group and falling in line with the Birla strategy. In the case of the G.D. Birla-directed group, when the colonial Raj applied sufficient pressure, they tended to compromise, as is clear from their attempts to tone down their nationalist stance during the second civil disobedience movement.[41]

(7) The nationalist group, including both Birla and the more moderate Thakurdas, attempted to balance between both imperialism and the nationalist movement. On occasion, as in 1931, while taking a more radical anti-British and nationalist stance publicly, they were prepared to compromise privately. Their efforts were directed at influencing the Congress leadership to go in for compromises acceptable to the British. Simultaneously, they sought concessions from the British, to meet the colonial government's proposals acceptable to the Congress.

(8) The colonial Raj, on its part, was unable because of imperialist imperatives to adequately follow a divide and rule policy. On at least two occasions, though, during their support to the Steel Protection Bill in 1924 (which favoured the Tatas) and particular during the Lees-Mody Pact of 1933, they succeeded in dividing Indian big business. But because of the nature of the contradictions between Indian capitalism and the British, this policy could not succeed in the long run.

(9) The Birla strategy of supporting the conservative Congress leadership had some apparent success. In particular, the shift in the character of the Congress towards its becoming a parliamentary party, considerably increased the leverage of Indian big business, who were the major fund providers. In turn, the conservative Congress leaders who were able to elicit big business funds, gained correspondingly in influence within the party.

(10)Despite diverging political approaches, all big business groups generally opposed mass agitations which they considered a potential threat, even in an independent India, particularly if they were permitted to be prolonged. While the Tata-led group was more forthright in its opposition, the Birla-led group sought to apply pressure on the Congress to withdraw mass agitations.

(11)Despite the evidence of substantial big business influence on the Congress, especially from the 1930s, there is far from sufficient evidence to substantiate any hypothesis that big business controlled the Congress, not to mention other sections of the nationalist movement.

(12)All big business groups were influenced by the nationalist movement. The Birla group within FICCI therefore, sought to identify itself with national aspirations as far as possible, without alienating the British. Once it was clear that independence was in the offing, all big business groups endeavoured to appear in fully nationalist colours.

REFERENCES

1. At the 1920 Nagpur session of the Congress, Bajaj was adopted by Gandhi as his "son" (cf. Parvate, 1962: 27). For almost the entire

period till his death in February 1942, Bajaj was the Treasurer of the Congress Party (cf. Sen, 1972: 101-102). In his authoritative history of the Congress, Sitaramayya claimed that, "During the last twenty years, there has been practically no important policy or programme of the Indian National Congress, in which Seth Bajaj has not had a significant part..." (cf. Sitaramayya, 1947: 308-309). Sitaramayya estimated that Jamnalal Bajaj has contributed more than Rs. 25 lakhs to the Congress and related causes during this period (Sitaramayya, 1947: 308).

2. Gordon notes the absence of the names of Bombay industrialists from various fund contribution lists such as the Jinnah Memorial Hall Fund list (1918) and the Tilak Swaraj Fund list (1921). From Gandhi's statement cited above, taken in conjunction with the absence of the names of industrialists from the above lists, Gordon believes that there was no large-scale anonymous contribution by Bombay industrialists, who were apprehensive of antagonising the government (cf. Gordon, 1978: 159). Markovits takes the opposite view and believes, largely on the basis of the contributions by Godrej, Bajaj and Podar, that during 1920 to 1922, Indian industrialists had begun to support the nationalist movement, despite a more pro-indigenous business policy by the British Government after 1918. Yet, he believes that the manipulation of the sterling -rupee ratio, and the lack of concrete protectionist measures left Indian industrialists dissatisfied.

   However, we do not agree with Markovits' assessment, regarding the support by Bombay industrialists for the reasons as given by Gordon above. See also below. Markovits' understanding of the strategy of Indian industrialists vis-a-vis the government, is similar to that of other scholars (See Gordon (1978), Markovits (1978), Kochanek (1974), Ray (1979), and Chandra (1979).

3. P. Thakurdas to A. Sarabhai, 18 November 1930, *PT Papers*, File No. 42, Pt. VII, NMML.
4. S.K. Patil claimed in a May 1975 interview, that all the other Bombay big business groups contributed to the Civil Disobedience Movement in 1930-31 (cf. Markovits, 1978).
5. P. Thakurdas to Private Secretary of Viceroy, 31 January 1931, *PT Papers*, File 107.

   A week later Frederick Sykes, Governor of Bombay, cabled Lord Irwin, that businessmen were putting pressure on Gandhi to negotiate (Telegram, 7 February 1931, *Sykes Papers*, India Office Library, London, cited in Markovits, 1978). Thakurdas was actually following, at this stage, the strategy laid down by Birla in his January 1931 letter to him, wherein, the latter had written, "If we are to achieve what we desire the present movement should not be allowed to slacken. We should, therefore, have two objects in view: One is that we should jump in at the most opportune time for a reconciliation and the other is that we should not do anything which might weaken the hands of those through whose efforts we have arrived at this stage" (G.D. Birla to P. Thakurdas, 16 January 1931, *PT Papers*, File No. 42, Pt. VII, NMML).

6. Memo of conversation with G.D. Birla on 4 October 1931, *Benthall Papers*, Box XI File 1, South Asian Centre, Cambridge.
7. Birla to Sir Samuel Hoare, 14 February 1932.
8. Birla to Sir Samuel Hoare, 2 February 1932.
9. In February 1931, Phiroze Sethna wrote to Tej Bahadur Sapru that, "the Indian Merchants' Chamber is now entirely controlled by the Congress clique". Sethna to Sapru, 18 February 1931, *Sethna Diaries*, NMML; Gordon, 1978: 234).
10. Letter from G.D. Birla to Sir Samuel Hoare, 14 March 1932. Birla had already made this specific suggestion to Hoare earlier during the second Round Table Conference, but the latter had turned it down (see Hoare's letter to Birla of 27 January 1932).
11. G.D. Birla to Sir Samuel Hoare, 20 March 1932.
12. The full text of the resolution, and the changes made is given in Birla, 1953: 333-334, Appendix.
13. This account differs from that of Ray who attributes the compromise resolution adopted by "the Federation" as due to Shri Ram's "insistence". Thereafter, "relations between Birla and Shri Ram remained cool to the end of Shri Ram's life". No evidence for this break is provided in the reference Ray (1979) cited. In fact Singh and Joshi quoted Shri Ram as stating that: "A revision of the resolution was desired not only by myself but also by Birla himself though on different grounds..." (Singh and Joshi, 1968: 205).
14. Resolution of censured of 25 October 1932, and P. Thakurdas's resignation letter, *PT Papers*, File No. 126, NMML.
15. Lord Derby to P. Thakurdas, 27 to July 1953, *PT Papers*, File No. 142, NMML.
16. Lancashire, was to be allowed to import 700,000,000 yards of cotton cloth, twice its then imports; Kasturbhai Lalbhai, interview, 1973: cited in Gordon (1978).
17. That Mody had to campaign hard to convince the other Bombay millowners is clear from the reports in the *Bombay Chronicle*, 13, 14, 27 and 28 October 1933.

18. Indian capitalists were more united in their support to the Ottawa agreement signed between different members of the Commonwealth in July in 1932. Under the agreement, preferences of 7.5 to 10 per cent were given to a wide range of British goods exported to India. In return, the British allowed free entry for some Indian goods and margins of preference for the most important Indian exports, e.g. tea, cotton, jute and tobacco (see Markovits, 1978; Tomlinson, 1979: 133-135). Nehru was bitterly critical of the agreement and the role of Indian capitalists stating that,

    "The part that many capitalist elements have played in India during the past few years has been scandalous, even from the Congress and the nationalist view-point. Ottawa may have benefited temporarily some small groups, but it was bad in the interest of Indian industry as a whole, and made it more subservient to British capital and industry. It was harmful to the masses, and it was negotiated while our struggle was being carried on, and many thousands were in prison" (Nehru, 1962: 367).
19. P. Thakurdas to G.D. Birla, 10 April 1934; G.D. Birla to P. Thakurdas 12 April 1934, *PT Papers*, File No. 126, NMML.
20. P. Thakurdas to G.D. Birla, 10 April 1934, *PT papers*, File No. 126, NMML. In January 1934, Dr. Ansari (a prominent Muslim Congress leader and Gandhi's personal doctor) and Dr. B.C. Roy (leader of the Congress in Bengal who was also Gandhi's personal doctor) in a series of meetings in Delhi had already decided that the Congress should contest the elections due within the next year. Gandhi had blessed Ansari's efforts (see Tomlinson, 1976: 37-38).
21. This influence could only have been heightened by the fact that at the time Jamnalal Bajaj was an acting president of the Congress.
22. V. Patel to G.D. Birla, 4 October 1934, *AICC Papers*, File G-43.
23. Apparently, Patel was looking forward to expelling CSP and feared that Gandhi might stop him, as indeed he did (see P. Sitaramayya to Patel, 21 September 1934, *AICC Papers*, File G-43, 1934).
24. This clause was not invoked when in the case of Congressman who were members of the Hindu Mahasabha till 1939.
25. Prasad sought to cover up the shift in the Congress position by claiming on behalf of the Gandhian leadership in a letter to Nehru in December 1935 that:

    "It has been wrongly and unfairly assumed that the Working Committee has been thinking of nothing except offices under the new Constitution. We have not as a matter of fact given the matter any importance. On the other hand, it is others who have been trying to force our hands to come to a decision" (Rajendra Prasad to Jawaharlal Nehru, 19 December 1935, *Rajendra Prasad Papers*, File No. VI/36, and MML, cited in Tomlinson, 1976: 56).

26. Bhulabhai Desai's diary entry on 26 June 1936.
27. As we have seen above, Thakurdas on several earlier occasions had aligned with the Tata-led Bombay group. Bipin Chandra's contention therefore that,

    "the odd man out among the 21 was Purshotamdas Thakurdas whose growing anxiety had made him sign the manifesto but who was... in wider agreement with the larger and more sober (Birla-led) section of the capitalist class" (Chandra, 1979: 190).... would appear in an overstatement. Walchand Hirachand was also politically conservative and his group, though members of FICCI, did not support the Congress (cf. Mukherjee, 2 September 1978: 1524).
28. G.D. Birla to Walchand Hirachand, 26 May 1936, *PT Papers*, File No. 177, NMML.
29. Birla to Thakurdas, 1 June 1936, *PT Papers*, File No. 177, NMML.While reporting this conversation to Lord Linlithgow, the new Viceroy, on 5 August 1936, Birla stated referring to the relationship between Gandhi and Nehru that "so long as Mr. Gandhi lives there is no danger...of any split in the Congress" (Birla, 1953: 206; Chandra, 1979: 191).
30. Birla to Thakurdas, 20 April 1936, *PT Papers*, File No. 177, NMML (emphasis in original), After his London visit, Birla had reported to Gandhi about his talks. According to Birla though Gandhi, "found it difficult to accept the cheerful view that I took... yet he promised to see that at the Lucknow Congress no new commitments were made".

    While reporting this conversation to Lord Linlithgow, the new Viceroy, on 5 August 1936, Birla stated referring to the relationship between Gandhi and Nehru that "so long as Mr. Gandhi lives there is no danger…of any split in the Congress" (Birla, 1953: 206; Chandra, 1979: 191).
31. Despite Nehru support to efforts by the Congress socialists, the resolution dealing with the Congress attitude on the Constitution was framed and put forward by the Conservative Gandhian group was passed in the Subjects Committee and in the general session. In the official resolution the question of office acceptance was to be decided after the elections, in which the Congress would contest, by consultation between AICC and the PCCs (Tomlinson, 1976: 132).

32. P. Thakurdas to G.D. Birla, 23 April 1936, *PT Papers*, File No. 177, NMML.
33. Since after his frank exchange of views, Thakurdas together with Walchand Hirachand signed the 'Manifesto of 21', it appears that once again Thakurdas adopted a strategy different from that of Birla. Bipan Chandra appears to note the differences in this matter between Thakurdas and Birla, but plays them down. See for instance, Chandra, 1979: 190-196.
34. In the discussions, Birla sought to obtain concessions from the British, particularly some sort of 'gentleman's agreement' that the British would not use the constitutional safeguards against the Congress ministries. It was only on the bases of such an agreement that Gandhi prevailed on the Congress Working Committee to accept office. See Birla's letter to the Private Secretary to the Viceroy, 17 March 1937; and his updated letter (July 1937) to Mahadev Desai, Gandhi's Private Secretary.
35. See also, Indian Chambers of Commerce (Calcutta) Report 1937, Presidential address of M.L. Shah, 25 February 1938.
36. J.R.D. Tata to Jawaharlal Nehru, 10 August 1939, *Nehru Papers*, NMML.
37. Thakurdas, Shroff and Sarabhai figured in the original list of 11 non-official members; Walchand was one of the nine co-opted later. There was no similar representation of the NPC of trade union representatives.
38. Nehru rather perceptively noted in 1944 that though "big business was definitely apprehensive and critical (about the proposed planning exercises)... (it) probably joined up because it felt that it could look after its interests better from inside the committee than from outside" (Nehru, 1972: 395).
39. This became clear from the very strong, even strident reaction by big business to the recommendations of the Economic Programme Committee Report, which were similar to these made by K.T. Shah. Mukherjee plays down the anti-monopoly character of the left nationalist recommendations, reducing it to a "possible anti-monopoly tinge" (Mukherjee, 2 September 1978: 1521).
40. A theory of P-C-P could perhaps be constructed for an analysis of the colonial government strategy on the lines attempted by Bipan Chandra (1979). The Raj also applied pressure tactics and compromised on occasion. Of course, for such a theory too, the same criticisms would hold.

4

The Formulation of Industrial Policy, 1944-1949

The industrial policies adopted in the early years after independence for instance, the April 6, 1948 Industrial Policy Statement, and the April 6, 1949 Statement On Foreign Investments, have to be seen in the background of the pre-independence debates on the nature and pattern of the development that independent India would pursue. The National Planning Committee (NPC), though constituted by the Indian National Congress in 1938, could function only for a short period because its work was disrupted owing to a number of political events. In early 1944, a few of the leading Indian industrialists, some of whom had participated in the deliberations of the NPC, published a document which came to be popularly known as the 'Bombay Plan'.[42] An alternative to the Bombay Plan was provided by a plan formulated by some labour leaders affiliated to the Radical Democratic Party. The latter is popularly known as the 'People's Plan'. The salient features of these two plans are briefly brought out to show the alternative frameworks which were before the national political leadership. The chapter also presents an account of the Industrial Policy Statement, 1945; the Report of the Advisory Planning Board; and the recommendations of the AICC Economic Programme Committee. An assessment is also made of other important events pertaining to the sphere of industrial policy such as the Conference on Industrial Development in India, December 1947; the lifting and re-imposition of controls on foodgrains in the immediate post-independence period, etc. The above account should provide the background in which the nature and significance of the Industrial Policy Statement and the Statement on Foreign Investments need to be examined.

Throughout the discussion, an attempt is made to relate the events to the political conditions obtaining at the time, in particular to the relationship between Indian big business and the Congress leadership.

The Bombay Plan

The Bombay Plan presented by Purshotamdas Thakurdas, G.D. Birla, Shri Ram, Kasturbhai Lalbhai (all FICCI leaders), A.D. Shroff (also in FICCI but close to Tatas), John Matthai (later a Union Finance Minister), Ardeshir Dalal and J.R.D. Tata (Thakurdas, Tata, Birla, Dalal, Ram, Lalbhai, Shroff, Matthai, 1944); can be treated as an indication of the then big business attitude towards planning and governmental control over economy. According to the authors, the memorandum...(was) not in any sense a complete scheme nor ...(was) its scope to comprehensive as that of the National Planning Committee (Thakurdas et al. 1944: Part I: 10). Further it was stated that,

> Underlying our whole scheme is the assumption that on termination of the Second World War or shortly thereafter, a national government will come into existence at the Centre which will be vested with full freedom in economic matters (Thakurdas et al. 1944: Part I: 2, emphasis added).

The fifteen-year plan comprising three Five Year Plans envisaged a total investment of Rs. 10,000 crores (Thakurdas et al. 1944: Part I: 54). Basic industries accounted for 34.8 per cent of the total outlay in the Bombay Plan. This was intended to reduce "the dependence on external finance" as "the capital equipment required by consumption goods industries would be supplied to an increasing extent by our own industries...". The proposed investment in agriculture was to be only 12.4 per cent, on education 4.9 per cent and on health 4.5 per cent of the total outlay. The proposed outlay of Rs. 940 crores, i.e. less than 10 per cent on communications, considering the state of transport system, would also appear on the low side (Thakurdas et al. 1944: Part I: 54). Apart from the pattern of investments, the proposed sources of funding was itself a controversial aspect of the Plan.

As evident from Table 1 'created money' which was "to be created by borrowing against ad hoc securities from the reserve bank" (Thakurdas et al. 1944: Part I: 48), constituted 34 per cent of the total finance and almost 46 per cent of the internal finance. This quantum of deficit financing, as the authors themselves noted was,

> Likely to lead to a gap between the volume of purchasing power in the hands of the people and the volume of goods available. How to bridge this gap and to keep prices within limits will be a constant problem which the planning authority will have to tackle. During this period, in order to prevent the inequitable distribution of the burden between different classes which this method of financing will involve, practically every aspect of economic life will have to be so rigorously controlled by government that individual liberty and freedom of enterprise will suffer a temporary eclipse (Thakurdas et al. 1944: Part I: 48, emphasis added).

Deficit financing which is accompanied by inflation, invariably hits the lower income groups much more, and the rigorous controls that were indicated leading to a loss of individual liberties, was suspected by radical scholars, to be advocacy of an authoritarian big business controlled government. But, as Rajni Palme Dutt writing in 1947 noted, "Howsoever reactionary, the plan has attracted countrywide attention because it reflected the strong irresistible urge for industrialisation" (Dutt, 1947: 186).

However, the industrialist's notion of planning and of the "National Planning Committee" was not the same as that of the Congress (See Chapter IV above). The industrialists envisaged a committee "under the central government...in which the various interests concerned (obviously including business interests) will be represented" (Thakurdas et al. 1944: Part II: 2-3). The Bombay plan's support to the state sector was extremely qualified. In Part II, it was explicitly stated that, "from the point of view of maximising social welfare, state control appears to be more important than censorship management"

(Thakurdas et al. 1944: Part II: 26, emphasis added). Moreover, "it does not invariably follow that all enterprises owned by the state should also be managed by it" (Thakurdas et al. 1944: Part II: 29). It therefore, recommended a "compromise": "The simultaneous operations of both (public and private enterprise) systems in the same industry will provide a useful incentive and corrective to each system" (Thakurdas et al. 1944: Part II: 31). The author also considered a number of the controls to be "of a temporary character" and recognised that these "instituted during the planning period...(would) be similar to those which are in force at present under what conditions..." e.g. licensing, capital issues control, wage controls, etc. (Thakurdas et al. 1944: Part II: 32).

Table I: Bombay Plan: Source of Finance

External Finance	*Rs. in Crores*
a) Hoarded Wealth	300
b) Sterling Securities	1,000
c) Balance of Trade	600
d) Foreign Borrowing	700
Total	2,600
Internal Finance	
a) Savings	4,000
b) 'Created Money'	3,400
Total	7,400
Grand total	10,000

Source: Thakurdas, et al., (1944), *A Plan of Economic Development of India*, (Bombay: The Commercial Printing Press), Part I, pp. 44-47.

The inegalitarian aspect of the plan is also clear from the argument,

> That although gross inequalities are undesirable, total abolition of inequalities, even if feasible, would not be in the interest of the country... (as it was considered) desirable to leave... variations in income...to provide the necessary incentive for improvement of efficiency (Thakurdas et al. 1944: Part II: 4).

The Plan argued for "a steeply graduated income tax" including taxation of "agricultural income above a certain level...", remissions for depreciation and reinvested profits in industries were however advocated (Thakurdas et al. 1944: Part II: 17-20). To the industrialists it was "obvious that India's fiscal system will have to place more and more reliance on direct taxation in future" (Thakurdas et al. 1944: Part II: 21). Baldev Raj Nayar has noted that there are obvious contradictions within the Bombay Plan, between the proposed strict regulations of the economy on the one hand, and the business commitment towards protecting profits on the other (Nayar, 9 September 1971: 855). However, some of the contradictions are more apparent than real. Government controls, some of which already existed during the war period, were not supposed to operate against big business. In fact, according to the Bombay Plan, even the state sector could be managed by the private sector. The overall philosophy of the Bombay Plan was to strengthen Indian private big business. Significantly, though Nehru realised that the Plan was "conditioned by the ways of thinking of big industry and tries to avoid revolutionary changes as far as possible", yet he believed that,

> Revolutionary changes are inherent in the plan, although, the authors made themselves not like some of them. Some of these authors... were members of the National Planning Committee and they have taken advantage of a part of its work[43] (Nehru, 1972: 500-501).

However, it was precisely because of the criticism of the industrialists by various sections of the national movement, including within the Congress itself, that the authors of the Bombay Plan took pains to sound as "revolutionary" as possible, without actually suggesting any concrete measures that may have damaged their interests.[44]

The Bombay Plan was, as could be expected, welcomed by FICCI. Muthiah Chettiar, in his Presidential Address at the 17th Annual Meeting of FICCI on 4 March 1944 lauded the plan, (of which Part I has been published), as one which, "if wisely followed and firmly put into practice will... assure the happiness and welfare of the India of tomorrow..." (FICCI, 1951: 127-128). A resolution to the same effect was passed during the meeting which also endorsed the view that the establishment of a national government was essential for the economic development of India (FICCI, 1951: 127-128).

The People's Plan

The Bombay Plan was not the only non-Congress attempt at planning. In March 1944, the People's Plan was published. Three colleagues of M.N. Roy in the Radical Democratic Party, V.M. Tarkunde, G.D. Parikh, and B.N. Banerjee prepared a ten-year plan with an investment of Rs. 15,000 crores for the areas of British India, bypassing themselves on ideas set out by Roy earlier (Karnik, 1980: 101).[45] In contrast to the Bombay Plan the People's Plan placed its emphasis on the development of agriculture, enhanced the outlays on social services and was self-financed (Karnik, 1980: 101). The authors explicitly stated their belief in the Soviet type planning under a "genuine democratic state" (*Young Indian*, 1944, D72, D74). It was categorically pointed out that,

> The problem of distribution can neither be divorced from that of production nor from that of the kind of social structure and productive relationships that will be retained in the planned economy (*Young Indian*, 1944,D74).

The land and mineral wealth were to be national property, and the heavy industries and banks subject to state control. The state was directed to promote large-scale cooperative agriculture and to promote the increased productivity of labour. Further, all new industry started during the plan period which included the basic and heavy industries were to be financed, owned and controlled by the state. It was proposed that the private sector be subject to "rigid control" with the state permitting private industry at 3 per cent return on its capital (*Young Indian*, 1944, D76-D81).

From Table II it is clear that there is virtually no dependence on external finance in the People's Plan, unlike the Bombay Plan. The difference in the respective emphasis of the two plans is clear from the following Table III.

In both relative and absolute terms, the People's Plan had a greater emphasis on agriculture. The outlays on education, health and housing etc., were also substantially greater. This was apparently in consonance with the stated objectives of the Plan.

The People's Plan while providing a radical alternative to the Bombay Plan, was by no means as important as the latter. By 1944, M.N. Roy though prominent as a founder of the Indian Communist movement, and the Radical Democratic Party

Table II: People's Source of Finance (Footnotes)

	Rupees in Crores
Sterling Balances	450
Initial Finance: Estate Duty, Inheritance Tax, Death Duties	810
Income from nationalised land in the pre-first year of the Plan	90
Income from agriculture for reinvestment during the period of the Plan	10,816
Income from industries for reinvestment during the period of the Plan	2834
Total	15,000

Source: *Young Indian*, Special Independence Number 1972, Vol. II, Nos. 34-40, D. 94.

Table III: Showing Patterns of Investment under the Bombay and People's Plan

Rupees in Crores

S. No.	*Sector*	*Bombay Plan*	*Percent-age*	*People's Plan*	*Percent-age*
1	Agriculture	1,240	12.4	2,950	19.7
2	Industry	4,480	44.8	5,600	37.3
3	Communication	940	9.4	1,500	10.0
4	Health	450	4.5	760	5.1
5	Education	490	4.9	1,040	6.9
6	Housing	2,200	22.0	3,150	21.0
7	Miscellaneous	200	2.0	–	–
	Total	10,000		15,000	

Source:

(1) Thakurdas, et al., (1944), *A Plan of Economic Development of India*, (Bombay: The Commercial Printing Press), Part I, pp. 50-55.

(2) *Young Indian*, Special Independence Number 1972, Vol. II, Nos. 34-40, D. 86; D 87.

founded and led by him, was not a major political force.[46] The People's Plan therefore, was virtually ignored by Indian big business interests.

The People's Plan together with the recommendations of the National Planning Committee, and the Advisory Planning Board, provided alternative frameworks to that put forward by Indian big business in the Bombay Plan.

Business and the Industrial Policy Statement, 1945

Representatives of FICCI and big business participated in the Industrial Policy Committee set up by the British colonial government in October 1944. They included G.D. Birla, Shri Ram, Walchand Hirachand, Purshotamdas Thakurdas, Kasturbhai Lalbhai (the FICCI President), Padampat Singhania (all associated with FICCI), and John Matthai, Ardeshir Dalal, (both associated with the Tatas, although Matthai also maintained regular contact with FICCI), and J.R.D. Tata himself (See Mukherjee, 17 January 1976: 67-73). However, both the FICCI and the Tata group representatives made explicitly clear their commitment to a national government, which they realised would replace the colonial government, sooner rather than later. Ardeshir Dalal however, joined as a member of Planning and Development in the British Viceroy Executive Council in August 1944.[1]

At its Annual Meeting in March 1945, FICCI passed a resolution expressing anxiety over the absence of a well-defined industrial policy, and calling for an early declaration of the same by the government (FICCI, Vol. III, 1945: 132-133).

On 23 April 1945, the colonial government's Planning and Development Department issued a statement of India's future industrial policy. The objectives of Indian industrial development were stated to be: (a) to increase the national wealth by the maximum exploitation of the country's resources; (b) to make the country better prepared for defence; and (c) to provide a high and stable level of the employment (Roy, 1965: 47).

The main features of The Industrial Policy Statement were as follows:

(1) About 20 major industries were proposed to be brought under the control of the central Government;
(2) Basic industries of national importance i.e. aircraft automobiles and tractors, chemicals and dyes, iron and steel, prime movers, transport vehicles, electric machinery, machine tools, and electro-chemical and non-ferrous metal industries—would be nationalised if adequate private capital was not forthcoming, as it was considered as essential in the national interest to promote such industries;
(3) All remaining industries were to be left for private enterprise under varying degrees of control. The coal industry was to be examined and dealt with separately;
(4) In order to regulate industrial development in the national interest, the central government would have to take powers to license industrial undertakings. Control would also be required to secure for the workers a fair wage and decent conditions, to prevent excessive profits to private capital, and to ensure the quality of industrial products;
(5) The central government was to have the primary responsibility for assisting industrial progress by development of transport facilities, development of power, provision of facilities for industrial and scientific research, and provision of facilities for technical education. The central government could also assist industry by helping to raise capital, by tariff and taxation policy, and by the procurement of capital goods from abroad (Roy, 1965: 48).

Badridas Goenka, the FICCI president, in a press statement on 20 April 1945, while finding "the fundamental objective of industrialisation and economic development as laid down by (the) government commendable", stressed that "there are certain essential prerequisites for the fulfilment of these objects". For this,

> the first necessary condition... is the establishment of a National Government representative of and responsible to the people...

> (and) fully autonomous to pursue national economic policies in the interest of India, untrammelled by controls from Whitehall or constitutional restrictions on its sovereignty.

Significantly however, Goenka went on to state that the "fundamental issue for India today is not that of state versus private enterprise but of paramountcy of national interests". He went on to criticise the "system of controls and restrictions which... only tend to hamper industrial progress and dampen initiative and enterprise...", in the absence of a constructive plan (FICCI, Vol. II, 1945: 125-126). He made pointed criticism of the silence of the Industrial Policy Statement,

> in regard to the important problem of safeguarding Indian industries also from internal competition of non-Indian interests. There is no assurance on the part of the (colonial) government that they will not permit foreign enterprises from establishing themselves in India behind tariffs walls to compete unfairly with or even destroy Indian industries (FICCI, Vol. II, 1945: 126).

Regarding the statement's objective of "prevention of concentration of industries in the hands of a few persons or of a special community", Goenka argued,

> that while everyone would appreciate government helping backward communities in participating in the industrial development of the country, the conditions stipulated by government would in effect retard industrialisation unless particular communities come forward to undertake the risks of industrial enterprise (FICCI, Vol. II, 1945: 126).

These positions were to form a more or less constant refrain in FICCI's reactions to government policy even after independence. The criticism of controls, of anti-monopoly measures and of the government's latitudes towards private foreign capital was to continue throughout the period studied in this chapter. Therefore, it is not quite correct to infer as Kidron has, from some of the earlier statements in the Bombay Plan, that the FICCI "switched to an anti-controls policy" at its 19th Annual Meeting in March 1946 (Kidron, 1965: 73). In fact by 1944, the trend as regards India's political future was clear (as we have seen above).

Therefore, as noted above, the demands that FICCI was to make in the post-independence period one already articulated, though sometimes in a 'radical' guise. Earlier G.D. Birla's speech while moving a resolution on "the Industrial Development of India" at the March 1946 Annual Meeting, largely repeated the earlier sentiments expressed by Badridas Goenka in his April 1945 statement (see above). Birla alleged that through,

> the guise of planning... and in the name of targets, government has adopted a policy of allocation under which they decide as to which party and at what place a certain factory should be elected. The result is that nepotism and corruption are encouraged. I am therefore, dead against government deciding where and who should build up a certain industry (FICCI, Vol. III, 1946: 23).

Similarly, in their reactions to the budget, the FICCI E.C. in their press statement of 4 March 1946, welcomed the tax concessions given, i.e. withdrawal of the excess profits tax, the reintroduction of the special initial depreciation allowance, and reliefs on earned income. FICCI however urged the abolition of controls on capital issues (FICCI, Vol. II, 1946: 94-96). This was of a piece with the general FICCI attitude: concessions were welcome, controls were not.

Advisory Planning Board

In the last week of October 1946, the Advisory Planning Board of the Interim Government was appointed. K.C. Neogy was appointed Chairman, and members included Dr. Meghnad Saha, K.T. Shah, Dr. Zakir Husain, Nawab Ali Nawaz Jung and G.L. Mehta (FICCI), apart from half a dozen government officials. Although the Advisory Planning Board's Report evoked little response in view of the prevailing political uncertainty, (with the Muslim League having made its demand for the partition of the country) (Roy, 1965: 57-58), its recommendations were an important indicator of the direction of the industrial policy of the later national government which was to be formalised in the 6 April 1948 Industrial Policy Statement. According to the terms of reference of the Board, it was to make its recommendations in the light of its review of the work of the National Planning Committee and other

Congress proposals regarding planning (Roy, 1965: 57).

Of interest to our study, are the Report's recommendations regarding the nationalisation of certain basic industries. The Report warned,

> that if at the present juncture the state attempted to take into its own hands the ownership and management of a large range of industries, the industrial development of the country might not be very rapid.

It was, however, felt by the majority that "some basic industries" should be nationalised. These would include,

> apart from defence industries; and industry or branch of any industry which might be found desirable to start as a state enterprise through the reluctance of private capital to undertake it, the nationalisation of the following should be considered: coal, mineral oils, iron and steel, motor, air and river transport (GoI, 1947: 16-17).

It must be noted here that the majority desired nationalisation of industries wherever private capital was reluctant to invest.

However, G.L. Mehta (a FICCI member) disagreed with these recommendations as,

> any proposals for nationalisation are likely to retard industrial development and hamper initiative and enterprise... I believe that the machinery of the state can be more usefully and constructively employed in so far more urgent tasks such as, for example, the development of water resources and electric power as well as improvement and coordination of the transport system, apart from provision of technical aid and encouragement of scientific and industrial research.

He again reiterated that, "at the present juncture, it would... be impractical to launch upon any programme of nationalisation or specify any industries... as suitable for nationalisation" (GoI, 1947: 28, emphasis added). As noted earlier, this attitude against government control over, or ownership of, certain vital industries, was characteristic of the industrialists' views even in the Bombay Plan. Thus G.L. Mehta was only, somewhat bluntly, reiterating the FICCI position.

K.T. Shah on the other hand was critical of the majority view for not going far enough in the matter. He argued,

> I have no doubt about the rapid industrialisation of the country being promoted, rather than retarded, by a policy of planned, intensive, universal socialisation. I would not confine the programme of nationalisation to 'basic industries' or defence industries only; but extend the regime to every item in the field of production. Nor would I wait upon the readiness of private capital to take up any industry. Without public ownership, national control over industry would be nominal—if even that, and, without effective and rigid control of all productive enterprise, the success of any planned programme will be illusionary (GoI, 1947: 46-47 emphasis added).

Shah's positions though similar to those in Nehru's most radical rhetoric in the 1933-36 period (see Chapter III above), were obviously too concretely 'socialistic' to be acceptable to the large bulk of the Congress itself.

The Chairman of the planning advisory board, K.C. Neogy took a moderate stance relative to the majority. In principle he was in favour of state ownership (and some form of state management) of certain key industries. But,

> in the interest of rapid industrialisation... I should not like to make nationalisation a condition of development in certain spheres... I should like to take advantage of private enterprise for speeding up industrial progress, leaving it open to government to acquire such industries as may be found appropriate and desirable at a later date (GoI, 1947: 28; Roy, 1965: 62).

Neogy's position was in essence much closer to that of G.L. Mehta and of FICCI, as it proposed a larger, leading role for private enterprise.

The Industries Conference

Shortly after independence, a "Conference on Industrial Development in India" popularly known as the "Industries Conference" was held in New Delhi on 15 and 16 December 1947. FICCI which was invited by the Ministry of Industry and Supply to nominate a representative, nominated G.D. Birla as their representative (FICCI, Vol. II, 1947: 235-239). However, a large number of industrialists associated with FICCI were presented at the Conference in other capacities. They included apart from Birla, A.D. Shroff, Shri Ram, Padampat Singhania, S.P. Jain, Lalji Mehrotra and Kasturbhai Lalbhai (FICCI, Vol. II, 1948: 168; Ministry of Industry and Supply, n.d.: iv-vi). As FICCI's own Report on the Conference shows, the recommendations were quite acceptable to the industrialists (FICCI, Vol. II, 1948: 164-168). As the Report put it,

> The present crisis is described as essentially a crisis of confidence. Frequent conflicting pronouncements by Ministers of the Central and Provinces, threats of nationalisation, vacillating and indefinite (sic.) government policies, wild attacks on the industrial community in general, the political uncertainties arising out of the Kashmir and Hyderabad problems have all combined to discourage private enterprise and to cause serious lack of confidence which acts for the low tempo in business activity in the country (FICCI, Vol. II, 1948: 164-165).

To resolve the crisis of confidence, among other recommendations was the imposition of a ceiling on prices implying a control also over the distribution over the essential commodities, which the industrialists noted "has become unavoidable" (FICCI, Vol. II, 1948: 166). The industrialists present, must have been reassured by Nehru's statement,

> that far too much attention is often paid to acquiring existing industries... But it seems to me a far better approach to the problem for the state to concentrate more and more on new industries of the latest type and to control them in a large measure, because then the resources of the state go towards further... and controlled progress, instead of merely trying to get hold of something which exists (Ministry of Industry and Supply, n.d.: 88).

The industrialists also accepted a ceiling on the dividends which was not to exceed the average of the past three years, and 6 per cent in case of companies which had not earlier paid dividends (FICCI, Vol. II, 1948: 166). However, the business community obtained vital concessions from the government. The most important was stated thus in the report:

> The power vested in government to nationalise certain industries at the end of 10 years has proved a serious deterrent to the expansion of such industries. The removal of the time limit is recommended (FICCI, Vol. II, 1948: 167).

Together with this,

> The government should provide incentive both for expansion of the existing industries and the creation of new ones by permitting special depreciation allowances to make the higher replacement costs of plants and machinery. In case of new industries, relief from income tax should be granted for the first five years (FICCI, Vol. II, 1948: 167).

The Conference recommended a three-year industrial truce which was accepted by the trade unionists present. This idea had been suggested by G.D. Birla earlier in the year in his 18th April speech at the Fourth Ordinary General Meeting of the United Commercial Bank, wherein he had suggested that there be no strikes or lockouts for a specified period (*Eastern Economist*, 25 April 1947). The recommendations of the Conference were welcomed by the big business controlled press (see for instance *Eastern Economist*, 9 January 1948).

Removal of Controls

The war-time controls on a number of commodities including food grains, sugar, cotton and cloth were lifted in the period between December 1947 and January 1948. This was despite the "categorical recommendations" (Deshmukh, 1957: 43), of the Commodity Prices Board comprising A.D. Gorwala and D.R. Gadgil. The Board has stated that, "not abolition but the improvement of the system of controls would have to be undertaken especially as our long-term plans involved regulation and direction of economic activity by the state" (quoted after Deshmukh, 1957: 43). Earlier in late September 1947, the government appointed a Foodgrains Policy Committee under the Chairmanship of Purshotamdas Thakurdas. Its members included G.D. Birla and Shri Ram, apart from Dr. V.K.R.V. Rao, R.L. Gupta, D.S. Bakhle, S.Y. Krishnaswami and Dr. Ram Manohar Lohia (Deshmukh, 1957: 46-47). In view of the strong representation of FICCI stalwarts, it is not surprising that in its Interim Report of December 1947, the majority including the FICCI members and Dr. V.K.R.V. Rao, recommended an "orderly and planned" liquidation of existing controls (Deshmukh, 1957: 45-46). In late November 1947,

Dr. Rajendra Prasad, the Food Minister, had apparently received assurances from K.K. Birla in reference to the proposed sugar decontrol "that no undue advantage would be taken"[2] (cf. FICCI, Vol. II, 1947: 180-181). In December 1947, the government removed controls from sugar and foodgrains. In January 1948, controls were lifted on cotton and cloth. This was hailed by the *Eastern Economist* (23 January 1948) as "the one and only straight decision".

C.D. Deshmukh has, in his memoirs, admitted that "the removal of controls... was a political derivative of this pressure..." (Deshmukh, 1974: 59) i.e. pressure from businessmen who cited Gandhi's criticism of controls as leading to dishonesty and corruption. However, as Frankel has noted,

> Since the business community was not noticeably influenced by Gandhi's moral injunctions in other cases when their vital economic interests were opposed, it is difficult to interpret their deference to Gandhi's wishes on the issue of decontrol as anything but expediency (Frankel, 1978: 76n).

Because of this decontrol there was a "spectacular" rise in prices and profits.

> From December 1947 to July 1948, the wholesale price index for foodgrains rose by nearly 58 per cent. The prices of all other consumer goods increased by about 33 per cent. In the two years between November 1947 and November 1949, the general price index was permanently inflated by some 23 per cent to 29 per cent (Frankel, 1978: 76).

Dr. S.P. Mookerjee, the Minister for Industry and Supply, admitted in Parliament, that despite increased production of cotton textiles since December 1947, prices had increased from 50 per cent to 200 per cent. The government could not take effective steps to check profiteering under the system of decontrol (*Eastern Economist*, 20 August 1948). The government was thus forced to reimpose controls: on cloth in July, on cotton in August, on foodgrains in September, and on sugar in December 1948 (Frankel, 1978: 76; see also Deshmukh, 1974: 54-57).

The removal of controls and the other concessions to

business were accompanied by assurances to the business community. Sardar Patel addressing businessmen at a Calcutta Club luncheon on 5 January 1948 stated that,

> Our Finance Minister (Shanmukhan Chetty) belongs to your class... we deliberately appointed him to create confidence in the industrial future of India... Our Commerce Minister (C. H. Shabha) is also an experienced industrialist. Syama Prasad Mookerjee, the Minister for Industry and Supply, is not a Congressmen... I am quite certain that all these Ministers would like to secure your co-operation in making India industrially great (Vallabhbai Patel quoted in Natarajan, 1952: 247-248).

Economic Programme Committee

The euphoria generated by the Industrialists Conference was short-lived. Barely a month later in late January 1948, the Report of the Economic Programme Committee of the AICC, of which Nehru himself had been Chairman was released. The immediate background to this Committee's deliberations was provided by the "Resolution of Objectives" passed at the AICC meeting held in New Delhi on 17 November 1947[3] (*Young Indian*, 1972, Vol. II, Nos. 34-40: D 98). The resolution stated that,

> Our aim should be to evolve a political system which will combine efficiency of administration with individual liberty, and an economic structure which will yield maximum production without the operation of private monopolies and the concentration of wealth and which will create a proper balance between urban and rural economies. Such a social structure can provide an alternative to acquisitive economy of private capitalism and the regimentation of a totalitarian state (*Young Indian*, 1972, Vol. II, Nos. 34-40: D 98, emphasis added).

The Economic Programme Committee met in New Delhi on 22 and 25 January 1948 to prepare a final report on the basis of the reports of its sub-committee (*Young Indian*, 1972, Vol. II, Nos. 34-40: D 99). Of particular importance was the sub-committee headed by Gulzarilal Nanda as Convener, which included Jayaprakash Narayan, Shankarrao Deo and John Matthai as members. This subcommittee was "to consider (a) ownership development and control of large-scale industry including transport, (b) coordination of large-scale industry with cottage industry (c) priorities in planning and (d) industrial relations" (*Young Indian*, 1972, Vol. II, Nos. 34-40: D 99). The main committee included apart from Nehru who was the chairman, Maulana Azad, J.C. Kumarappa, N.G. Ranga, John Matthai and Shankarrao Deo as members and therefore represented important elements of the Congress leadership. The major recommendations with respect to the industrial sector were the following:

1) Industries producing/manufacturing food articles, clothing and consumer goods were "for the most part to be run on cottage or small-scale basis" (*Young Indian*, 1972, Vol. II, Nos. 34-40: D 101).
2) Where large-scale industry competed with the cottage and small-scale industries, the former was to be brought under "state control" (*Young Indian*, 1972, Vol. II, Nos. 34-40: D 102).
3) "New undertakings in defence, key and public utility industries should be started under public ownership. New undertakings which are in the nature of monopolies or in view of their scale of operation serve the country as a whole or cover more than one province should be run on the bases of public ownership". This was subject to the limitations of the state's resources and capacity and "the need of the nation to enlarge production and speed up development" (*Young Indian*, 1972, Vol. II, Nos. 34-40: D 102).
4) The existing undertakings in the areas reserved for the state would be transferred to public ownership after five years. "In special cases" that transfer could be effected earlier (*Young Indian*, 1972, Vol. II, Nos. 34-40: D 102). This transition to public ownership would "be controlled so as to avoid the dislocation of the economic life in the country, fall in production, uneconomic acquisition of inflated assets and the diversion of valuable resources from more urgent to less urgent uses". To ensure this the acquisition should

take place after the existing "excessive" profits had fallen due to decreased prices "or under pressure of appropriate legislation or administrative measures" (*Young Indian*, 1972, Vol. II, Nos. 34-40: D 102).

5) The managing agency system was to be abolished "as early as possible". Further, the necessary regulations and controls "needed for the realisation of the objective of national policy in the matter of industrial development" were to be imposed (*Young Indian*, 1972, Vol. II, Nos. 34-40: D 102).
6) A maximum of 5 per cent dividend in terms of capital employed (capital plus reserves) was also recommended. Surplus profits were to be shared between workers and shareholders "in proportions to be fixed by government" (*Young Indian*, 1972, Vol. II, Nos. 34-40: D 102- 103).
7) It was further recommended that, "all resources available for investment should be subjected to the control and direction of the state...(which) should set a Finance Corporations for financing industries". To ensure this, it was necessary that "Banking and Insurance should be nationalised" (*Young Indian*, 1972, Vol. II, Nos. 34-40: D 103).
8) A cooperative distribution system for consumer goods was envisaged as "necessary to secure a balanced progressive economy". In fact "cooperating consumer societies" were to be given government assistance "to control all large and growing volume of the retail trade in the necessities of life of the humbler section of the population" (*Young Indian*, 1972, Vol. II, Nos. 34-40: D 103).
9) "To implement the above programme...a permanent Central Planning Commission should be appointed to advise and assist the Congress governments in the practical steps that should be taken" (*Young Indian*, 1972, Vol. II, Nos. 34-40: D 103).
10) The country's foreign trade, the Report recommended, should be directed in a manner "to make it possible

for the nation to provide its primary needs and thus buttress its independent position".

11) Finally, regarding foreign capital, the Report recommended that "the place of foreign capital should be carefully examined so as to ensure the economic controls remained with the nationals of the country" (*Young Indian*, 1972, Vol. II, Nos. 34-40: D 103).

The Report of the Economic Programme Committee generated a storm of protest. M.A. Master, the FICCI President, on behalf of the FICCI E.C., sent a long telegram on 3 February 1948, protesting against the Report to Nehru, Patel and other members of the Cabinet (FICCI, Vol. II, 1948: 179-181). In the telegram it was stated that the Report's recommendations made by FICCI, "very apprehensive about the future economic structure and the industrial development of this country" (FICCI, Vol. II, 1948: 179). While FICCI recognised that the Report had not been submitted to the government but was only a Congress Party document it felt that as Nehru himself was a party to the recommendations, it was "likely to substantially influence the future economic and industrial policy of the Government of India". The proposed reservation and of the food processing, clothing and other consumer goods industries for the cottage and small-scale sector was opposed for ignoring the imperatives of increased production and for preventing "the equitable and natural extension of large-scale industries because of state action" (FICCI, Vol. II, 1948: 179). The recommendations for establishment of the new undertakings in the defence and key industries and in public utilities in the public sector only, as well as the transfer of the existing undertakings in these industries to state ownership, after five years, was strongly opposed. The acquisition of privately owned industries after their profits declined was decried as "tantamount to an act of virtual expropriation" (FICCI, Vol. II, 1948: 180).
The FICCI,

> "Deeply regretted that when some of the responsible Cabinet Ministers, for instance, the Finance Minister (Shanmukhan Chetty—a former FICCI E.C. member)... were trying to revive the

> incentive to private enterprise by assuring the country that for many years to come there was need and scope for private enterprise in industry...", The Economic Programme Committee should have made recommendations to the contrary (FICCI, Vol. II, 1948: 180-181).

The proposed state control over investment resources including the nationalisation of banking and insurance, it was claimed would "seriously retard the future industrial growth of India...". The proposed controls on the distribution and division of profits between the workers and investors, FICCI warned, would have "serious and far-reaching effects on the flow of capital..." (FICCI, Vol. II, 1948: 181). The FICCI argued the economic programme committee recommendations were virtually "short-circuiting... resolutions passed at the Industries Conference" to which the Government of India was itself a party. The telegram concluded with a dire warning, that if the recommendations of the committee were followed they would have "far-reaching and disastrous effects on the economic and industrial structure of this country" (FICCI, Vol. II, 1948: 181). The FICCI, therefore, suggested an early conference of all the concerned interests to evolve a suitable policy (FICCI, Vol. II, 1948: 181).

In particular the proposed dominance of the state sector, in terms of both ownership and control of a fairly large number of industries including consumer goods industries, was considered an immediate threat to the private sector. The setting up of a cooperative distribution system as envisaged in the report, would have severely limited the role of private trade. In view of the fact that a number of industrial groups associated with the FICCI had extensive trading interests (Levkovsky, 1966: 323), FICCI was bound to be perturbed by the limitation on the sphere of operation of private capital in trade. The abolition of managing agencies and nationalisation of banks and insurance was another major threat to the larger houses, as these proposed measures would have struck at the very roots of large-scale private enterprise. Thus, the very strong, even strident reaction, from FICCI and industry to the E.P.C. Report.

FICCI reactions to the E.P.C. Report were not confined to written representations. Their representatives met various members of the Cabinet and number of important bureaucrats in order to effect a reversal of the state policy (FICCI, Vol. III, 1948: 72).

The Political Balance of Forces

The mobilisation by FICCI against the recommendations of the EPC report must be viewed in the context of the actual balance of political forces in the country at the time. On the one hand, as indicated earlier, there were close relations between important sections of the Congress leadership and FICCI. For instance, after the assassination of Mahatma Gandhi, Nehru wrote to G.D. Birla regarding the acquisition of Birla House as a national monument. In his reply to Nehru on 12 May 1948, Birla pointed out that the Birla House was not only associated with Gandhi but it was a nerve centre of all nationalist activity. Apart from Gandhi, others who had resided at Birla House included Patel, Rajendra Prasad, Govind Ballabh Pant, Bhulabhai Desai, K.M. Munshi, Shankarrao Deo and Balasaheb Kher. Even Nehru himself had resided there "for a few days" (Das, 1973, Vol. VI: 69). Birla further pointed out that,

> Many important political decisions or far-reaching consequences have been taken in this house... Many important meetings of the (Congress) Working Committee were held... (as well as later) the first meeting of the Congress Cabinet... immediately after the Congress assumed power in 1946 (Das, 1973, Vol. VI: 70).

Patel was able to enlist the support of C. Rajagopalachari in opposing the proposed acquisition of Birla House (Das, 1973, Vol. VI: 73-74). In a letter to Nehru on 13 May, Patel wrote in Nehru that,

> I have known Ghanshyamdas (Birla) through Bapu (Gandhi) for more than 25 years. The relations between Bapu and him were those of father and son... But never throughout our long connections has he taken any undue advantage of these ties or exploited them.

Later in the same letter, Patel referred to his "very close and intimate connections with Birla" (Das, 1973, Vol. VI: 72). He also admitted the validity of Birla's claim of having hosted "so many prominent personalities... Through many years of valuable contacts with men, prominent in business and public life" (Das, 1973, Vol. VI: 73). Despite Patel's claim to the contrary, the extent of Birla's influence with him and other prominent leaders of the Congress that was a subject of public criticism, should be evident (see Chapters II and III above).

Patel's attitude towards business circles is reflected in his concern over the powers given to the Income Tax (Investigation) Commission in 1948. (Although the matter was finally resolved after the 1948 Industrial Policy Statement, the attitude of the government and of Patel in particular, is indicative of the influence that business circles were able to wield in the government. This would enable us to appreciate the conditions that proved conducive for the jettisoning of major recommendations of the E.P.C. Report). On 27 January 1948, Patel wrote to Nehru referring to the minutes of the Cabinet meeting of the 19 January, in which he claims that,

> The powers which we have now given to the Income Tax (Investigation) Commission are rather drastic and will have an unsettling effect on business. We can ill-afford to upset seriously the business world at this time of crisis. On the one side, we are straining every nerve to stimulate production by carrying the employers with us. If, on the other side, we make such drastic changes, it would virtually mean not only upsetting what we have so far succeeded in achieving in restoring confidence, but also creating further lack of confidence.

Patel therefore urged further discussion in the Cabinet "so that, if necessary, we could make suitable changes to relax the rigours of the law" (Das, 1973, Vol. VI: 278).

Earlier on 10 January 1948, the Secretary of Income Tax (Investigation) Commission had written to FICCI referring to the proposed amendments of Sections 34 and 46 of the Income Tax Act (FICCI, Vol. II, 1948: 65-71). After receipt of this letter, it is virtually definite that FICCI representatives including Birla would have approached senior Congress and government leaders, including Patel himself. Patel's letter to Nehru was probably occasioned by such a representation which made him aware that businessmen were "upset seriously", and which led him to bless the latter's case so forcefully to Nehru. The Prime Minister in his reply the next day, referred to the earlier discussion in the Cabinet where both Shanmukham Chetty and Justice Varadachari, the Chairman of the Commission, had urged the Commission be given "additional powers" without which it would be "completely helpless". Nehru also explained to Patel that to wind up the "Commission at this stage... would create a very bad public impression". In view of the "full consideration" of the matter, Nehru expressed his doubts about the likelihood of any changes being made after another Cabinet Meeting (Das, 1973, Vol. VI: 278-279). After this, Patel had no choice but to agree though he "still felt" that "the cumulative effect would be some lack of confidence in the business world" (Das, 1973, Vol. VI: 279-280).

On 5th February, C.H. Bhabha[4] then Commerce Minister wrote to Patel, after his earlier letter to Chetty of 27 January had elicited no reply. Bhabha referred to an earlier assurance by Liaquat Ali Khan that, "the names of the parties whose cases would be referred to the Investigation Commission would be put up to the Cabinet for approval". He also urged that "a few businessmen" be consulted before the proposed amendments were placed before the Constituent Assembly (Das, 1973, Vol. VI: 280). Later in June-July, Patel corresponded with K.C. Neogy, Bhabha's successor as Commerce Minister, and Chetty, in order to force the withdrawal of cases against "leading industrialist" from the Investigation Commission (Das, 1973, Vol. VI: 281-284). Patel also brought Nehru around to his point of view (see below). Patel's letters to Chetty were in some cases quite peremptory. On 16th July, Patel wrote to Chetty advising him to ensure "that the harassment of innocent persons is avoided". The letter made it clear that Chetty should "set matters right" by withdrawing some of the cases (Das, 1973, Vol. VI: 284).

Later on 27th July, Patel wrote to Chetty enclosing a copy of a telegram he had received from Kasturbhai Lalbhai (of FICCI). The telegram warned that if Section 34 of the Income Tax Act was amended by the Select Committee, it would "seriously interfere (with) business and industrial enterprises" (Das, 1973, Vol. VI: 286-287). Patel asked Chetty "whether there is any force in what he (Lalbhai) says?" (Das, 1973, Vol. VI: 286). However, as it turned out, Patel's insistence on the withdrawal of cases succeeded. On 19 February 1948, Chetty after consultations with the Chairman of the Central Board of Revenue, issued oral instructions with the actual written order issued only later on 12th March (Das, 1973, Vol. VI: 288-289). However, since he had not informed the Constituent Assembly of the proposed withdrawals, nor had he referred the matter to the Investigation Commission, Chetty was forced to resign as Finance Minister on 15 August 1948. Nehru accepted his resignation the next day (Das, 1973, Vol. VI: 289-290).

This episode demonstrates Patel's control over the Congress Party and his sympathies with the industrialists. In fact Patel had himself selected Chetty as the Finance Minister, only after another FICCI representative G.L. Mehta had refused (Venkatasubbiah, 1977: 70). Chetty had earlier on a number of occasions made his sympathies for private enterprise quite clear (See above). He promised the Indian Merchants' Chamber (IMC), an important constituent of FICCI, on 29 September 1947, that he would "not be a party to any policy of taxation that will discourage private enterprise" (quoted after Venkatasubbiah, 1977: 75).

The above discussion lends substance to what is fairly common, though debatable, view that "by 1946 the most powerful man inside the Congress Party organisation was neither Gandhi nor Nehru but Sardar Vallabhbhai Patel..."(Frankel, 1978: 75). Patel's position of strength within the party organisation enabled him to even overrule Gandhi and Nehru, in some vital instances. When Acharya J.B. Kripalani resigned as Congress President in 1947, Gandhi's suggestions that either Jayaprakash Narayan or Acharya Narendra Dev be elected to replace him, were rejected by the Congress Working Committee[5] (Frankel, 1978: 75; Weiner, 1957: 58). This was done despite Nehru's support to Gandhi. The relative strength of the conservative section of the Congress leadership was largely due to the relative weakness of the leftists within the party.

Weakness of the Left

In 1939, the events at the Tripuri Session of the Congress forced the resignation of Subhas Bose (Frankel, 1978: 71; Weiner, 1957: 54; and Sitaramayya, 1947: 109-118). Bose's decision to lead his followers out of the Congress to form the Forward Bloc, weakened the strength of the Leftists within the Congress (Frankel, 1978: 71; Weiner, 1957: 54-55).

Earlier, the June 1939 AICC meeting in Bombay had adopted "far-reaching changes in the Congress Constitution" (Sitaramayya, 1947: 120), which restricted admission to the party, and which were suspected to be directed against radical elements (Adhikari, Sen et al., 1974: 57). Unfortunately, for the Left, the Socialists and the Communists had their own conflicts and were unable to unite.[6] In the struggle between Bose and the conservative leadership, the Socialist group had played an "ambivalent" role (Weiner, 1957: 55). Interestingly, a Government Intelligence Report in 1940, also assessed the Leftists' strength in the AICC as being of only 26.6 per cent of the members, while the Rightists had the support of 73.4 per cent. The report also noted that the "Congress socialists at present are for all practical purposes closely allied to the right wing..."[7] (cited in Pandey, 1979: 161-162). After the expulsion and forcing out of the Communists in 1940 and 1945 (Pandey, 1979: 165), the strength of the Socialists declined further. Although outside the Congress, the Communist Party strength had increased with a membership of 89,263 by the second Congress of the CPI in February 1948, it was to decline very sharply thereafter. The CPI at its second Congress followed "a full-fledged left-sectarian, dogmatist and left-adventurist line" which led the party "to the verge of total collapse" by January 1950 (Adhikari, Sen et al., 1974: 76-81). The CPI termed independence in 1947 as a "fake independence", and treated the Congress leadership as "collaborationist" (with British imperialism), and therefore the "spearhead of counter-revolution".

In this political background, the balance of political forces did not favour radical, anti-big business elements. On the contrary, as we have briefly sketched out above, the political scenario in the immediate post-independence period favoured the conservative section within the Congress led by Patel. Representatives of the Socialist group in the E.P.C., e.g. Jayaprakash Narayan, N.G. Ranga and others were able to make the Committee pass radical, even revolutionary programmes and formulations. They were unable however to force their implementation.

In fact, from at least as early as 1936, when it became obvious that the Congress was likely to come to power after the provincial elections, a large number of the more prosperous rural elements joined the party. Almost half of all Congressmen who joined in the mid-thirties were from landed peasant castes, with landholdings between 21 and 100 acres (Kochanek, 1968: 337-338). By 1948, the Congress General Secretary received hundreds of complaints regarding bogus membership (Kochanek, 1968: 215). The AICC's attempt to curb bogus membership, by eliminating the four-anna fee for primary membership through an amendment of the party constitution in 1948, actually backfired. Between 1945-46 and 1949-50, primary membership of the Congress increased phenomenally from 55 lakhs to 170 lakhs (Kochanek, 1968: 222). The increased weight of these new landholding peasants in the Congress membership, acted against the radical elements in the party organisation.

The final blow to the Socialist group was dealt by Patel in the second half of February 1948, shortly after Gandhi's death. Under Patel's influence, the AICC approved an amendment to the party constitution which barred all Congressmen from membership "of any other political party, communal or other which has a separate membership, constitution, and programme" (quoted after Frankel, 1978: 72). This was a direct attack on the Congress Socialist Party (CSP). Shortly thereafter in March 1948, at the Socialist Party Convention at Nasik, the majority voted to sever their connections from the Congress and to form a new party (Weiner, 1957: 57). Thus at this stage, as Frankel has noted, "Nehru's socialist support inside the Congress Party was sharply attenuated" (Frankel, 1978: 72).

Nehru-Patel Relations

Nehru's lack of support within the Congress, complicated the problems of his relations with Patel within the Cabinet. Though Nehru was Prime Minister, he only held the portfolios of External Affairs and Commonwealth Relations. Patel, the Deputy Prime Minister held the more important portfolios of Home Affairs, States and Information and Broadcasting. Correspondence between Nehru and Patel between December 1947 and January 1948, centred around the precise delineation of their tasks. Patel even objected to Nehru's dispatching his Principal Private Secretary, H.V.R. Iyengar to Ajmer, in order to report on the communal rioting there (Das, 1973: 8-10). As Patel put it, there were "such vital differences of opinion" between the two relating to "the fundamental question of our respective sphere of responsibility, authority and action..." (Das, 1973: 12).

Gandhi intervened in the dispute, as both Patel and Nehru sought his guidance. In a note dated 6 January 1948, Nehru referred to Patel and his "difference in approach... to economic and communal matters..." which had persisted "ever since we worked together in the Congress" (Das, 1973: 17). Nehru believed, that as Prime Minister he was called upon "to play an outstanding role..." as the Minister "more responsible than anyone else for the general trend of policy and for the co-ordination of the work of various government departments". This role of "a coordinator and a kind of supervisor..." Nehru believed, was essential if he was not to be reduced to "only a figurehead..." (Das, 1973: 17-18). As was his wont, Nehru graciously offered to resign if a compromise was not acceptable (Das, 1973: 19-20). Of course, Nehru was aware that his resignation could not be accepted. This was however, a threat he had employed before and was to use again. In the same note, Nehru also expressed his concern that, "we have delayed too long already in laying down an economic policy and this has led to differing interpretations and statements by Ministers" (Das, 1973: 18).

Patel in his own note to Gandhi differed with Nehru's interpretation. He argued that the Prime Minister had "no overriding powers over his colleagues..." as that would render "a Cabinet and Cabinet responsibility... superfluous". He offered his own resignation, if matters came to that (Das, 1973: 20-24). Once Gandhi died Nehru and Patel decided to sink their differences and work together. Both generally accepted that public discussion of their differences were, in Patel's words "bad for the country" (Das, 1973: 29-30). Despite this compromise, the differences in the "Diumverate" were of political significance as Patel not only provided an alternative focus of power within the Cabinet, but as we have seen earlier, he was able to wield considerable influence over his colleagues. Patel was also influenced by some important bureaucrats, generally sympathetic to business. C.D. Deshmukh, who was Governor of the Reserve Bank in 1948-49, was in regular contact with Patel. During this period Chetty had tentatively proposed to nationalise the Imperial Bank, but this was opposed by Patel on the basis of Deshmukh's "confidential advice... that the time was not ripe for such a step" (Deshmukh, 1974: 155).

To sum up the above discussion, by February 1948, in the mobilisation and counter-mobilisation by various political forces, those sympathetic to private enterprise appeared to have gained the upper hand. Thus efforts by pro-business forces, including FICCI itself, succeeded in whittling down the recommendations of the E.P.C. shortly after they were made. The following discussion deals briefly with the events which highlighted the dilution of Congress 'radicalism' culminating in the April 1948 Industrial Policy Statement.

Nehru and the E.P.C. Report

On 17 February 1948, Kazi Syed Karimuddin moved a private member's resolution in the Constituent Assembly stating:

> "This Assembly is of the opinion that the economic pattern of this country shall be a socialist economy based on the principle of nationalisation of key industries and cooperatives and collective farming and socialisation of the material resources of the country and that the Government of India shall adopt the said principle immediately (CAD, Legislative, Vol. II, Part 2, 1948: 825).

Karimuddin cited the report of the EPC in his support (CAD, Legislative, Vol. II, Part 2, 1948: 826), and stated that his purpose in moving the resolution was to ensure "a declared and definite (economic) policy on the part of the Government of India" (CAD, Legislative, Vol. II, Part 2, 1948: 827).

Nehru strongly argued against the adoption of the above resolution (CAD, Legislative, Vol. II, Part 2, 1948: 828-834). He repeatedly stressed the importance of increasing production. As he put it, "everything that we do should be judged from the point of view of production first of all as well as other points of view" (CAD, Legislative, Vol. II, Part 2, 1948: 829). He warned that "such steps may often lead to some kind of petty disaster... (and) graver crisis may follow". Further, "in an attempt to change the economic system you may have a period of semi-disaster" (CAD, Legislative, Vol. II, Part 2, 1948: 829). Nehru emphasised the tentative nature of the E.P.C. Report, pointing out that it had not received "the final sanction" of the AICC. Even if it had, the AICC would only have laid down "the general policy", leaving it to the government to decide priorities (CAD, Legislative, Vol. II, Part 2, 1948: 830, 832-833). Nehru interpreted the Report as stating that the state's limited resources would be used in starting new industries or projects, e.g. hydroelectric projects, big reservoirs, irrigation canals, malaria prevention, prevention of erosion, etc., rather than being wasted in nationalising existing industries. This would also permit private enterprise to continue production in various fields (CAD, Legislative, Vol. II, Part 2, 1948: 830-831). He specifically referred to the proposed five-year period after which certain industries were to be taken over as of "little significance in the present changing dynamic world". Because of the unpredictability of changes "in the political and economic domain..." in the near future, this time period merely gave "some picture in our minds to which we can work up to". In fact, the proposed five-year period was intended to reassure "those who might be somewhat put out by the prospect of these changes" (CAD, Legislative, Vol. II, Part 2, 1948: 831).

Later in the speech, Nehru explicitly stated that, "obviously we want the good will of the industrialists of the country" (CAD, Legislative, Vol. II, Part 2, 1948: 833). Nehru finally assured the assembly that the government was "very anxious" to draw up an industrial policy statement (CAD, Legislative, Vol. II, Part 2, 1948: 833). While concluding, he appealed to Karimuddin "not to press a resolution which on the face of it cannot be given effect to" (CAD, Legislative, Vol. II, Part 2, 1948: 834). In response to Nehru's appeal, Karimuddin withdrew his resolution (CAD, Legislative, Vol. II, Part 2, 1948: 836). The speech was, as can be expected, welcomed by the financial press. The *Eastern Economist* in an article on "Nationalisation" referred to,

> Nehru's speech on economic policy... (as) very welcome, as it finally lays at rest any suspicion that government may be committed to hasty and ill-considered decisions on purely doctrinaire, or ideological considerations... the Prime Minister's speech will go a long way towards creating the right atmosphere which had deteriorated because of the rather drastic steps recommended by the Economic Programme Committee....

It expressed the "hope that the government will soon make a detailed announcement of their economic policy" (*Eastern Economist*, 20 April 1948).

FICCI's 21st Annual Session was held on 28th and 29th March, 1948, virtually on the eve of the Industrial Policy Statement. In his presidential address M.A. Master expressed the business community's "earnest anxiety to know where the private enterprise stands in the future industrialisation of this country..." (FICCI, Vol. III, 1948: 16). He also urged that the industrial policy be announced "at an early date" (FICCI, Vol. III, 1948: 18).

Nehru in his reply reassured the industrialists present. Referring to the question of nationalisation, he averred that, "in India today we cannot adopt any one 'ism'"... We do not have the strength to nationalise big industry... *We have to think and consider what to nationalise and what not to* (FICCI, Vol. III, 1948: 26, emphasis added). Nehru referred to the Karachi Congress resolution wherein it was stated that big industry should belong to the state as "theoretical talk". He stressed that "in our nation private enterprise has a definite role" (FICCI, Vol. III, 1948: 26, emphasis added).

In his inaugural speech at the FICCI session, Nehru clearly indicated the shape of things to come. He stated that the government had classified industries into three broad categories. The first was of industries like the defence industry, in which the private sector would not be permitted. The second group of industries would be those which would, gradually over a period of time, come under government control. The third group of industries would be wholly for the private sector (FICCI, Vol. III, 1948: 26).

In the two categories of industries in which the state would participate, Nehru felt that the government should not bother taking over the existing old privately owned enterprises run "in an old-fashioned manner". The government on its part, should be interested in setting up new enterprises (FICCI, Vol. III, 1948: 26).

While stressing the need for cottage industries, Nehru clarified that he had "never considered them as something opposed to the large-scale industry" (FICCI, Vol. III, 1948: 30). Significantly, Nehru stated that even those industries that were nationalised, should be run in the manner of private enterprise. Nationalised industries should be made into corporations, run as efficiently as private industry (FICCI, Vol. III, 1948: 27).

As for the problem of inequality, Nehru noted, as usual, that the country's wealth was in the hands of a select few. He however, argued that to increase the national wealth it was necessary not to cut the pockets of the rich, and that all work. He therefore stressed the need for increased productivity. Nehru's speech in effect outlined the Industrial Policy Statement that was to follow in a few days. The sentiments expressed must have greatly reassured FICCI and the big business community.

At the FICCI Annual Session 1948, a number of resolutions were moved opposing the recommendations of the E.P.C. (FICCI, Vol. III, 1948: 57-69; 69-73). While moving a resolution on the "Government's Policy of Nationalization: Need for Clear-Cut Pronouncement", the mover Chunilal Mehta approvingly referred to Nehru's speech at the Constituent Assembly in reply to Karimuddin's resolution (FICCI, Vol. III, 1948: 72-73). Mehta however referred to press reports that the forthcoming industrial policy statement would increase the period for transfer of private undertakings to the state, from 5 to 10 years.

This increased period was also considered too little (FICCI, Vol. III, 1948: 72).

Therefore, after Nehru's speech, the publication of various press reports, and their own discussions with the political leadership and bureaucracy[8], the industrialists had considerable, if not complete, information about the nature of the forthcoming Industrial Policy Statement. As stated earlier, this must have considerably reassured big business, and in itself was an indication of their influence on the government.

1948 Industrial Policy Statement

The Statement on Industrial Policy followed a few days later. Dr. Shyama Prasad Mookerjee, the Minister for Industry and Supply placed the statement before the Assembly (CAD, Legislative, III, Pt. 2, 1948: 3293-3297). The Statement formalised the shift in government policy from the recommendations of the E.P.C., indicated by Nehru's 17th February speech. The basic premise of the Statement was that, "a mere redistribution of existing wealth would make no essential difference to the people and would merely mean the distribution of the poverty". Emphasis, therefore, was given to all measures necessary for a "continuous increase in production" which alone could create conditions for the satisfaction of "the basic needs of the people". In view of the existing constraints, the state could not intervene in industry "as widely as may be desirable". Therefore, it was believed,

> that for some time to come, the state could contribute more quickly to the increase of national wealth by expanding its present activities wherever already operating and by concentrating on new units of production in other fields, rather than on acquiring and running existing units. Meanwhile, private enterprise, properly directed and regulated, has a valuable role to play (CAD, Legislative, III, Pt. 2, 1948: 3293-3297, emphasis added).

The industries to be the "exclusive monopoly of the Central Government" included (1) the manufacture of arms and ammunition; (2) the production and control of atomic energy; and (3) the ownership and management of railway transport. The industries where "new undertakings" were to be exclusively reserved for the state included: (1) Coal; (2) iron and steel; (3) aircraft manufacture; (4) shipbuilding; (5) manufacture of telephone, telegraph and wireless apparatus, excluding radio receiving sets; and (6) minerals' oils.

Even for these industries the possibility of private enterprise was not wholly excluded as,

> in the national interest, the state itself... (could find) it necessary to secure the cooperation of private enterprise subject to such control and regulation as the Central Government may prescribe.

The E.P.C. Report recommendation of a five-year period before takeover was replaced by the following, highly qualified statement:

> Government have decided to let existing undertakings in these fields develop for... ten years, during which they will be allowed all facilities for efficient working and reasonable expansion. At the end of this period, the whole matter will be reviewed and a decision taken in the light of circumstances obtaining at the time. If it is decided that the state should acquire any unit, the fundamental rights guaranteed by the Constitution will be observed and compensation will be awarded on a fair and equitable basis (CAD, Legislative, III, Pt. 2, 1948: 3293-3297).

The state had already invested in a number of very large multi-purpose projects including the Damodar Valley Scheme, the Kosi Reservoir, the Hirakund Dam, etc (CAD, Legislative, III, Pt. 2, 1948: 3295). Apart from the above industries which were reserved for the state it was stated that,

> The state will also progressively participate in this field (of industries left open for private enterprise); nor will it hesitate to intervene wherever the progress of an industry under private enterprise is unsatisfactory (CAD, Legislative, III, Pt. 2, 1948: 3294-3295; see Appendix 'A' Para 6).

In view of the several assurances given by Nehru and others before, this was not taken too seriously, particularly by the business community.

Another 18 industries "whose location must be governed by economic factors of all India import or which require considerable investment or a high degree of technical skill", were to be subject to "Central Regulation and Control". This list which was not "exhaustive" included: (1) salt; (2) automobiles and tractors; (3) prime movers; (4) electric engineering; (5) other heavy machinery; (6) machine tools; (7) heavy chemicals, fertilisers and pharmaceuticals and drugs; (8) rubber manufacturers; (9) non-ferrous metals; (10) electrochemical industries; (11) power and industrial alcohol; (12) cotton and woollen textiles; (13) cement; (14) sugar; (15) paper and newsprint; (16) air and sea transport; (17) minerals; and (18) industries related to defence.

For the directions of these industries, the government decided to associate "representatives of Industry and Labour in the proposed Industry Advisory Council as recommended by the Industries Conference" (CAD, Legislative, III, Pt. 2, 1948: 3295).

The statement referred to the resolution passed at the Industries Conference dealing with the relations between labour and management. It proposed to strengthen the Industrial Relations Machinery and to establish permanent Industrial Tribunals "for dealing with major disputes" (CAD, Legislative, III, Pt. 2, 1948: 3296).

Regarding foreign capital, it was,

> recognised that (while) participation of foreign capital and enterprise, particularly as regards industrial technique and knowledge, will be of value to the rapid industrialisation of the country, it is necessary that the conditions under which they may participate in Indian industry should be carefully regulated in the national interest.

For this legislation was to be introduced to,

> provide that, as a rule, the major interest in ownership, and effective control should always be in Indian hands; but power will be taken to deal with exceptional cases in a manner calculated to serve the national interest (CAD, Legislative, III, Pt. 2, 1948: 3296-3297).

The statement proposed to establish the "National Planning Commission to formulate programmes of development and to secure their execution" as "careful planning and integrated effort over the whole field of national activity are necessary" (CAD, Legislative, III, Pt. 2, 1948: 3294; see Appendix 'A' Para I).

The statement on industrial policy concluded with the government's "hope that this elucidation of their intentions on fundamental aspects of industrial policy will remove all misapprehensions" (CAD, Legislative, III, Pt. 2, 1948: 3297; see Appendix 'A' Para 12). In the case of the business interests, this hope was largely justified as we shall see presently.

While introducing the statement, Dr. Mookerjee noted that it envisaged "a mixed economy". He disregarded the ideological question of "ism" as "hardly necessary in the present context of things". He hoped that in the case of the industries which might be taken over aftar 10 years, "the representatives of the industries concerned, some of whom are extremely powerful in this land will reciprocate this gesture of the government" (CAD, Legislative, III, Pt. 2, 1948: 3390, emphasis added). Moorkerjee also referred to the provision for "a fair and equitable" compensation, pointing out that the government "obviously... cannot go further than that" (CAD, Legislative, III, Pt. 2, 1948: 3391). He denied that the Statement was "at variance with the policy enunciated by the Economic (Programme) Committee of the Congress" (CAD, Legislative, III, Pt. 2, 1948: 3395). Minoo Masani welcomed "this statement of policy because I consider it and understand it to be a categorical rejection of communism" (CAD, Legislative, III, Pt. 2, 1948: 3401). He thought it a "sound" policy if flexibly administered (CAD, Legislative, III, Pt. 2, 1948: 3402). Others including K. Santhanam, N.G. Ranga, Khandubhai Desai and Renuka Ray supported it (CAD, Legislative, III, Pt. 2, 1948). Jawala Prasad Srivastava who quite openly professed, "to place before the House the point of view of the much maligned and much abused class of capitalists and industrialists" (CAD, Legislative, III, Pt. A, 1948: 3414), did not find the statement "one-sided" (CAD, Legislative, III, Pt. 2, 1948: 3415). Though Srivastava believed the policy "is unduly biased against the capitalist", he had little criticism to make of the Statement (CAD, Legislative, III, Pt. 2, 1948: 3414-3415).

The most trenchant criticism of the proposed industrial policy was made by K.T. Shah, who as we have seen earlier, had been instrumental in the deliberations of the National Planning Committee (see Chapter IV above). Shah categorically expressed his "utter disappointment with everything that is contained in this Resolution" (CAD, Legislative, III, Pt. 2, 1948: 3402). He noted that the N.P.C.'s lists of industries proposed "to be exclusively under state management have been grievously curtailed". He regretted that Nehru who had chaired the N.P.C. should have "subscribed" to the Statement (CAD, Legislative, III, Pt. 2, 1948: 3403). He enumerated the three industries selected for state ownership and rather caustically stated that,

> it could not have been selected with greater care to make state enterprise the most objectionable, meddlesome, losing inefficient concern that could ever be imagined, because the worst examples are left to the state and the best examples are selected to be reserved for the capitalist profit-seeker (CAD, Legislative, III, Pt. 2, 1948: 3404).

He was critical of the policy statement for proposing the takeover of only the, "new undertakings (and) new units" in the six industries that were to be exclusively developed by the state. This, he argued, showed that the state would take up only such areas in which private capital was not interested (CAD, Legislative, III, Pt. 2, 1948: 3404).

Shah further argued that the policy left the large bulk of industry, "the total industry...in the hands of the capitalists" (CAD, Legislative, III, Pt. 2, 1948: 3404). He noted that despite "all the tall talk about equality...no mention has been made of any limitation of profit". He was sceptical about the proposed time limit of ten years for the takeover of the state-reserved industries, stating that, "if the capitalists think it so proper we may have the chance of getting a few more crumbs from their overladen table; but not otherwise". This particular statement was to prove prophetic as we shall see later on. Shah characterised the policy as "a character of exploitation for the vested interests who will take the kernel and leave the husk to posterity" (CAD, Legislative, III, Pt. 2, 1948: 3414-3405).

Others who would have criticised the statement, e.g. Kazi Syed Karimuddin and Maulana Hasrat Mohani, did not get permission to speak in view of the limited time for discussion (CAD, Legislative, III, Pt. 2, 1948: 3395). As Shah noted at the outset of his speech, the three and a half hours allotted for the debate on this important issue was not sufficient time for such an important matter (CAD, Legislative, III, Pt. 2, 1948: 3402). Despite this no extension was given.

Nehru sought to rebut Shah's criticism in his concluding remarks. He claimed, as he had on an earlier occasion, that in view of the country's limited resources it was not possible to "acquire a large number of industries" (CAD, Legislative, III, Pt. 2, 1948: 3420). Referring to the proposed 10-year period before takeover, he stressed the highly qualified nature of the proposition as "nobody can guarantee what will happen and when it will happen...". He stressed that this policy gave industrialists "a fair chance, a fair field and fair profit" (CAD, Legislative, III, Pt. 2, 1948: 3421).

Nehru's assessment of the Statement on Industrial Policy was, to a large measure, shared by business interests. Lalji Mehrotra in a press statement on 7 April on behalf of the FICCI E.C. (FICCI, Vol. II, 1948: 201-203), stated that the E.C. was "happy to note..." the government's stress on "increased production". To this, the FICCI assured its "whole-hearted cooperation and support". The proposed setting up of the Planning Commission was "indeed welcome". The FICCI however, "viewed with apprehension" the proposed progressive increase in state participation in the sector left for private enterprise. Mehrotra sought an assurance that the state would not participate in this sector unless private enterprise was "found wanting" (FICCI, Vol. II, 1948: 203). The FICCI wanted the proposed ten-year time period for takeover of private enterprises in the six industries extended to 20 years, so that private industrialists would be able to expand their activities in that sector. The Press Statement urged incorporation in legislation, of the market value and goodwill for the payment of compensation in the event of a takeover (FICCI, Vol. II, 1948: 202). The FICCI also noted that there were indications in the

Statement "that the ultimate objective is the nationalisation of all industrial activities in the country". This had caused "disappointment" in private industrial circles (FICCI, Vol. II, 1948: 201-202).

An editorial in *Commerce* stated that the Statement "has dispelled certain apprehensions..." with its "right emphasis on the expansion of production". It cited approvingly the government's statement that it should concentrate on expanding the production of state units "rather than on acquiring and running existing units", and its recognition of the "valuable role" of the private sector (*Commerce*, 10 April 1948). Sir Ardeshir Dalal, a signatory of the Bombay Plan and a Director of Tata Sons, was quoted as stating that, "I do not consider an industry like steel to be capable of satisfactory management through a public corporation". Dalal further stated that "it would be far better for the present government to omit all reference to a period after which the position of existing units in the industry will be considered" (*Commerce*, 10 April 1948). In view of the Tata investments in the Tata Iron and Steel Company (TISCO), Dalal's concerns are quite understandable. As it turned out, the government obliged. *Capital* in its editorial statement noted that,

> the Cabinet has obviously recognised the limitations of its administrative and financial resources and, while adhering to long-term objectives of socialisation, has had the good sense not to commit itself to impracticable proposals at this stage (*Capital*, 15 April 1949).

From the discussion, it should be clear that the 1948 Statement on Industrial Policy must have come as a considerable relief to business circles. A large number of the concessions that they had sought were granted. The period for takeover was extended to 10 years, and even that, it had been made clear, was not an inflexible deadline. The largest possible area had been left open for the private corporate sector. Areas that were taken over, were as, *Capital* had noted, industries where private capital was 'shy'. Moreover, in the unlikely event of takeover, industrialists were promised "fair and equitable" compensation. The Congress's radical pronouncements, as we have noted earlier, had made way for measures designed to develop capitalism.

And this was what the big business organised in FICCI had sought.

Statement on Foreign Investment in India

Exactly a year after the Statement on Industrial Policy, on 6 April 1949, Nehru made a "Statement on Foreign Investments in India" (CAD, Legislative, III, Pt. 2, 1948: 2385). In it he stated the principles that would govern the official policy in future.[9] The earlier regulation for foreign capital was discarded as that,

> arose from (the) past association of foreign capital and control with foreign domination of the economy of the country. But circumstances today are quite different... Indian capital needs to be supplemented by foreign capital not only because our national savings will not be enough for the rapid development of the country on the scale we wish, but also because in many cases scientific, technical and industrial knowledge and capital equipment can best be secured along with foreign capital (CAD, Legislative, III, Pt. 2, 1948: 2385; Kidron, 1965: 100-101).

The salient features of the policy were: (1) existing foreign investments would be treated on par with similar Indian enterprise; (2) new foreign capital would be encouraged "on terms and conditions that are mutually advantageous"; (3) profits and remittances abroad as well as capital remittances of concerns "compulsorily acquired" would be paid "if and when foreign enterprises are compulsorily acquired"; (4) although majority ownership by Indians were preferred, "government will not object to foreign capital having control of a concern for a limited period, if it is found to be in the national interest..."; (5) although "vital importance" was given to the employment of Indian personnel, "government would not object to the employment of non-Indians in posts requiring technical skill and experience, when Indians of requisite qualifications are not available ..." (CAD, Legislative, III, Pt. 2, 1948: 2386).

The shift therefore, in the official policy was quite marked. The earlier Industrial Policy Statement in the brief paragraph on foreign capital had explicitly stated that legislation would ensure "that, as a rule, the major interests in ownership and effective control, should always be in Indian hands..." (Industrial Policy Resolution, 1948).

FICCI reacted very strongly to the new policy on foreign capital. In a letter to the Ministry of Finance, the E.C. cited the earlier Industrial Policy Statement and the 1946 report of the Planning Advisory Board, in support of the FICCI argument that the new government policy was "a tragedy"[10] (FICCI, Vol. II, 1949: 367-370). As the letter noted,

> The policy of the Indian National Congress has all along been to encourage national enterprise and even boycott foreign goods. It is really a strange turn of the wheel, that a government representing that very National Congress is now inviting foreign capital to manufacture those goods here, the sure result of which would be that Indian enterprises would never be able to produce the same.

It therefore urged the government to reconsider its policy (FICCI, Vol. II, 1949: 369-370, emphasis added). The Indian government however, as Kidron has noted, adopted this policy largely because of the economic constraints. Poor harvests together with the loss of food marketing areas (to Pakistan), necessitated large-scale import of foodgrains, arising from less than 1,000,000 tons costing Rs. 26 crores for undivided India to a peak of 5-1/4 million tons valued at Rs. 254 crores in 1951-52 (Kidron, 1965: 97-98). Largely because of sharply increased consumer imports, India had a deficit of some $ 200 million in 1948-49. The earlier lifting of controls over foodgrains, sugar, cloth and cotton had culminated in the general price index being inflated by approximately 23 per cent to 29 per cent between November 1947 and November 1949 (see above). The Congress's publication, *Second Year of Freedom August 1948 – August 1949*, considered that,

> The most serious problem before the government was the stagnation in the capital market resulting from a deep underlying fear about the future of that market. Unless this stagnation was checked and the conditions were created in which the incentive to save and invest was revived, the industrial expansion in the country and the execution of the plans intended to raise the living standards of the people in general were bound to be delayed (quoted after Frankel, 1978: 76-77).

This lack of capital investment, forced the government to turn towards foreign capital (*Capital*, 22 September 1949). The urgency increased as the Congress leadership was aware that "something had to be done to start Indian industry moving lest social and political chaos engulf the country..."[11] (Kidron, 1965: 98).

Under these circumstances, the government was not inclined to reconsider its policy towards foreign capital despite FICCI pressure. It was also evident that even within FICCI, some of the larger industrial houses were not too perturbed about the new policy. The *Eastern Economist*, as we have cited earlier, had in February 1950, referred approvingly to Nehru's statement (see above). Even earlier in his Chairman's report to the Annual General Meeting of the United Commercial Bank, G.D. Birla welcomed the policy as he was ready to "supplement internal sources of capital with foreign capital...in our mutual interests" (*Capital*, 5 May 1949). In a paper for the India-America Conference later that year Birla wrote,

> I visualise collaboration only in big tasks, that is, things like steel, heavy chemicals, heavy engineering and things of that nature where large-scale investment...(of) a few scores of crores is needed and also where necessary technical skill is wanted in India... The collaboration which I visualise is between agencies of private enterprise on both sides (quoted after Natarajan, 1956: 61; see also Kidron, 1965: 106).

In view of the above constraints the Ministry of Finance in its strictly confidential reply to the FICCI representation, rejected the latter's arguments against foreign capital[12] (FICCI, Vol. II, 1949: 372-374). It categorically stated that,

> The Government of India do not think that permission to retain majority non-Indian interests in ownership and effective control in some cases, can be considered *ipso facto* as detrimental to the interests of the country (FICCI, Vol. II, 1949: 372).

The government therefore only promised to leave "a fair field" for "Indian industries" and trusted that FICCI would "agree that this is as far as the government can go consistent with their responsibilities to the country as a whole" (FICCI, Vol. II, 1949:

373). It was in fact claimed that foreign investment including the growth of foreign-controlled concerns would be "advantageous to the country...(and) in the interest of Indian industrialists in the long run" (FICCI, Vol. II, 1949: 374).

As it turned out, the second half of the above statement was to be accepted by industrialists some years later. In the immediate post-independence period, Indian businessmen feared the competition of foreign capital which was already well-entrenched in the Indian economy. In spheres where Indian capital was not interested, foreign capital was welcome. Kidron has put it succinctly, "business saw reason to attract foreign capital but still wishes to be protected against it" (Kidron, 1965: 103).

In response to the strong criticism from business lobbies, leading Cabinet members sought to reassure industrialists. In January 1950, Sardar Patel appealed for support for Swadeshi (*Hindu*, 31 January 1950; quoted in Kidron, 1965: 105). H.K. Mahatab assured the National Chamber of Industries that Swadeshi "would be the guiding policy of the Government of India today; and accordingly the entire policy will be formulated (*Statesman*, 28 June 1950; quoted in Kidron, 1965). He further promised Indian industrialists that they would be consulted prior to any invitation to a foreign investor and that their agreement would be necessary before any foreign enterprise could be granted "national treatment" (*Foreign Commerce Weekly*, 12 September 1949; quoted in Kidron, 1965). These assurances together with a few instances of the withdrawal by government from proposals for ventures with foreign capital did not mollify industrialists. Their protests, as well as those from the Left, continued (Kidron, 1965: 105-109).

However, despite the protests from FICCI, the Nehru government's policy towards foreign capital, was in no way anti-big business, much less anti-capitalist. This fact was apparently appreciated as we have seen above, by no less a big business leader, than G.D. Birla himself. In view of the paucity of internal resources, of capital and technology, the dominant Congress leadership considered the import of foreign capital necessary for the development of capitalism in India (Kidron,

1965: 97-103). The necessity for the inflow of foreign capital was later recognised by FICCI itself, whose own policy changed to come into conformity with that of the government, as we shall see below.

Conclusions

At the time of independence, two broad alternatives in the field of economic, particularly industrial, policy could be said to exist. The first, represented by the deliberations of the NPC, the People's Plan and the recommendations of the Planning Advisory Board, envisaged a major, even prominent role for the state, and concomitantly, a substantially limited role for the private sector. The second alternative provided by the Bombay Plan proposed a very substantial role for the private sector, including its management of state-owned companies.

Socio-political conditions at the time of independence and immediately thereafter, provided a rather grim background for the official formulation of industrial policy. The partition and the massive migrations that followed, the disruptions in economic life that were a consequence of both the Second World War and partition, rendered the task of economic development even more daunting. In the political sphere, the strength of the Left and anti-big business forces, both inside and outside the Congress, was sharply attenuated.

Indian big business had already established its influence with the Congress leadership. This relationship apparently bore fruit. At the December 1947 Industries Conference, Nehru clarified that the government's intentions were to concentrate on the development of new industries and undertakings rather than to nationalise the existing ones. Shortly thereafter, the wide-ranging recommendations of the E.P.C. were published, in late January 1948, which envisaged a predominant role for the state, with large areas of private sector activity being nationalised. Nehru however, reassured irate industrialists that the E.P.C. Report's recommendations were not mandatory and binding on the government.

The Industrial Policy Statement announced on 6 April 1948 clearly opted for a much larger role for the private sector, at the cost of the activities of the state. It therefore corresponded more to the industrial policy frameworks symbolised by the Bombay Plan. Nehru, in his defence of the Statement, referred to the existing social economic constraints:

> After all that has happened in the course of the last seven or eight months, one has to be very careful of what step one might take which might injure the existing structure too much. There has been destruction and injury enough and certainly... I am not brave and gallant enough to go about destroying much more (CAD, Legislative, III, Pt. 2, 1948: 3417).

Indian big business circles welcomed the statement, the FICCI assured its "whole-hearted cooperation and support" (FICCI, Vol. II, 1948: 203). As business circles were concerned, the official policy was a very marked improvement on earlier efforts.

Similarly, the shortage of capital, among other factors, forced the government to adopt a liberal policy towards foreign capital, that was explicated in the 6 April 1949 statement on foreign investment. In this particular case, Indian big business was evidently dissatisfied with the even-handed treatment proposed to be meted out to foreign capital. FICCI was however, unable to obtain a reversal of this policy.

In a word therefore, the close relationships that the Indian big business stratum had been able to establish with the political leadership, together with the circumstances obtaining at the time, which not only enabled but also encouraged the latter to make concessions, led to the formulation of an industrial policy framework which, in Nehru's words gave the private sector, "a fair chance, a fair field and a fair profit" (CAD, Legislative, III, Pt. 2, 1948: 3421).

REFERENCES

1. Part I was published in January and Part II in December, 1944. (Purshotamdas Thakurdas et al., 1944).
2. He however was aware that when the big industrialists "talk of state control of industry they think of the state more or less as it is today" (Nehru, 1972:501).
3. The difference between the positions of the left nationalists regarding planning and those of big business in the Bombay Plan,

should be evident from the foregoing discussion. We are therefore, unable to accept Mukharjee's contention that the two were "in no significant way very differing..." (See, Mukharjee, 2 September 1978: 1521).

4. The full text of the People's Plan is reproduced in *Young Indian*, Special Independence Number 1972, Vol. II, No. 34-40, D72-D95.
5. Karnik, who was the first General Secretary of the Radical Democratic Party admits that Roy's attitude towards World War II, "made him very unpopular and he became the target of many abusive and malicious attacks" (Karnik, 1980: 95)
6. This precluded him from being a signatory to the second part of the Bombay Plan.
7. This was reported to D.G. Mulharkar of FICCI by Rajendra Prasad when they met on 5 December 1947.
8. The full text of the Report is reproduced on pp. D 98-D 103.
9. Bhabha himself was linked with a number of companies. In 1948 he was Chairman of the Sholapur Spinning and Weaving Co., and of Apollo Mills Ltd, and a Director of the following concerns: Oriental Government Security and Life Assurance Co., Central Bank of India, Mill and Rubber Produce Co., Rajagiri Rubber Produce Co., New Galen Estate, and Barrackpur Electric Co., (cf. *Times of India*, n.d: 1143).
10. However, as we have seen above in Chapter III, Gandhi's influence within the Congress had diminished by 1947.
11. Jayaprakash Narayan put the blame on the communists. See his statement of 1941 reprinted in Pandey, 1979: 163.
12. Intelligence Report, Home Political, File No. 4/4/40, National Archives of India.
13. Mehta in his speech referred to a "deputation of prominent businessmen" who had met Nehru and other Ministers after the E.P.C. Report was published (FICCI, Vol. III, 1948).
14. Unlike The Industrial Policy Statement which was a policy document put before the Constituent Assembly (Legislative), this was a verbal statement by the Prime Minister which was made available in written form only later.
15. FICCI latter number F. 3751/771 dated 18 August 1947 to the Ministry of Finance.
16. As noted earlier during this period the militant armed struggle led by the CPI was underway in the Telangana area. The CPI was preparing for a nationwide insurrection (cf. Adhikari, Sen et al.: 1974).
17. The Ministry of Finance strictly confidential letter No. 15(83)/49, dated 10 September 1949 to FICCI.

5

Establishing the Institutional Framework for Industrial Policy, 1947-1951

The 1948 Industrial Policy Statement and the 1949 Statement on Foreign Investments provided an overview of the government's industrial policy. However the larger overall industrial framework, under which industrial policy could be implemented, was established between 1947 and 1951. During this period, the debate in the Constituent Assembly (CA) culminated in the enactment of the Constitution of India. The Planning Commission which was to formulate the broad guidelines of the country's economic policy and whose formation was announced in the 1948 statement was also established during the period, in 1950. Between 1949 and 1951, the Industries (Development and Regulation) Act,[13] was drafted after extensive discussions in the Constituent Assembly and Parliament.

The enactment of the Constitution and the Industries Act, as well as the establishment of the Planning Commission, were obviously of great concern to Indian big business. The events that transpired, are briefly analysed, so as to indicate the political and socio-economic orientation, both implicit and explicit, that marked the Constitution, the Industries Act, as well as the envisaged role of the Planning Commission. The analysis seeks to highlight the role of big business in influencing events germane of economic policy in general and industrial policy in particular.

The Constituent Assembly and the Business Interests: Historical Background

The CA was set up in accordance with the recommendations of the Cabinet Mission made in its statement of 16 May 1946. While the Cabinet Mission admitted that "the most satisfactory method (for constituting the Constituent Assembly) obviously would be election based on adult franchise", it argued that,

> any attempt to introduce such a step now would lead to a wholly unacceptable delay in the formulation of the new Constitution. The only practicable course is to utilise the recently elected Provincial Legislature Assemblies as the electing bodies (Rao, 1968: 124).

The plan also recommended that the indirect elections by Provincial Legislature Assemblies be organised so as to provide proportionate representation for the three main religious communities in India, i.e. the Hindus, Muslims and Sikhs, especially for the last two.[14] Moreover, it was provided that the representatives allotted to each community in a province would be elected only by members of that community in their respective Assembly (Rao, 1968: 124).

The Cabinet Mission's recommendations were only a continuation of the provisions of the Government of India Act, 1935 under which the election to the Legislative Assemblies had been held in 1937. The Congress had consistently opposed the communal division of the electorate under the 1935 Act, and had insisted that any Constitution for India, "must be based on the independence of India as a nation and it can only be framed by a Constituent Assembly elected on adult franchise or a franchise which approximates to it as nearly as possible"[15] (quoted in Rao, 1968: 80). Some months later in December 1936, at the Faizpur Session, the Congress "Resolution on (the forthcoming Legislative Assembly) Elections and the Constituent Assembly" (Rao, 1968: 82-83), reiterated the same sentiments and called upon a candidates to,

> take the earliest opportunity to put forward in the new Assemblies the demand for a Constituent Assembly, elected by adult suffrage, and (that) this demand should be supported by a mass agitation

> outside to enforce the rights of the Indian people to self-determination (Rao, 1968: 83).

Right upon its victory in 7 out of 11 provinces, the AICC in its meeting in Delhi on March 18, 1937, in a resolution, referred to its victories as indicative of popular approval for its policies regarding the formation of a Constituent Assembly elected by adult franchise and, it therefore demanded "that the new constitution (i.e. the Government of India Act, 1935) be withdrawn" (quoted in Rao, 1968: 84).

By the time the Cabinet Mission Plan was announced, the Congress Party had changed its policies regarding its demands for a Constituent Assembly elected through adult suffrage. Not only was the earlier demand not "supported by a mass agitation outside" the Assemblies,[16] but in effect, the Congress reactions to the Cabinet Mission were generally favourable. But Abul Kalam Azad, the Congress President, on behalf of the Congress Working Committee wrote on 20 May 1946, to Pethick-Lawrence, who headed the Cabinet Mission, stating that the Congress,

> look(ed) upon this (proposed) Constituent Assembly as a sovereign body which can decide as it chooses... The only limitation we recognize is that in regard to certain major communal issues that decisions should be by a majority of each of two major communities (quoted in Rao, 1968: 251).

The Congress decision to accept the proposals regarding the indirect elections to the Constituent Assembly were based on political expediency. In view of the virtual non-cooperation by the Muslim League and the growing communal tensions, the pressure on the national leadership as represented by the Congress to complete all preparations for independence, was tremendous (Rao, 1968: 64-80; Chaube, 1973: 31-45). However, by this the Congress not only accepted the mode of election of the Constituent Assembly, and thereby the representative character of the Provincial Assemblies elected under the heavily criticised Government of India Act, 1935. It in effect, acquiesced in the indirect election to a Constitutional Assembly by legislators, who themselves had been elected under the operation of an Act, under which only some 13 per cent of Indians had a right to vote. It was therefore an acceptance of a restricted franchise, limited to the relatively propertied Indians[17] (Tomlinson, 1976: 71).

Apart from the restricted franchise, the actual process of the Constitution of the advisory committees in the Constituent Assembly tended to favour the relatively propertied interests including big business. D.P. Khaitan, a founder member of FICCI and an industrialist closely associated with G.D. Birla (see Chapter II above), was one of the members of the original seven-man Drafting Committee of the proposed Constitution of India. This Committee which was later chaired by B.R. Ambedkar, was set up by a resolution of the Constituent Assembly on 29 August 1947, which empowered it to revise the Draft Constitution as submitted by the Constitutional Adviser, B.N. Rau, and to submit the revised Draft Constitution to the assembly for its consideration (Constituent Assembly Debates, Vol. V, 1948-1950: 336). When Khaitan died in 1948, his vacancy in the vital Drafting Committee was filled by another businessman T.T. Krishnamachari, a future Finance Minister (Rao, 1968: 114). Thus Indian big business was intimately associated with the drafting of the Indian Constitution.

Similarly, Homi Mody (a Director of various Tata Companies) and Kasturbhai Lalbhai (another founder member of FICCI), who were not Members of the Assembly, were nominated to the membership of the Assembly's Advisory Committee on Fundamental Rights, Minorities and Tribal and Excluded Area (Rao, 1968: Appendix II: 847). Leading members of Indian big business therefore, were closely associated with the drafting of the Constitutional sections on fundamental rights, (including the right to property), despite the fact that they were not able to secure election to the Assembly despite the restricted franchise.

This intimate association of leading representatives of Indian big business in vital advisory committees of the Constituent Assembly could not but have influenced the formulation of the draft Constitution as a whole, as we shall see below. The very fact that this sectional interest was represented to the exclusion of other sectional interests, (for example, no trade unionist was a member of the Drafting Committee), may by itself be considered indicative of the influence that Indian big business had with the political leadership.

The positions taken by leading Congressmen, who were later to form a government of independent India, during the Constitutional debates, must also have reassured the relatively propertied interests in general, and Indian industrialists in particular.

Aims and Objectives of Constitution

While moving the resolution regarding aims and objectives, of the proposed Constitution, Nehru argued:

> others might take objection to this Resolution on the ground that we have not said that it should be a Socialist State... But the main thing is that in such a Resolution, if in accordance with my own desire, I had put in that we want a Socialist State, we would have put in something which may be agreeable to many and may not be agreeable to some, and we wanted this resolution not to be controversial in regard to such matters (Constituent Assembly Debates, Vol. I, 1948-1950: 60; Gupta, 1979).

Dr. Ambedkar opposed any such formulation with greater vigour,

> "If you state in the Constitution that the social organisation of the state shall take a particular form, you are, in my judgement, taking away the liberty of the people to decide what should be the social organisation in which they wish to live... I do not see therefore why the Constitution should tie down the people to live in a particular form and not leave it to the people themselves to decide..." (Constituent Assembly Debates, Vol. VI, 1948-1950: 402).

V.D. Tripathi on the other hand urged that,

> we should declare it beforehand that our Constitution shall not be framed, and the state created under that Constitution shall not be established on a capitalistic basis... we should declare it now, that our Constitution shall be framed on a socialistic and positively

> not on a capitalistic basis (Constituent Assembly Debates, Vol. II, 1948-1950: 292-293; Gupta, 1979: 31-32).

Tripathi's proposal was not accepted and the preamble as accepted did not contain any reference to a Socialist society.

Fundamental Rights and Directive Principles

Members in the Constituent Assembly were also sharply divided into two groups on the question of the Fundamental Rights and the Directive Principles. One group was represented by K.M. Munshi, A.K. Ayyer, Thakurdas Bhargava and others, with generally conservative views who emphasised the need to guarantee a variety of fundamental rights against state intervention of any kind. The other group with more radical pro-socialist views consisting of K.T. Shah, Seth Damodar Swarup and V.D. Tripathi, among others wanted some basic socio-economic rights for the common man to be guaranteed through state intervention (Gupta, 1979: 34). The conflict between these two groups occurred first in the Sub-Committee on Fundamental Rights, then in the Advisory Committee, and finally on the floor of the Constituent Assembly itself.

The conflict centred around two issues: first, the question of justiciability of the Fundamental Rights and the Directive Principles; and the second over the question of the incorporation of economic rights in the category of Fundamental Rights (Gupta, 1979: 30-40). In their letter of 13 April 1947 to the Chairman of the Advisory Committee, the members of the Fundamental Rights Sub-Committee explained the division of the Rights into justiciable and not-justiciable, thus:

> Typical of the former is a right which requires that the state shall not deprive a citizen of his liberty without due process of law. It is obvious that if this right is infringed, the citizen can and should have redress for this in a court of law... Typical of the latter is the right which requires the state to endeavour to secure a decent standard of life for all workers. Obviously, it is as impossible for a worker to prove, as for the court to find, that a general right of this kind has been infringed in a given case. We have, accordingly, put justiciable rights and non-justiciable rights into separate chapters and have made it clear that the latter are intended to be

> direction for the general guidance of the state and are not cognisable by any court (Rao, 1968: 84; Constituent Assembly Debates, Vol. II, 1948-1950: 137).

The justiciable rights included the economic rights: the right to property and the right to carry on trade and commerce. The non-justiciable rights included substantive economic rights of the common man including the right to an adequate means of livelihood, the right to earn a living wage and provision for healthy conditions of work, the right of the common man to work and education and, of the most importance for our study, provisions for steps against concentration of wealth in the hands of a privileged few (Gupta, 1979: 43).

K.T. Shah, however, sharply criticised the report. He observed,

> "while appreciating the distinction between justiciable and non-justiciable rights, I feel that owing to the very fact of making the distinction, the latter are likely to be treated as so many pious wishes, which can have no very great binding effect in daily life (Rao, 1968: 154).

In his "Note of Dissent" to the Report on 15 April 1947, he described the non-justiciable rights as "mandates of the community to its organised representative, the state, to be carried into effect at the earliest possible opportunity" (Rao, 1968: 192). His "Note of Dissent" though it together with a number of his other comments proved prophetic later, had little impact. The Advisory Committee accepted this division of rights into two categories (Gupta, 1979: 43).

However, some members of the Assembly continue to argue for the justiciability of the Fundamental Rights even on the floor of the Assembly. B. Das during the discussion on the Supplementary Report on Fundamental Rights stated:

> I do not find anything that makes it obligatory on the government, on the state, to discharge their obligatory duties to the people of India about common welfare and well-being of the people... and if I, a Gandhite, am not satisfied with this draft, how can I expect Socialists and Communists and the others to be satisfied with it? (Constituent Assembly Debates, Vol. V, 1948-1950: 338-339).

V.D. Tripathi, during the debate on 30 August 1947, noted that "except for the right to vote, the poor man has not yet got any other right under the Constitution". He urged his fellow members,

> you must make such regulations as may prevent the domination of vested interests, capitalists and those who desire to keep the poor under subjugation. I would request you at least to prevent the capitalists and vested interests from standing for the membership of the legislature or from holding high posts or those in the Ministry... (Constituent Assembly Debates, Vol. V, 1948-1950: 345-346).

In a later debate, K.T. Shah, criticised the non-justiciabilty of the Directive Principles arguing that,

> it is a kind of provision which encourages the Court and also the executive not to worry about whatever is said in the Constitution, but to act only at their own convenience and on their practicability and go on with it (Constituent Assembly Debates, Vol. VII, 1948-1950: 479).

Despite these criticisms, the Constituent Assembly adopted the Supplementary Report on the Advisory Committee on the same day, and sent it to the Constitutional Adviser for its incorporation into the Draft Constitution (Gupta, 1979: 45).

A sharp debate also took place in the Constituent Assembly over the incorporation of the right to property in the Constitution. This right is meaningful and of primary importance to those who possess large amounts of property and wealth. For a vast majority of the Indian population, who possess little or no property the right has no relevance. The right to property as a fundamental right, could only ensure continuance of economic disparities and perpetuation of the privileges of the dominant economic elite or ruling class whose property holdings would be protected against nationalisation. Precisely because of this reasons, there were sharp differences on the right to property amongst conservatives and the more radical members.

The Report of the Sub-Committee on Fundamental Rights provided for the acquisition of private property for public purposes. The Sub-Committee however, on the basis of Section 299 of the Government of India Act, 1935 stated in Clause 27 of the Report,

> No property, movable or immovable, of any person or corporation, including any interest in any commercial or industrial undertaking, shall be taken or acquired for public use unless the law provides for the payment of just compensation for the property taken or acquired and specifies the principles on which and the manner in which the compensation is to be determined (Rao, 1968: 141, emphasis added).

The inclusion of the term "just compensation" clearly implied compensation in terms of the prevailing market value of the acquired property. In this case the very objective of acquisition for public purposes could be defeated by the payment of "just compensation" to the property owner. This term would also be open to judicial interpretation, as to whether the quantum of compensation fixed was 'just' or not. Thus all legislation involving acquisition and the payment of compensation could be subjected to judicial scrutiny (Gupta, 1979: 49-50).

This line of thinking was evidently espoused by a number of conservative members including K.M. Munshi and A.K. Ayyar.

In the Draft Report on Fundamental Rights Munshi's amendment was included which stated: "No person shall be deprived of his life, liberty or property without due process of law" (Rao, 1968: 75). Munshi argued that the,

> Right to property is one of the pillars on which democracy rests; remove it and the structure is sure to collapse... once it is denied under the name of any 'ism', however, glamorous, to secure social justice, individual freedom goes down with it; the citizen becomes helpless, impotent and without means to assert his individual rights against the state (Munshi, Vol. I, 1967: 302; Gupta, 1979: 50).

At the Advisory Committee stage, Govind Ballabh Pant and K.M. Panikkar criticised parts of the right to property clause. Pant criticises the phrase "due process" arguing that its inclusion would "fetter the discretion of the legislature... It will lead to a great deal of trouble" (Rao, 1968: 243). He felt that the inclusion of the above phrase would lead to "controversy, and will place the fate of the people on the whims and vagaries of the judges" (Rao, 1968: 243-244). Pant and Panikkar also objected to the qualifying adjective "just" before compensation. Pant insisted that,

> if it is a question of acquisition of property for social purposes, then... payment of compensation should not even be compulsory and it should be left to the government concerned to decide how they will achieve that purpose (Rao, 1968: 275).

Panikkar argued that the use of the term 'just' "made it open to question in a court of law whether the compensation is just or not. Therefore, I would urge taking away of the word 'just' from this clause" (Rao, 1968: 274). Despite Ayyar and Munshi's insistence (Rao, 1968: 272-276), the term 'just' was dropped (Rao, 1968: 276).

The Interim Report on Fundamental Rights was submitted by Vallabhbhai Patel, the Chairman of the Advisory Committee to the Constituent Assembly on 19 April 1947. While the adjective "just" before the term "compensation", Clause 19, on the right to property was dropped, the provision for payment of compensation remained compulsory. The principles governing compensation were not specified and consequently the assessment remained open to judicial scrutiny. The cumulative effect of these aspects of the clause were commented upon by a number of members during the debate in the Assembly.

Ajit Prasad Jain, later a Cabinet ministers, criticised the revised clause:

> Fundamental Rights are embodied in the Constitution with a view to protect the weak and helpless. The present clause will have just the contrary effect. It will protect the microscopic minority of apartheid propertied classes and deny rights of social justice to the masses (Constituent Assembly Debates, Vol. III, 1948-1950: 509).

Phool Singh brought up the question of advantages likely to be taken by the capitalist class:

> "many people have spoken on the question of zamindari, but there is a much bigger problem than zamindari. It is industry. Who does not know that during the last five or six years of the war, many millionaires have earned profits several times more than their invested capital?... During this (Second World War) capitalists of no other country have reaped as much profits as Indian capitalists. Therefore,... by passing the clause in its present form he would be running the risk of permanently obstructing the possibility of reform in the country forever... (Constituent Assembly Debates, Vol. III, 1948-1950: 517).

Because of the extensive criticism of Clause 19, the Drafting Committee had a second look at the draft. The Committee, however, did not make any material alteration: Two new sub-clauses, to form Article 24 of the Draft Constitution were added (Gupta, 1979: 53). The right to property remained the only economic rights to be included in the Fundamental Rights. As such it was made immune from ordinary legislation. Furthermore, with the Directive Principles remaining non-justiciable, the socio-economic rights of the common man were left non-enforceable.

During the discussion on the Draft Constitution, a number of members sharply criticised Article 24. Mahavir Tyagi observed that,

> to say in the Draft Constitution that people shall not be deprived of their property without adequate compensation means that India will ever belong to vested interests... before we sign this Constitution we should see that we do not sow seeds of bloody revolution in India... If we shut the door as we have done against future legislation... the youth of India will rise... and smash it and the result would be a bloody revolution. Therefore,... I would plead that we should scrap the sub-clause (sub-clause (2) of the Article 24 which reproduced Clause 19 of the earlier Interim Report) altogether and make it possible in future for the Parliament to socialise all property and all means of production without being compensated for (Constituent Assembly Debates, Vol. VII, 1948-1950: 361).

The concern expressed in Tyagi's speech was for certain 'radical' legislations to avoid a "bloody revolution".

Thus, as we have seen earlier (see Chapter IV above), the

Congress leadership and the industrialists, reacted in a manner, with what might be termed an exaggerated fear of Communist revolution in India, and took postures which were apparently radical, even anti-capitalist, without concretely harming capitalist interests. The proposed Article 24 was also criticised by a number of other members including K.T. Shah (Constituent Assembly Debates, Vol. VII, 1948-1950: 245) and A.C. Guha (Constituent Assembly Debates, Vol. VII, 1948-1950: 255). Because of the extent of criticism of the Article, its consideration was deferred from 9 December 1944 to a later date (Gupta, 1979: 55; Chaube, 1973: 194-196).

The discussion in the Constituent Assembly on Article 24 was initiated nine months later. On 10 September 1949, Nehru opened the debate in the Assembly by moving an amendment to Article 24. Nehru's amendment which became Article 31 contained nothing substantively new. The clause (1), (2) and (3) of Article 24 were left relatively unchanged in the Clause (1), (2) and (5) of the revised Article. Clause (3) of the revised Article actually restricted the authority of the state legislatures by stipulating that no law referred to in Clause (2) could have the effect unless it had been reserved for the consideration of the President and had received his assent (Gupta, 1979: 55-56; Chaube, 1973: 197). This, as Chaube notes, was "a very important amendment" (Gupta, 1979: 55; Chaube, 1973: 194-196 and Constituent Assembly Debates, Vol. IX, 1948-1950: 1191-1192). This amendment actually limited the powers of state legislatures as regards rationalisation and takeovers, making such acts conditional on the assent of the President. Such provisions were present in various other Articles.

Nehru observed that his amendment was a "compromise formula" between the conservatives and the more radical democratic groups. He also clarified that there would be no expropriation without compensation. Nehru in the concluding part of his speech added that,

> No Supreme Court and no judiciary can stand in judgement over the sovereign will of Parliament representing the will of the entire community... But we must respect the judiciary, the Supreme Court and other High Courts in the land. As wise people, their

> duty is to see that in a moment of passion, in a moment of excitement, even the representatives of the people do not go wrong; they might. In the detached atmosphere of the courts, they should see to it that nothing is done that may be against the Constitution, that may be against the community in the larger sense of the term" (Constituent Assembly Debates, Vol. IX, 1948-1950: 1195-1196).

In this classic equivocal statement by Nehru, what was stated initially about "the sovereign will of Parliament" is later ignored to accept the superiority of the "wise", "detached" judiciary in interpreting the Constitution and the common good. Despite the fact that the amended Article had the force of Nehru's prestige behind it, it was criticised by both sides. Some like Nazimuddin Ahmad (Constituent Assembly Debates, Vol. IX, 1948-1950: 1235) and Munshi continued to plead for the explicit recognition of the principle of 'just' compensation (Constituent Assembly Debates, Vol. IX, 1948-1950: 1300-1301). Munshi however, was relieved that through the recognition of judicial review "a aspect of the 'due process' clause survived in the Constitution" (Munshi, Vol. I, 1967: 303). Others like Shibban Lal Saksena realised that,

> the final decision lies with the Supreme Court in the amendment moved by Pandit Nehru and it can well declare that the principles specified by Parliament for determining compensation are 'fraudulent'. The Supreme Court and not the sovereign Parliament is thus the ultimate authority to decide what is 'fair and equitable compensation'... If the Article is passed in the form proposed by the Honourable Prime Minister, it will mean permitting the capitalistic system in the country to remain intact... this Article, if it is passed... will be the darkest blot on our Constitution. I say this, firstly because... This amendment takes away the sovereignty of the Parliament and secondly because it will be a negation of all that the Congress has stood for all these many years (Constituent Assembly Debates, Vol. IX, 1948-1950: 1202-1203, emphasis added).

Seth Damodar Swarup in his criticism claimed that,

> The Draft Constitution has... failed rather miserably to deal properly with the question of the economic rights of the people. This Article 24... is soon going to be a *Magna Carta* in the hands of

> the capitalists of India (Constituent Assembly Debates, Vol. IX, 1948-1950: 1199).

However, despite these and other criticisms of the Draft Constitution, the draft and controversial Article 24 were passed under the pressure of the dominant Congress leadership and incorporated into the Constitution of India.

From the above discussion, it should be evident that the Constitution as it was framed protected the economic 'rights' of the Indian industrialists. Nehru's role seems to have fully justified the confidence that Gandhi, Birla and Thakurdas had placed in him (see Chapter IV above). While resorting to radical phraseology, though by now considerably toned down, his efforts were to provide a constitutional basis for the capitalist order. In this attempt, despite some ideological divergence, the Congress leadership was more or less united. The Constitution of India as enacted provided protection and sanction for the rights "of the capitalists of India". Indian big business, as represented preeminently by FICCI, had therefore, reasons to be satisfied with the net result of the deliberations of the Constituent Assembly.

The Industries Act

On 6 April 1949, the Statement on Foreign Investment was placed before the House and the Industries (Development and Control) Bill were introduced in the Assembly. Dr. Shyama Prasad Mookerjee, Minister for Industry and Supply, who introduced the Bill said that its 'object' was "to create a suitable legislative framework or by virtue of which the industrial policy can be implemented" (Constituent Assembly Debates, Vol. IV, 6 April 1949: 2388). He claimed that the framing of the Bill had been preceded by discussion in the Industries Advisory Council, and also separately with "a small team of industrialists and labour representatives including Homi Mody, Mr. G.D. Birla, Lala Shri Ram, Mr. Khandubhai Desai and Mr. Asoka Mehta" (Constituent Assembly Debates, Vol. IV, 6 April 1949: 2390). This claim was contested by FICCI, as we shall see below.

Mookerjee pointed out that the Bill marked "the beginning of a planning for the industrial development of this country

(Constituent Assembly Debates, Vol. IV, 6 April 1949: 2388). He explained the background to the development of the concept of planning, i.e. the National Planning Committee, the (colonial) Government of India's Industrial Policy of 1945, the Report of the Advisory Planning Board, and the Industries Conference. He thus claimed "planning is nothing new even so far as this country is concerned". He explained as was evident in the Bill,

> that the object is to select certain industries consider(ed) to be of All-India importance, and to provide a missionary for... securing their regulation and development. Whether you look at it from the point of view of view of utilisation of the vast raw materials that this country possesses, or from the point of view of the development of other industries for which certain basic industries must develop, the list of industries... included in the schedule is... fully justified.

An exemption clause permitting the government to exempt from a certain period was included as it was realised, "that it may not be feasible for government to regulate immediately all the industries...mentioned". The Bill did not include cottage, small and medium-sized industries, though as Mookerjee put it "the prosperity of the country will be in...(their) development..." (Constituent Assembly Debates, Vol. IV, 6 April 1949: 2389).

It was in this Bill that the system of industrial licensing was introduced. This was to ensure "that the industries do develop in a way that we like them to develop" without "at the same time government...(interfering) in the day-to-day working and create(ing) dislocation by such interference". Licensing was to apply "to new undertakings and (to) substantial development of existing ones... Before any new industrial undertaking comes into existence, a license will have to be taken out". State undertakings were not to require a license, but Mookerjee assured the Assembly that there would not be "two different standards of approach..." to privately controlled and publicly controlled industries. The licensing scheme was to be in accordance with rules "which will have to be framed under the Act". The government suggested that this be done after securing "the opinion of the provincial governments, the opinion of industries and the opinion of the House...". The Advisory

Council was also to be consulted. The composition of this Council was not indicated in the Bill. Mookerjee stressed the purely advisory nature of the proposed Council as the responsibilities "for giving effect to this act must belong to government". However for the "major questions falling within the purview of the Bill, consultation with the Advisory Council will be compulsory" (Constituent Assembly Debates, Vol. IV, 6 April 1949: 2391 emphasis added). The reason for the government taking "the widest possible powers..." as framed in the rules was because it was "necessary for the purpose of enabling government to determine what the national industrial policy should be" (Constituent Assembly Debates, Vol. IV, 6 April 1949: 2392).

Mookerjee referred to a particularly controversial clause: Clause 7, which permitted the government "to direct the control and management of a particular industrial undertaking". Referring to the "misgiving in the minds of industrialists and less this power should be exercised arbitrarily", the Minister promised that powers under this clause would be exercised only after consultation with the Advisory Council "which will include industrialists themselves"(Constituent Assembly Debates, Vol. IV, 6 April 1949: 2392). Clause 11 dealt with the government's right to delegate its powers to the provincial government or some other authorities as was felt fit. A third clause, Clause 12 dealt with the provisions for penalties for violation of the act including imprisonment and fine. But under Clause 13, prosecution under Clause 12 could be launched only after previous sanction of the central government or some authority appointed by it. However Mookerjee clarified that the government did not feel that industry could be controlled "through police methods". Clause 12 was included because "there must be some penal clauses if there are breaches of the provisions of the law" (Constituent Assembly Debates, Vol. IV, 6 April 1949: 2392). Yet another clause dealt with the vicarious liability of the companies, and the particular executives nominated by the companies as responsible for carrying out the provisions of the Act (Constituent Assembly Debates, Vol. IV, 6 April 1949: 2392).

Premieres of some of the provincial governments had written letters expressing concern over some provisions of the Bill, which they felt led to the central government taking over "large powers" so that "the provinces may be placed in a more or less subordinate position" (reported by Mookerjee in Constituent Assembly Debates, Vol. IV, 6 April 1949: 2393). Mookerjee argued in answer that the Bill laid "down that there are certain industries in this country which can develop only if there is a centrally regulated policy". He referred to the likelihood of disputes between provincial governments over the location of industrial undertakings, particularly if the number of the proposed projects was limited (Constituent Assembly Debates, Vol. IV, 6 April 1949: 2393).

At the outset of his speech Mookerjee moved a motion,

> that the Bill to provide for the development, regulation and control of certain industries be referred to a Select Committee consisting of Shri Homi Mody, Shri M. Ananthasayanam Ayyangar, Dr. Bakshi Tek Chand, Shri Ramnath Goenka, Shri H.V. Kamath, Shri T. Ramalingam Chettiar, Pandit Lakshmi Kanta Maitra, Shri Khandubhai K. Desai, Shri R.L. Malaviya, Shri V.C. Kesava Rao, Shrijeet Kuladhar Chaliha, Shri Prabhu Dayal Himatsingka, Shri Biswanath Das, Shri Padampat Singhania, Shri Jaspat Roy Kapoor and the Mover, with instructions to report not later than the last working day of the first week of the next session, and that the number of members whose presence shall be necessary to constitute a meeting of the Committee shall be five (Constituent Assembly Debates, Vol. IV, 6 April 1949: 2388).

The composition of the Select Committee as originally proposed is indicative of the extent of business influence on government. Although K.T. Shah had been prominent in the National Planning Committee (he was Secretary), his name was not included. However, three leading businessmen: Homi Mody (of Tatas), Ramnath Goenka and Padampat Singhania (the last belonging of FICCI) were included in the original list. Of these, Ramnath Goenka was also an important functionary in the ruling Congress Party. In 1949 he was a member of the Executive Committee of the Congress Legislature Party (CLP). He was also the Auditor of the CLP (*Times of India*, n.d.: 472).

K.T. Shah in his trenchant criticism of the Bill noted that the representation granted to industrialists in the Select Committee (Constituent Assembly Debates, Vol. IV, 6 April 1949: 2200-2413). He linked this to the fact that "the great importance seems to be attached...(in) this Bill, to the owning class and to the proprietary class, and not so much to the consumer class, or... to the labour class" (Constituent Assembly Debates, Vol. IV, 6 April 1949: 2404). He noted that the cinema industry, the printing press and printing machinery industries have been left out of the purview of the Bill. He was also critical of the leaving out of cottage industries which Mookerjee had admitted earlier (Constituent Assembly Debates, Vol. IV, 6 April 1949: 2402-2403). Shah objected to the omission of "the distribution side of the industry..." as he felt that "to leave out either prices or wages from the scope of control makes the control very lopsided". This he attributed to the fact that this measure "most prominently considered" business interests (Constituent Assembly Debates, Vol. IV, 6 April 1949: 2404). Shah found fault with the "very general" wording of the Licensing Rules. He referred to the National Planning Committee which had passed a resolution in one of its earliest sittings, in which licensing was to be deliberately aimed against foreign capital taking advantage of the protected Indian market. He also warned that no precautions had been taken in the Licensing Clause against the development of monopolies. Shah stressed that unless the Bill laid down "very definite and stringent rules" against the development of monopolies "the measure will suffer the taint of being one-sided, of being partial to the big business and hard capitalists" (Constituent Assembly Debates, Vol. IV, 6 April 1949: 2406). He criticised the drafting of the Clause relating to the Advisory Council, as there was no evidence as to the nature, composition, working and jurisdiction of the body. He therefore suspected that its effectiveness will be "rather limited" (Constituent Assembly Debates, Vol. IV, 6 April 1949: 2406). Later in his speech he dealt with the Prime Minister's Statement on Foreign Investments in India which had been placed before the Assembly on the same day (see Chapter V above).

Homi Mody who "missed the greatest part of Shah's

speech... on principle...oppose(d) everything he has said". While supporting the motion to refer the Bill to the Select Committee (of which he himself was a member) he stated that "industrialists...are in general agreement with the principle of the Bill" (Constituent Assembly Debates, Vol. IV, 6 April 1949: 2413). He however repeated "certain reservations", that he had placed before the Government earlier during the consultations the latter had had with industrialists. He referred to the proposed Clause 10, in which Sub-Clause (b) referred to, "the regulation of the production of any industrial undertaking and the use of raw materials therein and the fixation of standards of production" and to Sub-Clause (c) which covered "the issue of directions for prohibiting any industrial undertaking from restoring to any act or practice which might reduce its production capacity or economic value". He claimed that these vested "very drastic powers" with the authorities which were "wholly unnecessary for the purpose in view..." and liable to misuse (Constituent Assembly Debates, Vol. IV, 6 April 1949: 2413-2414). He repeated what he had,

> said on previous occasions...that we have the fullest confidence in the integrity and ability of the present Minister for Industry and Supply, and I think the country as a whole, has got a large measure of confidence in him and in the present government (Constituent Assembly Debates, Vol. IV, 6 April 1949: 2414, emphasis added).

Mody however hoped, not without justification as later events showed, "that the select committee will modify it (the Bill) suitably and that my honourable Minister (Mookerjee) will agree to such suitable modifications" (Constituent Assembly Debates, Vol. IV, 6 April 1949: 2415).

The FICCI reaction to the proposed Bill was similar to that of Homi Mody. In this matter industrialists, whether they were affiliated to ASSOCHAM or FICCI, had similar reaction. S.K.D. Jalan, the FICCI President, in a letter to Mookerjee dated 2nd April urged the postponement of the Bill because of the "great misgivings" of Indian industrialists over the envisaged regulations and controls in the Bill. It, according to Jalan, far exceeding the proposed regulations and controls as envisaged in the 1948 Industrial Policy Statement. Mookerjee in his reply of 5th April, stated that the Bill was going to be referred to a Select Committee and that there was "no need for being unduly apprehensive". He claimed that the outline of the Bill had been approved (as he claimed the next day in the Assembly), and the provisions "discussed with some leading industrialists" (for the entire correspondence on the Bill see, FICCI, Vol. II, 1949: 471-499; and FICCI, Vol. I, 1949: 63-68). Jalan, in a letter to Mookerjee, on 24th May, rebutted the claim that the Industries Advisory Council had approved an outline Bill, as the proposed measure was "far more drastic" than what had actually been discussed (FICCI, Vol. II, 1949: 471-499; and FICCI, Vol. I, 1949: 63-68).

In a detailed note on the proposed Bill, dated 20th June, the FICCI E.C. argued that the measure included two separate proposals, the first being to bring certain important industries under central government purview from that of the Provincial Governments; and the second one vesting the central government with wide discretionary powers to enable control and regulation of the specified industries. While the E.C. found the first proposal to be in consonance with the Industrial Policy Statement, it claimed that the second was not. The E.C. cited some clauses as hampering private enterprise. Clause 4 and 5 which referred to registration and licensing were opposed as that rendered industrialists who based their entrepreneurial decisions on the technical advice of private experts, subject to the "whims" of government officers. Thus it was claimed would "effectively deter" prospective investors. Clause 7 and 10, were sharply criticised on the grounds that taken together they would lead to "nationalisation by backdoor methods ..." without compensation. The E.C. wanted the present Bill withdrawn and proposed that an Industrial Committee including officials and representatives of industries be constituted for the scheduled industries to regulate their development and planning. It was suggested that the Central Advisory Council for Industries (CACI) be appointed to lay down broad policy, and to periodically review the proposed industrial committee's working (FICCI, Vol. II, 1949: 471-499; and FICCI, Vol. I, 1949: 63-68).

A delegation largely of FICCI-related industrialists led by Tulsidas Kilachand including M.A. Master, B.M. Birla, Lalchand Hirachand, G.L. Bansal (FICCI Secretary), P.A. Narielwala and Naval Tata met the Select Committee on 5 August, 1949. At the end of the hearing, Mookerjee reiterated that the Government was not going to withdraw the Bill (FICCI, Vol. I, 1949: 65). He stated however, that the Select Committee "could modify it (the Bill) even beyond recognition". All that was necessary was that the title and Preamble of the Bill "remained intact" FICCI, Vol. I, 1949: 65-66, emphasis added). This statement by the Minister was also Chairman of the Select Committee reflected the attitude that made industrialists like Mody praised him so highly.

A sub-committee of the FICCI E.C. was appointed at 14 August, 1949 to suggest the details of FICCI comments on the proposed bill. The sub-committee was chaired by Kilachand and its members included Thakurdas, Sriram, Rahimtulla M. Chinoy, M.A. Master, D.N. Sen, B.M. Birla (special invitee) and G.L. Bansal (FICCI, Vol. I, 1949: 66). On the basis of the deliberations of this sub-committee, the E.C. sent a letter to the government on 26th September, giving FICCI's detailed suggestions on the modification of the Bill[18] (FICCI, Vol. II, 1949: 490-495). The letter *inter alia* suggested that in Sub-Clause 3(a) the term "controlled industry", should be substituted by the term "scheduled industry" throughout the Bill. The list of scheduled industries under the sub-clause should consist of only the following industries: (1) coal; (2) iron and steel; (3) aircraft manufacturing; (4) shipbuilding; (5) manufacture of telephone, telegraph and wireless apparatus including radio receiving sets; and (6) mineral oils. By this the FICCI sought to reduce the ambit of the Bill quite drastically, by including in the list of scheduled industries only those industries in which under the 1948 Industrial Policy Statement all "new undertakings" were to be reserved for the state (see above).

As regards Clause 4 of the proposed Bill, it was suggested that if registration was considered "absolutely essential, existing factories should be registered automatically". For Clause 5 and 6, the FICCI E.C. suggested that the Government of India should have powers to prescribe the establishment of scheduled industries for a period not greater than 12 months at a time. It however opposed licensing, and claimed that the above suggestions would permit government regulation of industry "without the evil effects" of licensing. The E.C. reiterated its earlier opposition to the provision for takeover of industrial units as incorporated in Clause 7. In the case of Clause 9, the earlier suggestions for the constitution of industrial committees and the CACI were reiterated. The E.C. suggested that the rules and regulations made by the government under Clause 10, be published in the Gazette of India and that the concerned industries and industrial associations be given the opportunity to express their views before the rules and regulations were finalised. As auditing and accounts already came under the Indian Company Act, the E.C. argued that this should not be included in the present Bill and that the statistics industrial units were required to submit, be simplified. Regarding Clause 12, the E.C. reiterated its earlier position that the provision for imprisonment for those guilty of violations of the proposed Act be removed, and that the proposed maximum amount of the fine, be reduced. With reference to Clause 15, it was suggested that the powers of inspection vested in officers authorised by the Government of India "be substantially curtailed" (FICCI, Vol. II, 1949: 490-495).

On 23 November 1949, the Secretary of the Department of the Legislative Assembly sent an immediate confidential communication to FICCI. A note was enclosed,

> containing certain suggestions made in the Select Committee of the Legislature on the Bill... with the general object of removing the major criticism against the Bill, viz. that it confers great powers on government under conditions in which they may be exercised arbitrarily.

The communication went on to state that "the Honourable Minister of Industry and Supply will be glad to have the FICCI views"[19] (FICCI, Vol. II, 1949: 496). However, the Select Committee note was "a privileged document" (FICCI, Vol. II, 1949: 496) it has not been reproduced in the FICCI volumes for the year. There is also no reference to it in the Select Committee Report. But the very fact that such an attempt was made to remove apprehensions of industrialists, itself indicates the extent of business influence in the Select Committee. The FICCI itself was not satisfied with the concessions offered. In response to repeated offers that they meet the Select Committee again, the E.C. in its reply of 9th December, regretted "that there has been no real attempt to radically modify the main provisions of the Bill". The E.C. "emphasised that the present is not the opportune time for proceeding with the Bill even in the amended form as suggested by the Federation"[20] (FICCI, Vol. II, 1949: 498-499). The E.C. felt that there was no point therefore in a delegation meeting the Select Committee. Despite this, the E.C. expressed the hope that Mookerjee "would find his way to accept the viewpoint of the Federation..." on the proposed Bill (FICCI, Vol. II, 1949: 499).

The Select Committee which considered the Bill was, as we have already noted, by its composition is a body in which a significant number of members had at least some sympathy for the viewpoints of big business. In its Report dated 10 February 1950, the Select Committee made certain changes that effectively diluted the original provisions, as we shall see below. In the first place, the name of the original Bill itself was changed in the Report to "the Industries (Development and Regulation) Bill, 1949" (Parliament of India, 1950: 1). As FICCI had suggested the expression "controlled industry" was replaced by the term "scheduled industry".

The Committee added Clauses 4, 5 and 6 which,

> provided for the establishment of an independent Central Industries Board, to which will be assigned the function of granting or refusing licenses under this Act and also of ensuring that powers of control vested in the central government are exercised after investigation by this body.

This obviously was a major fundamental change, as Shah and Kamath pointed out in their "Minutes of Dissent", (see below). In Clauses 7, 8 and 9 "references to conditions like those relating to equipment and technique...", were omitted. In Clause 11, it was stipulated that those "aggrieved by any order of the (Central Industries) Board should have the right to appeal to the central government". This proposed clause, however, also permitted "the central government to revoke any licenses granted by the board before effective steps are taken to establish the industrial undertaking" (Parliament of India, 1950: 1).

In Chapter IV of the Bill, the majority Report stated that,

> while we feel that the central government should have the power to issue directions to regulate production, distribution and prices, we think that the power should be exercisable only when it is necessary in the public interest and that the necessity for such control should be established after a proper inquiry by the Industrial Board.

Thus, the industries which earlier were specified in one schedule were split up into two parts, with provisions contained in Chapter IV not applying to the Part II industries (Parliament of India, 1950: 1). The Clauses 15, 16 and 17, were specified that the investigations that the central government could order into certain industries and undertakings could be exercised "only after a full investigation by the Board". Furthermore, it was stated that,

> the power of the central government takeover direct control of industrial undertakings is now restricted to cases where mismanagement is proved in the Industries Board has approved of the action to be taken. This procedure should... serve to free industries from any fear which may be legitimately entertained by them with respect to the scope of government control" (Parliament of India, 1950: 2).

The majority Report was signed by Mookerjee, Khandubhai Desai, Lakshmi Kanta Maitra, Tek Chand, Ram Narayan Singh, T.A. Ramalingam Chettiar, Jaspat Roy Kapoor, P.D. Himatsingka and B.L. Sondhi; who felt "that the Bill has not been so altered as to require circulation..." and therefore "recommended that it be passed as now amended" (Parliament of India, 1950: 2).

K.T. Shah and H.V. Kamath, who can be characterised as the two 'Leftists' on the Committee, wrote a joint "Minutes of Dissent" (Parliament of India, 1950: 3-5). They cited the sentence in the 1948 Industrial Policy Statement that,

> the state will also progressively participate in this field (left open for the private sector); nor will it hesitate to intervene whenever the progress of an industry under private enterprise is unsatisfactory (Parliament of India, 1950: 3; see above).

This aspect of increased state participation and the intention in the original Bill of licensing "was adopted to ensure proper planning and sound development... for a balanced and coordinated growth..." was, they alleged, "overlooked or underrated" by the majority. They criticised the changes made in the Bill by the majority who they believed,

> "have been unduly influenced by 'certain strong criticisms levelled against this Bill' by obviously interested quarters (i.e. big business) They have, therefore, agreed to minimise control, and even to exclude it from the title of the Bill". This, they believe "gravely militates against the very object the Bill was introduced to achieve" (Parliament of India, 1950: 3).

Shah and Kamath objected to the Clauses establishing an "Independent Industries Board" as "a needless addition" which would duplicate the work of the Tariff Board and the proposed Industrial Advisory Council. In fact, these Clauses rendered the latter "almost superfluous". The various restrictions the majority proposed regarding the operation of the licensing system, (which we have enumerated above), were also criticised. The modification removing the references to efficient equipment and up-to-date techniques was considered "unfortunate". The restriction on the powers of the revocation, amendment or modification of licenses only to the cases where "the licensee has failed, without reasonable cause, to establish... the undertaking within the prescribed period..." was also objected to. Shah and Kamath argued that cases of "gross mismanagement" should be included as "more enterprises fail... through mismanagement than through all other factors combined" (Parliament of India, 1950: 4). They felt, as they had stated in their general remarks, that in Clauses 7 to 10, the majority had "been unduly swayed by the criticism... from interested quarters, and (had) made concessions...". In particular, the restricting of the central government's power to "regulate production, distribution and prices" only in the public interest as established by a prior enquiry by the Industries Board was criticised for "limiting state authority..." (Parliament of India, 1950: 4-5). Similarly, the majority's observations on Clauses 15 to 17 were also criticised, as the two felt that the government's control in these matters "must be categoric(al) and unconditional"[21] (Parliament of India, 1950: 5).

Shah and Kamath pointedly noted that,

> No mention is made in the Bill, either in its original, or in its amended form, of the claims and the role of labour in the development of industries. Nor is the treatment of the labour made in any way a condition of licensing, or otherwise controlling and regulating an industry, or an undertaking... .

This was "consider(ed)... a fatal omission..." and it was "hope(d)" that it would be "duly rectified at the first opportunity". In view of the political background, of which the two were all too well aware, this was certainly a pious hope. Shah and Kamath also objected to the modification of the one schedule in the original Bill into two parts. This division, they alleged, "is brought about in the desire to minimise government control over those industries (i.e. those in Part II)". In their note, they concluded by pleading for "a uniform policy for the control and regulation of all important industries of a national character (as that) would be much more effective than the kind of the differentiation suggested by the Committee" (Parliament of India, 1950: 5).

Ramnath Goenka and Padampat Singhania submitted separate notes of dissent. The latter's note was much more comprehensive and more or less corresponded to the official FICCI position examined above. The former was perhaps constrained to soften his stance because of his position in the Congress Party. The important points made by Goenka dealt first with the various sub-sections of Clause 5 relating to the membership of the proposed Industries Board. He wanted the membership qualifications to be omitted and that "whole time" membership be optional. In Clause 8, he wanted the inclusion of a time limit of six months after receipt of an application, for the Board "to make a decision about...a license...". He found the explanation in Clause 10 of "substantial expansion", which as amended equated it to that extent of expansion which "amounts virtually to a new undertaking, but does not include any such expansion as is normal to the undertaking..." (Parliament of India, 1950: 3, of amended bill) unhappily worded, permitting "judicial interference" (Parliament of India, 1950: 7, of Report). He wanted Clause 22, which governed the transfer of industries from Part II to Part I, omitted as transfer should be done through "a parliamentary amendment". He further wanted the "bicycles" industry added to the Part II industries (Parliament of India, 1950: 8).

Singhania in his separate note, wanted Clause 5 to be amended so that the Industries Board "include(d) at least half its members to represent industry". Like Goenka, he was against the stipulated whole time membership. This he opposed,

> because the number of applications coming before it for licensing even if it (licensing) is retained in the face of severe criticism against it, is not likely to be such as to warrant the appointment of a permanent whole time Board (Parliament of India, 1950: 8).

In his remarks on Clause 8, Singhania categorically opposed licensing itself. He as a substitute, suggested that "Powers may...be vested in the Government of India to prohibit the establishment of any of the scheduled industries in the Union or any specific territories for a period not exceeding 12 months at a time" (Parliament of India, 1950: 8). He added that, "in case...licensing is retained, the central government should refer the applications of the Provincial Governments also for the establishment of a new undertaking to the Industries Board". He proposed a modification to Sub-Clause (2) of Clause 8, that the board "should have no power to impose any other conditions excepting those of location and size in granting a license".

Further amendments proposed to dilute licensing powers included: (a) an addition to Clause 9(2): "provided that such variation or amendment would not prejudice the interests of the licensee...", and (b) deletion of Clause 11(2) which authorised the central government to revoke licenses granted by the Board (Parliament of India, 1950: 9). Regarding Clause 20, Singhania proposed that "apart from the Central Advisory Council, there should also be Advisory Councils for each of the industries in the schedule...(which) should have their members nominated by the industry or the industries concerned" (Parliament of India, 1950: 10). In Clause 24, on penalties he proposed that, "the provision relating to imprisonment should be deleted. The fine should not exceed Rs. 2,000 and in the case of continuing contravention should not exceed Rs. 50"[22] (Parliament of India, 1950: 9). He also wanted the deletion of Clause 30 which guaranteed immunity for government servants seeking to enforce the Act "in good faith".[23] He argued that "government servants always enjoy immunity. Special provision for the same is not necessary in the Act which may have the effect of leaving the aggrieved party without recourse to a court of law" (Parliament of India, 1950: 9). For Clause 31 entitled "power to make rules", he proposed that "the rules to be framed should not only be published, but views on the same should be specifically invited from the industries concerned". Further, with the exception of Sub-Clause 2(a) of Clause 31, he proposed that it be explicitly stated "that the government shall consult the Advisory Council and Councils...in making the rules"[24] (Parliament of India, 1950: 9).

In another note of dissent, K. Chaliha, who generally praised the Bill as amended by the majority as "conceived with the best of intentions...", objected only to the inclusion of the tea industry in Part II of the scheduled industries. Chaliha, a leading Congressman from Assam and a tea planter himself, (*Times of India*, n.d.: 655) argued that the tea industry was already "controlled in every way from cultivation to manufacture". Therefore "further" control would be "a misfortune". Though, as already noted, the application of Chapter IV was only to industry listed in Part I, Chaliha was "strongly against inclusion of tea..." even in Part II (Parliament of India, 1950: 8, of Report).

The majority Report of the Select Committee, as Biswanath Das, in his note of dissent pointed out, "materially changed" the Bill. He therefore stressed the need for "republication of the bill" (Parliament of India, 1950: 5-6, of Report).

Dr. S.P. Mookerjee, placed the Report on the table of the Parliament on 10 February 1950 (Parliamentary Debates, Vol. I,

Part II, 10 February 1950, col. 40). As *Capital* (18 October 1951) later put it, the Report "was put on the shelf thereafter, but was revived by the Planning Commission, which insisted on its early enactment". Evidently, the pressures exerted by industrialists through ASSOCHAM and FICCI, apart from more informal channels of influence was very effective in delaying the enactment of the Bill.

Only on 4 September 1951, did Harekrishna Mahatab, the Minister for Commerce and Industry, move that the Bill be recommitted to a new Select Committee (Parliamentary Debates, Vol. XV, Part II, 4 September 1951, col. 1895). Referring to the delay since the Select Committee submitted its Report, Mahatab admitted that "this Bill happens to be perhaps the most ancient one in this House". He noted, that in the Select Committee recommendations "the whole structure of the Bill was completely changed". Further, the Bill as amended by the Committee did "not fit in with the scheme which had been put forth by the Planning Commission". Therefore, it was necessary to recommit the Bill to a reconstituted Select Committee including H.V. Kamath, Khandubhai Desai, A.C. Gupta, Thakurdas Bhargava, K.T. Shah, R.K. Sidhva, Panjabrao Deshmukh, T.A. Ramalingam Chettiar, Ramnath Goenka, Jaspat Roy Kapoor, B.L. Sondhi, P.D. Himatsingka, T.N. Singh, R. Venkataraman, D.P. Karmarkar, C.D. Deshmukh and Mahatab himself (Parliamentary Debates, Vol. XV, Part II, 4 September 1951, col. 1895). This new Select Committee was to report back to Parliament by 17 September.

In the discussion over the motion to recommit the Bill, Goenka raised a point of order, stating that under the Rules of Procedures and Conduct of Business in Parliament, the Bill could not be sent back to the old Select Committee. This was not accepted by the Deputy Speaker who cited an earlier ruling of February 1926 (Parliamentary Debates, Vol. XV, Part II, 4 September 1951, col. 1902-1903). In the discussion, Mahatab clarified that the government objected to the changes in the original Bill including: (a) the introduction of the Central Industries Board; and (b) the various provisions laying down conditions before the government could take over industries.

The Planning Commission suggested the institution of Development Councils for each industry or group of allied industries which would "enable private industry...to play its part..." in the planned development of the economy (Parliamentary Debates, Vol. XV, Part II, 4 September 1951, col. 1899-1900). These Development Councils were to "consist of representatives of the industries, the representatives of labour and technicians..." (Parliamentary Debates, Vol. XV, Part II, 4th September 1951, col. 1901). The existence of these Councils would obviate the need for the proposed Industries Board which would "have no purpose to serve in those circumstances" (Parliamentary Debates, Vol. XV, Part II, 4 September 1951, col. 1900).

Mahatab in his reply stated that regarding "as to what part of the public sector will play and what part the private sector will play..." in the economy "was not very clear when this Bill was introduced in 1949..." (Parliamentary Debates, Vol. XV, Part II, 4 September 1951, col. 1920). "Subsequently, gradually as the Planning Commission developed its own plan, the situation became very clear" (Parliamentary Debates, Vol. XV, Part II, 4th September 1951, col. 1920). Just before the end of the discussion, Renuka Ray's name was proposed for inclusion in the Select Committee, which Mahatab accepted, and the motion was adopted (Parliamentary Debates, Vol. XV, Part II, 4 September 1951; col. 1924).

From the published proceedings of the reconstituted Select Committee, it was evident that both the 'Leftists' nominated: H.V. Kamath and K.T. Shah refused to serve. Homi Mody had been appointed Governor of UP in May 1949 (*Times of India*, n.d.: 794) and thus was unable to serve on the earlier Select Committee. His appointment to the important Governorship is in itself an indicator of the high regard in which leading businessmen were held by the Congress government. Of the other leading industrialists, Padampat Singhania was not reappointed; and Ramnath Goenka who continued as Auditor of the Congress Legislators in Parliament (*Times of India*, n.d.: 529) did not serve in the Committee. The majority Report of the Committee dated 24 September 1951, was approved by 8 of the

13 members: H.C. Mahatab, C.D. Deshmukh, B.R. Ambedkar, B.L. Sondhi, A.C. Guha, P.S. Deshmukh, D.P. Karmarkar and R.K. Sidhva (Parliament of India, September 1951: 3).

The majority Report which "carefully considered the provisions of the Bill in the light of the suggestions made by the Planning Commission...(accepted) that there is no need for a full-time statutory Central Industries Board". The Planning Commission's suggestion regarding the institution of Development Councils on the lines of the British Industrial Organisation and Development Act, 1947, was accepted (Parliament of India, September 1951: 1).

The important recommendations of the majority included: (a) a new Clause 4 which excluded small industrial undertakings (where 'invested' capital did not exceed Rs. 1 lakh) from the operation of the Act; (b) a reworded Clause 5 replacing the old Clause 21 which "expressly provided the central government shall consult the Advisory Council before issuing any directions to an industrial undertaking or before exercising any power or control over it" (Parliament of India, September 1951: 1). (c) A new Clause 6 provided for the establishment of the Development Councils "for any scheduled industry or group of scheduled industries..." (Parliament of India, September 1951: 1-2); (d) A new Clause 8 provided for the summary dismissal of the Development Councils; (e) A new Clause 11 replace the old Clause 8, and provided that industrial undertakings with invested capital less than Rs. 5 lakhs would not require licenses. A time limit of four months for the issue of a license was also proposed; (f) Clause 17 (Parliament of India, September 1951: 2) was redrafted and a new Sub-Clause (5) was added "to ensure that when control of an industrial undertaking by the central government is no longer necessary...(it) shall hand over the undertaking to the owner"; (g) a new Clause 25 replace the old Clause 28 and "excluded from the power of delegation, the cover of issue directions to, or to take over control of, and industrial undertaking" (Parliament of India, September 1951: 2, emphasis added); and (h) the amended Bill provided two schedules, the first specifying the industries regulated by the Act and the second specifying the functions of the Development Councils.

The majority recommendation committed the tea industry from the first schedule because in their "opinion, whatever provisions may be necessary for regulating that industry should be made in the two Acts relating to that industry ...the Indian Tea Control Act, 1938 and the Central Tea Board Act, 1949". The majority did not consider that the Bill had been so altered so as to "require circulation...in Parliament..." and recommended "that it be passed as now amended" (Parliament of India, September 1951: 3).

In their note of dissent, R. Venkataraman and Khandubhai Desai, Renuka Ray and T.N. Singh opposed the majority report on the sole ground that the tea, coffee and rubber industries had been excluded from the First Schedule (Parliament of India, September 1951: 4-5). They cited in their support the fact, that "the government while recommitting the Bill to another Select Committee did not state that the Schedule required any alterations...". Specifically, the government never "propose(d) the exclusion of tea from the operation of the Bill". They argued, that "the Central Tea Board is mainly concerned with propaganda for tea in India and abroad and naturally the powers and functions fall far short of ...(what is) envisaged under the Bill". They referred to coffee and rubber as "also very important plantations..." and argued that as,

> The Industries (Development and Regulation) Bill has been conceived as a measure for expansion, growth and orderly development of the industries...there is no reason for the exclusion of important national undertakings like plantation products from the scope of the Bill" (Parliament of India, September 1951: 4).

Despite the major change in the Bill by the second Select Committee, which under pressure from the central government deleted the proposal for the creation of a Central Industries Board, it remained a piece of legislation which sought to accommodate business interests. Although the reconstituted select committee included leading Congress legislators, i.e. Renuka Ray, (Executive Committee member of the Congress legislatures) (*Times of India*, n.d.: 529), C.D. Deshmukh, R. Venkataraman, apart from Mahatab himself; it made sustained efforts to reassure business interests. This, of course, was in consonance with the approach of the Congress leadership, as we have seen above. In particular the new Clause 5, the new Sub-Clause (5) of Clause 17, and the new Clause 25 were evident concessions to business interests (see above). Moreover, the amended Bill still incorporated into a defect trenchantly criticised by Shah and Kamath in their minutes of dissent in the earlier Select Committee (see above).

Big business however, was not satisfied with the concessions made. Commenting on the Bill as it emerged from the First Select Committee, the *Eastern Economist* (17 February 1950) disputed the charge that the amendments had made the original Bill "an altogether new Bill". It claimed that despite the deletion of the term 'control' "the thing control is as firmly embodied as before". The Bill was sharply criticised as,

> a breach of promise to industry which underlay the assurances to private enterprise conveyed in the Industrial Policy Statement...(which) defects the objects of the concessions granted later in 1948...and the statement of last year (1949) intended to create the right climate for the entry of foreign capital.

It therefore urged the Bill to be scrapped.

During August 1951, the FICCI E.C. had sent a detailed note to the Ministry of Commerce and Industry, indicating its objections to the Bill as amended by the First Select Committee[25] (FICCI, Vol. II, 1951: 474-485). The E.C. objected to the wide coverage of the Bill, claiming that under the proposed regulation private enterprise would be "crippled and the industries... regimented". Various amendments to clauses were suggested. For Clause 7 it was proposed that existing undertakings be registered automatically. The note proposed drastic revision of the powers under Clause 15 and 16 enabling the government to investigate undertakings and to take action consequently. Clause 17 was sharply criticised as it was alleged that it allowed for virtual nationalisation without compensation (FICCI, Vol. II, 1951: 478). It reiterated earlier objections to Clause 24 proposing the deletion of the provision for imprisonment.

Under Part-I, it wanted only those six industries to be included, in which in accordance with the Industrial Policy Statement, new undertakings would be reserved for the state.

It however, referred to representations made to the E.C., by constituents of FICCI, that even coal should be deleted from the Part-I list. The E.C. proposed that the other industries listed in the amended Bill under Part-I be transferred to the Part-II list (FICCI, Vol. II, 1951: 479-480).

After the Second Select Committee Report was published, the FICCI sent another letter to Mahatab on 11 October 1951[26] (FICCI, Vol. II, 1951: 480-484). In this letter, the FICCI regretted that there had been no reply to its earlier letters. It expressed its unhappiness with the report of the Second Select Committee as it claimed that most "contentious provisions" had been retained (FICCI, Vol. II, 1951: 481). The earlier objections were reiterated.

Mahatab, while placing the amended Bill before Parliament on 11 October 1951, pointed out that no "other legislative measure has been subjected to so much consideration and examination as this measure has been" (Parliamentary Debates, Vol. XVI, Part II, 1951, col. 4646). He referred to the fact that, "much criticism has been made of this Bill by industrial interests and those who speak on their behalf". He pointed out that under the Industrial Policy Statement the private sector "would have a large field...". But the private sector "would be required to adjust itself to the national plan" (Parliamentary Debates, Vol. XVI, Part II, 1951, col. 4646). He referred to the final First Plan document and thought that "the self-created bogie of nationalisation of industries should have disappeared after the publication of the report of the Planning Commission".

Mahatab further argued that, "Regulation serves the best interest of the industry itself" citing in his support cases of closures of industrial units in the textile and other industries (Parliamentary Debates, Vol. XVI, Part II, 1951, col. 4647-4648). In view of "the miserable plight of the large number of industrial units", he stressed that "leaders of private industries themselves should volunteer to set up Development Councils to save the uneconomic units from utter ruin and also save the country from loss of production" (Parliamentary Debates, Vol. XVI, Part II, 1951, col. 4648).

From these extended quotations, the conciliatory attitude that Mahatab, representing the central government, exhibited towards business interests should be clear. Gulzarilal Nanda, the Minister for Planning displayed the same attitude, when in replying to the discussion on the Bill on 12 October, he asserted that "the best way to destroy private enterprise would be to leave it to shift for itself. Without the ministrations of the state, private enterprises cannot function". He went on to state that,

> private enterprise and the state have a mutually helpful role. The state cannot do without private enterprise today. That is absolutely clear. It cannot afford to abolish private enterprise (Parliamentary Debates, Vol. XVI, Part II, 1951, col. 4745).

Nanda rejected a policy of nationalisation as being counter-productive in the present situation. The government,

> "approach to nationalisation is to have certain things (i.e. national goals) in view and if it is possible to achieve those very things without giving it a certain name (i.e. nationalisation), we should try and secure that process and that result (Parliamentary Debates, Vol. XVI, Part II, 1951, col. 4747).

In the debate over amendments moved to the Bill, the government accepted a large number of amendments of a fairly minor nature. However, Syamnandan Sahaya, himself an industrialist, moved an amendment to Clause 10 of the Bill relating to the registration of industries. This was to ensure automatic registration of existing undertakings without payment of a registration fee as FICCI had suggested. This was not acceptable to the government spokesmen, and Sahaya did not press it (Parliamentary Debates, Vol. XVI, Part II, 1951, col. 4825-4828). But Khwaja Inait Ullah's amendment which permitted the registration "of any undertaking for the establishment of which effective steps have been taken..." was accepted without any objections (Parliamentary Debates, Vol. XVI, Part II, 1951, col. 4825-4828).

An important indication of business influence in the debate was an attempt by Mahatab to move an amendment to Clause 17, (relating to direct control of undertakings by the central government), which would have effectively diluted the clause as amended by the Second Select Committee. In Clause 17, on lines 17 to 19, the words "either to take charge of the whole or any part of the undertaking in suppression of any other person or body of persons in charge thereof or" (Parliamentary Debates, 12 October 1951, col. 4856); (which allowed the government to take over management without compensation), were according to Mahatab's proposal to be omitted (Parliament of India, September 1951: 7). The proposal including the deletion of Sub-Clause (2) (Parliament of India, September 1951: 7) which permitted the taking over authority to "take all such steps as may be necessary to take...under his control all the property, effects and auctionable claims to which the industrial undertaking is or appears to be entitled..."(Parliament of India, September 1951: 7). Further in Sub-Clause (5) the words "the industrial undertaking shall be released from any control under this section", was to be replaced by the original words: "the control of the industrial undertaking shall vest in the owner of the undertaking" (Parliament of India, September 1951: 7; Parliamentary Debates, Vol. XVI, Part II, 1951, col. 4646).

The amendments passed would have effectively prohibited the takeover of management without compensation, and corresponded to the sentiments expressed earlier by FICCI (see FICCI, Vol. II, 1951). Mahatab justified these changes as necessary in the light of "the recent judgments of the Supreme Court in the Bihar Estates Abolition Act and the Sholapur Mill Case". He further claimed that management takeover without compensation "will conflict with the provisions of the Constitution..."[27] (Parliamentary Debates, Vol. XVI, Part II, 1951, col. 4857), i.e with Article 31(2).

This amendment was not acceptable to Venkataraman and T.N. Singh, who had themselves served on the Select Committee (Parliamentary Debates, Vol. XVI, Part II, 1951, col. 4856-4857). Singh pointed out the original provisions were not *ultra vires* of the Constitution, as these were in the public interest. Further the,

> Government does not expropriate them (the industrialists), does not deprive them of the industry...or the undertaking itself...(it) only takes over the management for the specific object of increasing the production for benefiting both the country and the industry.

He was thus provoked to state that, "I am really getting... suspicious as to why this last-minute opinion has been advanced on this point" (Parliamentary Debates, Vol. XVI, Part II, 1951, col. 4859-4860). Singh, of course, like the other MPs was well aware of the pressures exerted by industrialists, for effecting changes in this vital clause. After further discussion, D.P. Karmarkar's proposal that the term "charge" be substituted by the words "over the management" was accepted (Parliamentary Debates, Vol. XVI, Part II, 1951, col. 4865-4866).

However, Syamnandan Sahaya's amendment that the takeover be "authorised for a period not exceeding five years" was accepted by Mahatab and passed in Parliament (Parliamentary Debates, Vol. XVI, Part II, 1951, col. 4866-4867). Therefore, although the government representatives were unable to dilute Clause 17 as they had earlier planned, they did accept an industrialist representative's amendment that sought to repair some of the damage.

An effort was made by Sahaya and Thakur Krishna Singh to remove the provision under Clause 24 stipulating "imprisonment which may extend to 6 months...". After considerable discussion, the amendment which was moved by Krishna Singh, (Sahaya withdrew his), was defeated (Parliamentary Debates, Vol. XVI, Part II, 1951, col. 4879-4896). However, in defending this provision, Mahatab rhetorically asked: "how many prosecutions of that type have been launched? How many have been successfully prosecuted?" He admitted that "if we take statistics, I am sure the charge will be that of all those provisions have not been fully given effect to. That charge will probably be correct" (Parliamentary Debates, Vol. XVI, Part II, 1951, col. 4895).

This statement must have reassured industrialists, as it was doubtless intended to. It also indicated that the governments' real attitude towards the industrialists charged with violations of the Act in later years, as the events following the Vivian Bose Commission Report were to reveal (see Chapter III above and Chapter VIII below).

In winding up the discussion, Mahatab reacted to a telegram from the All India Manufacturers Organisation (AIMO) read out by C.D. Deshmukh criticising the Bill, by calling upon it and "prominent industrialists like Shri Syamanandan Sahaya and others to come forward and help the government in making this measure a success" (Parliamentary Debates, Vol. XVI, Part II, 1951, col. 4912). Here again the government's effort to placate business circles is indicated.

Despite all the above attempts to soften the bill, which became the Industries (Development and Regulation) Act, 1951, the reaction of business circles was considerably hostile, even strident. In *Capital*[28] (18 October 1951), the reaction was quite muted. It traced the ideological basis of the measure to the Congress election manifesto, but noted Nanda's reassurances about the necessity of private enterprise in his maiden speech while supporting the Bill (c.f. Kochanek, 1974: 221; Registrar of Newspapers for India, 1968: pt. 1).

A more balanced and perceptive appreciation of the entire situation followed in the next issue a week later. In a "Leading Article" (editorial) in the 26 October issue entitled "The State of the Revolution", the *Eastern Economist* noted that, "at least until the elections are over, the right wing in the Congress is content to play a subordinate role; this is no more than a concession to political realities". Because, "the widespread belief that the Prime Minister is far and away the largest factor in the elections is indubitably true...".

While it wanted that, "prejudices against the business community resulting in more regulation will mean less initiative and less production" it concluded, on the above lines that "in effect, the country is less left than it is assumed and so, indeed, is the government" (*Eastern Economist*, 26 October 1951).

In the *Commerce* also there was sharp criticism of the Bill. In a leading article in the 20th October issue, it stated that the Bill was passed,

> In the teeth of country-wide opposition to certain objectionable features of the Bill, even the last-minute frantic appeal of the Federation of Indian Chambers of Commerce and Industry...was of no avail.

It is necessary to note here, that the FICCI attitude towards the government's industrial policy, prior to the passing of the Bill, was essentially one of satisfaction. At the 24th Annual Session of FICCI held from 31st March to 2nd April 1951, Sri Ram while moving a resolution on "Industrial Development" stated that,

> I find that there are number of good points in the situation today. For instance, not only the Congressmen but even the Socialists today say that only the basic industries should be nationalised. The bogey of nationalisation has more or less disappeared...".

He admitted that though FICCI had,

> protested against government starting factories... I think this starting of factories by the government has done a lot of good and probably is to a great extent responsible for their taking a realistic view (FICCI, Vol. III, 1951: 98).

He believed "it is a matter of satisfaction that the government have realised the importance of financing industry..." and referred to the case of TISCO (FICCI, Vol. III, 1951: 100-101). He stressed "that it is our government... We must have confidence in our own government and the government must have confidence in at least some of us" (FICCI, Vol. III, 1951: 103).

Too much should not be made of the FICCI criticism of the Bill and later Act. In fact a couple of years later, R.G. Saraiya, the then FICCI President, in a letter to T.T. Krishnamachari (TTK), then Minister for Commerce and Industry, noted that the two Select Committees had "both improved on the original provisions, which were objectionable in the extreme"[29] (FICCI, Vol. II, 1953: 545). Thus, taken with the earlier evidence adduced above, it is clear that industrialists in general, and FICCI in particular, had managed to considerably influence the formulation of the Industries (Development and Regulation) Act.

This was in a sense inevitable, in view of the existing political balance of forces, which as Shyama Prasad Mookerjee had admitted, led to some industrialists being "extremely powerful in this land" (See Chapter III above). As the government spokesmen had emphasised time and again, during the debates and discussions prior to the passing of the Act, state regulation of the economy, and specifically of important industries, was necessary for the development of a viable capitalist system, and therefore the measures incorporated in the Industries Act were necessary for the survival of the existing politico-economic system as a whole. Moreover as Nanda and others had stressed, the measures to be taken under the Act, would guarantee the viability of private enterprise. In fact as we shall see below, industrial policy measures actually contributed to a disproportionate growth of the larger industrial groups and consequently of their influence on the political leadership.

Constituting the Planning Commission

As we have seen above, the recommendations of the newly constituted Planning Commission led to the government action in taking the Industries Bill off the shelf, as it were, despite FICCI pressures. The establishment of the Planning Commission itself occurred only after Nehru was able to overcome resistance "from Sardar Patel and senior government officials" (Frankel, 1978: 84). Although the Report of the Advisory Planning Board and the deliberations of the National Planning Committee had led to an explicit statement in the 1948 Industrial Policy Statement to establish "a National Planning Commission to formulate programmes of development and to secure their execution..." (Paranjape, 1964: 5-12; see also Appendix A), no action was taken until the Congress Working Committee (CWC) was forced to take action in January 1950.

The almost chaotic conditions prevailing in the economy forced Nehru to push for the establishment of the Commission at the end of 1949 (Kochanek, 1968: 139). At the 15th of January 1950 Congress Working Committee meeting, a note by Shankarrao Deo (who had served in the National Planning Committee and in the Economic Programme Committee), was discussed which,

> contained a severe indictment of government (economic) policy...(and) warned of the possibility of grave social disorders unless definite steps were taken to improve economic conditions. To avert this danger, the note called for a Gandhian program(me) based on austerity and a planned economy[30] (Kochanek, 1968: 140).

On the basis of discussion on the note, G.L. Nanda, who was later to become Planning Minister was asked to prepare a draft resolution. The introductory paragraphs of his note were designed to appeal to the Gandhians, the Congress Socialists and the right wing. The operative part of the resolution called for the immediate creation of a Planning Commission[31] (quoted in Kochanek, 1968: 140). Despite this conciliatory strategy, the draft resolution was subjected to considerable debate and criticism.

The two major points of dispute in the CWC meeting on 19 January were firstly over the objectives of planning, and secondly over the proposed Planning Commission's role vis-a-vis government. A passage supported by Nehru himself in the original draft prepared by Nanda which included in the principles of planning,

> the progressive elimination of social, political and economic exploitation and inequality, the motive of private gain in economic activity or organisation of society and the anti-social concentration of wealth and means of production... (Kochanek, 1968: 140).

...was deleted under pressure from the right wing led by Patel and Rajendra Prasad. According to Kochanek,

> As was evident from the note later submitted by Nanda, there was pressure from the right wing members of the Working Committee to drop the passage on the ground that such broad objectives could create enough anxiety within the business community to alienate it from the Congress[32] (quoted in Kochanek, 1968: 141).

The second major debate in the CWC took place over the role of the Planning Commission. The majority wanted the proposed Commission to be a purely advisory body making recommendations to the Cabinet. This was opposed by Nanda, who argued,

> A Plan is not a body of recommendations of a reporting committee which may be accepted or rejected in part. The part which will be rejected may be found by the Planning Commission to dissolve the entire structure of its creation, rendering the Commission incapable of taking further responsibility (cited in Kochanek, 1968: 142).

The CWC did not endorse Nanda's views and left the matter of the relationship between the Planning Commission and the government to the Cabinet to resolve (Kochanek, 1968: 142). The entire discussion over the resolution highlights the determination of the dominant Congress leadership to curb any policy or moderate any statement that might alienate business interests.

Conclusions

The composition of the Constituent Assembly, and the inclusion of the business representatives on its important Committees, contributed to the Constitution being framed in a fairly conservative manner. The Directive Principles, which included the important socio-economic objectives, were not made justiciable. On the other hand, the Fundamental Rights, including the right to property, were made subjected to judicial scrutiny. This resulted, as some critics noted in the Constituent Assembly, in the perpetuation of the privileges of the few who had substantial amounts of property. This evidently was also in the business interest.

The prolonged process of formulation of the Industries Act, provides further indications of the measure of business influence on the political leadership. At virtually every stage of the proceedings, attempts were made to reassure Indian big business. The act expressly provided for the return of units taken over to the original owner within a period of five years. At the final stage of the debate, H.K. Mahatab attempted to dilute the takeover clause resulting in angry protests from leading Congressmen. On its part, Indian big business, which was initially very hostile to the proposed Act, moderated its own stance later.

The debate over the constitution of the Planning Commission also reveals the anxiety on the part of the conservative sections of the Congress leadership not to displease big business.

From the above examination it is apparent that in the framing of the Constitution, the Industries Act, and the objectives of the Planning Commission, big business influence was able to play a substantial part. Despite some criticism of these measures, by FICCI as well as by individual businessmen, the institutional framework that was established during this period from 1947 to 1951, for the implementation of industrial policy, provided considerable latitude for the protection, and growth, of Indian big business.

REFERENCES

1. For the sake of brevity, we shall refer to the Industries (Development and Regulation) Act, 1951, as the Industry Act. It is also referred to, in some citations, as the I(D&R)A or IDRA.
2. The Hindus were implicitly equated with the "general group" which was defined as "all persons who are not Muslims or Sikhs".
3. Resolution on the Government of India Act, 1935 adopted at the 49th session of the Indian National Congress at Lucknow on 12-14 April 1936.
4. As promised at the Faizpur Session.
5. Under the Act there were only 35,982,000 voters, 13.3 per cent of the total population, and an average of 25,406 electors per seat.
6. FICCI, E.C. Letter No. F.4448/760 dated 30 August 1949.
7. Confidential Immediate Communication No. 7466/49A dated 23 November 1949.
8. E.C. letter No.F-5763/760 dated 9 December 1949.
9. The reference in the text is to Clauses 16 to 18, but from the statements it is clear that this is an error (perhaps of printing), which remained uncorrected in the final printed record.
10. In the text instead of Clause 24, Clause 23 is printed, evidently a printing error.
11. In the text, Clause 28 is printed which in the amended Bill refers to delegation of powers.
12. In the text, Clause 29 is printed which is Clause 31 in the amended Bill.
13. FICCI letter No. F.4536/760 dated 10 August 1951 to the Ministry of Commerce and Industry.
14. FICCI letter No. F.5539/760 dated 11 October 1951 to H.K. Mahatab.
15. The conservative, even status-quoist nature of Supreme Court judgements on property matters is well-known. For analysis see Gupta, 1979.
16. Capital at that time was largely controlled by the British dominated managing agency houses in Calcutta.

17. R.G. Saraiya D.O. letter No. 24/5354 dated 24 March 1953 to T.T. Krishnamachari.
18. This is a summary of Deo's "Note on Economic Policy", prepared for the CWC meeting, unpublished Rajendra Prasad papers.
19. Unpublished Rajendra Prasad papers, G.L. Nanda, "Draft Resolution on the Formation of the Planning Commission".
20. Unpublished Rajendra Prasad Papers, G.L. Nanda, "Special Move to the Working Committee", 19 January 1950; G.L. Nanda, "Corrected Final Draft Resolution".

6

The Development of Industrial Policy, 1951-1956

In the first four years after independence, the first Industrial Policy Statement of 1948 had been made, the Constitution adopted, the Industries Act enacted, and the Planning Commission set up. The period from 1951 to 1956, witnessed the initiation of the planning process through the formulation of the First Five Year Plan. During the course of the implementation of the First Plan, the need for a more rigorous industrial policy framework became more obvious. In a sense therefore, the First Plan period provides the background to the evolution of industrial policy which culminated in the 1956 Industrial Policy Resolution.

First Plan

In mid-1951, the Draft Outline of the First Plan was circulated. Shortly afterwards, the FICCI submitted a memorandum to the Planning Commission.[33] It welcomes the "modest targets" and the "very limited reliance" on foreign aid in the Draft Outline. The FICCI was critical of the fact that there was no discussion in the Draft regarding implications of the plan outlay for generating additional employment and of the physical resources necessary for implementation. Instead of the proposed reliance on revenue surpluses, FICCI wanted policies to encourage private savings (FICCI, Vol. I, 1951: 29). It was also critical of the "limited targets" for the private sector and pleaded for a more important role for this sector. FICCI advocated an upward revision in the targets of certain industries, especially pig iron and steel.

FICCI opposed the proposal for a State Trading Corporation and what is considered comprehensive controls over the mixed economy. It noted that as a number of government-sponsored schemes were already underway, the Planning Commission had "little choice" in distributing financial resources, and therefore the Plan was a "draft of planned expenditure instead of a national plan for economic development" (FICCI, Vol. I, 1951: 30). The FICCI noted with satisfaction that its memorandum was "widely circulated" and that the Draft Plan was being revised by the Planning Commission ((FICCI, Vol. I, 1951: 31).

Later, at the FICCI Annual Meeting held from 29-30 March 1952, in New Delhi, where Nehru as usual inaugurated the session in the presence of a member of his Cabinet colleagues, the FICCI-government dialogue on the Plan and other industrial policy matters, was continued. The meeting, (which was also the FICCI Silver Jubilee Session), was the first held after the results of the 1952 General Elections, and in his Presidential speech, C.M. Kothari stated that though he was "gratified" at the Congress victory, he was unhappy at "the stray success of disruptive (at another point he used the term 'extremist elements') which he believed had made headway where "the populace has been suffering the most" (FICCI, Vol. III, 1952: 9). The reference was to the success, in particular, of the CPI which was returned as the second largest party in the Lok Sabha. Kothari was critical of the modest plan targets particularly in view of the existing steel shortages, and he therefore found the Planning Commission's outlook "almost pedestrian" (FICCI, Vol. III, 1952: 12). He considered the proposed Rs. 200 crores per annum "a very low target" for the public sector and private sector combined, and cited the Bombay Plan estimates of Rs. 2,000 crores per annum as more appropriate (FICCI, Vol. III, 1952: 13).

Nehru while inaugurating the meeting, defended the Draft Plan as subject to modification (FICCI, Vol. III, 1952: 30-31). With the background of the relatively good showing of the Left (Communists and Socialists) in the General Elections, he was constrained to be more critical of the private sector. He disagreed with Kothari's claim "that private enterprise is part of democracy..." But argued that,

> "private enterprise is good only as long as it serves the people; and when it ceases to serve the nation, it will itself cease to exist... We are ready to view it (private enterprise) with suspicion..." He asked, "Are you not unaware that private enterprise is today the target of attacks from all sides" (FICCI, Vol. III, 1952: 33).

Nehru noted the importance of creating "an atmosphere in which people can be inspired with hope and faith..." as "when they find the future holds no promise for them, they naturally will get desperate". It was, therefore, necessary to view the Plan in that context (FICCI, Vol. III, 1952: 34). He defended the lack of emphasis in the plan on industrialisation, on the grounds that "top priority should been given to food production... (as) insufficiency in food can any day endanger our national existence. Any day we may succumb to foreign pressure" (FICCI, Vol. III, 1952: 34). Referring to the Bombay Plan he stated,

> we did experiment a bit on it, but soon realised that circumstances have changed, and we will not be able to implement it... I think it was better if we could have taken up a part of that Plan and finish it rather than giving up the whole venture (FICCI, Vol. III, 1952: 35).

Significantly, Nehru did not refer to the reactionary features of the Bombay Plan of which he must have been well aware. Nehru later in the speech, spoke of the need for self-reliance, extending it even to the sphere of armaments" (FICCI, Vol. III, 1952: 35-36). While moving the vote of thanks for the Prime Minister, Thakurdas stated that the elections had "gone aright". He believed that, "as far as this Federation is concerned we cannot expect more from him than this" (FICCI, Vol. III, 1952: 39).

On the second day of the FICCI session, there was a discussion on FICCI's resolution on the Planning Commission's First Five Year Plan. G.L. Nanda, the then Deputy Chairman of the Planning Commission, and G.M. Mehta (Members, Planning Commission, who was FICCI President in 1942), participated in the discussions. Nanda during his speech defended controls and the Plan Draft, but invited FICCI to discuss their suggestions with the Planning Commission FICCI, Vol. III, 1952: 105-112). Mehta claimed that,

> when you look at the Planning Commission's Report, you will find that with the exception of the Industries (Development And Regulation) Act and a reference to state trading, there is hardly anything we could arouse the apprehensions of businessmen (FICCI, Vol. III, 1952: 118-119).

The preparation for meeting the Planning Commission, the FICCI representatives met at Birla House on 30th May. Those present included G.D. Birla, Shanti Prasad Jain, Tulsidas Kilachand, B.M. Birla, G.D. Somani, Charat Ram, R. Poddar, Syamnandan Sahaya and G.L. Bansal (then FICCI Secretary) (FICCI, Vol. II, 1952: 246-256).[34] At any preliminary meeting, G.D. Birla suggested that the Commission should be appraised of the difficulties Indian industry was facing as a result of the recent fall in prices and its implications to the fulfilment of targets in the private sector industries. He saw two problems. The first, of ensuring that goods which were produced be sold so that unduly large stocks would not accumulate with the manufactures; and the second, of finding finance for industrial undertakings which he considered very difficult. After some discussion, it was decided by the industrialists present that G.D. Birla (who held no official FICCI position, but was then, as later, regarded as one of the elder statesmen among industrialists), should act as the main spokesman of the group representing the FICCI E.C. (FICCI, Vol. II, 1952: 247).

At a meeting with the Planning Commission on 14th May the government was represented by Nanda himself, C.D. Deshmukh, G.L. Mehta, T.T. Krishnamachari and Tarlok Singh among others. Birla stated that the main idea of the industrialists participating in the meeting "was to place the doubts and misgivings of the business community before the Planning Commission. He repeated the points he had made at the Draft Outline, because of the marketing difficulties (FICCI, Vol. II, 1952: 248). He suggested "that to sustain and expand economic activity... (a) thought-out spending programme..." by the government was necessary. He urged the Commission to allocate more expenditure on education and such items, which would lead to increased utilisation of local materials and goods indigenously manufactured. He approved of the Commission's stand which accepted a modest rate of inflation as necessary to fulfil the targets (FICCI, Vol. II, 1952: 249).

Referring to the fall in prices, Nanda pointed out that the common man "had not gained any tangible benefits of (the) price fall". To this Birla replied claiming that there was always a time lag between a fall in wholesale prices and a fall in retail prices (FICCI, Vol. II, 1952: 250). When Birla raised the possibility of deficit financing, Deshmukh expressed doubts about the viability of such a policy and warned that further rising prices "would not be tolerated by the common man", e.g. the recent rise in food prices. Birla claimed that the Draft Outline had underestimated the performance of Indian industries of the last few years. He cited FICCI calculations that private industrial enterprises had invested approximately Rs. 450 crores over the previous five years (FICCI, Vol. II, 1952: 250-251). During the discussions, Deshmukh suggested that FICCI and the Planning Commission experts exchange views and information. This was welcomed by Birla (FICCI, Vol. II, 1952: 253).[35]

In the concluding part of the discussion, Deshmukh and Mehta argued that although FICCI had every right to point out defects or dangers in government policy or legislation enacted, it should be accepted by FICCI and the latter should make efforts to find the best working methods under the circumstances. Mehta referred to the FICCI criticism of the Industries Act and characterised it as "futile". Shanti Prasad Jain in reply assured the members of the Planning Commission "that they (FICCI) were doing their best to make constructive suggestions" (FICCI, Vol. II, 1952: 256). Jain thanked Nanda and the commission members for organising the meeting and hoped that such exchanges of views would be more frequent as they "would help both government and the business community" (FICCI, Vol. II, 1952: 256).

After the preparations of the final draft of the First Plan, Nanda wrote to Shanti Prasad Jain, the FICCI President, on 26 October 1952. In his letter, Nanda referred to FICCI's "valuable suggestions"at the earlier meeting and asked for further suggestions by the 7th November as the National Development Council was to meet on 8th November to finalise the Plan (FICCI, Vol. II, 1952: 261).[36]

The revised first plan provided for the major role in industrialisation to be played by the private sector. While envisaged investment in public sector industries was Rs. 173 crores the planned investment in private sector industries was of the order of Rs. 477 crores (Planning Commission, 1952:80). Moreover, it was explicitly stated that "the rate of investment, and therefore of development in this (industrial) sector as a whole, will depend however primarily on the implementations of the working plans of private industries..." (Planning Commission, 1952: 81). As it turned out, of the total fixed investment amounting to Rs. 293 crores made in the manufacturing sector during the First Plan Period, as much as Rs. 233 crores was in the private sector, and only Rs. 60 crores in the public sector (Planning Commission, 1957: 182).

The FICCI reply dated 6th November, welcomed the fact that the revised plan was "somewhat bolder" than the Draft Plan (FICCI, Vol. II, 1952: 261).[37] This was a reference to the considerable increase in the total outlay, and the increased allocation for industry. The FICCI reiterated some of its earlier criticisms on the draft outline as the revised plan had not taken full note of their suggestions. It argued for an increased expenditure outlay as this was considered necessary to reduce unemployment which was "rising", leading to "intense... discontent and unrest..." among the "middle and lower classes". It again reiterated the need for deficit financing (FICCI, Vol. II, 1952: 262). It advocated import of foodgrains, i.e. wheat, because of the prevailing high prices of foodgrains in the domestic market. FICCI as usual criticised existing controls (FICCI, Vol. II, 1952: 263-264) and opposed the proposal for state trading (FICCI, Vol. II, 1952: 270). In reply, Nanda's private secretary stated that Nanda was "grateful for the letter... (which) will of course receive careful consideration in the Planning Commission (FICCI, Vol. II, 1952: 271).[38]

The revised Plan as it was passed by the National Development Council, must have been a cause for some satisfaction to the entire business community. As a number of scholars have noted, in the Plan the "major reliance for development was placed on the private sector" (Nayar, 1972: 31; Ranadive, 1953: 1-2 and 107-171).[39] The ideological formulations in the Plan were also far from "socialistic". The government resolution of March 1950 setting up the Planning Commission referred to the Directive Principles of state policy stating that the state,

> shall direct its policy towards securing, among other things, (a) that the citizens, men and women equally, have the right to an adequate means of livelihood; (b) that the ownership and control of the material resources of the community are so distributed as best to subserve the common good; and (c) that the operation of the economic system does not result in the concentration of wealth and means of production to the common detriment (Planning Commission, 1952: 80).

This section was drafted by Nehru himself (Singh, 1969: 253). It however was a considerably diluted version of the draft proposed earlier by Nanda which had been rejected by the Congress Working Committee (Kochanek, 1968: 140). Moreover though the Plan was intended to reduce "economic inequalities", it categorically stated that,

> while it would be wrong... to condone the existence or accentuation of sectional privileges, it is no less important to ensure a continuity of development without which, in fact, whatever measures, fiscal or other, might be adopted for promoting economic equality might only end up in dislocating production and even jeopardising the prospects of ordered growth (Planning Commission, 1952: 31).

As in Nehru's earlier speeches in the Constituent Assembly, the emphasis was on increased production, which through a 'trickle-down effect' would in turn raise the living standards of the masses.

This approach was evident also in the section "Fiscal Policy as an Instrument of Planning". Here it was stated that,

> Direct taxation of the rich is likely to impinge more on their savings than on their consumption. There is a need for balancing the advantages of a greater equality of incomes and wealth against

> the disadvantage of a possible fall in private savings and capital formation (Planning Commission, 1952: 40).

In the matter of controls the plan warned against "a doctrinaire approach..." (Planning Commission, 1952: 42). It is clear that ideologically there was nothing in the plan that could be to the dislike of businessmen, as G.L. Mehta had told the FICCI representatives earlier.

FICCI had however, wanted even greater financial support for the private sector. This was to be a constant refrain. This apart, prominent FICCI leaders welcomed the revised plan. Tulsidas Kilachand in his Chairman's Address at the Annual General Meeting of the Bank of Baroda on 2 May 1953 stated, "it is admitted by all sections (sic) that the targets and priorities fixed in the Plan are more realistic now then they were while in the draft stage..." (Quoted from Ranadive, 1954: 244). Speaking about the Plan G.D. Birla stated that,

> I am glad the government have confined their task to the undertaking of a few economic programmes of basic and public character... Excepting the branches of economic activity, agriculture, irrigation and transport reserved for its work it has left the entire field of economic enterprise to private effort. And this is the right thing that they have done... (Ranadive, 1954: 244).[40]

The policy orientation explicit in the First Plan clearly corresponded more to that expressed in the Bombay Plan, rather than to the consciously egalitarian, distribution-oriented strategies expounded in the National Planning Committee, the Advisory Planning Board, and the People's Plan (see Chapters IV and V above). The emphasis in the first plan, as in the 1948 industrial policy statement, was on increased production, at the cost of the radical anti-big business measures suggested earlier. The notion of planning that was incorporated in the First Plan therefore, had much more in common with that of Indian big business, then with the radical tradition within the Congress. Nehru's praise for the Bombay Plan can therefore be taken as an indication of the similarity of official and big business positions on the content of Indian planning.

The business press also praised the Plan. The *Eastern Economist* (12 December 1952) stated that,

> It (the Plan) has given confidence and courage to both Bombay and Calcutta. There is even greater optimism to be found in the sound approach which Ministers of economic affairs in Delhi are now displaying... implementation here at least is in good hands. C.D. Deshmukh, Mr. T.T. Krishnamachari and Mr. Rafi Ahmed Kidwai presents together in the ablest triumvirate which has ever held sway over India's economic policy.

The lavish praise is an indication of the happiness with which the business viewed the First Plan and the activities of the Ministers in charge of the important economic portfolios.

The 1952-53 Economic Crises and Indian Business

Around February 1952, consequent to a recession in the capitalist world economy, there was a marked slump in commodity prices in the Indian economy (Ranadive, 1954: 1). As we have seen earlier, this point was also raised by G.D. Birla in FICCI's discussions with the Planning Commission. This "spectacular break in prices which... has all the appearance of a crash..." (*Eastern Economist*, 7 March 1952; see also *Capital*, 13 March 1952), caused considerable worry to both the capitalists as well as to the government. This crisis did not lift as was expected, after a few months, but continued well into 1953. In July in 1953, the *Eastern Economist* again referred "to the new and unexpected crisis which is coming over our economic affairs" (*Eastern Economist*, 3 July 1953). *Capital* (13 August 1953) expressed similar sentiments in a leading articles in August.

The crisis of the domestic market again forced FICCI to sharpen its criticism of the government's policy towards foreign capital. At its 26th Annual Meeting, FICCI adopted a "Swadeshi Resolution" in which it deplored the present indifference to the importance of Swadeshi in the social and economic regeneration of the country..." urging,

> that the purchase of (the) government's own requirements... should be confined to goods of Indian origin, wherever available and possible, and more liberal price preference in favour of Indian goods and a substantial reference to Indian banking, Indian insurance and Indian shipping should be accepted as part of the official stores purchase policy (FICCI, Vol. III, 1953: 38-39).

Later in a confidential communiqué to the government, FICCI reiterated its earlier criticisms of the official policy (FICCI, Vol. II, 1953: 603-608).[41] it pointed out, that foreign capital had created difficulties for indigenous industries "without any substantial gain to the country". "In...fact to the extent Indian units are placed at a disadvantage, to that extent considerable harm will be done to the larger and permanent interest of the country also (FICCI, Vol. II, 1953: 606).

The E.C. therefore "urged, with all the emphasis at their command, that foreign capital, new or existing, should not be permitted to adversely affect the parallel Indian industry (FICCI, Vol. II, 1953: 608). The E.C. concluded by reiterating its earlier stand and foreign capital should be allowed only into the new and highly technical sectors of the economy where there was no previous Indian industry (FICCI, Vol. II, 1953: 608).[42]

In the same period, some relatively minor changes were made in the licensing procedure under the Industrial Act. In June 1952, changes were made, in the draft rules for the registration and licensing of industrial undertakings. Before making these, the government took note of the FICCI suggestions made in the Central Advisory Council of Industries (CACI) meeting held on 10th May, a fact that FICCI appreciated (FICCI, Vol. II, 1952: 457-463).[43] In 1953, the government proposed further amendments to the Industries Act (FICCI, Vol. II, 1953: 543-544)[44] which included provisions for;

(a) allowing government to take over management (not ownership) of an industrial concern without first issuing directions to it; (FICCI, Vol. II, 1953: 543-544)

(b) allowing government to extend the existing provisions for controls over prices and distribution to similar industrial undertakings and to imported goods; and,

(c) adding to the list of industries in schedule 1, the ferro-manganese industry (FICCI, Vol. II, 1953: 544).

R.G. Saraiya, the FICCI President (FICCI, Vol. II, 1953: 545-546)[45], wrote to TTK that the proposals went against the recommendations of both the Select Committees that had examined the Industries Bill (FICCI, Vol. II, 1953: 545). In particular reference to the proposal (b) above, Saraiya stressed that there was no need for any change. In conclusion he,

> urge(d) that, at a time when there is a generally better understanding between governmental and those engaged in industry and commerce, no action should be taken, however warranted it may seem, on purely theoretical considerations, which is likely to disturb that understanding (FICCI, Vol. II, 1953: 546).

Shift in FICCI Stand on Foreign Capital

By 1954, the economic situation eased (Kidron, 1965: 109). In that year itself, the FICCI attitude towards foreign capital softened. A FICCI publication of May 1954 on imports and industrial development, omitted all proposals for the regulation of foreign firms (FICCI, 1954; *Eastern Economist*, 21 May 1954). In January 1955, a FICCI sub-committee including B.M. Birla, J.R.D. Tata, A. Ramaswami Mudaliar, Tulsidas Kilachand and Shantilal Managaldas met in Bombay to consider a fresh the FICCI attitude towards foreign capital. The subcommittee,

> generally welcomed the flow of foreign capital into India, particularly in those industries which are not pursued by Indian nationals even after due notice by the Government, like oil refineries, where there are difficulties of obtaining technical know-how etc. It also welcomed foreign capital in the consumers industries, like textiles, cement, paper etc., where India has already established herself (*Hindu*, 28 January 1955; Kidron, 1965:109-110).

A FICCI press statement in March, expressed its broad agreement with the government policy statement on foreign capital. Foreign capital was welcomed "as being of value to the rapid industrialisation of the country". However, while FICCI accepted the entry of foreign capital into the consumer goods industries, where Indian industrial units "are fairly established", it proposed that the entry be permitted only if Indian capital was not forthcoming after "say one year's" notice (FICCI, Vol. II, 1955: 218-219). FICCI moreover, stressed the need for foreign capital to offer equity participation to Indian investors and to utilise Indian services e.g. banking, shipping, insurance etc. The crucial test of the utility of foreign investment was "how rapidly it builds up local enterprise". Significantly, FICCI defined Indian units as those where: (a) foreign held equity capital was not more than 49 per cent (in exceptional cases 50 per cent); (b) the majority of the board of directors active in management were Indians; and (c) where the majority control of the managing agency, company or firm was Indian (FICCI, Vol. II, 1955: 219).

Kidron (1965: 110) is perhaps, not quite correct in arguing, that, "the new policy (towards foreign capital) was not accepted wholeheartedly (by the FICCI) as yet".[46] The policy as stated in the March press statement, was clearly one of "collaboration" and not of "hostility" (to use Kidron's categories). The FICCI definition of Indian enterprises clearly allowed for substantial foreign participation, and its policy therefore was one of collaboration with foreign private capital.

The shift in the attitude of larger Indian industrialists towards private foreign capital, was due to their increased confidence after eight years of growth in independent India, that they would not be swamped by foreign companies. Indian business circles therefore, as represented by FICCI, were interested in mutually advantageous collaboration with foreign capital, even if it meant vesting in the latter, a considerable measure of control over the giant enterprise. Indian capitalists were fully aware that a 49 per cent equity participation by a foreign collaborator, together with the various agreements relating to the supply of foreign technology and the payment of royalties, would amount to handing over a large measure of control to foreign private capital. Nonetheless, they were prepared for a partnership with foreign capital, unlike their position in the earlier period.

The 'Leftist' Shift in Congress Rhetoric

In July 1953, the Praja Socialist Party won the by-election for the Agra parliamentary seat. The crucial factor contributing to the Congress defeat was a phenomenon of increasing unemployment (Planning Commission, 1956: 110), which led to public dissatisfaction with the ruling party. This was noted by the FICCI leadership who discussed this with the government on a number of occasions (see above). At the FICCI Annual Session in March 1954, a Resolution on "Unemployment and Economic Development" was moved by G.D. Birla (FICCI, Vol. III, 1954: 92-93). In the resolution, FICCI expressed concern over the rising unemployment, especially amongst the educated "which is a potent cause of political and social unrest" (FICCI, Vol. III, 1954: 92).

The Congress was also aware of the political threat from the Left (PSP and CPI), and this, as Kidron has noted, "determined to some degree both Congress's choice and solutions—industrialisation—and a method—state production. Congress had to compete, on their (the Leftists') terms" (Kidron, 1965: 128). In May 1953, the Congress Working Committee warned that "the major test of the success of any plan is the measure in which one deals with the problem of unemployment". The focus was not yet on the role of the state in promoting industrialisation, as the resolution stated that the unemployment problem "should...be tackled on all fronts and more particularly by the organised growth of Cottage and Village Industries (Indian National Congress, n.d.: 79-80). The AICC meeting held at Agra in July, around the time of the by-election, passed a resolution on "Unemployment". The AICC expressed, "it's concern at the increase in unemployment... notwithstanding the fact that generally there has been an upward trend of production... during the last 18 months (sic)" (Indian National Congress, n.d.: 81). The AICC moreover, stated that "the state must accept an increasingly active and positive role in regard to the development of industries" (Indian National Congress, n.d.: 83).

At the meeting of the National Development Council (NDC) in November 1954, Nehru in a rather lengthy speech about his planning philosophy said,

> The picture I have in mind is definitely and absolutely a Socialistic picture of society. I am not using the word in a dogmatic sense at all, but in the sense of meaning largely that the means of production should be socially owned and controlled for the benefit of society as a whole. There is plenty of room for private enterprise

> there, provided the main aim is kept clear (*Commerce*, 4 December 1954).

Just six months earlier, at the FICCI session, he had categorically stated that "if we have a private sector, it should be allowed a certain obvious freedom of functioning". He further assured FICCI "that no one in government is against big industry. We want big industry to develop" (FICCI, Vol. III, 1954: 31-32).

FICCI on its own part, was happy with the government policy. R.G. Saraiya in his Presidential speech at the March 1954 session recorded, "our (FICCI's) appreciation of cordial relations that exist between the various Ministries of Government and the Federation" (FICCI, Vol. III, 1954: 19). He welcomed the recent changes in government policy including the relaxation of food controls, higher depreciation allowances, decreased excise and export duties, etc. (FICCI, Vol. III, 1954: 14). In August 1954, in a leading article on "Industrial Policy", *Eastern Economist* approvingly noted,

> the fact that what was regarded as a grand instrument of industrial policy in 1949, namely the Industries (Development and Control) Bill, was never put into full use even after its belated enactment in 1951 and its amendment last year. The law is still on display on the shelf—except for some action on the more routine and less objectionable sections like registration, licensing and the establishment of the Development Council (*Eastern Economist*, 13 August 1954).

A few weeks after Nehru's espousal of socialism at the NDC meeting, C.D. Deshmukh addressed the ASSOCHAM annual meeting. *Capital* (16 December 1954) headlined its report on the meeting "Mr. Deshmukh reassures the private sector". Deshmukh reassured business circles about the Companies Act Amendment Bill, the Report of the Taxation Enquiry Commission, and generally about "how the private sector stands with government". *Capital* therefore concluded that, "it is not difficult to agree with him (Deshmukh) that these proposals cannot spell such grave disasters on the private sector as is now prophesied in some quarters".

Deshmukh's reassurance to ASSOCHAM, was followed a few days later, by the Lok Sabha's acceptance of the goal of the "socialistic pattern of society". This, as a perusal of the debate in the House shows, occurred virtually spontaneously and even unexpectedly. On 20th December, Deshmukh moved a motion "that the present economic situation in India be taken into consideration" (Lok Sabha Debates, 20 December 1954, Vol. IX, Part II. col. 3463). His speech in support stated little that was new, and merely repeated the recommendation of the Planning Commission that, "a rapid expansion of the economic and social responsibilities of the state alone will be capable of satisfying the legitimate expectations of the people" (Lok Sabha Debates, 20 December 1954, Vol. IX, Part II. col. 3470). He further stated, that the governments' industrial policy "will be announced very shortly" (Lok Sabha Debates, 20 December 1954, Vol. IX, Part II. col. 3465). As it turned out, the new Industrial Policy Resolution was announced only on 30 April 1956. He explicitly reassured business that if the then privately owned banks were nationalised to form a State Bank of India, compensation would be given on the basis of market value (Lok Sabha Debates, 20 December 1954, Vol. IX, Part II. col. 3481). Deshmukh in a reference to the unemployment problem, stressed the need to increase the employment in the non-agricultural sectors and therefore justified incentives for the cottage and small scale industries and handicrafts (Lok Sabha Debates, 20 December 1954, Vol. IX, Part II. col. 3475-3476). Significantly, throughout his speech he never used the term 'socialistic' but instead use the usual term 'Welfare State' (Lok Sabha Debates, 20 December 1954, Vol. IX, Part II. col. 3467).

Only after his speech T.S.A. Chettiar ((Lok Sabha Debates, 20 December 1954, Vol. IX, Part II. col. 3484-3487) and N.M. Lingam (Lok Sabha Debates, 20 December 1954, Vol. IX, Part II. col. H HII. col. 3487), citing Nehru's speech at the NDC meeting, moved amendments that the objective of industrial policy be explicitly stated as a "socialistic society". Speaking of the amendments were moved, Hiren Mukherjee, a CPI leader, after referring to Nehru's recent statements about "his socialistic faith", expressed his resentment over,

> the Prime Minister's trying to bluff our people into feeling that socialism is being constructed in this country when, on the

> contrary, the vested interests are being perpetuated in a different way (Lok Sabha Debates, 20 December 1954, Vol. IX, Part II. col. 3489-3503).

Asoka Mehta also criticised the government noting that "even the industrial policy resolution (of 1948), inadequate as it was, has not been properly implemented (Lok Sabha Debates, 20th December 1954, Vol. IX, Part II. col. 3514). In this connection, he cited the government's vacillation over nationalisation of TELCO's boiler and locomotive manufacturing units (Lok Sabha Debates, 20 December 1954, Vol. IX, Part II. col. 3522), while both the public and the privately owned financial institutions had given less credit than before to the small sector (Lok Sabha Debates, 20 December 1954, Vol. IX, Part II. col. 3523-3524). Because of the government's industrial policy, Mehta claimed, "we find that the same handful of big business houses are growing everywhere. It is Tatas, Birlas and the Dalmias" (Lok Sabha Debates, 20 December 1954, Vol. IX, Part II. col. 3525). During this period of discussion, as Mehta noted Prime Minister Nehru, the Finance Minister and the Minister for Commerce and Industry were not even present in the House (Lok Sabha Debates, 20 December 1954, Vol. IX, Part II. col. 3529).

Meghnad Saha also cited various deviations from the Industrial Policy Statement. For example, foreign companies were operating petroleum refineries, while the private sector continued to control the coal industry (Lok Sabha Debates, 20 December 1954, Vol. IX, Part II. col. 3449-3451). He cited T.T. Krishnamachari's recent statement at the Indian Merchants' Chambers (a constituent of FICCI) meeting at Bombay, where the latter had stated that "the government are not wedded to any doctrinaire policy on the sustainability or otherwise of nationalisation for the development of Indian industries" (Lok Sabha Debates, 20 December 1954, Vol. IX, Part II. col. 3551), in support of his charge that the Minister for Finance, and, Commerce and Industry were "friends" of the Tatas, Birlas, Dalmias and Kasturbhai Lalbhai (Lok Sabha Debates, 20 December 1954, Vol. IX, Part II. col. 3555). He noted that the Development Councils (the advisory bodies for various industries), were "filled up mostly by industrialists and their nominees", which in fact was responsible for various pro-big business decisions of those bodies (Lok Sabha Debates, 20th December 1954, Vol. IX, Part II. col. 3556).

When such deviation continued Nehru sought to defend the government's industrial policies. He, as before, explained government policy in terms of the 'class conciliation' approach to the class struggle (Lok Sabha Debates, 20 December 1954, Vol. IX, Part II. col. 3590).[47] He stated that the government would follow a policy in which "we always try to win over even those who suffer from that policy" (Lok Sabha Debates, 20 December 1954, Vol. IX, Part II. col. 3604). While reiterating his faith in socialism: a "casteless, classless society", Nehru also argued that socialism did not mean that all industry must be nationalized (Lok Sabha Debates, 20 December 1954, Vol. IX, Part II. col. 3602). He stressed that "our policy must be, inevitably, one of raising production and increasing employment as rapidly as possible". For this it was necessary that the public sector "should grow rapidly as possible" (Lok Sabha Debates, 20 December 1954, Vol. IX, Part II. col. 3607). Immediately afterwards, he reassured business circles stating that the "private sector should function under certain broad strategic controls but otherwise the freedom, the initiative, etc., within those limits" (Lok Sabha Debates, 20 December 1954, Vol. IX, Part II. col. 3607).

The assurances by Deshmukh and Nehru, were appreciated by G.D. Somani, (an industrialist and a leading FICCI member), who hoped that their speeches would dispel all doubts and fears over industrial policy (Lok Sabha Debates, 20 December 1954, Vol. IX, Part II. col. 345). He praised, "the policies of the Government of India on economic matters during the last few years (which) have stimulated and have imparted strength to our economy" (Lok Sabha Debates, 20 December 1954, Vol. IX, Part II. col. 3647), further evidence of which were the "very favourable" conditions in the Stock Exchange (Lok Sabha Debates, 20 December 1954, Vol. IX, Part II. col. 3647).

After the debate, the motion as amended by N.M. Lingam (Coimbatore), which was acceptable to the government, was passed. The amended motion stated:

> the House having considered the economic situation in India and the policy of the government in relation thereto, is of the opinion that (i) the policy of government is in harmony with the policy statement of 6 April 1940; (ii) the objective of our economic policy should be a socialistic pattern of society; and (iii) towards this end the tempo of economic activity in general and industrial development in particular should be stepped up to the maximum possible extent (Lok Sabha Debates, 20 December 1954, Vol. IX, Part II. col. 3692).

As should be evident from the preceding discussion, this notion in claiming that government policy was in harmony with the Industrial Policy Statement, was a conscious attempt to legitimise the existing industrial policy as we have seen above, there were considerable divergences from the letter and spirit of the 1948 statement. The extremely vague nature of the "socialistic pattern of society" was evident from Nehru's speeches, even before the Lok Sabha debate.

The financial press was thus not agitated over the statement. *Commerce* (8 January 1955) noted that Nehru was generally opposed to further nationalisation, and further that, "He says that it is a advantageous to have a competitive private sector to ensure the efficiency of the public sector". The article also noted that in his later speech to the Congress MPs, Nehru had warned "his countrymen from entertaining exaggerated hopes that socialism is just round the corner" and had stressed that socialism can come only gradually (*Commerce*, 8 January 1955). The Parliament had accepted the goal of a "socialistic pattern" of society, but the ruling party, despite a number of statements by its undisputed leader, had not. This, together with the additional factor of the ensuing election in Andhra, where the CPI was the major electoral threat, provided the necessary impetus to the Congress to adopt its famous Avadi resolution in January 1955.

The Avadi Session

At the 60th Session of the Indian National Congress, held on 21 January 1955 at Avadi (Madras), as many as 14 resolutions were passed (Indian National Congress, 1956: 7). In what was later to be considered a landmark, a resolution defined the Congress objective as,

> the establishment of a Socialistic Pattern of Society, where the principal means of production are under social ownership or control, production is progressively speeded up and there is equitable distributions of national wealth (Indian National Congress, 1956: 7).

In the resolution on "Economic Policy", while it was stated that the public sector would play a progressively greater role, particularly in the establishment of basic industries, it was emphasised that the private sector had also "a definite place in our economy at present and should be encouraged to play its part within the broad strategic control of the plan. In its concluding section, the resolution implicitly acknowledged the threat to the Congress because of popular dissatisfaction, as it stated:

> India is faced today by a great challenge. Not only the urge of the people to progress, but also the compulsion of circumstances necessitate rapid advance so as to bring about far-reaching social, economic and industrial changes. The challenge is to bring these about speedily and effectively by peaceful and democratic processes (Indian National Congress, 1956: 8-9).

The Congress offered its "peaceful and democratic" road to socialism to counter Leftist propaganda, especially that of the CPI. It however also reassured the private sector.

In his report to the session as the outgoing president, Nehru referred to the resolutions passed and reiterated his earlier arguments[48] that,

> In our present state to limit resources to the public sector means restriction of our opportunities for production and growth...it becomes necessary, therefore, to have a private sector also and to give it full play within its field... within the larger framework that we lay down, the test always is fuller production and fuller employment (AICC Economic Review, 21 January 1955: 86).

The business press understood the political compulsions behind the resolutions quite well and was not unduly perturbed. *Capital* (27 January 1955) in its commentary on the session noted that,

> The need to give a new battle-cry well in advance of the 1956-57 General Elections, and to rally the wobbling middle third behind the Congress in the name of socialism and secure employment, was recognised by Mr. Nehru and his associates.[49]

Further, all these moves "might it is stated, isolate the Communists and effect a situation of polarisation of forces—a situation in which the Reds cannot win a parliamentary majority in any state" (*Capital*, 27 January 1955). *Commerce* (29 January 1955) in its comment on the session, noted that "Neither the objective nor the policy constitutes any fundamental departure from the ideals to which the Congress has all along subscribed. It however stressed that,

> The change of bottle, with a new level on it, need not, however, cause any alarm in the private sector. A careful analysis of the two resolutions...will show that there is hardly anything in it to which any enlightened businessmen can object.

The new 'Leftist' slogans at Avadi arose because the failure of the old slogans has necessitated the launching of a new high-powered campaign of deception" (*New Age*, February 1955: 1-3).

The 'Leftist' shift in Congress rhetoric had almost immediate success. In the assembly elections held in Andhra between the 11th and 27th of February, the Congress was returned to power with a comfortable majority. As the CPI admitted, "the election results constituted a political defeat for the Party and a setback for the democratic (i.e. Leftist-led) movement in the whole country" (*New Age*, April 1955: 1-3). Though the CPI candidates secured some 27 lakh votes, approximately 31 per cent of the total, in terms of seats it was a poor second (*New Age*, April 1955: 1-3). On the other hand, the Congress which polled 42.65 lakh votes, approximately 49.5 per cent of the total, won 146 of the 196 seats (Indian National Congress, 1956: 76). This result, the CPI ascribed to the fact that the economic situation had improved and to the effectiveness of the Congress's use of the "socialistic" ideology, which led the middle strata to vote for the Congress candidates (*New Age*, April 1955: 1-3).[50]

However, as business representatives admitted, despite the

resurgence of 'Leftist' rhetoric, the government's industrial policy continued to favour the private sector (as we have seen above). Various proposals for nationalising particular industries or firms had been turned down, e.g. EELCO in October 1954, commercial banking in December 1954, foreign trade, cement, jute, and plantation in early 1956 (Kidron, 1965: 133). The manner in which the major acts of nationalisation were actually implemented, e.g. air transport in 1953, the Imperial Bank in May 1955,[51] life insurance in January 1956, and the Kolar Gold Fields in November 1956, showed that the government's policy was not one of "socialistic" nationalisation which was part of an overall anti-private sector strategy (Kidron, 1965: 133-134). As Kidron had noted, air transport was weakly organised, unable without government support to extend services to many cities within India, let alone abroad (Kidron, 1965: 134). Thus, when the companies themselves requested long-term loans at nominal interest from the government, the latter nationalised them and appointed J.R.D. Tata, who controlled the largest private air company, Chairman of the new Air Corporation. Regarding the belated nationalisation of the Imperial Bank, A.D. Shroff (a leading FICCI member, and later founder of the Forum for Free Enterprise), admitted that the act was a consequence of the "unresponsive attitude of bankers to the nation's requirements" for a network of small-town branches (*Capital*, 6 January 1955).[52] Further, in response to a proposal for the nationalisation of commercial banking, T.T. Krishnamachari emphasised that this "should be the last thing in nationalisation" (*Hindu*, 1 January 1955; Kidron, 1965: 134).

The nationalisation of life insurance was intended to concentrate savings for the large industrial investment proposed in the Second Plan. Moreover, C.D. Deshmukh, the Finance Minister, reassured business that the private sector would continue to receive "at least as much money as today made available to it" (*Economic Weekly*, January 1956: 52). Although FICCI protested against the nationalisation of life insurance, because of FICCI pressure, the private shareholders received sizeable compensation (FICCI, Vol. II, 1956: 328-351), which as *Commerce* (23 March 1956) admitted, "many in the business community felt (was)...all things considered, a reasonable and fair bases of compensation."[53]

Similarly, generous compensation provisions were provided both under the Air Corporation Act, as well as for the takeover of the Imperial Bank. In the latter case, the compensation was computed on the basis of the average market price over the previous 12 months (Kidron, 1965: 135).

This led to protests even from the ruling party members in the Lok Sabha (Kidron, 1965: 135). The quantum of compensation paid to the Kolar group, was almost doubled by the Centre to £1.23 million (the original provision by the Government of Mysore was for £6.5 lakhs), which the group's managing director accepted as a "fair and reasonable" sum (*Financial Times*, October 10, 1956; quoted in Kidron, 1965). Hence, while the government was constrained to nationalise a number of industries and firms mainly because of the insufficiency and non-viability of the concerned undertakings, together with the need to expand the resources available with the state for investment in the Second Plan (Kidron, 1965: 133-136), private sector industrialists, both Indian and foreign, were compensated very generously. In this sphere also, therefore, despite the Leftist rhetoric, government policy was designed to accommodate business interests as far as possible.

The Second Plan and FICCI

This spirit of accommodation, or to put it more sharply of collaboration, with the Indian private sector, manifested itself in the process of the formulation of the Second Five Year Plan. As it had even earlier in the instance of the First Plan (see above).On 17 March 1955, the Second Plan Frame was published (Planning Commission, 1955: 33-58). Mahalanobis's draft explicitly stated that,

> Key industries would be established and developed in the public sector generally in accordance with the Industrial Policy Declaration of 1948 as interpreted in December 1954. Government would also take up the factory production of certain consumer goods which are of strategic importance for the growth of the national economy.

Therefore it was necessary that,

> The public sector must be expanded rapidly relatively faster than the private sector for steady advance to a socialist economy. In order to make available large capital resources for investment and national development and to facilitate the implementation of the plan, government will be prepared to enter into such activities as banking, insurance, foreign trade our internal trade in selected commodities (Planning Commission, 1955: 47).

Further, in order to accomplish the above stated aims, the Plan Frame proposed a development expenditure of Rs. 4,300 crores in the public sector and Rs. 2,248 crores in the private sector, approximately a ratio of 2:1 (Planning Commission, 1955: 61).

Four days later, "Tentative Framework" for the Second Plan was published, based on the working paper prepared jointly by the Economic Division of Ministry of Finance and the Planning Commission, in consultation with the Central Statistical Organisation and the Indian Statistical Institute (Planning Commission, 1955: 69-107).

This document advocated that "emphasis must be placed on the extension of public ownership or control over the strategic means of production", as well as on the "achievement of social justice..."(Planning Commission, 1955: 72). This framework proposed a public sector outlay of Rs. 4,300 crores and a private-sector outlay of Rs. 2,200 crores, again a ratio of 2:1 in favour of the public sector (Planning Commission, 1955: 92-93). The proposed allocations for industries and mining were Rs. 1,100 crores in the public sector and Rs. I00 crores in the private sector (Planning Commission, 1955: 92-93).

The FICCI immediately made representations to increase the outlay of the private sector (FICCI, Vol. II, 1995: 233-239).[54] In their note on the Plan, FICCI referred to the expansion of TISCO, and the private sector entry into the manufacture of mixed fertilisers as well as the development of synthetic chemical units, as contributions of the private sector, apart from the First Plan targets (FICCI, Vol. II, 1995: 239). The permission to the private sector, to take up fresh investments in these areas was, of course, a deviation from the Industrial Policy Statement.

The FICCI pressures for the increase in the Plan outlay for

the private sector, proved effective. In the final approved version of the Second Plan, the ratio of public to private investment was markedly changed. The investment programme for the public sector was Rs. 3,800 crores, while for the private sector this was increased to Rs. 2,400 crores (Planning Commission, 1956: 92). The shift did not pass uncriticised. When the Draft Plan, incorporating the changes was in the Lok Sabha, the deviation from the Plan Frame were sharply criticised.

In terms of ideological formulations, there were no consistent 'socialist' policy statements in the Plan. In the Chapter on the "Approach to the Second Five Year Plan", it was stated that the objective was the "socialist pattern of society" and that,

> The benefits of economic development must accrue more and more to the relatively less privileged classes of society, and there should be a progressive reduction of the concentration of incomes, wealth and economic power (Planning Commission, 1956: 239).

Later, in the same chapter it was stated that,

> it is important to ensure that in reducing inequalities no damage occurs to the productive system as would jeopardise the task of development itself, or imperil the very processes of democratic change which it is the objective of policy to strengthen (Planning Commission, 1956: 33).

Furthermore, "it has to be recognised, however, that some of the measures which might reduce inequalities are apt to react to live and adversely on incentives" (Planning Commission, 1956: 33-34). Although the planners recognised that "the most important single factor responsible for inequalities of incomes and wealth is the ownership of property" (Planning Commission, 1956: 34), no measures for removing or even reducing, inequalities through the expropriation of the very rich, (i.e. through nationalisation, etc.) are advocated. In fact with reference to the Indian taxation structure it was explicitly stated that,

> Experiences in more advanced countries seem to indicate that progressive income taxes on the scales that are now prevalent are in reality not so effective, firstly because the income by way of capital gains escape such taxation, and secondly because there is

a great deal of evasion in various ways (Planning Commission, 1956: 34).

Therefore, the document recommended the substitution of expenditure tax for income tax, since the former "may encourage saving and, in theory at any rate, it is a more effective instrument than an income tax for moderating inflationary and deflationary tendencies (Planning Commission, 1956: 34). Thus, even the fiscal measures that were recommended were pragmatic rather than radical.

The general thrust of the industrial policy was, despite the occasional diluted 'socialist' rhetoric, similar to that of the First Plan. The accent was on increase production which would enable a rise of the "Floor to incomes", and thus bring about a quicker...advance towards the socialist pattern..." (Planning Commission, 1956: 36). The planners advocated the,

"Promotion of a cooperative forms of production, elimination of functionless rent-receivers, substitution of private usurious credit by institutional credit, control a private monopoly and enlargement of the public sector in strategic lines of production and trade..." so that,

an increasing proportion of the community's surpluses (are placed) directly in the hands of public authorities (so) that an effective reduction in the incomes and spending power accruing to a few can be brought about (Planning Commission, 1956: 36).

However, no concrete and comprehensive measures for controlling the private monopolies were put forward (Hanson, 1966: 139). Hanson has noted that, "a predominantly public and cooperative economy was a very distant ideal, and in the meantime the selective stimulation and regulation of private enterprise was of the highest importance. Of this the planners were well aware, and they might have done better to emphasise it more heavily". The dependence on the private sector and the fact that socialism was realisable only in the distant future was, of course, something the planners could not emphasise because of the political compulsions, discussed above.

On the other hand, the attitude to controls was ambivalent. It was stated that "it would...be desirable on psychological as well as administrative grounds to avoid as far as possible control and rationing of the necessities of life", though it was acknowledged that "controls on essential consumption cannot be ruled out in particular situations" (Planning Commission, 1956: 39). Thus, the plan as a whole, was quite acceptable to the industrialists, as the socialist rhetoric had not been transformed into socialist controls and curbs on the private sector.

This is borne out by the reactions of various groups to the second plan. In the Lok Sabha debate, A.K. Gopalan (CPI) noted that, "the monopoly elements of the private sector after the publication of the Plan Frame went all out to denounce and scuttle the Plan Frame". In effect they succeeded as, "The Planning Commission and the government tampered with the Plan Frame" (Lok Sabha Debates, Vol. V, 25 May 1956, col. 9420-9421). He believed that there was "some advance" in the Second Plan over the preceding one as it contained "proposals for economic and developmental activities on a scale larger than that in the First Plan" (Lok Sabha Debates, Vol. V, 25 May 1956, col. 9422). While the Plan Frame had embarked Rs. 1, 100 crores for industry and mining in the public sector, the outlay in the Second Plan, excluding that for the steel plant, was only Rs. 350 crores. This allocation, Gopalan noted was "very much negligible". He also observed that the ratio of investment in the public sector and the private sector of 2:1, "has been abundant" (Lok Sabha Debates, Vol. V, 25 May 1956, col. 9423). Therefore he concluded,

> From the proposals of the Second Plan, it would seem that instead of the public sector gradually securing an ascendancy over the private sector, it is the private sector that continues to maintain its preponderance in the economy. This is contrary to what the Plan Frame had suggested" (Lok Sabha Debates, Vol. V, 25 May 1956, col. 9424).

This was evident from the fact that the second line changed the plan frame's stress on the cottage and small-scale industry, which were to meet a substantial amount of the demand for consumer goods, by sanctioning an increase in the investment in the consumer goods industries dominated by the large industrial houses. It further sanctioned fairly heavy investments in the aluminium, steel, ferro-manganese, and cement industries in the private sector, as well as in the silk and rayon industries (Lok Sabha Debates, Vol. V, 25 May 1956, col. 9425).[55]

G.D. Somani, a leading industrialist and a FICCI leader as well as a Congress MP was on the other hand full of praise for the Plan. He called upon all sections "to cooperate whole-heartedly with the government in making the Plan the grand success which it deserves" (Lok Sabha Debates, Vol. V, 26 May 1956, col. 9473). He further welcomed a previous,

> statement of the Prime Minister in which he deprecated the condemnation of the private sector and in which he visualised an important role which the private sector will continue to play during this historical period when we are building a new India (Lok Sabha Debates, Vol. V, 26 May 1956, col. 9473).

Even earlier, the private sector had welcomed the increase in the private sector outlays. As *Capital* put it, this, together with the other feature of the plan was "a welcome step towards a more balanced economic development all round" (*Capital*, 12 January 1956).

The Industrial Policy Resolution

The government's policy was, as we have seen above, conciliatory to the private sector. Despite the socialist rhetoric, concessions to the private industrial interests had been systemically granted. Moreover, the rhetoric was never anti-capitalist or even anti-big business. Nehru himself, time and again, had stressed the indispensability of private enterprise.

It is evident from C.D. Deshmukh's statement in the Lok Sabha on 20 December 1954, wherein he had stated that the government's industrial policy "will be announced very shortly" (see above), that a new Industrial Policy Resolution had been under preparation, at least since mid-1954. With the new strategy of the public sector obtaining "the commanding heights" as enunciated in the Second Plan, the need for a new Industrial Policy Resolution, was even more manifest.

On 27 April 1956, just three days before the Industrial Policy Resolution was placed before Parliament, M.S. Gurupadaswamy moved a resolution for the nationalisation of scheduled banks. He was however, not of the view "that the whole network of production, distribution and exchange should be socially owned and controlled..." because,

> If we try to do that we may achieve (the) socialist objective but we will be annihilating democracy in part. So, to achieve (the) socialist objective it would be enough to control the peaks or the commanding heights of our economic pyramid (Lok Sabha Debates, Vol. IV, 27 April 1957, col. 6612).

A.C. Guha, the Minister for Revenue and Defence Expenditure, who replied to the debate on behalf of the government, rejected the resolution, although its proponents had supported bank nationalisation, as necessitated as in the earlier instance of nationalisation of life insurance, by the need to increase the resources available to the state for investment in the Second Plan (Lok Sabha Debates, Vol. IV, 27 April 1957, col. 6643). Guha in his reply to Gurupadaswamy Sammy's speech accepted the government's views were "pragmatic". He further argued that as "90 per cent or more of the production of our national wealth even now comes from the private sector", the nationalisation of banks could not be justified in terms of the Congress's pragmatic ideology (Lok Sabha Debates, Vol. IV, 27 April 1957, col. 6661). Guha further opposed bank nationalisation, even if it was justifiable on monetary considerations, by arguing that such an act would not be to the credit for the good reputation of any government.

Significantly none of the participants referred to earlier Congress resolutions, e.g. the recommendations of the Economic Programme Committee, which had proposed the nationalisation of banks. Perhaps they were aware that these resolutions were now dead-letters, no longer to be taken seriously, now that the Congress had to rule without losing its "credit" or "good reputation" with big business, its main financier. At any rate, on the eve of the Industrial Policy Resolution, the government's policy remained stubbornly pragmatic even when verbally 'socialistic'. The stream of concessions to private industry, were now to lead to a rather remarkable attempt to combine socialistic rhetoric with a charter for the continued expansion of the private sector.

The language of the 30 April 1956, Industrial Policy Resolution was more radical than that of its precursor of 1948, for the reasons stated above. It was categorically stated that,

> The adoption of the socialist pattern of society as the national objective, as well as the need for planned and rapid development require that all industries of basic and strategic importance, or in the nature of public utility services, should be in the public sector... (together with) other industries which are essential and require investment on a scale which only the state, in present circumstances, could provide... (Appendix, B, para 6).

These industries, numbering 17 in all, were put in schedule 'A' of the Resolution (Appendix, B, Schedule 'A'), for which "the future development...will be the exclusive responsibility of the state" Appendix, B, para 7).

Even regarding these industries, it was stated "This does not preclude the expansion of the existing privately owned units, or the cooperation of private enterprise in the establishment of new units when the national interests so requires". Only "Railways and air transport, arms and ammunition and atomic energy... (were to) be developed as central government monopolies ". For the other industries,

> whether cooperation with the private enterprise is necessary, the state will ensure, either through majority participation in the capital or otherwise, that it has the requisite powers to guide the policy and control the operations of the undertaking (Appendix, B, para 8).

In this new policy statement therefore, the private sector participation in schedule 'A' industries was explicitly provided for. Thus in effect, as S.K. Goyal has noted, "some of the industries exclusively reserved for (the) public sector under the Industrial Policy Resolution of 1948 were thrown open to the private sector" (Goyal, 1972: 3). Furthermore, the clause in the 1948 statement that specified that privately owned units in the industries reserved for the state, would be taken over after 10 years was deleted, as FICCI had consistently demanded (Appendix, B, para 4; Goyal, 1979: 8).

The Industrial Policy Resolution included a second category

of 12 industries in Schedule 'B',

> which will be progressively state-owned and in which the state will generally take the initiative in establishing new undertakings, but in which private enterprise will also be expected to supplement the effort of the state (Appendix, B, Schedule 'B' para 7, emphasis added).

For the third category of industries, not listed in either schedule, "their future development will, in general, be left to the initiative and enterprise of the private sector" (Appendix, B, para 7).

Therefore in the Schedule 'B' industries, private sector participation was explicitly "expected" to supplement public investment. Thus, it is apparent that in this Resolution, apart from a few industries, all others were explicitly left open for private sector participation. In comparison, therefore, with the 1948 Statement, it represented further concessions to private sector interests, rather than a "socialist" advance.

As could be expected, industrialists reacted favourably to the Resolution. G.D. Somani while participating in the discussion on the Second Plan stated,

> that even under the revised Industrial Policy there is more than enough to do for the private sector, and I therefore do not in the least feel disappointed or worried about the future of the private sector under the revised Industrial Policy Resolution.

In a press communiqué on 6 May 1956, the FICCI E.C. generally welcomed the Resolution and stated that,

> They are in full agreement with the objectives of accelerating the rate of economic growth and spreading of industrialisation and, in particular, to develop heavy industries and machine making industries, and they offer their whole-hearted support to the government in promoting and achieving these objectives (FICCI, Vol. II, 1956: 582-583).

In a reference to the Schedule 'A' and 'B' industries, the FICCI recommended a flexible approach in order to facilitate economic growth and increased production (FICCI, Vol. II, 1956: 583). Regarding the proposal for "state trading on an increasing scale" (Appendix B, para 5), the FICCI recommended "that the activities of the state should not result in displacing normal trade channels (FICCI, Vol. II, 1956: 584)". It also suggested that, "it would perhaps have assisted a better understanding of government's future industrial policy if the Resolution assured the investors that enterprises in private hands will be nationalised" (FICCI, Vol. II, 1956: 584).

The FICCI could not have entertained very serious fears about nationalisation after the numerous reassuring statements made by Nehru and others around that period, which we have referred to above. And the "flexibility" they wanted regarding the interpretation of Schedule 'A' and 'B' was already explicit, as we have seen.

The business press was also generally appreciative of the Resolution. The *Eastern Economist* (4 May 1956) noted that, "Bombay and Calcutta (the areas where large industrialists are concentrated), it is true, have heaved a large sigh of relief...". By their standards the resolution was,

> a splendid piece of ideological tight-rope walking... There is nothing which should terrify private enterprise in this Socialism. On the other hand, there is nothing in this mixture which enables the public sector to do any job for which it was not otherwise qualified.[56]

Leftist circles were, as could be expected, quite critical of the Resolution. A.K. Gopalan (CPI), speaking in the Lok Sabha, referred to the Resolution noting that,

> It does not promise us any radical change in their relative position of the two sectors in our economy. It does not recognise...that in order to strengthen and expand the public sector it is necessary not only to start new state-owned industries but also to nationalise big industries and units in the private sector.

He disputed Nehru's earlier statement in Parliament where the latter had opposed nationalisation of private sector units on grounds of the "payment of the compensation" required, arguing that under the Constitution, as amended, Parliament could decide that big compensation should not be given (Lok Sabha Debates, Vol. V, 25 May 1956, col.9424; Gupta, 27 May 1956).

Also in this period (1956), the Companies Act was amended,

four years after the Bhabha Committee Report was submitted (Ministry of Finance, 1952). FICCI made a number of recommendations starting from 1952, seeking to reduce the powers of the government to control the affairs of privately owned companies (various Reports of FICCI).[57] However, the Companies Act as amended, failed to curb the growth of managing agency companies or their malpractices, as the Patel Committee Report of 1965, showed (Ministry of Law, 1966).

Conclusion

From the preceding discussion, it is apparent that there is a discernible trend in the development of industrial policy from 1951 to 1956. From the debates on the formulation of the First Plan to the April 1956 Industrial Policy Resolution, the marked tendency in the Congress government's industrial policy was to facilitate the growth of the private corporate sector, including the large industrial houses. The 1956 Industrial Policy Resolution, despite some socialistic phrases, contained, as we have seen above, significant concessions to the private sectors. In particular, the clause in the 1948 Industrial Policy Statement that specified that privately owned units in industries reserved for the state, would be taken over after 10 years was deleted, evidently in a response to the consistent business demand for its removal.

The various shifts in the Congress's ideological stance can be related to the political compulsions on the Congress leadership in specific situations. At no stage however, was a 'Leftist' shift in Congress rhetoric translated into a 'Leftist' industrial policy, which restricted the area of operation of the private sector as a whole, or of Indian big business in particular. On its part, Indian big business was apparently able to exploit the socio-political situation in its own favours, in order to wrest policy concessions from the Congress government. As we shall show in the following chapter, with the help of statistics pertaining to the 1951 to 1958 period, the objective result of the industrial policies followed in these years, was the impressive growth of big business, both in absolute terms, and also in relation to the rest of the private corporate sector.

REFERENCES

1. FICCI memorandum dated 25 September 1951 to Planning Commission, FICCI, volume 1, 1951, pp. 29-31; FICCI, volume 2, 1951, pp. 151-190.
2. As mentioned in Confidential Report of meeting with Planning Commission.
3. Deshmukh repeatedally made this proposal at the meeting; cf. FICCI, Vol. II, 1952: 225.
4. Nanda, D.O. letter No. PC(p053/52), dated 26 October 1952 to Shanti Prasad Jain.
5. FICCI D.O. letter dated 6 November 1952 to Nanda.
6. D.O. letter No. 1329/HMP/52 dated 10/11 November, 1952 to Shanti Prasad Jain.
7. B. T. Ranadive's book is a Communist Party critique of the Plan.
8. G.D. Birla's speech to the Annual Meeting of the United Commercial Bank, Quoted in Ranadive, 154: 244.
9. FICCI E.C. confidential communiqué No. F. 4000/777 dated 19 May 1953 to the Ministry of Commerce and Industry.
10. FICCI representatives made similar criticisms at the Central Advisory Council of Industry (CACI) meetings held on 29 May and 12 October 1953 in New Delhi; cf. Confidential Reports submitted by FICCI representatives in FICCI, Vo. II, 1953:797-805, 806-813.
11. FICCI letter No. F. 37/35/760 dated 14 June 1952 to the Ministry of Commerce and Industry.
12. Ministry of Commerce and Industry circular No. 4(3)-LA(G)/52 dated 12 March 1953 to members, CACI.
13. R.G. Saraiya D.O. letter No. 24/5354 dated 24 March 1953 to T.T. Krishnamachari.
14. As Kidron consulted only the reporters of the press statement in the *Hindu* and *Capital*, he may have been unaware of the FICCI definition of Indian enterprises, which allowed for very substantial participation by foreign private capital.
15. For example, Nehru stated that: "In the economic field there are classes. We want to do away with the classes. Our approach has been, by and large, trying to win over people... I admit class struggle... but... I want to get rid of it as far as possible without aggravating that struggle, by other means."
16. See, for instance, that the debates in the Constituent Assembly in 1948, as analysed in Chapter V above.
17. The "wobbling middle third" referred to the middle class base

of the Congress, that was effected by unemployment, etc. and whose electoral support therefore was uncertain.

18. The Congress took this campaign very seriously. Nehru addressed a number of mass meetings within the state. c.f. Issues of the *Hindu* and *Times of India*, February 1955.
19. This was done more than six years after Chetty's original proposal was turned down. See Chapter V above.
20. Speeches at the Rotary Club, Ahmedabad.
21. (See also India, Ministry of Law, 1956: 22-27), The First Schedule, wherein the principles for computation of compensation are given.
22. P. Chentsal Rao D.O. letter No. F.1722-1735/803 dated 18 March 1955 to Ministers of Government of India, Planning Commission Members and some government officials.
23. Since Iron and Steel was included in the Schedule 'A' industries under the Industrial Policy Resolution of the previous month, the allocation of funds to the private sector units in the steel industry was a violation of stated policy. The Resolution will be discussed in detail below.
24. Comments in *Commerce* and *Capital* were critical of the Resolution, because of the enhanced role of the state, cf. *Capital*, 3 May 1956; *Commerce*, 5 May 1956.
25. FICCI, Vol. II, 1952: 318-368; FICCI, Vol. II, 1953: 263-274; FICCI, Vol. II, 1954: 279-278; FICCI, Vol. II, 1955: 186-201; FICCI, Vol. II, 1956: 432-438.

7

Industrial Policy and Big Business, 1956-1963

The big business interests, through FICCI, sought to keep up the pressure to influence the formulation of industrial policy at all levels.

This chapter seeks to examine the changes in stated industrial policy during 1956 to 1963 and the advantages, if any, reaped by the large industrial houses dominating the Indian organised private sector. The cumulative effect of policy changes and the extent, to which these may have altered some of the basic features of the industrial policy framework established by 1956, is examined.

Pragmatism and the 1966 to Industrial Policy Resolution

In September 1957, an industrialists' delegation went to the USA, Canada and Western Europe. The delegation was led by G.D. Birla and included Babubhai Chinai (FICCI President), G.L. Bansal (FICCI Secretary-General), and a few other important industrialists including B.D. Garware, D.P. Goenka, Shriyans Prasad Jain, S.S. Kanoria, S.L. Kirloskar, D.C. Kothari and Ramnath A. Podar. The composition of the delegation was largely from among the FICCI-associated industrialists.

Prior to the departure of the delegation to the USA, there was a meeting between T.T. Krishnamachari (TTK), the then Finance Minister, Morarji Desai, the Commerce and Industries Minister, and Nehru. The Industrial Licensing Policy Inquiry Committee (ILPIC), found in its investigations into the development of the aluminium industry, a noting on a file by

Dr. Nagaraja Rao, Chief Industrial Adviser in the Ministry of Commerce and Industry which revealed:

> That the question of permitting the private sector to develop the aluminium project was considered just before the Finance Minister (TTK) went to the USA for the visit... There was a discussion between the Prime Minister, the Finance Minister and the Commerce and Industry Minister, so as to evolve a picture of the specific industries which could be thrown open for development in the private sector even among those which had been included in Schedule 'A' and Schedule 'B'. The adviser (Dr. Nagaraja Rao) thought that it was on the basis of the decisions taken during this discussion that both Shri G.D. Birla and Shri Venkataswami Naidu were encouraged to contact possible American collaborators for the two proposed aluminium plant (Goyal, 1979; IPR, 1956).[58]

The aluminium industry had been included in Schedule 'B' of the 1956 Industrial Policy Resolution which consisted of industries, "which will be progressively state-owned and in which the state will therefore generally take the initiative in establishing new undertakings..." (IPR, 1956). The throwing open of the aluminium industry to the private sector, and that to the Birla and V.R. Naidu groups, amounted to a clear deviation from the Industrial Policy Resolution of the previous year.[59] Moreover, the fact that at the above high-powered meeting involving the Prime Minister, the Finance Minister, and the Commerce and Industry Minister, there was a discussion of the "specific industries which could be thrown open for development in the private sector even among those which had been included in Schedule 'A' and Schedule 'B'..." (See above), clearly indicates that wide-ranging deviations from the Industrial Policy Resolution had been approved by the political leadership, barely a year after the announcement of the new industrial policy.

When the Indian Industrial Delegation (the industrialists' delegation), left India in September 1957, they departed with the "full blessings" of the Ministers of Commerce and Industry, and of Finance (FICCI, Vol. II, 1957: 546-547). TTK was already in the USA on an official visit when the industrialists arrived. The FICCI report claims that the two delegations worked "as a team". TTK assured prospective foreign investor (as well as Indian private entrepreneurs), "that the future role of the private sector would be double that of the public sector". This statement FICCI noted, "caused much satisfaction" (FICCI, Vol. II, 1957: 552).

In March 1957, at the 5th meeting of the Reviewing Sub-Committee of the Central Advisory Council for Industries (CACI), it was reported that a licence had been granted to M/s Textool Company Ltd., Coimbatore to manufacture 750 tonnes of pig iron per mensem. L.K. Jha, Secretary Ministry of Heavy Industries explained that though iron and steel was in the Schedule 'A' industries, this was "no absolute bar to government allowing privately owned units in this field in exceptional and special circumstances" (FICCI, Vol. II, 1957: 776).[60] Thus apart from the continuance of the privately owned Tata Iron and Steel Company (TISCO) and Indian Iron and Steel Company (IISCO of the Martin Burn group), a new privately owned unit was allowed entry into the iron and steel industry.

Within a year of announcement of the 1956 Industrial Policy Resolution, a government spokesman had stated that there was "no absolute bar" to private sector entry even into the Schedule 'A' industries. The deviations from the industrial policy framework as earlier planned in the high-powered meeting referred to the above had begun.

FICCI and the 1957 General Elections

Some leading members of FICCI viewed the result of the 1957 General Elections with some disquiet. At the 1957 Annual Session S.S. Kanoria (who in 1971 was to become FICCI President), referred to the "contempt, hatred and suspicion" with which big business was,

> looked upon... in a country. It is therefore no surprise that no political party in India ventured to advocate and support our cause in the general elections. As things are now moving, we cannot deny that our days appear to be numbered and our system is on the way out in India. And if the end comes, I am afraid it may go unwept, unsung and unhonoured.

Kanoria also warned that,

> The recent elections have clearly indicated a Leftist trend, and any further delay in the economic advancement of the common man... may turn the country entirely red. It is therefore the bounden duty of the businessmen to join hands with the government...(to) make the plan a success (FICCI, Vol. III, 1957:16).

The FICCI president, Lakshmipat Singhania differed with Kanoria, and claimed that "the Federation has been showing very good results and success and (has been) helping trade, commerce and industry". He further disagreed with Kanoria that the days of the business community were limited. He however agreed that the policy of criticising the government was "wrong" (FICCI, Vol. III, 1957: 32).

Nehru, in a speech at the session, reassured the business community that the government was "not rigid...(or) dogmatic" (FICCI, Vol. III, 1957: 58). While speaking in Hindi, he clarified that his government had accepted a very flexible concept of socialism (FICCI, Vol. III, 1957: 52-53). Thus while moving the vote of thanks, Babubhai Chinai was able to offer the business community's help in achieving the goal of a socialistic pattern of society (FICCI, Vol. III, 1957: 61-62).

Of course, as we have already seen in the preceding section, the industrial policies of the "socialist pattern" had already been diluted to favour business interests. Thus FICCI would obviously have been only too happy to offer its "help" to the government.

FICCI and the 1957 Budget

Yet another instance of the effectiveness of FICCI lobbying during this period is that of the 1957 budget (Kochanek, 1974: 246-249).[61] The 1957 budget was introduced only on 15 May 1957; a delay occasioned by the General Elections. The Minister of Finance, TTK, had introduced a number of tax measures which included a sharp increase in company taxation, increases in excise duties, as well as in wealth and expenditure taxes. The wealth tax was to be levied both on individuals and companies (Minister of Information and Broadcasting, 1957 alone 22-23; quoted after Kochanek, 1974: 246n).

FICCI reacted fairly sharply to the texts and Babubhai Chinai, the FICCI president as also a Congress MP, in a press statement on 15th May, described the budget "as a bold and imaginative one". He however criticised the new tax measures (FICCI, Vol. II, 1957: 389). A more detailed critique of the budget was contained in a FICCI E.C. press statement of 22nd May, copies of which were sent to the ministers and the concerned officials (FICCI, Vol. II, 1957: 390-395).

Later meetings were held between FICCI delegations and TTK in Calcutta and Bombay. In Calcutta on 18th June, Chinai led a FICCI delegation which included G.D. Birla, Kasturbhai Lalbhai and B.D. Garware, among others to meet the government representatives who apart from TTK, included the Governor of the Reserve Bank of India, the Chairman of the State Bank of India, as well as H.M. Patel, the Minister's Principal Secretary (FICCI, Vol. II, 1957: 395). At the meeting, TTK agreed that some adjustments in wealth and in expenditure tax could be made, particularly as the Select Committee level (FICCI, Vol. II, 1957: 396-397). Thereafter, the FICCI secretariat prepared a detailed memorandum on the "1957-1958 Budget – Taxation Structure and Second Plan", for submission to TTK as well as to the Select Committee of Parliament (FICCI, Vol. II, 1957: 397-453). Later on 1st August, a FICCI delegation testified before the Select Committee (FICCI, Vol. II, 1957: 453-455).

A major concession sought was the exemption of the shipping industry from the wealth tax. Shortly after the budget speech, representatives from the shipping industry had sought this exemption from TTK on the grounds that the wealth tax as levy would have a devastating impact on the industry's growth. TTK refuse to grant the concession. Thereafter, Sumati Morarji, a director of the Scindia Steam Navigation Company, who was newly elected President of the Indian National Steam Ship Owners Association (INSOA)[62] (Jog, 1969: 213), went to Delhi to discuss the matter with various ministries. Several days before the Select Committee meeting Mrs. Morarji and the INSOA delegation arrived in Delhi to meet privately with ministers and influential Select Committee members (Scindia Steam Navigation Company Ltd., 1957: 35; quoted after Kochanek,

1974: 247). During these discussions, Mrs. Morarji and the delegation which included M.A. Master, a former director of Scindias and a former FICCI president (1947-48), succeeded in enlisting the support of the Transport Minister Lal Bahadur Shastri, Director-General of Shipping Nagendra Singh, and several key members of the Select Committee, notably Feroze Gandhi, Nehru's son-in-law.

When the INSOA delegation met the Select Committee, its Chairman Asoke Sen, the Law Minister, told the delegation that the Committee apart from receiving the INSOA memorandum, had already heard the testimony of the FICCI delegation who had presented the views of the shipping industry. Sen therefore stated that, since "it is impossible at present to make a distinction between shipping companies and other companies", he saw little point in hearing the delegation (Scindia Steam Navigation Company Ltd., 1957: 23; quoted after Kochanek, 1974: 248). At this stage, Feroze Gandhi and Minoo Masani, another member of the Select Committee intervened and requested the Chairman to hear the delegation's case, to which the latter agreed.

Master spoke of INSOA. He stated that Indian shipping which was not subsidised by government, lacked the fund to finance even the limited development proposals under the Second Five Year Plan. He claimed that the proposed wealth tax would reduce the industry's investible resources and hence slow down its long-term growth, while providing only limited revenues for the government (Scindia Steam Navigation Company Ltd., 1957: 11-18; quoted after Kochanek, 1974: 248).

After Master's testimony, according to Mrs. Morarji,

> some (select committee members)" like Shri Feroz Gandhi and others said that they were convinced that they (the shipping industry) should not be only exempted from... the wealth but must be given further relief such as exemption from the capital gain tax, and so on (Scindia Steam Navigation Company Ltd., 1957: 23; quoted after Kochanek, 1974: 248).

The shipping industry lobby also obtained the support of Lal Bahadur Shastri, then Transport Minister, who supported the former's case before the Lok Sabha (Scindia Steam Navigation Company Ltd., 1957: 20; quoted after Kochanek, 1974: 249).

Shastri also strongly advocated the industry case in private discussions with TTK, the Finance Minister. As Master later admitted, "had it not been for the strong pressure that was brought from Shri Lal Bahadur Shastri... We may not have achieved the results that we have achieved today" (Scindia Steam Navigation Company Ltd., 1957: 42; quoted after Kochanek, 1974: 249).[63]

As a consequence of the lobbying by the INSOA, and by the FICCI itself, the Select Committee made several concessions to private enterprise. These were the exemption from taxation of shares held by one company in another company; the provision of a tax holiday of five years from the date of incorporation for new companies and new units of existing companies; and the exemption of the shipping industry from wealth tax (Kochanek, 1974: 247). TTK accepted only some of the recommendations including the exemption of the shipping industry from wealth tax which was a "major concession" (Kochanek, 1974: 247).

This entire episode is a revealing instance of lobbying by business associations. FICCI and its constituent INSOA, lobbied at both the select committee level and with select ministers. Moreover, they, particularly FICCI, must have ensured the compliance of the rest of the Congress Party leadership, to ensure that the concessions were made.

However, business lobbying at this stage succeeded also because of the extent of the Congress with three in the second General Elections, and the relative weakness of the Opposition, particularly from the Left. In later attempts of lobbying, when the Left, both inside and outside the Congress was relatively stronger, concessions were not granted (see below).

Abridgement of Public Sector Expenditure

In May 1958, the Second Plan was cut by 20 per cent (Kidron, 1965: 141). The proposed shift towards stated dominance in public investment did not materialise. Instead of the projected 55 per cent of all monetised investment during the First Plan and the 61 per cent during the Second, the actual investment worked out to only 43.7 per cent and 51.5-54.1 per cent in the respective plan periods (Kidron, 1965: 142). On the other hand, the private sector investment considerably exceeded targeted investment. In the First Plan this amounted to Rs. 1,800 crores, or Rs. 200 crores more than the target. In the Second Plan, private investment was Rs. 1,300 crores, some Rs. 900 crores or nearly 40% more than the projected target (Kidron, 1965: 142). Thus the proposed dominance by the public sector of the "commanding heights of the economy" was already curbed a couple of years after the Plan was announced.

Further Deviations in Industrial Policy, 1958-1959

Of the seventeen industries listed in Schedule 'A', no less than seven were thrown open to the private sector around 1958. These included arms, the heavy plant and machinery, a large part of whose output was produced by ACC-Vickers-Babcox, Larsen and Toubro and Walchandnagar Industries—all of these were licensed in early 1959 (Kidron, 1965: 143-144). Heavy electrical plant machinery, where there was already substantial private sector production, was also thrown open to English Electric in early 1959 (Kidron, 1965: 144). The processing of the lead and zinc was opened to the private sector in 1958-1959; the production of telephone cables and telegraphic equipment, and the generation and distribution of electricity and coal (in which there was already considerable private sector participation), were also open to further private investment in this period (Kidron, 1965: 144).

In the schedule 'B' list, of the total of twelve industries, in as many as nine, the bulk of the production was in the private sector since 1957-1958 (Kidron, 1965: 144). Though expansion in aluminium production was allocated for the public sector in the second plan, a private sector project was announced in March 1958 (Kidron, 1965: 144), and in early October the same year, a collaboration agreement was reached between Kaiser (USA) and Birlas to set up a 20,000 tonne aluminium plant[64] (Kidron, 1965: 144). The meshing tools, ferro-alloys and the tool steels industries were also further opened to the private sector. In 1961, of the 261,000 tonnes licensed capacity, fully 160,000 tonnes were in the private sector (Kidron, 1965: 144). The basic chemicals and intermediates, and the antibiotics and other essential drugs industries followed a similar pattern, as public sector projects were drastically curtailed, and the industries opened to the private sector in 1958-59 (Kidron, 1965: 144). The fertilisers industry was also open for private sector investment, as was the production of synthetic rubber. Production in the latter was wholly in the private sector (Kidron, 1965: 145-146).

Furthermore, though in 1950-51, the nationalisation of road transport was accepted as government policy, this was finally rejected in early 1958. Private operators were in fact, assisted to set up viable operations (Kidron, 1965: 146). In the case of sea transport, the private sector was helped to grow through the Shipping Development Fund (Kidron, 1965: 146).

From the above discussion, it is apparent, that the 1956 Industrial Policy Resolution was consistently changed within a few years of its enactment. These deviations from the Resolution enabled the private sector to grow rapidly and allowed the large industrial houses to become a leading force in the private corporate sector, as would be evident from Table I and II below.

GROWTH OF THE INDUSTRIAL HOUSES 1951-58

Table I: Share Capital of 20 Groups (Public Companies Only)

(Rs. in Crores)

	Share Capital		*Gross Capital Stock*	
	1951	1958	1951	1958
Net Complex (of 20 groups)	202.7	310.3	462.6	1,033 .8
All Non-Government Companies	591.0	765.0	1,396.0	2675.0

Source: India, Planning Commission, *Report of the Committee on Distribution of Income and Levels of Living*, "Distribution of Income and Wealth and Concentration of Economic Power" (Delhi: Manager of Publications, 1964), Part I, p. 39, Statement (7).

Table II: Share of the 20 Groups in the Share Capital and Physical Assets of All Non-Government Public Companies (Percentages)

	Share Capital		*Net Fixed Assets*		*Gross Capital Stock*	
	1951	1958	1951	1958	1951	1958
Net Complex (of 20 Groups)	34.30	40.56	37.81	39.90	33.14	38.65
Net Complex (of 13 Groups)	33.09	38.41	36.31	38.13	31.69	36.35
All Government Public Companies	100.00	100.00	100.00	100.00	100.00	100.00

Source: India, Planning Commission, *Report of the Committee on Distribution of Income and Levels of Living*, "Distribution of Income and Wealth and Concentration of Economic Power" (Delhi: Manager of Publications, 1964), Part I, p. 39, Statement (8).

As can be seen from Tables I and II, the top twenty groups markedly increased their share of share capital, net fixed assets and gross capital stock in the private corporate sector, between 1951 and 1958. The top thirteen groups also increased their share in these three areas. Therefore, the government's industrial policies over the period only served to strengthen the hold of the monopoly houses over the private corporate sector, as the other table shows. Thus, the industrial policy framework as it evolved, and the deviations from it, heightened socialist rhetoric in the second half of the 1950, actually served, in large measure, the interests of the industrial houses largely represented by FICCI.

The growth of the monopoly stratum of the private corporate sector was also facilitated by the credit policies of the larger scheduled banks. A survey conducted by the Mahalanobis Committee revealed that in the top 14 banks in 1959-60, no less than 51 per cent of the directors were from industrial houses. For eight banks, the corresponding figure was nearly 77 per cent. Significantly, the government-owned State Bank of India had no less than 48 per cent of its directors connected to industrial houses (Planning Commission, 1964: 46-47, Statement (12). Given this composition of the board of directors, it was inevitable that the credit policies of these banks would favour the private corporate sector.

The Ideological Retreat

The 1958-59 period was also marked by a considerable softening of the ideological postures of government. Addressing the 31st Annual Session of FICCI in March 1958, Nehru said, "you (FICCI) represent a very important section of opinion...(to which it is) desirable for any government to pay the greatest attention..." (FICCI, Vol. III, 1958: 12). He reassured the industrialists that the government accepted that, "the private sector is of great importance and fulfils an important purpose in the development of the country...it should be encouraged in every way..." (FICCI, Vol. III, 1958: 12).

During this period various important Congress leaders, explained the existence of public sector projects, as necessitated only by the inability of private enterprise, and not due to ideological or policy reasons. While opening Tata's ferro-maganese plant in Orissa, H.K. Mahatab, the Chief Minister,

> pointed out that even the three steel plants under the public sector would have gone to the private sector if (only a) sufficient number of private people had come forward... (*Hindu*, 21 April 1958; cited in Kidron, 1965: 147-148).

It is sometimes argued that this ideological shift, as well as the deviations from the Industrial Policy Resolution, was occasioned by the foreign exchange crisis, which in this period had become quite acute (*Eastern Economist*, 30 May 1958).

The ideological shift continued in 1959. Commenting on a resolution on planning and economic development finalised by the Congress Working Committee (CWC) and adopted by the 64th Session of the Congress, Commerce (17 January 1959) noted that "the socialism of the Congress Party is the vaguest of its kind in the world, for it has never been fully defined".

At the 32nd Annual Session of FICCI, its President B.P. Singh Roy praised Nehru's 19th February Statement in Parliament wherein the latter had stated,

> "A great majority of the people in the private sector had tried

> their best to cooperate with the government. The private sector has a great domain to work in this country. Just to push it out will be utterly wrong and injurious to this country at the present moment and for a considerable time to come". This Roy noted, had "put heart in those who...apprehended a reversal of governmental policy" (FICCI, Vol. III, 1959: 11).

Nehru in his speech at the session welcomed the "friendly approach" of Roy's speech (FICCI, Vol. III, 1959: 15). He further played down the public versus private sector controversy (FICCI, Vol. III, 1959: 19).

In a speech at the 8th March FICCI Luncheon Meeting, G.B. Pant, the Home Minister stressed the "supplementary and complementary" nature of the public and private sectors (FICCI, Vol. III, 1959: 74).

The ideological shift was accompanied by a relaxation in the industrial policy towards the private sector. In January 1959, *Commerce* noted that, "the Government of India has taken certain welcome steps to expedite the issue of licenses for the expansion of industries in the private sector" (*Commerce,* 31 January 1959). These included the removal of the earlier mandatory reference to the Licensing Committee, for the production of new articles by existing undertakings, if these did not involve the installation of additional machinery and use of imported materials (*Commerce,* 31 January 1959).

The budget also contained concessions for the private sector. *Commerce* praised the concessions in the budget noting that, "it is apparent that the private sector has heaved a sigh of relief" (*Commerce,* 7 March 1959). It praised Morarji's "proposal to abolish the wealth tax on companies and the access dividends tax... (as) a courageous step for a Minister of Socialist (sic) Government to take" (*Commerce,* 7 March 1959).

The Swatantra Party and FICCI

On 4 June 1959, the formal decision to establish the Swatantra Party was made public at a meeting held in Madras (Erdman, 1967: 65). However the origins of the Swatantra Party, which was to be the most openly pro-business party in the Indian political scene, went back to the foundation of the Forum for

Free Enterprise (FFE) in 1956 (Erdman, 1967: 65).

Active in the founding of the FFE had been a group of Bombay businessman led by A.D. Shroff, (who as we have seen earlier had been active in FICCI), as well as Minoo Masani, a former Tata executive (Erdman, 1967: 66).

Both Shroff and Masani were associated with the Tatas, who were generally known to have provided "strong support" to the FFE (Kochanek, 1965: 182, n. 14). The FFE was unabashedly pro-private enterprise, as its name itself indicates, and it sought to educate the public "on the fundamentals of free enterprise and on the contributions which it can make to national welfare" (Forum for Free Enterprise, 1966; quoted after Kochanek, 1965: 204). Though the FFE claimed to be a "non-political and non-partisan organisation" it was in effect, anti-Congress.

Shortly after its formation, at the FICCI Annual Session, Lalchand Hirachand, a senior and influential FICCI leader, supported the FFE, and rhetorically asked why it could not "be organised on a large scale" by the Federation[65] (FIICI, Vol. III, 1957: 19). N.S. Siamwala, and others who spoke, rejected this proposal, with Siamwala noting that the FFE had been formed to "put up a fight and (to) challenge the government" (FIICI, Vol. III, 1957: 21). Winding up the discussion, Lakshmipat Singhania (the FICCI President), rejected the policy of criticising one's own government as "wrong" (FIICI, Vol. III, 1957: 32).

The FICCI reaction to the Swatantra Party was similar. As Kochanek has noted,

> Although the vast majority of the industrialists shared pro-Swatantra Party sentiments... (their) lack of enthusiasm for the Swatantra Party is based on the conviction that, attractive though its program (me) may be to the business, it has little hope of becoming a major political force in India (Kochanek, 1965: 39, ; Erdman, 1967: 141).

This was recognised by Minoo Masani himself, who considered,

> it would be futile... to wait for Big Business to make up its mind to give us support... The reason for this state of affairs...lies in a controlled economy...(which necessitates) the supine attitude to government and the pathetic desire to clutch at any straw that may come their way in the shape of soft words thrown at them

occasionally by government spokesmen, displaced by certain sections of business... (Swatantra Party Preparatory Convention, 1959: 10).

The business elite as organised in FICCI, was not only aware of the constraints of the controlled economy, as somewhat bitterly stated by Masani, but also of the political reality of virtually unchallenged Congress rule[66] (Kochanek, 1965: 223). The FICCI strategy therefore continued to be one of influencing the ruling party. Support to the Swatantra Party was low key and directed only at putting pressure on the Congress.

The Third Plan

As in the case of the Second Plan, a FICCI delegation had a meeting with the Planning Commission on the formation of the Third Plan. The 12-member FICCI delegation led by its President M.R. Ruia, met members of the Planning Commission and the Minister of State for Industry on 7 July 1959 (FICCI, Vol. II, 1959: 188). Ruia proposed a greater emphasis on industry in the Plan, without neglecting agriculture (FICCI, Vol. II, 1959: 188-189). Lakshmipat Singhania urged that in view of the shortfall in the Second Plan on the employment creation front, the Third Plan should increase the employment potential (FICCI, Vol. II, 1959: 190). Both Bharat Ram and Babubhai Chinai emphasised the need to modernise industry, and for this the latter suggested larger imports of capital goods and raw materials (FICCI, Vol. II, 1959: 190).

Later, in a response to Nehru's monthly press conference on 3 December 1959, FICCI reiterated its positions. It repeated its earlier stand that the overall outlay of the Third Plan could be larger than that of the Second Plan. It further emphasised the need for various incentives for the private sector, failing which the country would have to satisfy itself with a smaller plan (FICCI, Vol. II, 1959: 192).

The very fact that FICCI had detailed consultations with the Planning Commission regarding the formulation of both the Second and Third Plans, an opportunity denied other pressure groups, e.g. trade unions, consumer associations, agriculturists unions (Kisan sabhas), etc., is in itself a significant indicator of the extent of the influence FICCI was able to wield in the formation of India's industrial policy.

In October 1959, the Third Plan was discussed at the AICC Session at Chandigarh. *Commerce* (3 October 1959) noted that, "there was no tirade against this (private) sector, as such, nor was there an insistent demand for a larger scale extension of state control and its ownership". It approvingly cited Nehru's speech at the session where he had stated,

> "we have deliberately kept a wide field for the private sector... I have not done it under pressure, but I think, in the present circumstances, it is desirable. I want to give initiative to private enterprise provided it does not throttle the public or private interest. Because I want to encourage every aspect of production..." (*Commerce*, 3 October 1959). Nehru in emphasising the need for increased production, at the cost of any emphasis on the distributive aspect, was only reiterating his earlier positions of the immediate post-independence period.From the above report, it is evident that the ideological retreat which had commenced in 1958 continued through 1959.

On 31 March 1960, a FICCI delegation led by A.M.M. Murugappa Chettiar (FICCI Vice-President) met members of the Planning Commission (FICCI, Vol. II, 1960: 171-176). The discussion revolved around the estimated investment in the private sector in the Third Plan. The FICCI representatives called for an investment outlay of Rs. 3,000 crores in the private sector. T.N. Singh, the Planning Commission Member (Industry), argued that the investment in the private sector should be around Rs. 1,000 crores, as an increase in that outlay could only be at the cost of other sectors (FICCI, Vol. II, 1960: 176). He referred to the public versus private sector controversy and stated that the private sector was expanding relative to the public sector, and enough scope was left for the initiative of private sector under the Industrial Policy Resolution (FICCI, Vol. II, 1960: 176).

FICCI representatives met on a number of occasions with government representatives in order to influence the final formulation of the Third Plan, and other aspects of industrial policy. As the FICCI E. C. Report for 1960 put it,

> The relations of the Federation with government continued to be cordial. There was a considerable increase in activities by way of informal discussions with Ministers and officers of the government (FICCI, Vol. I, 1960: 78).

These meetings met with a marked success, especially as the outlay for private sector investment was considerably increased in the final Third Plan document. The private sector outlay was increased to Rs. 4,100 crores in the final Plan document, (an exponential increase over the Planning Commission's earlier estimate of approximately Rs. 1,000 crores (Hanson, 1966: 206). This was an important success for the private sector, and for FICCI in particular[67] (FICCI, n.d.).

Liberalisation of Licensing Policy, 1960

In early 1960, the government liberalised its industrial licensing policy. A letter from the Ministry of Commerce and Industry to FICCI stated that these decisions had been taken after discussions between FICCI representatives and "officers of this Ministry"[68] (FICCI, Vol. II, 1960: 300). The government decided to exempt industrial undertakings employing less than 100 workers, and with fixed assets of less than Rs. 10 lakhs, from applying for industrial licenses (FICCI, Vol. II, 1960: 300-301). A subsequent letter from the Ministry of Commerce and Industry to FICCI clarified that there could be exceptions even under the list of 'banned' items, as applications could be put up by officers of the concerned Ministries to the Licensing Committee for approval[69] (FICCI, Vol. II, 1960: 309).

Later, in July, September and November, further concessions to private entrepreneurs were announced. In industrial undertakings where production was increased because of "balancing equipment" utilising the excess intermediate product of the main plant, which did not exceed 10 per cent of the value of the installed machinery or to Rs. 2 lakhs, whichever was less, licenses were to be issued without reference to the Licensing Committee. In the earlier relaxation, (see above), 49 industries had been put on the 'free' list, i.e. their licenses would be readily granted[70] (FICCI, Vol. II, 1960: 312-314). Even earlier in January 1960, the Ministry of

Commerce and Industry in a letter to FICCI, communicated a government decision to allow industrial units allotted foreign exchange for import of components, intermediates or new materials, to increase their production within their foreign exchange allotment, even when production exceeded licensed capacity. The excess capacity was to be automatically regularised (FICCI, Vol. II, 1960: 315-316).

During this period licenses were issued liberally in his Chairman's address at the 11th meeting of the Central Advisory Council for Industries, Lal Bahadur Shastri, the Minister for Commerce and Industry, stated that whereas 773 licenses had been cleared in 1958, this increased to 997 in 1959, and was as much as 542 in the six-month period from January to June 1960 (FICCI, Vol. II, 1960: 498). Thus not only were licensing rules relaxed but then increasingly large number of licenses were sanctioned every year. Hence the operation of the licensing system could only have been a matter of satisfaction for FICCI and its constituents.

The 1960 budget was also favourably received by the business circles. *Commerce* (5 March 1960) found that Morarji's budget "makes pleasant reading... The quantum of fresh tax burden (is) very much less than the anticipation of even optimists..."

Industrial Policy in 1961: Further Concessions to the Private Sector

Writing on industrial policy in late September 1961, the *Eastern Economist* (22 September 1961) noted that "of late...some new pragmatism has been discernible in the Union Government's industrial policy". In this connection it referred to the private sectors being allowed to participate in the manufacture of heavy electrical machinery (a Schedule 'A' industry). It also referred to the government decision to allow increased private sector production of nitrogen fertilisers (a Schedule 'B' industry), excess of the plan targets (*Eastern Economist*, 22 September 1961).

The budget in 1961 also came in for favourable comment. FICCI "express(ed) their appreciation of the lucid Budget proposals which afford the elements for strengthening the

Indian economy...", in particular welcoming the reduction of taxes on companies and on bonus shares (FICCI, Vol. II, 1961: 288-291). FICCI also "appreciated" the reduction of taxes on royalties from 63 per cent to 50 per cent, the reduced taxes on inter-corporate dividends on minority shareholdings of foreign companies, and the tax exemptions for the hotel industry (FICCI, Vol. II, 1961: 291).

In response to a FICCI request in May 1960, to the Planning Commission for more than 0.7 5 million additional spindles in the cotton textile industry targets during the Third Plan (FICCI, Vol. I, 1960: 29-30), the government in a press note on 25 August 1961 announced that it would license an additional 3 million spindles during the Plan period (FICCI, Vol. I, 1961: 57; see also FICCI, Vol. II, 1961: 380-381). This was an important concession to FICCI, in view of the importance of the cotton textile industry to the private sector.

At the meetings of the Import Advisory Council held in New Delhi on 6th March and 11th September 1961, Manubhai Shah,[71] the Minister for State for Industry clarified that priority for purposes of industrial and import licensing would be given to the following: (1) export-oriented industries; (2) machine-building industries; (3) industries producing raw materials; (4) industries producing component parts; and (5) vital consumer goods industries (FICCI, Vol. II, 1961: 555).

As the 12th Meeting of General Advisory Council of Industries, K.C. Reddy, Minister for State for Commerce, stated that as compared to the 2,640 industrial licensing applications received during 1960, as many as 3,268 applications had been received during the January to September 1961 period. There was also an increase in the number of licenses granted (FICCI, Vol. II, 1961: 562). Karam Chand Thapar, the FICCI President, welcomed the government's industrial licensing priorities (FICCI, Vol. II, 1961: 565). While concluding the discussions, Reddy referred to the role of the public sector in the expansion of the private sector, noting that the prosperity of the latter largely depended on the services of the former (FICCI, Vol. II, 1961: 570).

In terms of industrial policy therefore, 1961 was another

good year for privately owned industry. A number of concessions were given and the industrial licensing policy favoured the private sector, and as such, was welcomed by FICCI.

In a survey of the private corporate sector, Raj K. Nigam estimated that its output had increased by over 50 per cent during the 10-year period which ended in 1957-58. Nigam also calculated the extent of the concentration in the corporate sector. The larger companies with a paid-up capital of Rs. 50 lakhs or more, constituted in terms of numbers approximately 1.5 per cent of the total, but accounted for nearly 60 per cent of the paid-up capital of all companies (Nigam in *Commerce*, 12 August 1961). Thus, as the Monopolies Inquiry Commission, and the Industrial Licensing Policy Inquiry Committee, were to conclude later, the government's industrial policy had facilitated the growth of monopolies which dominated the private corporate sector in India (and which dominated FICCI itself).

Government Policy Towards Foreign Capital, 1961

In early May 1961, the government made a statement on "the Role of Foreign Capital in India's Economic Development" (FICCI, Vol. II, 1961: 408). The Press Note issued on 8th May by the Ministry of Commerce and Industry, specified that foreign capital would be allowed into a number of industries including iron and steel structurals, iron and steel castings and forgings, iron and steel pipes, special steels, (the iron and steel industry is in Schedule 'A') (Appendix 'B'), boilers and steam generating plants, etc. (FICCI, Vol. II, 1961: 408-409). It was clarified that Indian majority shareholding was not necessary in "on merits" cases. It was further stated that the "exceptions" may be made to the Schedule 'A' of the Industrial Policy Resolution "in the public interest" (FICCI, Vol. II, 1961: 408-409).

The statement was appreciated by the big business controlled financial press. *Commerce* (13 May 1961) considered it a "welcome advance on the existing position". It also appreciated the "softening of the rigour of the government's policy in relation to Schedule 'A'industries..." (*Commerce*, 13 May 1961).

Therefore the industrial policy in this period, encompassed premeditated deviations from the earlier announced industrial policy framework, in the interests of both foreign and indigenous private capital.

Industrial Policy in 1962: Liberalisation Continues

On 8 February 1962, the government issued a press note stating that all industrial undertakings having fixed assets not exceeding Rs. 10 lakhs, would not be required to obtain licenses, irrespective of the number of persons employed; (the earlier policy stipulated that no more than 100 persons could be employed) (FICCI, Vol. II, 1962: 280-281).

At the 13th meeting of the Central Advisory Council of Industries held in New Delhi on 27th March, K.C. Reddy, the Minister of State for Commerce and Industry, revealed that as many as 1,042 licenses for setting up new units and far substantial expansion had been issued to the private sector in 1961-62 (FICCI, Vol. II, 1962: 546-547). Reddy also noted that the government had adopted a pragmatic approach towards the development of industries like fertilisers (Schedule 'B' industry) (See appendix 'B'), which was thrown open to the private sector. Swaran Singh, Minister for Steel Mines and Fuel, referred to the licenses granted to the private sector for the production of special steels (FICCI, Vol. II, 1962: 552).

On its part, the private sector welcomed the government's liberal industrial policy. In a commentary on the FICCI session, *Commerce* (31 March 1962) noted appreciatively that "liberal interpretation (of the 1956 Industrial Policy Resolution) has enabled the private sector to secure a foothold into reserved fields like the fertiliser industry".

The 1962 budget also contained some concessions for the private sector. A FICCI press statement on 27th April welcomed the abolition of the expenditure tax and the proposed transport subsidy for furnace oil, though it felt that increases in other taxes "more than counterbalance(d)" the concessions granted (FICCI, Vol. II, 1962: 169).

At the 35th FICCI Annual Session Karam Chand Thapar's Presidential speech welcomed the Congress's victory in the 1960

General Elections (FICCI, Vol. III, 1962: 2). Nehru on his part was conciliatory towards the private sector. He categorically stated that, "private enterprise is a good thing for India...(and that) suppression of private enterprise will be bad..." (FICCI, Vol. III, 1962: 15), although at two points in his speech he criticised monopolies (FICCI, Vol. III, 1962: 16-21), claiming that "monopolies put an end to private enterprise..." (FICCI, Vol. III, 1962: 15).

The Dalmia-Jain Controversy

An event which caused much embarrassment to FICCI, including organisational problems,[72] was the publication in early 1963 of the Vivian Bose Commission Report (Ministry of Commerce and Industry, Department of Company Law Administration, 1963). The Report found the management of the Dalmia-Jain companies responsible for losses amounting to Rs. 2.6 crores to the investing public (Ministry of Commerce and Industry, Department of Company Law Administration, 1963, Chapter IX: 43). Shriyans Prasad Jain, the then FICCI President, was indicted for being "directly concerned with the fraud..." in a number of instances ((Ministry of Commerce and Industry, Department of Company Law Administration, 1963, Chapter X: 47). The Report caused considerable public outcry and embarrassed big business in general, and FICCI in particular.

Speaking at the 36th Annual Session of FICCI in March 1963, Nehru referred to the difficulties he had had in accepting FICCI's invitation as "many people, my colleagues and friends..." had not wanted him to accept (FICCI, Vol. III, 1963: 10). Referring to the Vivian Bose Commission Report and the public response to it, he warned that if the private sector suffered "in public estimation" it would not be able to grow (FICCI, Vol. III, 1963: 14).

The government however took virtually no action on the basis of the Vivian Bose Commission Report. M.N. Govindan Nair (CPI), speaking in the Rajya Sabha, noted that Dalmia-Jain concerns had been awarded 3 licenses after the publication of the Report (Rajya Sabha Debates, Vol. XLIV, No. 2, 14 August

1963, col. 304). The Daphtary-Shastri Committee appointed by the government, recommended that no further action should be taken against the accused, and was sharply criticised for the same by Arjun Arora (Congress) in the Rajya Sabha (Rajya Sabha Debates, Vol. XLIV, No. 2, 14 August 1963, col. 675). Speaking in the same debate, M.M. Mehta deeply regretted that Nehru had chosen to address the FICCI Annual Session in which Shriyans P. Jain himself was the outgoing President (Rajya Sabha Debates, Vol. XLIV, No. 2, 14 August 1963, col. 909).

The FICCI reacted to the Dalmia-Jain controversy by preparing in E.C. from April 1963 onwards, a statement on "Obligations and Responsibilities of Businessmen". In it,

> The Federation...(urged) upon the business community to run their industrial enterprises and business in the context of the wider public policy. It is equally important that the prestige of commercial and industrial organisations is maintained and enhanced.

It further stressed the need for businessmen "to exercise a great measure of self-restraint..." and "for commercial and industrial organisations" to secure the "observance of high standards in the public life of businessmen and in their business practices" (FICCI, Vol. I, 1963: 111-112). However no operational procedures to ensure the above aims were finalised (FICCI, Vol. I, 1963: 112).

Notwithstanding the above episode, the FICCI President and its representatives met the Prime Minister "many times", as well as the Ministers holding the various economic portfolios. According to FICCI records, "the meetings and discussions were very useful" (FICCI, Vol. I, 1963: 119).

Success Despite Embarrassment, 1963

The FICCI lobbying over the 1963 budget, is yet another example of its efficacy in influencing industrial policy in the interests of business groups. FICCI had strongly criticised the proposed super profits tax on company profits. A FICCI E.C. Press Note while welcoming Moraraji's approach to increasing economic capacity, called for a revision of the companies taxation proposals (FICCI, Vol. II, 1963: 131-132).

Later when FICCI representatives met Morarji to plead for the removal of the super profits tax, the latter told them that they "were asking him to commit political suicide" (*Commerce*, 30 March 1963). The industrialists then asked for a modification of the proposals, which was "regarded as the most realistic by official circles" (*Commerce*, 30 March 1963). Consequently, on 16th April, Morarji announced a modification of the original proposals, reducing the super profits tax, which was welcomed by FICCI as helping to restore the "badly shaken" confidence of the business community (FICCI, Vol. II, 1963: 131-136; *Commerce*, 20 April 1963).

In early 1963, the government decided to transfer the licensing of the commercial sheet rolling units of the non-ferrous metals industry from the Directorate General of Technical Development (DGTD) to the State Directors of Industries. On 9th May, FICCI wrote to the Ministry of Commerce and Industry urging a reconsideration of the decision[73] (FICCI, Vol. II, 1963: 278). On 17th September, the Ministry replied that the *status quo ante* was being maintained for the time being[74] (FICCI, Vol. II, 1963: 279).

On 12th October, the FICCI President wrote to T.T. Krishnamachari praising the latter's speech over All India Radio on the previous night as "a thorough, excellent, analytical account of the present economic situation..."[75] (FICCI, Vol. II, 1963: 111). The letter stressed that T.T. Krishnamachari's "real and bold" approach and his emphasis on "the requirements of rapid growth", was the same as that of FICCI (FICCI, Vol. II, 1963: 111). It offered FICCI's "full support"[76] (FICCI, Vol. II, 1963: 111-112). T.T. Krishnamachari in his reply of 14th October, stated that he was "very happy to hear" of FICCI's support for his views[77] (FICCI, Vol. II, 1963: 112).

From the above discussion of the industrial policy for the year 1963, it is evident that the identity of views held by FICCI and a senior Minister holding the vital Finance portfolio, was matched by the concessions made to the private sector by the government. Further, by this year, the various concessions in industrial policy led to the licensing of a number of industries for the private sector, in areas reserved under Schedule 'A' and

'B' of the Industrial Policy Resolution of 1956, for the public sector.

By 1963, the Kamani Engineering Corporation was granted a license to produce one lakh tonnes of special quality pig iron in Rajasthan: three foreign-owned oil refineries (including Burmah Oil, Philips Petroleum and Mobil Oil) were set up; Brown Boveri of Switzerland was permitted to collaborate with Hindustan Electricals to manufacture heavy electrical equipment; and International General Electric was given licenses for smaller electrical equipment (all Schedule 'A' industries) (Kust, 1964: 131-132). In the list of Schedule 'B' industries, a significant number were thrown open for foreign collaboration. Synthetics and Chemicals collaborated with Firestone Tire and Rubber (USA) in the production of synthetic rubber; Kaiser Aluminium (USA) and Chemical Corporation (USA) collaborated with Hindustan Aluminium in the production of aluminium. In the nitrogenous fertilisers industry, as we have noted earlier, as many as nine private projects were licensed (Kust, 1964: 132).

In view of the above interpretation by the government of the Industrial Policy Resolution, Kust characterises government industrial policy as one marked by "pragmatism" (Kust, 1964: 133). However, as we have noted earlier, these concessions as well as those analysed above, constituted a consistent series of deviations from the earlier industrial policy framework, as established by the 1956 Industrial Policy Resolution.

In late 1963, business was given further concessions. Bank credit was liberalised in November, and the price and distribution control on 16 commodities were removed in December, the same year. This, of course was welcomed by FICCI[78] (FICCI, Vol. III, 1964: 66).

Changes in the Companies Act

As a result of the Vivian Bose Commission Report, the Attorney General C.K. Daphtary and Justice A.V. Visvanatha Shastri, were appointed by the government, to recommend preventive action in the form of changes in the Companies Act. The Daphtary-Shastri Report made several proposals which FICCI considered highly controversial (FICCI, Vol. II, 1963: 201-215). In particular, the provision that a clause be inserted in the Company Act enabling the government to convert its loans to private sector companies in the equity share capital, thus giving the former a certain measure of control over management, was highly controversial. FICCI accused the government of proposing backdoor nationalisation (FICCI, Vol. II, 1963: 236).

The Company Law Amendments Bill was sent to a Select Committee of Parliament in December 1963. Some Congress members of the Select Committee amended the loans conversion clause by making it only applicable to future loans and not retroactive, as originally stated (Kochanek, 1965: 251).

At that time, the Congress was embroiled in sharp ideological conflicts. In spring 1963, in Parliamentary by-elections held in Amroha, Farukhabad (both in UP, Nehru's home state) and Rajkot, all three considered safe seats for the Congress prominent Opposition stalwarts, Acharya J.B. Kripalani, Ram Manohar Lohia and Minoo Masani won. Later in August 1963, in what was generally considered part of Nehru's "counter-attack on his conservative opponents inside the Congress Party" (Frankel, 1978: 228), the Kamaraj Plan was announced. Named after K. Kamaraj, the then Chief Minister of Madras, the Plan called for the resignation of senior Congressmen from government office in order to take up organisational work to revitalise the Congress organisation in the wake of the earlier humiliating by-election results. Two of Nehru's leading opponents inside the Congress, Morarji Desai and S.K. Patil were among the six Cabinet Ministers removed. Patil, in an interview at that time, claimed that Nehru "wants a leftist (sic) pattern. He practically gave everything to the leftists. All six (Cabinet Ministers) removed were considered from the communists' side to be on the right"[79] (cited in Frankel, 1978: 229).

In December 1963, therefore, within the Congress, leftist elements, largely organised in the Congress Forum for Socialist Action, led by K.D. Malaviya, a Congress Working Committee member, were fairly influential. These congressmen challenged the recommendations of the Select Committee. When the

Congress Parliamentary Executive upheld the recommendations, the leftists at the requisitioned general body meeting of the Congress Parliamentary Party, charged that some Congressmen "under the influence of big business lobbies, are trying to water down the bill" (Kochanek, 1965: 252). Under their pressure, Nehru, after consulting his Cabinet, decided to reverse the Congress Parliamentary Party's Executive's decision to support the Select Committee recommendations. This was accordingly announced in Parliament by T.T. Krishnamachari, who however sought to reassure businessmen by hinting that the loans given to TISCO and to the Indian Iron and Steel Company (IISCO) would not be converted into equity (Kochanek, 1965: 255).

Hence the success of business lobbying depended, as we have seen in several instances earlier, on the political balance of forces, including that within the ruling party. The loan-equity conversion clause, as well as other potentially anti-big business measures that were under pressure enacted, were however, due to the influence of business lobbies never implemented, or implemented only in a very limited way.[80]

The growth of monopolies in the private corporate sector was a fact that Nehru was forced to admit. In the autumn of 1963, he stated, "Monopoly is the enemy of socialism. To the extent it has grown during the last few years, we have drifted away from the goal of socialism" (Congress bulletin, No. 9-11, 1963: 55). However, as we have noted above, the industrial policies of Nehru's government consistently contributed to the growth of monopolies, while simultaneously paying lip-service to the goal of socialism. The drift away from that goal therefore, was inevitable under the circumstances, as Nehru himself was doubtless aware.

Conclusion

The deviations from the 1956 Industrial Policy Resolution started almost within a year of its announcement. In the above-mentioned meeting between Morarji, T.T. Krishnamachari and Nehru, the entry of the private sector in both Schedule 'A' and Schedule 'B' industries was discussed. Starting with the opening up of the aluminium industry to the private sector in 1957, a large number of other industries in Schedule 'A' and 'B', were thrown open to the private sector. By 1963 therefore, the 1956 Industrial Policy Resolution was honoured more in its breach than in its practice.

In other areas of economic policy of importance to Indian big business, significant concessions were made. The planned investment in the private sector under the Second Plan, was exceeded by nearly 40 per cent. In a response to the business pressure, the private sector outlay for the Third Plan period was increased from the initially proposed Rs. I,000 crores to Rs. 4,100 crores when the Third Plan was finalised. Various concessions were made in the budgets during the period under study, in order to accommodate business interests.

In the sphere of industrial licensing, the general trend was one of consistent liberalisation favouring the private sector. In 1960, as many as 49 industries were added to the 'free' list of industries, i.e. the licenses would be readily granted. Other changes in the licensing rules significantly increased the size of the industrial units permitted to operate without licenses.

The cumulative effect of the liberal, pro-private sector industrial policy of this period, was the impressive growth of the large industrial groups. As the Mahalanobis Committee has shown, between 1951 and 1958, the dominance of the 20 large business groups within the private corporate sector actually increased. Whereas the 20 groups accounted for 33.14 per cent of the gross capital stock of the private corporate sector in 1951, the percentage increased to 38.65 by 1958 (see Table I above). In absolute terms, the increase was exponential; the gross capital stock figures for the 20 groups being Rs. 462.6 crores and Rs. 1033.8 crores in 1951 and 1958 respectively.

It clearly emerges from the foregoing analysis therefore, that the deviations from the 1956 Industrial Policy Resolution, which itself had incorporated concessions to the private sector (see Chapter VIII below), were indicative of the considerable influence wielded by Indian big business in the area of industrial policy. This influence was evidently enhanced by the fact the potentially countervailing forces, including the Left parties and the trade unions, were not sufficiently strong politically to counter the business pressures during this period.

REFERENCES

1. Extracts from the Second Industrial Licensing Policy Inquiry Committee Report (1969). The second ILPIC Report is still unpublished and Goyal's book contains the only published extracts.
2. The term 'deviation' here, as throughout the study, is used in a non-pejorative sense. It is used in the same manner as in the ILPIC Report which in reference to the above case stated that, "the (government) approach seems to have been that such deviations could be permitted without affecting the long-term pursuit of the (Industrial) Policy". c.f. India, Ministry of Industrial Development, Internal and Company Affairs, (1969) Report of the Industrial Licensing Policy Inquiry Committee (Delhi: Manager of Publications), p. 107.
3. Minutes of the meeting of the Reviewing Sub-Committee of the CACI, held on 18 March 1957.
4. This has been analysed in Kochanek's work (1974), but our analysis is more detailed.
5. INSOA is a member-body of FICCI.
6. See also Jog, 1969: 213, n. 22, wherein it was stated, "INSOA... Made out a strong case for exempting shipping companies from the tax and succeeded in getting an exemption".
7. This was a consequence of the earlier decision taken by Nehru, Morarji and TTK.
8. Hirachand later became the treasurer of the Swatantra Party in 1969, together with H.P. Nanda (of the escorts group, who was a member of the rival ASSOCHAM).
9. The Congress defeat of 1967 is outside the purview of our study. Even then, the Congress control of the central government remained. At that time however, a significant section of Indian big business, including members of FICCI apparently supported the Rightist Opposition parties.
10. FICCI presented its own Third Plan framework earlier, c.f. FICCI, The Third Five-Year Plan: A Tentative Outline (New Delhi: FICCI, n.d.).
11. D.O. letter No. A.S.(I)-71/60 dated 4 February 1960.
12. Letter No. 6(4)-IA(IG)/60 dated 11 April 1960.
13. Press Note dated 13 July, 27 September and 20 November 1960.

14. Manubhai Shah prior to joining politics had served in high technical and administrative posts in the Delhi Cloth and General Mills (Shri Ram group) for more than 12 years (c.f. *Times of India*, n.d.: 1209). He may therefore be considered to have reasons to be sympathetic to Indian big business.
15. Tata and Mafatlal representatives resigned from FICCI, over the refusal of Shriyans P. Jain, then FICCI President, to resign from his post, although he had been implicated in the Vivian Bose Commission Report. See Chapter III above.
16. FICCI letter No. F.7907/1/2(2) dated 9 May 1963 to the Ministry of Commerce and Industry.
17. Reply from the Ministry of Commerce and Industry (Metals Section) letter No. 8(11)Met./63 dated 17 September 1963.
18. D.O. letter from FICCI President dated 12 October 1963 to T.T. Krishnamachari.
19. This statement was also favourably received by the financial press. See for instance, *Commerce*, 19 October 1963, " T.T.K. Engenders Optimism", leading article, which stated that "the Finance Minister's talk contains clear indications that the authorities are not thinking in terms of curtailing the score for private enterprise".
20. T.T. Krishnamachari's D.O. letter No.2442-FM/63 dated 14 October 1963 to FICCI President.
21. These decontrolled commodities included: (1) rayon yarn; (2) staple fibres; (3) caustic soda; (4) soda ash; (5) hydrochloric acid; (6) chlorine; (7) calcium carbide; (8) bleaching powder; (9) Chilean nitrate; (10) muriate of potash; (11) sulphate of potash; (12) washing soap; (13) tyres and tubes; (14) sheet glass; (15) paper boards; and (16) natural rubber. c.f. Ramanbhai Amin's (FICCI President) letter to d. Sanjivayya, Minister of industry, dated 5 May 1966 (FICCI, Vol. II, 1966: 261-269).
22. S.K. Patil, Interview, 27 August 1963.
23. See for instance S.K. Goyal, "Joint Industrial Sector", a paper presented at the seminar on "Industry and the Fourth Plan", University of Bombay, 29-31 March 1971, mimeo. Goyal shows how the loan-equity conversion clause, as well as other recommendations of ILPIC were not implemented, even in the post-1966 period (which is outside the scope of our study).

8

Liberalisation of Industrial Policy and the Growth of Monopoly, 1964-1966

In the 1964 to 1966 period, the process of liberalisation of industrial policy was accelerated by the government's acceptance of the recommendations of the Swaminathan Committee.[81] The process culminated in the relicensing of a substantial number of industries in 1966; and in the decontrol of a significant number of industries during the period.

In the meanwhile, the Report of the Mahalanobis Committee was published in February 1964.[82] This Report was the first official disclosure of the existence of a high concentration of wealth and income in Indian society, and as such sparked off considerable debate. The next year, the Report of the monopolies inquiry Commission was published. This further revealed the consequences of the actual operation of official industry policy.

In a sense therefore, two aspects of the process of Indian industrialisation, were sharply highlighted in these years. The first, was the culmination of the trends in the development of industrial policy. The second, was the consequence of such an industrial policy as well as its implementation. This chapter therefore, treats with tendencies already examined in the preceding chapters, but which were accentuated in the 1964 to 1966 period.

The Mahalanobis Committee

On 13 October 1960, the Planning Commission had appointed a nine-member committee, of which P.C. Mahalanobis was to be Chairman. Its terms of reference were:-

i) "to review the changes in levels of living during the First and Second Five Year Plans;
ii) to study recent trends in the distribution of income and wealth; and in particular
iii) to ascertain the extent to which the operation of the economic system has resulted in concentration of wealth and means of production" (Planning Commission, 1964: 1).

The Report of the Committee, popularly known as the Mahalanobis Committee, was published in February 1964. Its findings provided a wealth of data to show that the largest 20 industrial houses or groups had grown relatively to the other groups in the private corporate sector, in the period 1951-1958 (See Chapter VII above).

The Report categorically stated that:

> It is... evident that the working of the planned economy has contributed to this growth of big companies in Indian industry. The growth of the private sector in industry and especially of the big companies has been facilitated by the financial assistance rendered by public institutions like the Industrial Finance Corporation (IFC), the National Industrial Development Corporation (NIDC), etc. (Planning Commission, 1964: 46-47, Statement, 12).

The Report also brought out the major element of control the industrial houses had over the top 14 privately owned scheduled banks and over the government-owned State Bank of India. It noted that:

> the banking sector itself presents a picture of a high degree of concentration. The aggregate share of the 15 top banks having deposits of 363 was 78 per cent. If the government–owned State Bank is excluded—and looking to the composition of its Board of Directors there is really no adequate reason for doing so—the percentage comes to 60 (Planning Commission, 1964: 48).

This latter statement about the State Bank was made because as many as 48 per cent of its directors held directorships in firms controlled by industrial houses in the private sector (Planning Commission, 1964: 46-47, Statement 12).

If from the list of 14 major banks, we exclude the three banks: the Canara Bank, the Canara Industrial and Banking Syndicate, and the Bank of Maharashtra, which have no private sector directors, the percentage of industrial directors in the remaining 11 Banks is 63 per cent, in 1959-60. In the first eight banks, the dominance of directors from the private sector is even more marked, nearly 77 per cent. From this evidence, the Committee concluded "that there is a significant link in the form of common directors between the leading banks and the large-sized industrial undertakings" (Planning Commission, 1964: 47), which may be considered an understatement.

The Mahalanobis Committee showed that in the top 15 scheduled banks, 14.1 per cent of the total advances were given to companies or firms in which the directors of the banks were interested. The Committee noted that, "It is significant that this proportion is the highest (i.e. 26.9 per cent) for the State Bank of India" (Planning Commission, 1964: 47).

Basing itself on a study undertaken by R.K. Hazari, the Mahalanobis Committee examined the concentration of control in the structure of the private corporate sector. At that time under the existing company law, corporate groups or industrial houses had "no separate legally-identifiable existence" (Planning Commission, 1964: 38). Hazari defined corporate groups:

> as consisting of units which are subject to the decision-making power of a common authority. It takes policy decisions on prices, profits, investments, production, purchases and sales on behalf of a number of companies and determines responses to particular economic and political developments (Planning Commission, 1964: 38).

Hazari noted that it was not necessary for the controlling group "to own the majority of shares in every company in the group", as this could be done by a process of inter-corporate investment. As an example it was stated:

> a Controlling Interest which owns the majority of shares in a comparatively small concern A may gain control over the affairs of large concern B in which A holds the majority of shares, a second still larger concern C in which B holds the majority of shares, and

> so on; even in the original concern A, the Controlling Interest's investment may be partly financed by borrowings from banks on the security of that investment itself. The picture could be made complicated by spreading the investment of each company among several companies of the group and by changing the pattern of investment over time. The control acquired by inter-corporate investment is supplemented by powers obtained under managing agency agreements and by the buying and selling of shares by Investment Companies belonging to the group (Planning Commission, 1964: 38).[83]

According to Hazari's definition, the "complex" of companies belonging to a group include both the "Inner Circle" and the "Outer Circle" companies. The former "consists of sole control and majority companies...", while the latter "consists of fifty-fifty, minority, and under-management companies in which the decision-making authority of the group has a material influence but not the controlling voice" (Planning Commission, 1964: 38). We have already noted above the growth of the top twenty groups over the 1951-1958 period. Hazari also showed that the controlling blocks of share capital owned by the groups in the "Inner Circle" companies was often less than 50 per cent. According to his study as reported in the Mahalanobis Committee Report, the average shareholding necessary for control declined from 48 per cent of the ordinary share capital and 22.7 per cent of the preference share capital in 1951, to 43.1 per cent and 17.3 per cent respectively in 1958 (Planning Commission, 1964: 42, Statement 11).

The study also discovered that,

> All complexes except Martin Burn, Shri Ram, Kasturbhai, Seshasayee and Kirloskar, have a large number of subsidiaries and joint subsidiaries, In 1958 the Tata Complex had 73 subsidiaries and joint subsidiaries, Birla had 105, Dalmia – Sahu – Jain 30, Bird Heilger 44, Andrew Yule 20, Bangur 47, Thapar 31, J. K. (Singhania) 27, Shapoorji (Pallonji) 15, Khatau 14, Walchand 16, and Mafatlal 13... In the aggregate... there were 163 subsidiaries and 266 joint subsidiaries out of the 1079 sample companies in 1958. In most of the remaining companies, also, inter-corporate investment played a key role but individuals and trusts too were important holders (Planning Commission, 1964: 43, Statement 11).

It was evident to the Mahalanobis Committee that the provisions of the company law were unable to curb the control of companies by a group, through inter-corporate investments open, stating,

> whether the Administration could deal more effectively with such investments with suitable modifications in the existing laws is a question of policy which has to be left to the appropriate authorities (Planning Commission, 1964: 43, Statement 11, emphasis added).

The Committee drew attention to the then recently published Vivian Bose Commission Report on the Dalmia-Jain Companies (see Chapter VIII above),

> and the lessons that flow from it in regard to the possibilities of the anti-social consequences that can follow from both the attempts to build up concentration of economic power as also from an exercise of this power (Planning Commission, 1964: 44).

The Committee also examined the extent of inter-locking of company directorship through case studies of six companies in six leading Indian and foreign business groups. These included: (i) Andhra Valley Power Co. Ltd., in the Tata Group; (ii) Century Spinning and Weaving Co. Ltd., in the Birla Group; (iii) Standard Mills Ltd., in the Mafatlal Group; (iv) Mcleod and Co. Ltd., in the Surajmull Nagarmull Group; (v) Kamarhatti Ltd., in the Jardine Henderson Group; and (vi) Bengal Coal Co. Ltd., in the Andrew Yule Group (Planning Commission, 1964: 48-49).

The case studies revealed "wide prevalence of inter-locking of directorships in companies belonging to long-established and reputed houses". It was also noted that, "the seven companies studied are often linked with non-profit making associations and even government companies through their directors" (Planning Commission, 1964: 49, emphasis added). The Department of Company Law Administration undertook a further study to explore the inter-locking of directorships, which covered 74 marketing companies with paid-up capital of Rs. 5 lakhs and above. These companies were found to be connected with a further 1,111 companies, through 233 directors out of a total of 341 directors of the 74 marketing companies studied (Planning Commission, 1964: 44).[84] Out of the 1,111 companies inter-linked with the marketing companies, 414 were manufacturing companies, 382 trading companies, 113 banking and financial companies, 19 electricity companies, and the remaining 183 companies belonged to miscellaneous industrial groups (Planning Commission, 1964: 49). The study found "that the inter-locking of marketing companies does not depend much on their size" (Planning Commission, 1964: 50).[85]

The Committee also referred to another study by the Department of Company Law Administration of the inter-locking of directorships between central government companies and non-government companies. The sample studied was of 49 companies with a paid-up capital investment of Rs. 620 crores, amounting to 95 per cent of the total paid-up capital of all central and state government-owned companies (Planning Commission, 1964: 50). There were a total of 428 directorships in the 49 central government companies, and they were held by 311 persons of whom 86 were 'non-official' (Planning Commission, 1964: 51; 101-102, table 4.18 and 4.19); 42 of the 'non-official' directors did not hold directorships in any non-government company. The remaining 44 'non-official' directors held 50 directorships in 308 non-government companies (Planning Commission, 1964: 51, Statement 15).

The Committee was very equivocal in its conclusions from the above evidence arguing that,

> It is not possible to draw conclusions regarding the economic and social consequences of this inter-locking...without a careful examination of the growth and working of the government companies vis-à-vis as undertakings where such common directorships exist. How far this helps the public sector by enabling it to obtain business expertise and how far it helps to increase the concentration of economic power in the hands of selected individuals in big business are questions that are pertinent but that we are not in position to answer. Perhaps these constitute a part of the puzzle that characterises a mixed economy such as the country is building through its planned development (Planning Commission, Part I, 1964: 51, emphasis added).

It would appear that this paragraph was drafted to obtain a consensus among the members.[86] Because the very fact, that influential private sector or big business representatives held directorships in the majority of the public sector companies that comprised the bulk of the public sector investment, is itself a telling commentary on the inter-linking and interpenetration of the two sectors. Together with earlier cited findings relating to the extent of public financial institutions' support to the private sector (see above), this exposed the private sector orientation of the public sector.

The Report further noted that,

> Economic power is exercised not only through control over production, investment, employment, purchases, but also through control over mass media and communication. Of these, newspapers are the most important and constitute a powerful ancillary to sectoral and group interest. It is not, therefore, a matter of surprise that there is so much inter-linking between newspapers and big business in this country, with newspapers controlled to a substantial extent by selected industrial houses directly through ownership as well as indirectly through membership of the boards of directors. In addition, of course, there is the indirect control exercised through expenditure on advertisement which has been growing at a pace during the Plan periods. In a study of concentration of economic power in India, one must take into account this link between industry and newspapers which exists in our country to a much larger extent than is found in any of the other democratic countries in the world.[87]

Basing itself on the 1960 Annual Report of the Registrar of Newspapers for India, the Committee found that,

> there were 10 owners representing five chains (*Express* Newspapers, *Times of India*, *Hindustan Times* and Allied Publications, *Amrita Bazar Patrika* and *Jugantar*, and *Anand Bazar Patrika*), three groups (*Malayalam Manorma*, *Free Press Journal* and *The Hindu*) and to Multiple Units (*Thanthi* and *Statesman*) which published 37 dailies with a circulation of 18.11 lakhs and thus controlled 39.3 per cent of the total circulation of daily newspapers in the country. Taking the three categories separately, dailies forming part of the chains commanded 34.7 per cent of the total circulation of dailies, those belonging to groups 23.8 per cent, and those coming under Multiple Units 9 per cent (to give a total of 67.5 per cent) (Rao, 1979: 52).

The detailed Table 4.20 in the Appendix of the Report, brought out the control of the Ramnath Goenka-headed family over Express Newspapers, director of the Sahu-Jains over Bennett Coleman & Co. Ltd (Times of India Group), and that of the Birlas over the Hindustan Times and Allied Publications (Rao, 1979: 103-106). Thus this section of the Report exposed how the 'free press', a purported defender of 'public interest' was largely controlled by private interests, i.e. big business houses.

The conclusion of the Committee after evaluating the evidence collected, the highlights of which we have given above, was quite equivocal, in tune with the policy statements of Nehru and others at that time. It is necessary to quote the Report at length:

> Despite all the countervailing measures taken which have been recounted above (e.g. industrial licensing, price and distribution controls, and companies and industries acts, etc.), concentration of economic power in the private sector is more than what could be justified as necessary on functional grounds, and it exists both in generalised and in the specific forms. It is not within our terms of reference to suggest what should be done to remedy the situation and combine economic development with a steady diminution of the concentration of economic power. Undoubtedly the scope and intensity of countervailing measures to alleviate the incidence and offset the effect of economic concentration indicates the general direction of attack on the problem.

However, the committee concluded:

> The task is not easy. The country has a mixed economy; and the private sector has an important role to play in its planned development. Industrialisation has its own logic, and neither the economies of scale nor that of full utilisation of scarce talent can be ignored with impunity. Economic development within a democratic framework remains the paramount objective of national policy. At the same time, the country is pledged to the realisation of a socialist pattern of society; and diminution and the eventual elimination of concentration of economic power in private hands is a part of that society. The task has to be attempted in terms of harmonious progress towards these goals; and the sooner the government sets up the necessary machinery for collection, examination and analysis of all relevant data on the

subject, the easier it would be for it eventually to formulate the necessary policy that will combine industrialisation with social justice and economic development with this dispersal of economic power (Planning Commission, 1964: 54-55, emphasis added).

The equivocal nature of the Mahalanobis Committee's recommendations is explicit in the above extended quotation. In the first place, because of the nature of their terms of reference the Committee did not consider it advisable to suggest concretely "what should be done to remedy the situation" of the concentration of economic power; although it did enunciate "the general direction of attack on the problem". Secondly, it was stated, in accordance with government policy, that since in a mixed economy "the private sector has an important role to play..." the "logic" of (capitalist) industrialisation demands that "neither the economies of scale nor that of full utilisation of scarce talent can be ignored...". But as is well-known, the economies of scale are not synonymous with private ownership—even the public sector can provide economies of scale. The belief that the development of the monopoly stratum within the private sector facilitated the full utilisation of "scarce talent", was repeated in the Monopolies Inquiry Commission Report of the following year. In both cases these conclusions were unsubstantiated.

Finally, it appears that the Committee accepted that a "democratic" socialist path of development would have to, in some unstated way, reconcile harmoniously the conflicting goals of industrialisation and economic development, on the one hand, with social justice and the dispersal of economic power, on the other. This growth versus justice dichotomy, it may be argued, would apply only to private-profit oriented, capitalist economies and not to truly socialist economies directed in the larger public interest (Myrdal, 1968, Vols. I-III). At any rate, as we have seen above, even the diluted socialist rhetoric was not translated into concrete industrial policy. The actual purpose was to give an increasingly inequitable capitalism a "socialist face".

As could be expected, the Mahalanobis Committee Report generated a storm of protest. Critics of official industrial policy, and specially from the Left, used its findings to indict the Congress government. On its part, the private sector representatives including FICCI, tried to discredit the Committee's findings and to play up the ambiguities in its Report.

In the latter half of February 1964, shortly after the Committee's Report was published, its findings were cited in both Houses of Parliament. The CPI MP in the Rajya Sabha, P. Ramamurthy cited the data collected by Hazari and the Committee, that the Birla and Tata groups together controlled Rs. 600 crores of the total capital invested in the corporate sector, to support his party's contention that "we have not been progressing towards socialism, we have been progressing towards capitalism of an intensely monopoly character" (Quoted in *New Age Weekly*, 23 February 1964). M.N. Govindan Nair (CPI), reacted sharply to the Vice President's claim that India was moving towards socialism, by asserting, in the light of the above studies that, "there cannot be more blatant travesty of truth than this" (*New Age Weekly*, 23 February 1964). During the Raja Sabha discussions on the budget on 16th March, Govindan Nair regretted that T.T. Krishnamachari had not yet placed the Committee's Report before the House (Rajya Sabha Debates, Vol. XLVI, No. 26, 16 March 1964, col. 4501).

In fact, the Report was presented to the Parliament only in late April and early May 1964, although it had been published in February (Goyal, 9 May 1964: 9). Significantly, the government never moved a motion to allow discussion on the Mahalanobis Committee Report. Nor did it do so for the Monopolies Inquiry Commission Report published the next years.

On 30 April 1964, the government replied to a question asked by Ramachandra Ulaka and four others, which had *inter alia* asked what decisions the government had taken on the Mahalanobis Committee Recommendations (Lok Sabha Debates (III Series), Vol. XXXI, 30 April 1964, col. 13599). In reply, B.R. Bhagat, Minister of State for Planning stated that as the Committee itself had wanted its Report to be considered as a whole, the government would decide on further action only after the concluding Part II was received (Lok Sabha Debates (III Series), Vol. XXXI, 30 April 1964, col. 13599-13600).

However, Part II of the Report entitled "Changes in the Levels of Living" was submitted and published only in July 1969 (Planning Commission, 1964), despite the earlier belief that it would be submitted "in a few weeks"[88] (Planning Commission, 1964). The delay, according to Mahalanobis himself, was occasioned by the fact that "controversial issues emerged which made it necessary to retabulate and examine a great deal of new statistical data and to extend the scope of analysis"[89] (Planning Commission, 1964). Thus, the government was provided with an excuse to take virtually no action on the basis of the findings of the Committee.

The government did however, on the basis of the findings and recommendations of the Mahalanobis Committee Report, announce the setting up of the Monopolies Inquiry Commission (MIC). T.T. Krishnamachari in his Budget speech on 29 February 1964 announced the proposal to set up the MIC (FICCI, Vol. II, 1964: 79), and under a government notification dated 16th April, the MIC was appointed under the Commission of Enquiry Act, 1952 (we shall deal with MIC and its Report below).

The big business controlled press and FICCI tried, as indicated above, to question the database of the Mahalanobis Committee's findings and to highlight it's more ambiguous and equivocal statements. In a long leading article entitled "Concentration in Corporate Sector - Mahalanobis Committee Findings", *Commerce* (30 May 1964) characterised the Committee's conceptualisation of concentration and its findings as "arbitrary". It highlighted the admission in the Report that,

> We have not been able to assess whether and how far the undoubtedly larger area of concentration of industry was balanced to any extent by a dilution of the intensity of control associated with a decline in the ratio of share capital in the controlled sector owned by the Controlling Interests (Planning Commission, 1964: 43).

FICCI in its brochure, "FICCI on Mahalanobis Committee Report ", highlighted the ambiguities in the report that we have referred to earlier. FICCI claimed that there was not "any significant interlocking or directorships" (FICCI, Vol. I, 1964: 46). The brochure also reiterated, the usual FICCI argument that the large companies in India were small by international standards, and that their size was related to planning, and was determined by the industrial licensing system. It further claimed that competition was "pervasive" in the private sector, and that as the ownership of assets was diffused over a large number of shareholders, no significant concentration of economic power existed (FICCI, Vol. I, 1964: 46). The FICCI warned that, "too much preoccupation with ideological values would check, if not prevent, possible enterprise and depress the growth of the economy" (FICCI, Vol. I, 1964: 46).

This was clear warning to the government against the latter imposing anti-monopoly measures, because of ideological considerations, following the public outcry over the findings of the Mahalanobis Committee Report. The FICCI also tried to refute the Committee's findings, that though,

> the degree of inequality in income distribution is not higher in India than in some other developed or under-developed countries, the distribution of income in the urban sector is more unequal, as in the other countries, than that in the rural sector (Planning Commission, 1964: 22).

The brochure stated that,

> it should be noted that there is a general feeling, though the Committee could not collect the required data to support it, that an average person, whether in urban or rural areas, is better fed, better clothed and even better housed in the 1960s than in the 1950s and that the working conditions have also improved generally over this period. On the other hand, since there is also some evidence that the rate of growth in income for certain high income groups has been as high as or higher than the rate of growth for the country as a whole, it has not been possible for the Committee to pronounce a definite judgement, even of a broad nature, on the changes in income distribution. However, it can be stated that there is no clear indication of a significant change in income distribution over the Plan decade (quoted in *Commerce*, 18 July 1964, emphasis theirs).

Commerce, in its commentary on the FICCI brochure, was

sarcastically critical of both the Mahalanobis Committee Report and of FICCI's attempted refutation. It stated,

> what a blissfully vague and ambivalent observation this is: It is this unenlightening statement that the Federation claims to have refuted. But how unenlightening in its turn, the Federation's refutation is.

Commerce was also critical of FICCI for not getting its own research department, (the Economic and Scientific Research Foundation), to counter the Mahalanobis Committee's statistics. This last criticism was perhaps unfair. In view of the real trends in the economy, FICCI would have had to fabricate statistics, to produce some which could counter those cited by the Committee. And if it had done so, it would undoubtedly have been caught out.

The criticism of the Mahalanobis Committee Report however, for its admitted inadequacies of data was well taken. The Committee drew mainly on information from the Reserve Bank of India, the National Council of Applied Economic Research, the National Sample Survey, the Department of Company Law Administration, as also on individual studies notably those by R.K. Hazari, Raj K. Nigam, Iyengar and Mukerjee. As a commentator pointed out at the time, "the Committee has based most of its conclusions on studies already well-known". Furthermore,

> The relevant question to ask would be why the Committee itself could not undertake the collection of data or institute a survey wherever it felt there were lags in data. In the present situation since these studies are not co-extensive temporarily, it would appear to be a patch-work and compilation of a time-series based on data from different sources, having differing concepts and definitions (Goyal, 9 May 1964: 9-10).

Although the report was to cover the period 1951 to 1961, it mainly took into account statistics up to 1959 or 1960, despite being published in 1964. As S.K. Goyal (9 May 1964: 10) pointed out in the above cited article,

> there is no doubt that (the) situation in the middle of 1964 must be very much different from what the Report presents. Contrary to

> the hesitancy shown in the Report to accepting the tendencies (of increased concentration of wealth), they seem now to have become visible and significant trends.

The same commentator, after examining the divergence between 'official' ideological statements and the actual industrial policy, the latter resulting in the trends hesitantly, and ambiguously, stated by the Mahalanobis Committee, predicted "we are afraid the place of the Report is clearly written on the wall—(the) National Archives" (Goyal 9 May 1964: 11). For all the effect the Report had on industrial policy, it might as well have been placed in the National Archives.

The Swaminathan Committee

On 24 September 1963, the government had set up the "Industries Development Procedures Committee", popularly known as the Swaminathan Committee, after its chairman T. Swaminathan, Secretary, Department of Supply and Technical Development (Ministry of Industries, 1964: 6). According to the government resolution constituting the Committee, it had been suggested to it,

> that there is need to simplify the procedures and regulations relating to the approval of schemes of industrial expansion. It is important that controls operate speedily and efficiently in order that they may serve as instruments for the achievement of a high rate of industrial growth. Government have accordingly decided that the operation of the controls applicable to the establishment of additional industrial capacity under the Industries (Development and Regulation) Act, 1951, the import of capital goods, the issue of capital and foreign investment and collaboration should be examined by a Committee which will suggest such modifications as would reduce delays in decision (Ministry of Industries, 1964: 6).

Significantly, the government resolution made no reference to its socialist goals or even to more equitable industrial development. The membership of the committee, however, starkly brought out its pro-private sector character. All five non-official members were from ASSOCHAM and FICCI mainly the latter. They were Bharat Ram (FICCI president), A.R. Foster

(ASSOCHAM President), Lakshmipat Singhania (FICCI) A.M.M. Murugappa Chettiar (FICCI), and P. Chentsal Rao (FICCI). The official members, excluding Swaminathan including N.C. Srivastava, Advisor Planning Commission; P. Govindan Nair, Additional Secretary, Department of Economic Affairs; V.K. Ramaswami, Economic Adviser, Ministry of Industry; and K.J. George, Deputy Secretary, Ministry of Industry, who was a Member Secretary of the Committee (Ministry of Industries, 1964: 6-7).

Thus of the total of 10 members in the Committee, as many as 5 were representatives of big business, including 4 from FICCI itself. The weightage given FICCI representation in the Committee relative to that of ASSOCHAM (4:1), was indicative of the influence the two contending chambers wielded with the government. Although, under its terms of reference, the Committee was to deal with procedures relating to, amongst others, imports of capital goods, foreign investment and collaboration; ASSOCHAM, which represented foreign capital interests (much more so than FICCI), had only one representative. However, the very fact that the Swaminathan Committee had only representatives of big business as the non-official members, is itself a clear indication of the business influence on the government's industrial policy. Moreover, as we shall see below, the Swaminathan Committee Report did not get the same treatment as the Mahalanobis Committee Report. Unlike the latter, the former's recommendations were accepted and implemented.

The Interim Report of the Swaminathan Committee was submitted to the government and then a summary was published on 13 January 1964, by the Ministry of Industry in a Resolution in the Gazette of India (Ministry of Industries, 1964: 13-15; Kidron, 1965:7-13). There were two main recommendations: (i) In the Committee's view in order to enable private entrepreneurs to "know as early as possible where the government would...consider favourably..." their proposals, further enabling the former to negotiate with foreign collaborators and suppliers of machinery, it was advisable that the government issue a "letter of intent" in the first instance, within about a month of the receipt of the application (Ministry of Industries, 1964; Kidron, 1965: 8). It further recommended that the Directorate General of Technical Development (DGTD), and the Director of Industries of the concerned state government, be asked to submit their views on the administrative Ministry within three weeks. In the case of the latter,

> "if no comments from the state government are received within this period, it will be presumed that...(they) have no objections and that this (application) will be further processed on this assumption (Ministry of Industries, 1964; Kidron, 1965: 8, emphasis added).

The Committee further recommended that there should not be a "rigorous or time-consuming scrutiny" of applications "from the point of view of availability of fuel, power, rail transport and other facilities" (Ministry of Industries, 1964; Kidron, 1965: 9). This was because it considered that "It would be reasonable to assume that the entrepreneur gives an adequate measure of consideration to these factors before deciding on the project and a particular location". Moreover, since "in practice very few applications", were turned down on this ground, it was believed that it would be sufficient if the Ministry of Industry, the co-coordinating Ministry could "arrange to send periodically, to the authorities concerned, consolidated statements giving refinements of fuel, power, etc., in respect of approved schemes..." (Ministry of Industries, 1964; Kidron, 1965: 9, emphasis added).

Therefore, the "letter of intent" to be issued by the government was to broadly indicate the conditions on which it was prepared to grant an industrial license. Of these conditions, it was suggested, that in case where any of the following applied: 9a) terms of foreign collaboration; (b) import of capital equipment; (c) capital issues; the application should come up with definite proposals within a period of "6 to 12 months depending on the nature of the industry" (Ministry of Industries, 1964; Kidron, 1965: 9). The period to be allowed to the applicant to submit further applications regarding foreign collaboration, etc., was to be "determined by the (proposed) Licensing Sub-

Committee while considering the case" (Ministry of Industries, 1964; Kidron, 1965: 9).

The proposed Subcommittee of the Licensing Committee was to consist of the Secretary, Ministry of Industry, as Chairman; the Secretaries of the administrative Ministries concerned or their representatives; the Secretary, Department of Economic Affairs and his representative; the Secretary, Department of Technical Development or his representative; a representative from the Company Law Division; and a representative of the Planning Commission. The Sub-committee, it was recommended, would scrutinise and pass orders on applications for "letters of intent", and it would meet at least once a fortnight (Ministry of Industries, 1964; Kidron, 1965: 9). The Swaminathan Committee claimed that the new procedure proposed by them would reduce the incidence of the "infructuous licensing", i.e. the "large number" of unimplemented licenses (Ministry of Industries, 1964; Kidron, 1965: 9).

Because under the new procedure, "if the party does not make adequate progress within the stipulated time, the letter of intent would be automatically deemed to have become inoperative" (Ministry of Industries, 1964; Kidron, 1965: 9-10).

The second major recommendation of the Swaminathan Committee, related to a proposed "special procedure" for licensing of "key" industries. The list of key industries, which it stated was "by no means exhaustive" (Ministry of Industries, 1964; Kidron, 1965: 10), included no less than 22 industries. These were: (1) Pig Iron; (2) Alloy Steel; (3) Malleable Iron Castings; (4) Steel Castings; (5) Steel Forgings; (6) Structurals (heavy); (7) Industrial Machinery; (8) Cranes; (9) Ferro-Chrome and other Ferro Alloys except Ferro-Manganese and Ferro Silicon; (10) Machine Tools including Small Tools, Dies, Jigs, and Fixtures; (11) Automobile Ancillaries; (12) Fertilisers; (13) Sulphuric Acid; (14) Caustic Soda and Soda Ash; (15) Rubber Chemicals; (16) Petro-Chemicals including Synthetic Rubber; (17) Pulp (Cellulosic); (18) Coated Abrasives; (19) Electric Winding Wires; (20) Pesticides; (21) Paper and Paper Board; and (22) Cement (Ministry of Industries, 1964; Kidron, 1965:

12-13). Of these the first two were Schedule 'A' industries, as were the sixth, seventh, and eighth listed (Appendix B). The third, fourth and fifth listed industries would fall into Schedule 'A' category, if they included heavy castings and forgings (Appendix B). The industries numbering (9) to (17) in the above list all came under the category of Schedule 'B' industries (Appendix B).

In all, of the 22 "key" industries, 17 were Schedule 'A' and 'B' industries under the 1956 Industrial Policy Resolution, and as such should not have been thrown open to the private sector. However, in view of the composition of the Swaminathan Committee itself, and given the background of earlier deviations from the earlier stated industrial policy, this could hardly be considered surprisingly. The special procedure for these "key" industries was intended to hasten the process of industrial licensing in these cases. The committee recommended that once a "letter of intent" was issued, the proposed licensing subcommittee should simultaneously consider all other clearances required.

Thus, taken as a whole, the Swaminathan Committee's recommendations were clearly pro-business. In the first place, the list of 22 "key" industries included a large number which under the terms of the industrial policy resolution were either reserved exclusively for the public sector (Schedule 'A'), or where new enterprises were reserved for the public sector (Schedule B) (see above).

Secondly, the changes introduced to speed up the licensing procedure would simultaneously reduce the scrutiny of applications by the DGTD, the state government and other bodies. Moreover, the fact that entrepreneurs would be issued "letters of intent" before they presented definite proposals regarding foreign collaboration, import of capital equipment and the issue of capital, meant that the licensing procedure was virtually divided into two stages. This would benefit those entrepreneurs, especially from the influential big business houses, who were able to wield sufficient influence to obtain the required "letter of intent" initially. Armed with that, they would be able to negotiate with potential foreign collaborators under the new procedure, entrepreneurs who had already definite proposals regarding foreign collaboration, would have no advantage over others in obtaining licenses.

Thirdly, the explicit "special preferential treatment" to be given to the "key" industries in obtaining all clearances, was tantamount to facilitating the deviations from stated industrial policy, (as the bulk of the "key" industries were listed in Schedule 'A' and 'B' of the 1956 Industrial Policy Resolution) (see above).

However, as stated earlier, the very composition of the Swaminathan Committee as well as its terms of reference, made its pro-business recommendation inevitable. And, as could be expected, the government accepted its major recommendations. In its notification, the government announced its acceptance of the special procedures for "key" industries, thus in effect accepting what was a clear deviation from the Industrial Policy Resolution of 1956. Regarding the Committee's proposal for a Licensing Sub-Committee, the government's decision was "that the other members of the Licensing Committee stationed in Delhi may also be associated with the work of the Sub-Committee..." (Ministry of Industries, 1964: 14). Thus, the government gave its seal of approval to the recommendations, even though they constituted major departures from official industrial policy as enunciated in the 1956 Industrial Policy Resolution. The entire affair only served to demonstrate the considerable extent of the big business influence on official industrial policy (*Eastern Economist*, 17 January 1964)

A significant admission of the influence of the business interests represented by FICCI, as well as the opportunist reasons for the Congress's espousal of socialism, was made by Asoka Mehta, then Deputy Chairman of the Planning Commission, in a speech to FICCI on 9 March 1964. Mehta noted that, "In India, the surge of our situation itself will make the socialist appeal increasingly attractive for a considerable time to come" (FICCI, Vol. III, 1964: 66).

As we have shown earlier, precisely because the 'socialist appeal' was politically rewarding, the Congress used it to enlist mass support. However the socialism was confined to the realm of rhetoric, the policies remained pro-capitalist in general, and pro-big business in particular. This as we have shown above, was especially true of the industrial policies.

In his speech, Mehta acknowledged that "In the choice (of development) that the nation makes, the decision of the industrial elite gathered here will prove crucial" (FICCI, Vol. III, 1964: 67, emphasis added). Thus, Mehta formally admitted the "crucial" influence FICCI had on the choice of economic policy. Moreover, as we have shown above, this statement was only an admission of the existing realities, and not mere flattery.

On the same day as the announcement of the Swaminathan Committee's Interim Report, i.e. 13 January 1964, the government announced yet another relaxation in industry licensing policy. Following the Finance Minister's announcement in Parliament on 16 December 1963, it was notified that all units with fixed assets valued at Rs. 5 lakhs to Rs. 25 lakhs had only to register with the appropriate government agency. For those not requiring items in short supply, registration was to be "automatic" (FICCI, Vol. II, 1964: 269).

The final report of the Swaminathan Committee which was submitted on 18 March 1964, was released for publication nearly 3 months later on 10th June (Ministry of Industries, 1964: 1). Its major recommendations had already been made, and acted upon, in the Interim Report. It recommended that in the cases of licensing of raw materials and components, the government should issue licenses within three months from the commencement of the licensing period. This was accepted by the government, as were the other recommendations (Ministry of Industries, 1964: 2). Of these the most important was "priority treatment" (as for the "key" industries), for 8 industries which were import-saving or substantially export-oriented" (Ministry of Industries, 1964: 4, emphasis in original). These included (1) industrial chains; (2) transformer oil; (3) insulating papers; (4) high tensile galvanised steel wires; (5) laboratory glassware; (6) detonators and detonating fuses; (7) synthetic fibres; and (8) caprolactum (Ministry of Industries, 1964: 4).

At the 9th meeting of the Central Advisory Council for

Industries held on 21 March 1964, K.P. Goenka, the FICCI President, welcomed the recommendations of the Swaminathan Committee as stimulating the growth of the decontrolled industries (FICCI, Vol. II, 1964: 375-376). From the nature of the recommendations, as analysed above, it is evident that there was much that big business in general, and FICCI in particular, could appreciate. The government's acceptance of the Swaminathan Committee recommendations, represented major concessions for Indian big business. Hence, 1964 was marked by a further, very significant concession for big business, in clear deviation from both the letter and the spirit of the 1956 Industrial Policy Resolution.

The Monopolies Enquiry Commission: FICCI's Memorandum

In August 1964, FICCI sent a detailed memorandum to the Monopolies Enquiry Commission (MIC) (FICCI, Vol. II, 1964: 78-93). FICCI argued that the number of units in particular industries were restricted, because of controls and because of the transitional stage of economic development, together with the technological considerations in new industries (FICCI, Vol. II, 1964: 80-81). FICCI argued that there was no monopolistic ownership because of the existence of the large number of shareholders. Further, the memorandum argued against the imposition of further controls, claiming that industrial growth had been "impaired" by them. According to FICCI, "the issue really is how pervasive control exercised by authority over industry should be reduced rather than to think in terms of adding to the existing body of restrictive law" (FICCI, Vol. II, 1964: 81-82).

Citing the National Council of Applied Economic Research (NCAER) statistics, FICCI argued that no group or unit controlled even one-third of production of capacity in an important industry (FICCI, Vol. II, 1964: 82-83). It claimed, that the existing market structure was the "optimum" and that "any violation" of it, would have "adverse repercussions on industrial growth", as the existing "comprehensive" regulating measures made it "impossible" for firms and groups "to achieve monopoly power" (FICCI, Vol. II, 1964: 86). The memorandum, approvingly cited T.T. Krishnamachari's statement in the Lok Sabha on 16 December 1963 that, "we (government) have come to the conclusion that gradual and orderly relaxation of some of the controls would be in the interest of stimulating economic growth" (quoted in FICCI, Vol. II, 1964: 89). The citation was used to put forward FICCI's case for reforms in the Industries Act, particularly in sections relating to industrial licensing, foreign collaboration agreements, price revision, etc. (FICCI, Vol. II, 1964: 89). FICCI also cited Nehru's 23 April 1963 statement in Parliament, that only 182 out of 4211 licenses issued in the three years ending 31 March 1963, had gone to the leading industrial houses, as evident that the "scarcity in some sectors..." was not due to the existence of monopolies but to the "imbalance between the state of progress and the size of a emerging demand" (FICCI, Vol. II, 1964: 93).

Later the same year Asoka Mehta, the then Deputy Chairman of the Planning Commission, met members of the FICCI E.C. on 18th August at the Federation House, the data having been suggested by G.L. Bansal, FICCI Secretary-General. Earlier, Mehta had met leading industrialists at Federation House on 23rd December of the previous years (FICCI, Vol. II, 1964: 96-97). On 26 November 1964, a 10-man FICCI delegation led by K.P. Goenka (President), including among others Padampat Singhania, Babubhai Chinai, A.M.M. Murugappa Chettiar, Bharat Ram, Ramnath A. Podar and G.L. Bansal met Nehru's successor as Prime Minister, Lal Bahadur Shastri (FICCI, Vol. II, 1964: 101). The delegation which met the Prime Minister for 45 minutes, urged the relaxations of the gold control policy, taxation policy and industrial licensing (FICCI, Vol. II, 1964: 101-102).

Nehru's Death

Earlier in late May 1964, Nehru had passed away. In a press statement of on 25th May, the FICCI E.C. stated in a resolution that "the Committee... have always felt that there was much in common in his approach and ours, to economic goals and perspectives" (FICCI, Vol. II, 1964: 401-402). While laudatory and appreciative references in such statements are customary, there was indeed much in common between the approaches of Nehru and the FICCI leadership to the economic development of India (as we have seen above).

FICCI had maintained its relations with the dominant 'Syndicate' in the ruling Congress after Nehru's death. On 1 July 1964, it hosted a reception in Calcutta where Kamaraj, P.C. Sen and Atulya Ghose were present (FICCI, Vol. II, 1964: 403-404). Speaking on the occasion, K.P. Goenka called for a "new look "to "economic policies" and found Kamraj the "most competent person to initiate a process"(FICCI, Vol. II, 1964: 104).

Industrial Policy in 1965: Further Concessions to Big Business

The budget proposals for 1965-66 were welcomed by FICCI. The FICCI E.C. in a press statement on 6th March congratulated T.T. Krishnamachari for recognising that "the resources available to the public sector enterprises sector... are all part of the same pool" (FICCI, Vol. II, 1965: 108). This FICCI considered "heartening" as it itself had emphasised this commonality "for many years" (FICCI, Vol. II, 1965: 108). The 50 per cent decrease in excise duty and "marginal" decreasing personal taxation were welcomed as proposals "in the right direction", but FICCI claimed that they were "not to the right extent" "(FICCI, Vol. II, 1965: 110). It urged reductions in the levels of wealth, gift and expenditure taxes and in estate duties "(FICCI, Vol. II, 1965: 110-112).

The supplementary budget proposals of late August 1965 were also welcomed by FICCI. Its press statement found "that the budget has some favourable aspects..."(FICCI, Vol. II, 1965: 128), but FICCI wanted further concessions, e.g. removal of taxes on dividends, bonus shares, super profits, etc. "(FICCI, Vol. II, 1965: 128-130).

Further concessions in industrial licensing policy, were announced in a government press note on 26th July the same year" (FICCI, Vol. II, 1965: 177). These included: (a) permission for substantial expansion and new undertakings in power alcohol, if the director of industries in the concerned state certified the availability of molasses; (b) diversification in engineering goods and the production of new articles was allowed with existing plant and machinery if (i) the article was not on the banned list, (ii) it was not specifically reserved for small-scale industry, and (iii) there was no substantial reduction in the production of the already licensed items; and (c) new articles in three non-engineering industries were allowed. These relaxations were to be reviewed after one year" (FICCI, Vol. II, 1965: 177).

In mid-April 1965, S.K. Patil, Minister of Railways, and a prominent leader of the Syndicate, in a speech at the Punjab and Delhi Chambers of Commerce, complimented the business community "on having contributed significantly to industrial production and industrial expansion despite the difficulties in their way..."(*Eastern Economist*, 16 April 1965). In other words, the monopoly houses had contributed to national economic development despite being fettered by the government's industrial policy. This was precisely the argument of big business interests, including FICCI. Of course, the shift in government rhetoric as exemplified by Patil's speech was inevitable in view of the pro-big business shifts in industrial policy, that we have examined above. The efforts of big business had to be lauded if industrial policy shifts had to be justified.

Steel and Cement Decontrol

In early 1965, the government decided to decontrol steel. Thereafter in April 1965, G.D. Somani, a former Congress MP, the new President of the Cement Manufacturers Association began lobbying with Prime Minister Shastri with T.N. Singh, the Industries Minister, and with State Congress leaders, to ensure that cement was also decontrolled (Kochanek, 1974: 254). In May 1965, a delegation of the Cement Manufacturers Association (CMA) met T.N. Singh, to plead for the decontrol of cement (Cement Manufacturers Association, 1965: 7, quoted in Kochanek, 1974). In early August, the CMA broke from the past policy call openly for a partial decontrol of cement, on the grounds that this was necessary for the generation of extra funds for the expansion of cement industry (Kochanek, 1974: 254-255).

On 26th August, Shastri abruptly announced in Parliament the government's decision in principle to decontrol cement, with details to be worked out later. T.N. Singh defended the decision later, as one necessitated by the disruption of foreign aid resulting from the Indo-Pakistan war of 1965, which had made the role envisaged for the public sector Cement Corporation impossible to achieve (*Times of India*, 17 November 1965; Kochanek, 1974: 255). Nonetheless, some MPs called the decontrol a sell-out to the private sector (*Statesman*, 19 November 1965; Kochanek, 1974: 255).

Shastri faced strong opposition within the Congress. The Congress Parliamentary Party's executive committee expressed grave misgivings over the decontrol of cement. Some members urged the government to reconsider its decision, and if necessary, to reverse it (Kochanek, 1974: 255).

At this stage, unlike in December 1963, the Left within the Congress, was not sufficiently influential to provide a counter check however limited, to business influences. Therefore, in consonance with the trends of concessions to industry, of which the Swaminathan Committee recommendations were the watermark, cement was also decontrolled in the following years.

Monopolies Inquiry Commission

The monopolies Inquiry commission (MIC) Report was published in December 1965. S.L. Kirloskar, the FICCI President, in a press statement welcomed those of its findings that were not critical of big business. He noted that the MIC's "analysis of some important issues..." was similar to that of FICCI's, e.g. the recognitions of the fact that the business sources by providing managerial skills, etc. (Kochanek, 1974: 56).

Even R.C. Dutta's 'Note of Dissent', where a "more radical approach" towards monopolies was advocated, conceded that the pioneer ventures in new industries were inevitably "monopolistic". Kirloskar argued that since there was "no evidence" to show misuse of power by "large units", their expansion should be permitted. The statement opposed the recommendation that a permanent commission be set up to give prior sanction for expansion to "inter-connected undertakings" with Rs. 1 crore and above of assets, as one likely to lead to a "delay" in economic "progress". Therefore, Kirloskar urged that implementation of only those recommendations, which would ensure that industrial progress, was "not... hampered by further legislative barriers" (Kochanek, 1974: 57).

A trenchant critic of the MIC Report was made by R.K. Hazari shortly after its publication. The MIC Report had at a number of places praised the contribution of Indian big business. It stated for example, that, "big business has done much for the country's economic betterment and as a consequence, for the alleviation of the poor man's misery" (Report of the Monopolies Inquiry Commission, 1965: 135; Hazari, 18 December 1965: 1843). However, as Hazari noted, the MIC lacked "the benefit of tangible and analytical evidence..." in support of the above statement (Hazari, 18 December 1965: 1845). He further noted that though "for many years, government spokesmen vehemently denied that concentration had increased and was probably increasing...", the commission took "growth of concentration as a proved fact...", even though it is related only to March 1964 (Hazari, 18 December 1965: 1845).

The general recommendations of the MIC (majority) were as follows:

1) self-discipline by political parties, i.e. rejection of assistance from business houses;
2) removal of corruption from administration;
3) liberalisation of licensing since it could not be abolished and preference in favour of small business without sacrifice of efficiency;
4) insistence on proper distribution of goods imported under licenses;
5) higher imports to stimulate efficiency;
6) countervailing action by the public sector through public units to prevent monopoly; and
7) promotion of small industries and preferential government purchases from small units, strong consumer cooperatives and organised consumer resistance ((Hazari, 18 December 1965: 1846; see also Chapter VII of the MIC Report, 1965: 139-146).

The MIC Report included a recommended Draft Bill entitled "The Monopolies and Restrictive Trade Practices Bill, 1965", intended:

> to provide that the operation of the economic system does not result in the concentration of economic power to common detriments for the control of monopolies and the prohibition of monopolistic and restrictive trade practices when found contrary to the public interest and for matters connected therewith or incidental thereto (MIC Report, 1965: 166).

However, despite the public debate over the Report, this bill in a greatly modified form was not discussed till 1967, and did not become an Act until 1969.

R.C. Dutt, a member of the MIC and Chairman of the Company Law Board, wrote a lengthy "Note of Dissent" to the Majority Report (MIC Report, 1965: 190-206). In that he argued that the "harmful effects" of the concentration of economic power had been "underestimated" in the Majority Report (MIC Report, 1965: 191). He referred to the ability big business had to "influence the decisions of government", through "their predominance in the press" (MIC Report, 1965: 194). Dutt noted that "economic disparity which is a consequence of under concentration of economic power... affects economic growth itself in the long run and inhibits it" (MIC Report, 1965: 198).

However, as stated earlier, the release of the MIC Report led to no anti-monopoly legislation or even to discussion of the Draft Bill as presented in the Report. Moreover as we have noted earlier, the Report was not even discussed in the Parliament. But, in a larger sense, this was only to be expected. In view of the consistent policy of concessions to big business, when even anti-monopoly rhetoric had been toned down, any anti-monopoly legislation, given the political balance of forces was improbable.

In December, a 12-man FICCI delegation led by Kirloskar, met the Prime Minister Lal Bahadur Shastri. The delegation complained about the "paucity" of bank credit, the high interest rates in the market, the extent of non-productive expenditure by the government, and above all the purported wage-push inflation. According to the FICCI report, Shastri gave them "a patient hearing", stating that "solutions had to be found" (FICCI, Vol. II, 1965: 62-63).

Earlier that year, Neelam Sanjiva Reddy, Minister for Steel and Mines, speaking at a FICCI lunch on 22nd March, pointed out that "most" pig-iron plants had been put up by the private sector and further asserted that "we are trying to encourage the private sector to put up more plans" (FICCI, Vol. III, 1965: 65). Since pig-iron was a Schedule 'A' industry, this amounted to another deviation of the industrial policy framework, as laid down in the 1956 Industrial Policy Resolution.

Industrial Policy in 1966: Culmination of the Process of Liberalisation

In February 1966, the reconstituted Swaminathan Committee submitted its Report. The Committee had been reconstituted in August 1965, in pursuance of recommendations by the original Swaminathan Committee that:

> this Committee, with the same composition as far as may be, be reconstituted after a year to study the results of the working of the revised procedures and asked to make a report and suitable recommendations to government[90] (Ministry of Industries, 1964: 6; Ministry of Industry, February 1966; para I).

As one of the original members, A.M.M. Murugappa Chettiar had expired, the strength of the Committee was reduced to 9 members, and the representation of industrialists to 4 (as Chettiar's vacancy was not filled) (Ministry of Industry, February 1966; para III). A.R. Foster, who was President of ASSOCHAM in 1963, when the original Swaminathan Committee was constituted, was replaced as the ASSOCHAM representative by H.K.S. Lindsay, President of ASSOCHAM in 1965. Similarly, Bharat Ram, President of FICCI in 1963, and a member of the original Committee, was replaced by S.L. Kirloskar, FICCI President in 1965, as a member of the reconstituted Committee. Apart from T. Swaminathan who was the Chairman of both Committees, K.J. George continued as the Member Secretary, but the three other official members were replaced by other government nominees.

The reconstituted Swaminathan Committee in its fresh examination of the licensing policy procedures arrived at the conclusion:

> that generally speaking, industries which do not involve the import of capital goods or raw materials should be exempted from the licensing provisions of the act by the issue of an exemption notification under Section 28-9 of the Industries (Development and Regulation) Act. It should, by and large, be left to the economic judgement of the entrepreneur to decide whether or not he will enter these fields and make an investment and to what extent. In these fields the targets laid down by the Planning Commission would serve as indicative targets and as a factor to be considered by the prospective investor in his assessment of demand and other economic data (Ministry of Industry, February 1966; para IV, Section: X).

As Bhagwati and Desai have noted,

> from an economic view-point, this criterion made no sense. Even if the sole purpose of industrial licensing were to consist in preserving foreign exchange, the rule of the thumb proposed was naive in so far as it took into account only the direct foreign exchange requirements and ignored other foreign exchange repercussions (Bhagwati and Desai, 1970: 478).

However, on the basis of this questionable economic argument, the reconstituted Committee proposed illustratively the delicensing of the following 10 industries; (1) cotton textiles; (2) sugar; (3) cement; (4) toilet preparations; (5) paper and newsprint; (6) fire bricks; (7) hand tools; (8) plywood; (9) furniture components; and (10) milk foods (Ministry of Industry, February 1966; para IV, Section: X).

After the Report of the reconstituted Swaminathan Committee was submitted, a large number of industries were delicensed at various points of time in 1966. The delicensing was preceded by reassurance to the business community. In a radio talk over All India Radio in late April 1966, the Prime Minister Mrs. Indira Gandhi while reiterating her government's commitment to "the objective of the socialist and democratic society...", stressed that this did not involve any doctrinaire adherence to some dogmas (*Commerce*, 30 April 1966). The speech was welcomed by the financial press. *Commerce* put it, "a pragmatic approach to economic problems is sought to be adopted..."(*Commerce*, 30 April 1966).

The developments in the sphere of industrial policy had their repercussions also within the business community. On 25th February G.D. Birla, speaking at the Annual Meeting of Indian Merchants' Chamber, urged his fellow businessmen to support the Congress. He argued:

> that it is very easy to score points and (to) criticise this government. There is no doubt that they have made a mess in many things. But do not forget that this is the best government that you can get under the circumstances. This is the only government which can give you stability—political stability—law and order".

Birla went on to state that he "entirely agree(d)" with the "slogan" of democratic socialism, as interpreted by Nehru. This, he took to mean, "more consumer goods for the people, more education, better health, more houses and more of this and more of that. This is all right" (*Eastern Economist*, 4 March 1966).

In his speech, Birla was only reiterating arguments made earlier. Speaking before the Indian Chamber of Commerce, Calcutta, in April 1965, he had warned fellow businessmen:

> you can break the Congress but it is not going to help. You will be replacing this government by a communist government and they will be the first to cut your throat. Do not make that mistake... It is a question of self-interest[91] (Indian Chamber of Commerce, 11 April 1965: 8-9).

Birla's speeches were in line with what Kochanek has termed "the Birla strategy", which was one of pressurising the government to make concessions, without confronting the Congress openly or directly (Kochanek, 1974: 188). This strategy, as we have seen above, was the one dominant in FICCI. As we have seen in the preceding analysis, FICCI leaders generally did not criticise the government or the Congress Party as a whole, even when they disagreed with official policies. The FICCI strategy was generally one of selective criticism of particular policy measures which were perceived to be against the interests of Indian big business. This Birla or FICCI strategy was apparently successful, as starting from May 1966, a large number of industries were delicensed.

In May 1966, 11 industries were delicensed: (1) iron and steel castings and causing; (2) iron and steel structurals; (3) electric motors up to 10 hp; (4) pulp; (5) glue and gelatin; (6) glass; (7) power alcohol; (8) solvent extracted oils; (9) fire bricks and finance linings; (10) cement, gypsum, and insulating boards; and (11) timber products (Lok Sabha Secretariat, 1967: 179). The Minister of Industrial Development and Company Affairs while announcing this, this policy concession in the course of his statement in the Rajya Sabha, on 9 May 1966, on 'Liberalisation of Industrial Licensing Policy', referred to the fact that:

> the Prime Minister has also on more than one occasion, recently reiterated government's policy that controls would be maintained only where it is necessary in the public interest to do so. Government has been there for keeping under review the various controls in existence... Two basic considerations which have been kept in view in the preparation of this list (of delicensed industries) are:-

(i) The items are those in respect of which there is no substantial import of components or new materials.

(ii) Industries in respect of which protection to the small and cottage industries is of importance have been left out (Lok Sabha Secretariat, 1967: 179).

The minister went on to state that,

> the above list (of delicensed industries) is by no means exhaustive. It is proposed to examine the schedule to the Industries (Development and Regulation) Act with a view to announcing further additions to this list from time to time. Apart from the two considerations mentioned above, an additional factor which will be taken into account in preparing further lists will be the need for the accelerated development of industry with export potential (Lok Sabha Secretariat, 1967: 179-180).

In the official statement to delicense 11 industries, the first consideration which referred to the foreign exchange component, was the same as that argued by the reconstituted Swaminathan Committee. Thus, as Bhagwati and Desai (1970:479) have noted, "the government, therefore, appeared to have accepted the (reconstituted) Swaminathan Committee's criteria".

Some months later, on 20th July, the paper and newsprint, and hand tools industries were delicensed (FICCI, Vol. II, 1966: 296). Following this relaxation, in early October 1966, some FICCI representatives including their President, Ranabhai Amin, and G.L. Bansal (FICCI Secretary-General) met D. Sanjivayya, the Minister for Industry. At the meeting, further delicensing of industries was discussed. In pursuance of the earlier discussions, Bansal on 19th October wrote to Sanjivayya enclosing a list of 25 items which FICCI recommended to be delicensed[92] (FICCI, Vol. II, 1966: 290).

On 14th November, Sanjivayya announced in both the Houses of Parliament a list of 23 items which were to be delicensed. A comparison of the FICCI proposals and the list of delincensed industries, reveals that a significant number of items figured in both lists. These included: (1) bicycles and components; (2) sewing machines and components; (3) mixed fertilisers (FICCI had recommended delicensing of all chemical fertilisers); (4) power-driven pumps; (5) electric motors upto 40 hp; (6) weighing machines; (7) items of industrial machinery, (i.e. air and gas compressors upto 6 c.mm., tea machinery, mathematical, surveying and drawing instruments and electric furnaces); (8) drugs and pharmaceuticals (i.e. barium chloride, barium nitrate, barium sulphate, blanc fixe, activated bleaching earth, activated carbon, metallic stearates, and sodium aluminates); and (9) furniture components, (i.e. hard board including fibre board, chip board and particle boards)[93] (FICCI, Vol. II, 1966: 290, 293-296).

Earlier, on 28th October, there had been another liberalisation of licensing policy. Industrial units were allowed to manufacture new articles without obtaining licenses if: (a) only minor balancing equipment was procured indigenously and added; (b) there was no increase in foreign exchange expenditure; (c) the diversified production did not exceed 25 per cent of the total licensed production; and (d) these did not include any of the 71 items reserved for the small-scale sector. Moreover, licensed industrial units were permitted to increase production upto 25 per cent over earlier licensed production, subject to the above conditions together with the further stipulation that there would be no additional demand by the unit for scarce raw materials (FICCI, Vol. II, 1966: 290-293).

The liberalisation of industrial licensing policy in 1966, following the submission of the reconstituted Swaminathan Committee Report, taken as a whole amounts to a substantial liberalisation for, as well as a significant deregulation of, the private corporate sector. Yet this liberalisation of industrial licensing policy, was only a culmination of the policy of piecemeal concessions to the private sector, increasingly adopted by the government from 1957 onwards, as we have seen above.

The 1966 Budget

The Budget which had been announced at the end of February 1966, had also incorporated concessions to the private sector. Significantly, the tax concessions made in the Budget, corresponded to the recommendations made in the confidential FICCI note "on (the) Present Economic Situation and the Budget", which had been appended to the confidential letter of 28th January from S.L. Kirloskar to Sachin Chaudhuri, Minister of Finance (FICCI, Vol. II, 1966: 191, 192-195). In the note, FICCI proposed the abolition of the tax on bonus shares and the equity dividend tax as well as reductions in the surtax on company profits and the taxes on inter-corporate dividends (FICCI, Vol. II, 1966: 193-194). Thus in a press communiqué on 28th February, S.L. Kirloskar, The FICCI President, appreciated the fact that the Budget had "removed some irritants", e.g. expenditure tax, and the tax on bonus shares (FICCI, Vol. II, 1966: 179-180). The FICCI E.C's press communiqué on 4th March also expressed its appreciation of the removal of the above taxes, as well as the reduction in the surtax on company profits and the liberalisation of dividend taxes (FICCI, Vol. II, 1966: 180-181). The E.C. however, objected to the proposals for additional taxation, through other or enhanced taxes in both the corporate and personal sectors (FICCI, Vol. II, 1966: 181).

Deviations from the 1956 Industrial Policy Resolution, 1956-1966

The cumulative effect of the deviations from the 1956 Industrial Revolution was brought out by the most comprehensive study of the actual operation of the industrial policy measures from 1956 to 1966, undertaken by the Industrial Licensing Policy Inquiry Committee (ILPIC). The ILPIC Report revealed very substantial deviations from the industrial policy framework as represented by the 1956 Industrial Policy Resolution. The Report noted, "that the licensing system... provides considerable scope for favour to be granted and... these favours mostly... are secured by firms belonging to the Large Industrial Sectors"[94] (Ministry of Industrial Development, Internal Trade and Company Affairs, 1969: 74). It catalogued the actual extent of the issue of licenses to the private sector for industries reserved for the state under Schedule 'A' and 'B' of the 1956 Industrial Policy Resolution, which we have reproduced in Tables I and II below.

The ILPIC Report also found after an examination of the financial assistance rendered to the private sector, by the three main all India financial institutions: the Industrial Finance Corporation of India (IFCI), the Industrial Development Bank of India (IDBI), and the Industrial Credit and Investment Corporation Of India (ICICI), that "the share of the large industrial sector is predominant, that of the 20 large houses is very large and a few individual houses get a major share"[95] (Ministry of Industrial Development, Internal Trade and Company Affairs, 1969: 170). In the case of the public sector banks, its findings were substantially the same:

"The public sector banking institutions are also found to extend favoured treatment in the credit facilities offered by them to the Large Industrial Sectors. Not only does large-scale assistance go to the Large-Scale Industrial Sector but the share of the 20 Larger Houses, is very large" (Ministry of Industrial Development, Internal Trade and Company Affairs, 1969: 179).

The ILPIC Report also brought out the very considerable growth in the assets of the large industrial houses. Table III below shows the increase in assets between 1951 (Hazari's estimates) and 1966 (ILPIC estimates)[96].

Table I: Licenses Given in Schedule 'A' Industries to the Private Sector Between 1956 and 1966

Sr. No.	*Industry*	*Public Sector*	*Private Sector*	*Total*
1	Iron and Steel	4	42	46
2	Heavy Castings and Forgings of Iron and Steel	6	306	312
3	Heavy Plant Machinery required for Iron and Steel Production, for Mining, Machine Tools Manufacture and for such other Basic Industries as specified by the government	3	103	106
4	Heavy Electrical Plant including Large Hydraulic and Steam Turbines	3	58	61
5	Coal and Lignite	46	344	390
6	Mineral Oils	3	7	10
7	Aircraft	2	2	4
8	Ship Building	-	12	12
9	Telephones and Telephone Cables, Telegraph Apparatus (excluding Radio Receiving Sets)	3	17	20

Source: Ministry of Industrial Development, Internal Trade and Company Affairs, Department of Industrial Development, *Report of the Industrial Licensing Policy Inquiry Committee* (Delhi: Manager of Publications, 1969), Main Report, p. 105, Table II.

Table II : Licenses Given in Schedule 'B' Industries to the Private Sector, 1956-1966

Sr. No.	*Industry*	*Public Sector*	*Private Sector*	*Total*
1	Machine Tools	9	226	235
2	Ferro-Alloys and Tool Steels	2	9	11
3	Basic and Intermediate Products required by Chemical Industries, such as Drugs, Dyestuff	17	233	250
4	Plastics, Antibiotics and other Essential Drugs	1	334	335
5	Fertilisers	12	42	54
6	Synthetic Rubber	-	3	3

7	Aluminium	-	46	46
8	Non-Ferrous Metals (other than Aluminium)	-	87	87

Source: Ministry of Industrial Development, Internal Trade and Company Affairs, Department of Industrial Development (1969), *Report of the Industrial Licensing Policy Inquiry Committee* (Delhi: Manager of Publications), Main Report, p. 106.

Table III: Illustrative List of Growth in Assets of Large Houses, 1951-1966

Rs. in Crores

Sr. No.	*Name of House*	*Net Fixed Assets in 1951*	*Net Fixed Assets in 1966*
1	Tata	54.31	505.36
2	Birla	24.23	457.84
3	Martin Burn	17.87	153.06
4	Bangur	3.53	104.31
5	Thapar	3.52	99.80
6	Dalmia Jain	14.32	58.75
7	Bird Heilgers	7.96	68.62
8	J. K. Singhania	4.33	66.84
9	Walchand	18.01	81.11
10	Shri Ram	4.98	74.13
11	Mafatlal	3.98	92.70
12	Andrew Yule	10.03	46.75
13	Kasturbhai Lalbhai	2.95	51.19
14	Kirloskar	0.64	43.02
15	Mahindra and Mahindra	0.86	38.58
16	V. Ramakrishna	0.99	18.78
17	Khatau	11.44	40.09

Sources:

(1) For 1951 figures which referred to net fixed assets, Hazari, R.K. (1966), *The Structure of the Private Corporate Sector* (Bombay: Asia), pp. 33-35, Table 2.1.

(2) For 1966 figures for assets, Ministry of Industrial Development, Internal Trade and Company Affairs, Department of Industrial Development (1969), *Report of the Industrial Licensing Policy Inquiry Committee* (Delhi: Manager of Publications), Vol. II, pp. 1-93.

What emerges quite starkly from the ILPIC Report is that the state-controlled industrial policy mechanism operates substantially in favour of big business. The extent of the deviations from the 1956 Industrial Policy Resolution, catalogued in the ILPIC Report, further highlights the considerable measure of the business influence on industrial policy as it developed from 1956.

Conclusion

In the 1964 to 1966 period, the earlier policy of making piecemeal concessions to the private corporate sector, including Indian big business, continued, despite the findings of the Mahalanobis Committee and the Monopolies Inquiry Commission (MIC), which had revealed that government policies had resulted in the absolute and relative growth of the large Indian industrial houses, or 'monopoly groups', as they are popularly known. Significantly, the government never moved a motion to allow a discussion of either the Mahalanobis Committee Report or that of the MIC, in Parliament, despite the obvious importance of both the Reports. If this is examined in the context of the actual measures adopted in the area of industrial policy during this period, the government's action in shelving discussion on these Reports, was in keeping with its now overt policy of concessions to the Indian private corporate sector, including its monopolistic upper crust.

The representation given to big business, especially to the representatives of FICCI, in both Swaminathan Committees, was another telling indication of the orientation sought to be imparted to industrial policy. In view of the composition of the two Swaminathan Committees, their recommendations, which incorporated a substantial measure of licensing, were only to be expected. The acceptance by government of the fairly far-reaching recommendations of the Swaminathan committees, including the simplifications of licensing procedures for "key" industries, (which included a number of industries in Schedules 'A' and 'B'), apart from the delicensing of a number of industries, amounted to substantial deviations from the industrial policy framework envisaged in the 1956 Industrial Policy Resolution and in the Second Plan document. The decontrol of various commodities and the concessions made to the private corporate sector in successive budgets, further highlight the clear bias in changes in official industry policy, which were directed at accommodating private sector interests, including those of Indian big business.

In the case of liberalisation of industrial policy, particularly in 1966, it would appear that internal factors were not the sole cause. Pressure from the World Bank, as well as the Aid-India Consortium, which culminated in the devaluation of the rupee in June 1966, probably contributed to the developments in 1966[97] (Bhagwati and Desai, 1970; Bhagwati and Srinivasan, 1976; Payer, 1974). Of course, external factors also impinged on developments in industrial policy which however are outside the scope of this study.

The process of liberalisation of industrial regulation which begins from the very inception of the system itself (see Chapters 5, 6 and 7 above), culminated in the far-reaching concessions made between 1964 and 1966. The large-scale private corporate sector or Indian big business, was facilitated as a consequence of the liberal economic policies to grow exponentially, and not only its economic strength but apparently its political leverage, and its ability to wrest concessions from the government, also increased correspondingly. Writing in November 1960, D.R. Gadgil, an eminent economist who later served as the Deputy Chairman of the Planning Commission, already considered that the consequence of such policies was that "the actual possessors of the politico-economic power in the country", were "the large business interests". While this may be considered an overstatement, it was by no means wholly incorrect. Because of their increased politico-economic power, large business interests had been able to significantly shape industrial policy in their favour in these years, from 1964 to 1966.

REFERENCES

1. This Committee was officially known as the Industries Development Procedures Committee, but is generally referred to as the Swaminathan Committee, after its Chairman, T. Swaminathan.
2. India, Planning Commission (1964), Report of the Committee

on Distribution of Income and Levels of Living (Delhi: Manager of Publications), Part I, "Distribution of Incomes and Wealth and Concentration of Economic Power." Mahalanobis was the Chairman of the Committee, which is thus popularly known as the Mahalanobis Committee.

3. Hazari's study which is cited by the Mahalanobis Committee i.e. Hazari, R.K. (1966), The Structure of the Corporate Private Sector (Bombay, Asia).
4. "Duplications of inter-linked companies as between directors of the same marketing company have been removed but not as between marketing companies".
5. Apart from this statement itself, no further evidence is cited in support of this contention. Three years earlier, however, two studies by the Department were published which examined the problem, cf. Nigam, Raj K. and Chaudhuri, N.C. (1961), *The Corporate Sector in India: A Factual Presentation of Long and Short-Term Trends* (Delhi: Manager of Publications); and Nigam, Raj K. and Joshi, N.D. (1961), *The Pattern of Company Directorships in India* (Delhi: Manager of Publications).
6. That there were divergences of opinion among the members is admitted by P.C. Mahalanobis himself. (c.f. Planning Commission, 1969, Part II of the Report). Furthermore in the second part of the Report, two members wrote notes of dissent. V.K.R.V. Rao, writing more than 15 years after the publication of the Report, stated that he had drafted Chapter IV of the Report on "Concentration of Economic Power". In his draft, which was not accepted, it was stated that there is: "The existence of a prima facie case for a Commission of Inquiry into Concentration of Economic Power especially in the private sector in industry, commerce, banking and finance. Such a Commission should have brought terms of reference, and (be) given both the necessary legal authority and competent full-time staff to carry out its task... Only after its Report becomes available would it be possible for government to chalk out a form policy regarding concentration of economic power" (c.f. Foreword to S.K. Goyal, *Monopoly Capital and Public Policy* (New Delhi: Allied, 1979: xii-xiii) (emphasis added). However, Rao has not explained why he did not write a note of dissent to Part I of the Report. (Planning Commission, 1964: 55).
7. The published paragraph is much less critical of the relationships between big business owned newspapers and the government than V.K.V.R. Rao's original draft. (Rao, 1979: xiii).

8. Forwarding Note to Jawaharlal Nehru by P.C. Mahalanobis dated 25 February 1964.
9. Forwarding Note to Indira Gandhi by P.C. Mahalanobis dated 25 July 1969.
10. Interestingly, the Final Report of the reconstituted Committee was never printed, and few mimeographed copies are available. The Licensing Policy Section of the Ministry of Industry, when contacted in November 1982, was not even aware of the existence of this Report, and one of its officers insisted that there was no reconstituted Committee Report (personal conversation with the author, New Delhi, November 1982).
11. Birla was apparently referring to the fact that the Communists CPI and CPI (M) posed an alternative to the Congress in West Bengal.
12. D.O. letter No. F.11710/1/2 dated 19 October 1966.
13. We have grouped the delicensed items together under broad heads. The number of items common to the two lists is not only 9, but well over half of the 25 recommended for delicensing by FICCI. This is evident from an examination of the individual items grouped in the above list.
14. The term 'Large Industrial Sector' referred to the top 73 industrial houses, with assets of Rs. 5 crores or more in 1964.
15. The '20 Larger Industrial Houses' all had assets of Rs. 35 crores or more in 1964.
16. Strictly speaking the two are not comparable as there are divergent definitions of assets, and differing methods of attributing house affiliations. Nonetheless, the data in this Table III may be considered generally indicative of the trend in the increase in assets.
17. Bhagwati and Desai do not refer to the liberalisation of industrial licensing policy as a consequence of Western pressure. Similarly, Cheryl Payer does not refer to the decontrol of the industrial sector as a consequence of World Bank pressure. She is however aware that the IMF and its sister organisation the World Bank, pressurise debtor governments to reduce or to jettison state controls over the private sector in the respective economies.

9
Conclusion

FICCI, as is evident from the study undertaken, is the most important apex body of Indian big business. Though it is very often asserted that FICCI represents commercial and industrial interests, in its operations it is dominated by a few large industrial houses, in which the Birla House plays the prominent role. For varying reasons, a few of the top industrial houses (including the Tatas, Mafatlals, Khataus and the Sarabhais) have generally kept themselves out of FICCI. A number of smaller industrialists and traders, made unsuccessful efforts at various stages of the Federation's history, to make the Federation a more representative body of the private sector in general, instead of a mouthpiece of Indian big business. In contrast to the FICCI, the ASSOCHAM has included some of the prominent Indian business houses who choose to remain out of FICCI. The government has, invariably, assigned greater weight to FICCI than to ASSOCHAM particularly, when nominating representatives of the private sector on official committees. The fact that FICCI has been recognised as a representative of the Indian big business emerges very clearly.

FICCI and Indian Big Business Influence on the Congress: Pre-Independence Period

Indian big business has sought to influence the Congress leadership of the nationalist movement, particularly from 1905-1907 onwards. The Indian big business, however, has no one strategy towards the nationalist movement. From the available evidence, it does not emerge that Indian big business, particularly the individual houses, were hostile to the British, and in turn faced the hostility of the Raj. The main difference appears in the degree of the support to the Congress Party.

Differences within the Indian big business cannot however, be reduced to what has been symbolically called the Bombay strategy and the Birla strategy. If the Bombay industrialists did not form a unified bloc, this was equally true of FICCI. While a majority of those who joined FICCI followed the lead of G.D. Birla; there were strong voices of dissent. For instance, while G.D. Birla generally supported the Congress openly, Purshotamdas Thakurdas, on a number of occasions opposed the Congress Party particularly when the party gave a call for mass agitations. Kasturbhai Lalbhai, who generally followed Birla's lead, was involved in the negotiations over the Lees-Mody Pact of 1933, which was later condemned by FICCI itself. Walchand Hirachand, though a founder member of FICCI, generally aligned with the Tatas, and opposed the Congress. Shri Ram, his biographers report, fell out with G.D. Birla over FICCI's initial support to the second Civil Disobedience Movement.

It is quite evident therefore, that though the Bombay strategy and Birla strategy may be considered the dominant strategies of Indian big business, individual business leaders adopted differing stands on many occasions. The Indian business community cannot be said to have had just one dominant strategy, purportedly represented by Purshotamdas Thakurdas and G.D. Birla.

The existence of close contacts and relationships between the Indian business and the Congress Party need to be seen in their historical context. Starting with the 1937 elections to the Provincial Assemblies, the conservative sections of the Congress leadership generally depended on Indian big business, particularly through the Birlas, to raise funds for election campaigns. Quite apart from the support provided to the individual leaders by individual industrialists, some of the financial support was overtly for constructive work by the party. Indian big business has also accepted crucial positions in the Congress Party. For instance, Jamnalal Bajaj was treasurer of the party for many years. A number of industrialists accepted the membership of the National Planning Committee. For instance, membership of the NPC Sub-Committee on Industrial Finance, headed by A.D. Shroff, enabled the Indian big business representatives to play an important role in evolving the party's policies in favour of the private sector. Shroff was able to get sub-committees to reject the proposals made by the left nationalists in the NPC for the nationalisation of key industries, public utilities and defence industries.

The Bombay Plan

By the mid 1940s, in the aftermath of the Quit India movement, it was apparent that the attainment of independence was only a matter of time, and that the future ruling party would be the Congress. This awareness seems to have forced Indian big business to have a more sympathetic approach towards the Congress Party. One indication of this was provided by the fact that the Bombay Plan of 1944 was signed by both FICCI and the Bombay group of industrialists. The Bombay Plan contained, in an encapsulated form, big business's attitudes towards the role of the state in the economic development of India. While the Bombay Plan envisaged a significant amount of state intervention in the economy, this was explicitly intended to subserve the private sector, including indigenous big business. In their Plan, the industrialists stressed that the emphasis and orientation, in the policies of industrialisation, was to maximise production, by simultaneously eschewing policies of radical reconstruction of the economy directed at the redistribution of national wealth.

The convergence between different factions of Indian big business, as exemplified by their leadership coming together in formulating the Bombay Plan, did not, however, mean the sinking of differences or the emergence of a unified group. The group of Indian industrialists aligned with foreign private capital in ASSOCHAM, maintained their alignment with the apex body, and did not join the larger Indian group represented in FICCI.

Industrial Policy in the Early Post-Independence Period

With the advent of independence in August 1947, Indian big business interests sought to use their influence in the formulation of industrial policy. The Industries Conference convened by the government in December 1947, brought together representatives of labour and industry, apart from those of the government. The resolutions adopted at the conference, as well as the ideological stances taken by the Congress leadership, were reassuring to the FICCI

In 1947-1948, the political balance of forces clearly favoured private sector interests. The left including the CPI and the socialists was divided. Whereas the CPI had opposed the Congress government as a "lackey" of British imperialism, and had considered independence to be "fake", the socialists particularly because of their approach to national problems were themselves isolated within the Congress. From the mid-1930s onwards, the class complexion of the Congress membership had changed, with the weightage of landholding peasants increasing sharply. This had acted against the more radical, anti-big business elements within the Congress. These factors had helped the conservative sections of the Congress leadership, headed by Sardar Patel, to establish a stronghold over the party organisation. This conservative section had strong links with Indian big business, which had been forged during the nationalist movement.

Within the Congress, as in the government, Nehru was the pre-eminent figure. He however, despite his predilections as evident from flashes of leftist rhetoric, had to adopt as head of a composite government, a policy of conciliation towards the private sector. The dislocations in the Indian economy, a consequence of Partition, added to the enormity of the tasks facing the political leadership. This was an added factor in Nehru's accommodation of the private sector. Faced with the compulsions of the circumstances, Nehru did resile from some of his odd positions and statements. For instance, during the course of the freedom struggle, Nehru had been bitterly critical of the Indian Civil Service (ICS), and had advocated its virtual elimination. He had categorically stated that

"Of one thing I am quite sure, that no new order can be built up in India so long as the spirit of the ICS pervades our administration and our public services... Therefore it seems to me quite essential that the ICS and similar services must disappear completely, as such, before we can start real work on a new order". However, the exigencies of the post-independence situation apparently obviated any possibility of eliminating the ICS; the "steel frame" was considered as necessary for governance.

As Mydral has noted, the ICS-dominated civil servants, in view of their background, and training in the colonial period, as well as the constraints of the inherited structure of administration were, "a regulating and stabilising influence that...worked against radical departures from the status quo—in other words, a conservative force". The upper echelons of the administration, were not only crucial in the process of implementation of government policies, but also contributed to the formulation of national policies. The dominance of the ICS cadre within the civil service administration, was another important factor strengthening the conservative, generally pro-business forces.

In this environment, the recommendations of the Economic Programme Committee (EPC) published at the end of January 1948, came as something of a shock to conservative sections. These recommendations were clearly anti-monopoly, in so far as they severely restricted the area of operations, not to speak of the possibilities of growth, of Indian big business. As could only be expected, the EPC Report generated a storm of protest. FICCI objected to the proposed restrictions, which it claimed made Indian big business "very apprehensive about the future economic structure and the industrial development of this country".

Apart from written representations, FICCI representatives met various members of the Cabinet, and some senior administrators, in their effort to lobby against the EPC Report's proposals. The lobbying by Indian big business interests against the EPCs recommendations was facilitated by the existing balance of political forces, referred to above. Shortly after the submission of the EPC Report, in the second half of February 1948, the socialists in the Congress, organised in the CSP, were virtually forced out of the ruling party. Thus, the strength of the countervailing forces against big business pressures, was significantly weakened in the months following the submission of the EPC Report.

The shift in the political balance of forces was reflected in Nehru's own stances on the EPC recommendations. For instance, in his speech at the Constituent Assembly, barely three weeks after the submission of the EPC Report, Nehru reassured the business community, alarmed by the EPC recommendations, by explicitly stating that, "obviously we (government) want the good-will of the industrialists of the country". This speech evidently reassured the business community, as it was apparently intended to.

Nehru had reassured FICCI members about the shape of future industrial policy, on the eve of the Industrial Policy Statement. In his speech at the FICCI Annual Session on 28 March 1948, Nehru virtually dismissed the 1931 Karachi Congress resolution, the progenitor of the EPC report, wherein it was stated that large industry should belong to the state, as "theoretical talk". During the course of his speech, Nehru clearly indicated the broad outlines of the forthcoming Industrial Policy Statement, in the presence of FICCI members.

(a) The 1948 Industrial Policy Statement

The Industrial Policy Statement was placed before the Constituent Assembly, about a week later, on 6 April 1948. The Statement marked a substantial retreat from the recommendations made in the EPC Report. The number of industries which were to be state monopolies were only three; while in six others "new undertakings" were to be exclusively reserved for the state. Even for these industries, the possibility of the entry of private enterprise was not ruled out. Further, the EPC proposal of a five-year period before the takeover of privately owned units in industries reserved for the state, was replaced by a highly qualified statement at the end of a ten-year period,

"The whole matter will be reviewed and a decision taken in the light of circumstances obtaining at the time. If it is decided that the state should acquire any unit, the fundamental rights guaranteed by the Constitution will be observed and compensation will be awarded on a fair and equitable basis".

The 1948 Industrial Policy Statement was, as K.T. Shah, the former Secretary of the National Planning Committee had noted, a significant dilution of the recommendations made in various committees of the NPC. He pointed out that the Statement left the large bulk of industry "in the hands of the capitalists". On their part, business circles approved of the Industrial Policy Statement. The dilution of the recommendations of the NPC and the EPC (both committees of which Nehru himself was the chairman), in the Industrial Policy Statement, was a consequence of increased big business influence on the formulation of official industrial policy, for the reasons enumerated above.

(b) 1949 Statement on Foreign Investments

The only really discordant note struck in the government-big business relationship in the immediate post-independence period, was the April 1949 Statement on Foreign Investments. The shift in the official policy from pre-independence stances of the Congress which were discriminatory against foreign capital, to one treating foreign and Indian capital on equal terms, was opposed by FICCI. Somewhat ironically, the divergence in the Congress policy on foreign capital from its stances during the nationalist movement, was pointed out to the Congress by FICCI, with the latter representing itself as the defender of the Swadeshi spirit. Concluding that the new policy on foreign capital was "a tragedy", FICCI called upon the government to reconsider it.

The serious economic situation, including the balance of payments deficit and the lack of capital investment, had forced the government to turn towards foreign capital. Moreover, within FICCI, despite the apparent unanimity on this issue, there were differences. Shortly after the announcement of the new policy, G.D. Birla welcomed it. Under the circumstances, the government rejected FICCI's demand for a reconsideration of the policy on foreign capital, and in doing so was doubtless strengthened by Birla's support.

The government however, sought to reassure the agitated industrialists, through conciliatory statements by various ministers. Although these postures did not mollify Indian industrialists whose protests continued, the very fact that they were made, is itself indicative of the respect with which the government treated the former's views. Furthermore, a few years later, when the economic situation eased, and Indian capital was more confident of its ability to compete with foreign capital, FICCI came around to accepting the government policy.

(ii) The Constitution and the Rights of the Propertied

The debates in the Constituent Assembly, and later in the Provisional Parliament, over the framing of the Constitution and the Industries Act, also reflected the pro-business attitudes of the Congress leadership. The Constitution as finally enacted enshrined the right to property as a fundamental right, and enjoined upon the state to give due compensation in the event of nationalisation of private property. Despite the urging of several members of the Constituent Assembly, the Directive Principles were not made justiciable, and were therefore potentially inoperative, if the requisite political will was lacking. Even the advice of the Constitutional Adviser, B.N. Rau, wherein he proposed certain amendments to the clauses relating to the Directive Principles, as a result of which laws made by the state in the discharge of its fundamental duties would prevail over the fundamental rights guaranteed to individuals was not accepted.

As we had already seen above, the Constituent Assembly was constituted on the basis of an indirect election by legislators who themselves had been elected on the basis of the Government of India Act, 1935, which restricted the right to vote to only some 16-18 per cent of the Indian population. The Assembly, in this sense, therefore actually represented only the relatively propertied electorate. Moreover, Indian big business was intimately associated with the process of the formulations of the Indian Constitution, as D.P. Khaitan, a founder member of FICCI and an industrialist closely associated with G.D. Birla, was a member of the original seven-man Drafting Committee, set up by a resolution of the Constituent Assembly on 29 August 1947. After D.P. Khaitan's death in 1948, his vacancy in the Drafting Committee was filled by another businessman, T.T. Krishnamachari. Under the circumstances therefore, particularly in view of the general influence of conservative and pro-business forces during this period, the rejection of the Constitutional Adviser's recommendations on such a matter affecting all propertied interests, was only to be expected.

The Constitution of India, as it was finally enacted, with the involvement of leading Indian businessmen including Homi Mody and Kasturbhai Lalbhai, who were not members of the Constituent Assembly, but were nominated to its advisory committees, contained a number of provisions favouring the propertied interests but did not include any economic rights for the people.

The Industries Act

The prolonged process of the formulation of the Industries (Development and Regulation) Act, 1951, clearly revealed the substantial influence wielded by Indian big business in the sphere of industrial policy. The two Select Committees set up to examine the Industries (Development and Control) Bill, 1949, included prominent businessmen. The first Select Committee, constituted on 6 April 1949 included among its members, three important businessmen: Ramnath Goenka (the Auditor of the Congress Legislature Party), Homi Mody and Padampat Singhania (who had been FICCI President in 1935). Ramnath Goenka was also nominated to the Second Select Committee set up on 4 September 1951.

The government consistently sought to reassure business interests who were critical of the proposed Bill. When a delegation of largely FICCI-affiliated industrialists met the First Select Committee on 5 August 1949, Shyama Prasad Mookerjee, the Minister for Industry and Supply, who was the Chairman of the committee, sought to reassure the business representatives present by stating that his committee, "could modify it (the Bill) even beyond recognition". All that was necessary was that the title and preamble of the bill "remained intact". Further, after the first select committee submitted its Report on 10 February 1950, the government just shelved the Report, and only referred it to the second select committee in September 1951, and then too, according to *Capital*, because of pressure from the Planning Commission.

During the final debate prior to the provisional Parliament's ratification of the Industries Bill, H.K. Mahatab the Minister for Commerce and Industry, sought to introduce an amendment which would have in effect prohibited the takeover of the management of a privately owned unit without compensation, and which was evidently a concession to the FICCI demand for the same. Because of the opposition from various MPs including T.N. Singh and R. Venkataraman, who had been members of the second select committee, Mahatab's attempt failed. However the businessman Syamnandan Sahaya's amendment that the takeover of management by the government be "authorise(d) for a period not exceeding five years", was accepted by Mahatab and passed by the Parliament. This was clearly a concession to business interests.

Whereas business circles were quite critical of the Industries Act initially, they later toned down their criticism. Further, a couple of years after the enactment of the Industries Act, R.G. Saraiya, the FICCI President, in a March 1953 letter to TTK, then the Minister for Commerce and Industry, noted that the two select committees had "both improved on business successes in obtaining concessions in the formulation of the industries that, were again a reflection of the prevailing political balance of forces, which as Shyama Prasad Mookerjee had admitted in Parliament, led to some industrialists being "extremely powerful in this land".

Similarly, the discussion in the Congress Working Committee on the resolution on the formation of the Planning Commission, revealed the anxiety on the part of some of the important sections of the Congress leadership to reassure the business community. Thus a passage in the original draft resolution which is referred to,

> the progressive elimination of social, political and economic exploitation and inequality, the motives of private gain in economic activity or organisation of society and the anti-social concentration of wealth and means of production..., was deleted.

Hence, during the process of what we have termed the establishment of the institutional framework for industrial policy, between 1948 and 1951, big business was able to wrest several vital concessions. These concessions and other lacunae in this institutional framework, allowed sufficient leeway in the implementation of industrial policy for the growth of the industrial houses, largely organised in FICCI, in later years.

Post-1951 Dilutions in Industrial Policy

Our examination of the industrial policy formulation and implementation in the First Five Year Plan period, also revealed significant concessions favouring Indian big business. In the First Plan, the investment for private sector industry was increased by more than 72 per cent over what was envisaged in the Draft Plan. Moreover in the revised First Plan, the major reliance for development was placed on the private sector. While planned investment in public sector industries was to be only Rs. 94 crores, it was to be as much as Rs. 383 crores in the private sector. It was, therefore, no surprise if FICCI leaders like Tulsidas Kilachand and G.D. Birla praised the revised plan.

The 1952-53 economic crisis aggravated Indian industrialists' fears of the competition from foreign private capital. At its Annual Session in 1953 therefore, FICCI adopted its famous "Swadeshi Resolution" deploring the government's attitude towards foreign capital. By May 1954 the economic situation eased, the FICCI attitude towards foreign capital softened. By January 1955, a FICCI sub-committee in its report "generally welcomed" the inflow of foreign capital. Thereafter the positions of FICCI and the government on the inflow of foreign private capital into India, more or less coincided. After eight years of continued growth in independent India, Indian industrialists had sufficient confidence that they would not be swamped by foreign competitors. Moreover they were interested in mutually advantageous collaborations and foreign private capital. Therefore, the earlier antagonism towards foreign capital, which was articulated on behalf of the Indian business circles by FICCI, no longer remained.

The 'Leftist' shift in Congress rhetoric, fuelled by the party's defeat in the Lok Sabha by-election in Agra, did not result in anti-business shifts in industrial policy. Nehru the 'Leftist' of the Congress leadership, at the FICCI Annual Session held in March 1954, reassured industrialists present "that no one in government is against big industry. We want (private) big industry to develop". In fact the acceptance in Parliament of the goal of a "socialist pattern" of society was a spontaneous move, of which the Left (Communist) MPs were sceptical.

The ensuing assembly elections in Andhra Pradesh, where the Communists posed a serious threat to the Congress, provided impetus for the Avadi Resolution of January 1955, where the Congress adopted the resolution on a "Socialistic Pattern of Society". At the Avadi Session however, Nehru had categorically stated the necessity "to have a private sector... and to give it full play within its field...".

Business circles were not perturbed by the 'Leftist' rhetoric at Avadi. *Commerce*, in its comment on the session, which was typical of the reactions of business circles, stated that the change of rhetoric "need not... cause any alarm in the private sector".

The satisfaction of business circles had been due to the manner in which industrial policy was implemented. Various proposals for nationalising particular industries or companies had been turned down by the government, for example TELCO in October 1954; commercial banking in December 1954; and foreign trade, cement, jute and plantations in early 1956. The manner in which major acts of nationalisation were undertaken, e.g. Air transport in 1953, the Imperial Bank in May 1955, life insurance in January 1956, and the Kolar Gold Fields in November 1956, revealed that the government's policy was not one of 'socialistic' nationalisation with an overall anti-big business orientation.

As has been brought out above, generous compensation was provided for in each case. A similar spirit of accommodation between the government and the Indian private sector, manifested itself in the process of the formulation of the Second Five Year Plan. The changes between the proposals in the Second Plan Frame of March 1955, and the finalised Second Plan, clearly exhibited concessions to business interests. The proposal that the state should "take up the factory production of certain consumer goods which are of strategic importance for the growth of the national economy", as well as proposed state entry "into such activities as banking, insurance, foreign trade or internal trade in selected commodities", made by Mahalanobis's proposed development expenditure of Rs. 4,300 crores and Rs. 2,248 crores, in the public and private sectors respectively, i.e. approximately a ratio of 2:1 in favour of the public sector, was also drastically modified, as the FICCI proposals to increase the plan outlay on the private sector apparently proved successful. The investment programme for the public sector was reduced to only Rs. 3,800 crores, while for the private sector it was increased to Rs. 2,400 crores, in the final Plan.

The 1956 Industrial Policy Resolution

The government's industrial policy in the entire period following the 1948 Industrial Policy Statement, had encouraged the growth of the private sector in general, and large industry in particular. However, at least by December 1954, the government had realised the need for a new industrial policy, which it was officially stated in Parliament "will be announced very shortly". With the new strategy enunciated in the Second Plan, of the public sector attaining "the commanding heights", a new Industrial Policy Resolution became even more imperative.

The Industrial Policy Resolution of the 30 April 1956, despite its socialist rhetoric contained major concessions to the private sector. Even in the case of the 17 industries listed in Schedule 'A', whose future development was reserved for the state, it was explicitly stated, "This does not preclude the expansion of the existing privately owned units, or the cooperation of private enterprise in the establishment of new units when the national interests so require". Moreover the clause in the 1948 Industrial Policy Statement that had stipulated that privately owned units in the industries reserved for the state, would be taken over after 10 years, was dropped, as FICCI had consistently demanded.

The Resolution referring to the 12 industries in Schedule 'B' stated that in these "private enterprise will also be expected to supplement the effort of the state". The industries not listed in either schedule were, of course, left open for the private sector. Therefore, apart from "Railways and air transport, arms and ammunition and atomic energy... (which was to) be developed as central government monopolies...", all other industries were potentially open to the private sector. G.D. Somani, MP and a FICCI leader, appreciated this Resolution, stating that there was more than enough left for the private sector. Compared therefore, with the 1948 Industrial Policy Statement, the 1956 resolution represented further concessions to business interests, rather than any genuine "socialist" advance.

Further Concessions to Big Business, 1956-1963

The 1956 Industrial Policy Resolution was reinterpreted in favour of Indian big business, almost on the morrow of its birth. Prior to the departure of the G.D. Birla led industrialists delegation to the USA, Canada and Western Europe in September 1957, a vital meeting between Nehru, TTK. (Finance Minister) and Morarji Desai (Commerce and Industries Minister) took place. As later recorded by the then Industrial Adviser to the government, it was decided to throw open certain industries included in Schedules 'A' and 'B', to the private sector. Thus the top circles of government decided, more or less secretly, to substantially modify the Industrial Policy Resolution, which was then barely a year old.

The concessions that were granted in the 1957 Budget when it was finalised, in response to FICCI pressure, is another instance of the influence of business circles. On the basis of the lobbying by FICCI and INSOA, one of its constituents, several concessions were made to the private sector in the finalised Budget, including the exemption of the shipping industry from wealth tax. The manner, in which business lobbies were able to enlist the support of influential MPs and Ministers, reflected the pervasive influence of business circles.

Of the 17 industries reserved for the state and Schedule 'A', no less than 7 were thrown open to the private sector around 1958. These included arms; heavy plant and machinery; heavy electrical plant machinery; processing of lead and zinc; the production of telephone cables and telegraphic equipment; and the generation and distribution of electricity as well as the production of coal.

Of the 12 industries listed under Schedule 'B', in as many as 9, the bulk of the production was in the private sector since 1957-58. Although expansion in the aluminium industry was allocated to the public sector in the Second Plan, the Birlas were allowed to conclude a collaboration agreement with Kaisers (USA) to set up a 20,000 ton plant. The machine tools, and the ferro-alloys and to steels industries were also further opened to the private sector. In the last, out of the total 261,000 tons licensed capacity, as much as 160, 000 tons were in the private sector. The basic chemicals and intermediates, as well as antibiotics and other essential drugs industries followed a similar pattern, as public sector projects were drastically curtailed, and the industries opened to the private sector in 1958-59. The fertiliser industry was also opened for private sector investments, as was the production of synthetic rubber. Production in the latter was wholly in the private sector.

Moreover, although in 1950-51, the nationalisation of road transport was accepted as government policy, this was finally rejected in early 1958. Private operators were in fact, assisted to set up viable operations. In the case of sea transport, the private sector was helped to grow through the Shipping Development Fund.

Thus within a few years of its enactment, the 1956 Industrial Policy Resolution was consistently reinterpreted, in order to facilitate the rapid growth of the large industrial houses.

The Ideological Retreat

The years 1958-59 were also marked by a considerable softening of the ideological postures of the government. While addressing the March 1958 session of FICCI, Nehru reassured industrialists that his government accepted that,

> the private sector is of great importance and fulfils an important purpose in the development of the country...(so that) it should be encouraged in every way.

Later, in March 1959, during a FICCI Luncheon Meeting, G.B. Pant, the Home Minister, stressed the "supplementary and complementary" nature of the public and private sector.

The ideological shift was accompanied by further relaxations in industrial policy towards the private sector. The earlier mandatory reference to the Licensing Committee, for the production of new articles by existing undertakings, if this did not involve the installation of additional machinery and the use of imported raw materials, was dropped.

The 1959 Budget contained concessions for the private sector. *Commerce,* praised Morarji Desai's proposals to abolish the wealth tax on companies and the excess dividends tax... "(as) a courageous step for Minister of a Socialist (sic) Government to take."

FICCI and the Swatantra Party

The Swatantra Party despite the pro-big business views did not elicit much support from the business community. As Minoo Masani himself noted big business was not inclined to support the new party. This, as Kochanek has shown was due to the conclusion of industrialists that the Swatantra Party had little hope of becoming a major political force in India.

The FICCI strategy continued therefore to be one of influencing the ruling party instead of direct participation in the political process, in the form of standing for elections or creating a new political party. Support to the Swatantra Party was low-key, and directed only at putting indirect pressure on the Congress.

Liberalisation of Licensing Policy, 1960

In early 1960, the government liberalised its industrial licensing policy. A letter from the Ministry of Commerce and Industry to FICCI, stated that these decisions had been taken after discussions between FICCI representatives and "officers of this Ministry". The government had decided to exempt industrial undertakings employing less than hundred workers, and with fixed assets of less than Rs. 10 lakhs, from applying for industrial licenses. It was later clarified that there could be exemptions even under the list of banned items, as applications could be put up by officers of the concerned Ministries, to the Licensing Committee for approval.

Later in July, September and November 1960, further concessions in industrial licensing were announced. These included the inclusion of as many as 49 more industries on the 'free' list, i.e. where licenses would be readily granted. Because of all these concessions, the period witnessed a liberal issue of licenses. Whereas, according to official figures, 773 licenses had been cleared in 1958, this increased to 997 in 1959 and was already 542 in the first six months of 1960.

The budget was also favourably received in business circles. *Commerce* found that Morarji Desai's budget "makes pleasant reading...the quantum of fresh tax burden (is) very much less than the anticipation of even optimists...".

Industrial Policy Concession in 1961

The policy of concessions in industrial policy to the private sector continued in 1961. Writing on industrial policy in late September 1961, the *Eastern Economist* noted that "of late... some new pragmatism has been discernible in the Union Government's industrial policy". In this connection it approvingly referred to the private sector being permitted to participate in the manufacture of heavy electrical machinery (a Schedule 'A' industry), in excess of the plant target.

The 1956 budget also contained concessions for Indian business. FICCI welcomed the reduction of taxes on companies, bonus shares, royalties, on inter-corporate dividends on minority shareholdings of foreign companies, and tax exemption for the total industry.

Even in the case of the Third Plan, a major concession was made to private industry, in the case of the targets in the cotton textile industry. In response to a FICCI request in May 1960, to the Planning Commission for more than 0.7 5 million additional spindles, the government agreed to license an additional 3 million spindles during the Plan Period. This was an important concession to FICCI, in view of the importance of the cotton textile industry to the private sector.

1962: Relaxations Continued

In February 1962, the government further liberalised licensing policy, allowing all industrial units having fixed assets not exceeding Rs. 10 lakhs, exemption from licensing, irrespective of the number of persons employed. A Schedule 'A' industry, special steels, and a Schedule 'B' industry, fertilisers, were thrown open to the private sector in 1962. This, as could be expected, was welcomed by business circles.

The government consistently displayed a conciliatory ideological attitude during this period. On its part, the business circles welcomed the Congress victory in the 1962 General Elections. Nehru at the 1962 FICCI session categorically stated that "Private enterprise is a good thing for India...(and that) suppression of private enterprise will be bad...".

The Dalmia-Jain Scandal

An event which caused much embarrassment to FICCI, including organisational problems, was the publication of the Vivian Bose Commission Report in early 1963, which indicted the management of the Dalmia-Jain companies as responsible for losses amounting to Rs. 2.6 crores to the investing public. Shriyans Prasad Jain, the then FICCI President, was indicted for being "directly concerned with the fraud..." in a number of cases. The Report caused a considerable public outcry and embarrassed big business, and FICCI in particular, considerably. Because of the furore over the Report, Nehru had difficulties in coming to inaugurate the FICCI Annual Session in 1963. However, the government took virtually no action on the basis of the Vivian Bose Commission Report. Evidently big business interests were sufficiently powerful to influence the government to take no action against a FICCI President and his family, despite their indictment on charges of fraud and other malpractices by a judicial officer.

Despite the embarrassment caused by this episode, FICCI

representatives succeeded in extracting concessions in the 1963 budget. FICCI had pleaded for a reduction in the proposed super profits tax on company profits. The concession was later granted in April 1963, by Morarji Desai, the then Finance Minister.

In December 1963, FICCI lobbied against a proposed change in the Companies Act under which a clause was to be inserted enabling the government to convert its loans to private sector companies into equity share capital, thus giving the former some control over the management. Because of business pressures, the Select Committee of Parliament to whom the Bill was sent, amended the loans conversion clause, making it prospective and not retrospective, as originally. Leftist Congressmen immediately put counter-pressure on the Congress leadership. Under their pressure, Nehru decided, after consultations with his Cabinet, to reverse the Select Committee recommendations.

This instance, like others examined before, demonstrates that the success of business lobbying depended on the political balance of forces, including within the ruling party. However, business circles were able to lobby excessively to virtually reduce the loan conversion clause to a dead-letter.

Industrial Policy and the Growth of Monopoly, 1964-66

In February 1964, with the release of the Mahalanobis Committee Report, the actual effect of the government's industrial policy, in encouraging the growth of the large industrial houses, was revealed. The Report categorically stated that,

> It is... evident that the working of the planned economy has contributed to this growth of big companies in Indian industry. The growth of the private sector...and especially of the big companies has been facilitated by the financial assistance rendered by public (financial) institutions....

Thus the official industrial policy including the policies of financial assistance by public financial institutions had contributed to the growth of Indian big business. The Report quite categorically noted that "concentration of economic power in the private sector is more than what could be justified as necessary on functional grounds...".

Not altogether surprisingly, the government chose not to have a discussion on the Mahalanobis Committee Report in Parliament. This in itself indicated its lack of interest in any discussion of how the officially sanctioned and financial growth of large private sector companies, and the concomitant increase in the concentration of economic power, could be curbed.

Just before the publication of the, Mahalanobis Committee Report, the Interim Report of the Swaminathan Committee was published in January 1964. In the Committee, all five of the non-official members were representatives of business: four from FICCI, and one from ASSOCHAM. Of the total of 10 members, fully half therefore, were from the private sector. As noted earlier, the very composition of the Committee was indicative of the government's sympathetic attitude towards big business. Moreover, the fact that FICCI had as many as four representatives on the Swaminathan Committee, clearly indicated the extent of its influence on government.

The major recommendations in the Interim Report were: (i) the government was advised to issue a "letter of intent" in the first instance to entrepreneurs applying for licenses, within about a month of receipt of the application. (ii) The second major recommendation related to a proposed "special procedure" for the licensing of "key" industries. In the list of 22 "key" industries, as many as 17 were Schedule A or B industries. For these industries, the entire licensing process was to be speeded up. Yet since the large bulk of these "key" industries were under the 1956 Industrial Policy Resolution, reserved for the public sector, these should not have been thrown open to the private sector at all.

Thus, the recommendations of the Swaminathan Committee were clearly pro-business, and represented a clear deviation from the stated industrial policy framework as symbolised even in the 1956 Industrial Policy Resolution. Yet, in view of the big business representation on the committee, such recommendations were inevitable.

In marked contrast to its attitude towards the Mahalanobis Committee Report which it virtually shelved, the government accepted the major recommendations of the Swaminathan

Committee. In so doing, it in effect accepted what was clear and considerable deviation from the Industrial Policy Resolution of 1956.

Industrial Policy in 1965: Father Concessions to Big Business

In this year the government decided to decontrol steel. Later from April onwards, FICCI leaders started lobbying for the decontrol of cement. The lobbying proved effective, and on 26th August, the Prime Minister Lal Bahadur Shastri announced the government's decision, in principle, to decontrol cement (decontrol was formalised later in 1966).

Shastri faced strong opposition within the Congress. The Congress Parliamentary Party's executive committee expressed grave misgivings over the decontrol of cement. Some members urged the government to reconsider its decision, and if necessary, to reverse it. However, at this stage, unlike December 1963, the Left with the Congress, was not sufficiently influential to provide a counter-check to business influences. Therefore, in consonance with the trend of concessions to business, of which the acceptance of the Swaminathan Committee's recommendations was the watermark, cement was decontrolled in the following year.

The publication of the Monopolies Inquiry Commission (MIC) Report in December 1965, did not change the situation. The MIC Report accepted the growth of concentration of economic power as a proved fact. Its recommendations included a proposal for the establishment of countervailing power against monopolies by the public sector through public sector units. However, these recommendations were never implemented. Like the Mahalanobis Committee Report before it, the MIC Report was never discussed in Parliament. This fact itself is indicative of the government's disregard for even limited anti-monopoly measures.

1966: Culmination of the Process of Liberalisation of Industrial Policy

The report of the reconstituted Swaminathan Committee, (which like its predecessors had very substantial big business representation), in February 1966, provided impetus to the further liberalisation of industrial policy. In the course of his statement in the Rajya Sabha on 19 May 1966, D. Sanjivayya, the Minister of Industrial Development and Company Affairs, accepted the faulty foreign exchange criterion as put forward by the reconstituted Swaminathan Committee, as a justification for the delicensing of 11 industries.

In late April 1966, Prime Minister Indira Gandhi in a speech over All India Radio, while reiterating her government's commitment to "the objective of a socialist and democratic society...", stressed that this did not involve any doctrinaire deal adherence to some dogmas. This statement was probably a justification for the liberalised pro-business industrial policy of the Congress government. This speech was welcomed by business circles, which was perhaps what the Prime Minister intended.

On 20th July, the paper and newsprint, and the handtools industries were delicensed. On 14th November, after a meeting with FICCI representatives, 23 more items were delicensed, of which most had been recommended for delicensing by FICCI. Earlier, on 28th October, there had been another significant liberalisation of licensing policy. Industrial units were permitted to manufacture new articles without obtaining licenses, if they fulfilled certain conditions.

The budget announced at the end of February 1966, contained several tax concessions for big business, largely on the lines proposed earlier by FICCI.

The liberalisation of industrial policy in this year, was only a culmination of the policy of piecemeal concessions to the private sector, increasingly adopted by a government, which throughout this period did not have to face any substantial countervailing pressure.

1947 to 1966: Industrial Policy for Big Business Growth

The entire post-independence period is marked by a significant and secular increase in the assets of the large industrial houses. This however, is not peculiar to India, but is a consequence of the capitalist path of development. As Marx first noted, with the development of capitalism there is a tendency for the centralisation and concentration of capital, which leads to the development of monopolies (Marx, *Capital,* Vol. 1, 586-589; 714-715).[1] This according to Marx, is a feature of the general law of capitalist accumulation (Marx, year of publication not defined, 586-589). In the development of capitalism in India, the growth of the monopoly stratum would appear to be a consequence of the operation of this general law. As we have noted on a number of occasions, there has been a secular growth in the assets of the large industrial houses, during the period of this study. In this respect, the general prediction by Zakir Husain (who later became the third President of India), made in 1944, about the development of Indian capitalism appears quite perspicacious. He predicted that,

> the stage seems to...(be) set for the growth of an Asian capitalism in which India appears marked for a big role—that this new capitalism, although it will have its distinct individuality, will not be very much different from its Western predecessor can be easily assumed. The forces that can be great to range themselves against the will... not be strong enough stop the new growth (Husain, 1967: 199-200).

It is evident from the preceding analysis, that apart from its specific features, Indian capitalism has not been very different from Western capitalism, in as much as it has led to the continued growth of the large monopoly houses and monopoly stratum of the Indian capitalist class. While it is quite apparent that this growth of big business or the big bourgeoisie, has been very substantially facilitated by the manner in which industrial policies were formulated and implemented, the objective nature of this continued growth, rising as it does from the very dynamic of the development of capitalism should not be lost sight of. The subjective factor, in this case the role of the state, in promoting the growth of Indian big business, was not the only factor, of development pursued by the political leadership of free India. There was an obvious interconnection between the two factors. The growth of big business increased its economic and political power and consequently its leverage with government, leading to further pro-big business concessions in the development and enforcement of industrial policy.

The consequence of the operation of these two factors in the development of capitalism in India in general, and in industrial policy in particular, was that, as Timberg (1978: 81) has put it, "essentially the period from 1951 to 1962 might be described as the Golden Age of Indian private capital". However, as we have seen above, the entire period from 1947 to 1966, may be described as a "Golden Age" for Indian big business, in particular. Writing in 1963, Bharat Ram, the then FICCI President, found it possible to state, probably with considerable satisfaction, that,

> "Politically, the last 25 years or more (after independence) may be called the period of the Indian National Congress. Economically, the period may be called the period of the Federation which aligned itself with the political movement for Independence and translated national aspirations into economic terms" (Ram, 1963: 420).

This happy position for the Federation, and the stratum of Indian big business is represented, was also a consequence of the generally astute policies followed by the Birla-led elite that dominated FICCI. During the national movement for independence, FICCI was able to play a mediating role between the British Raj and the Congress, without provoking the hostility of the former or losing the sympathy of, or influence with, the latter. Particularly, starting from the 1930s, the Federation was able to establish a close relationship with the conservative sections of the Congress leadership, and later with Nehru himself. This relationship enabled FICCI to start with an advantage vis-a-vis other pressure groups, in their efforts to influence government policy, following the advent of Independence.).

In the entire period from 1947 to 1966, there appears to be no marked change in the pattern of the development of industrial policy, specifically in the context of the events favourable to Indian big business. While it seems clear that FICCI's relationships with the Congress government's leadership enabled this constituent of Indian big business to influence the formulation as well as the implementation of industrial policy in its own favour, there appear to be no significant discontinuities in this process. In the light of the evidence brought out in this study, it appears that the process of interaction between Indian big business and government, resulted in a more or less continuous process of piecemeal concessions from 1947 onwards to the private sector in general, and to Indian big business, in particular. These processes finally culminated in the wide-ranging liberalisation of industrial licensing policy in 1965 and 1966. The consequence of these processes: of both the process of interaction between FICCI and government, and the process of change in industrial policy, was the dilution of those elements of earlier stated industrial policy, which acted as impediments to the growth and development of Indian big business. During the post-independence years, from 1947 to 1966, there appears to be a secular trend of piecemeal concessions in the sphere of industrial policy by the Congress government to Indian big business. This entire process apparently culminated in the wide-ranging decontrol and delicensing carried out in 1965 and 1966. By 1966, the industrial policy framework that existed, embodied major deviations from the 1956 Industrial Policy Resolution, and was, of course, a far cry from the radical anti-monopoly policy formulated in the Report of the AICC's Economic Programme Committee of January 1948. This development of industrial policy, as we have noted on several occasions above, was not a fortitious, autonomous or inevitable process. The manner in which industrial policy was formulated and implemented during these post-independence years, was very largely a consequence of the sustained lobbying by Indian big business, of which FICCI was the pre-eminent lobby. In that sense, to reiterate Bharat Ram's somewhat self-satisfied statement, "Economically, the period may be called the period of the Federation...".

REFERENCES

1. This was a process also examined by later Marxists cf. Bukharin, Nikolai (1973), *Imperialism and World Economy* (New York and London: Monthly Review Press), pp. 116-121; and

Preobrazhensky, E. (1965), *The New Economics* (London: Oxford University Press), pp. 150-160. Contemporary discussions are by Sweezy, Paul M. (1968), *The Theory of Capitalist Development* (New York and London: Monthly Review Press); and Mandel, Ernest (1971) *Marxist Economic Theory* (Calcutta and Delhi: Rupa Publications), pp. 162-166. According to Marx's definition, the 'concentration' of capital is the more important process, and refers to the combining of capitals already in existence with the expropriation of smaller capitalists by larger ones. Cf. Marx, year of publication not dated, 586-587.

Bibliography

(A) PRIMARY SOURCES

1. India: Official Reports and Publications

Government of India (1947), *Report of the Advisory Planning Board* (Government of India: New Delhi).

Government of India (1965), *Report of the Monopolies Enquiry Commission* (Manager of Publications: New Delhi).

Government of India, Industrial Policy Statement, 1948 to 1991, all available at: http://www.dcmsme.gov.in/policies/iip.htm

Hazari, R.K. (1966), *Industrial Planning and Licensing Policy, Interim Report to Planning Commission* (Manager of Publications: New Delhi).

Hazari, R.K. (1967), *Industrial Planning and Licensing Policy, Final Report* (Manager of Publications: New Delhi).

Ministry of Commerce and Industry (1952), *Economic Controls in India* (Manager of Publications: New Delhi).

Ministry of Commerce and Industry, Department of Company Law Administration (1963), *Report of the Commission of Enquiry on the Administration of Dalmia-Jain Companies* (Manager of Publications: New Delhi).

Ministry of Finance, Department of Economic Affairs (1952), *Report of the Company Law Committee, 1952* (Manager of Publications: New Delhi).

Ministry of Industrial Development, Internal Trade and Company Affairs, Department of Industrial Development (1969), *Report of the Industrial Policy Inquiry Committee, Main Report*, Vol. I-IV (Manager of Publications: New Delhi).

Ministry of Industry (1964), *Final Report of the Industries Development Procedures Committee* (Manager of Publications: New Delhi).

Ministry of Industry (1966), *Final Report of the Reconstituted Industries Development Procedures Committee* (Manager of Publications: New Delhi).

Ministry of Information and Broadcasting, Publications Division (1949), *Independence and After, Speeches by Jawaharlal Nehru, September 1946 to May 1949* (Publications Division: New Delhi).

Ministry of Information and Broadcasting, Publications Division (1957), *Speeches of TTK Krishnamachari* (Manager of Publications: Delhi).

Ministry of Law (1959), *The Life Insurance Corporation Act, 1956,* (Manager of Publications: Delhi).

Ministry of Law, Department of Company Affairs (1966), *Report of the Managing Agency Enquiry Committee* (Manager of Publications: New Delhi).

Namjoshi, M.V. (1969), *Licensing and Planning, 1956-1966, Report Submitted to the Industrial Licensing Policy Enquiry Committee.*

Planning Commission (1951), T*he First Five Year Plan, A Draft Outline* (Manager of Publications: New Delhi).

Planning Commission (1952), *The First Five-Year Plan* (Manager of Publications: New Delhi).

Planning Commission (1955), *Papers Relating to the Formulation of the Second Five Year Plan* (Manager of Publications: New Delhi).

Planning Commission (1956), *The Second Five Year Plan* (Manager of Publications: New Delhi).

Planning Commission (1957), *Review of the First Five Year Plan* (Manager of Publications: Delhi).

Planning Commission (1958), *Appraisals and Prospectus of the Second Five Year Plan* (Manager of Publications: New Delhi).

Planning Commission (1959), *Main Issues Relating to the Third Five Year Plan* (Manager of Publications: New Delhi).

Planning Commission (1962), *The Third Five Year Plan* (Manager of Publications: New Delhi).

Planning Commission (1963), *The Planning Process* (Manager of Publications: New Delhi).

Planning Commission (1964), *The Report of the Committee on Distribution of Income and Levels of Living, Part I* (Manager of Publications: New Delhi).

Planning Commission (1966), *The Fourth Five Year Plan: A Draft Outline* (Manager of Publications: New Delhi).

2. India: Parliament

Constituent Assembly Debates (1948-50), Official Report in 12 Volumes (Manager of Publications: New Delhi).

Constituent Assembly Debates (Legislative) (1948-50), (Manager of Publications: New Delhi).

Lok Sabha Debates (Lok Sabha Secretariat: New Delhi).

Lok Sabha Secretariat (1967), *Ninth Report of the Estimates Committee on Industrial Licensing* (Lok Sabha Secretariat: New Delhi).

Parliament of India (1949), *Report of the Select Committee on the Industries (Development and Regulation) Bill, 1949* (Parliament Library: New Delhi).

Parliament of India (1950), *Report of the Select Committee on the Industries (Development and Regulation) Bill, 1950, as amended* (Parliament Library: New Delhi).

Parliamentary Debates (1950-52), (Manager of Publications: New Delhi).

Rajya Sabha Debates (Rajya Sabha Secretariat: New Delhi).

3. Proceedings, Reports, Pamphlets of Chamber of Commerce, Industrial Associations, other Associations and Political Parties

Associated Chamber of Commerce and Industry of India, Proceedings of the Annual General Meeting of the Associated Chamber of Commerce (ASSOCHAM: Calcutta).

Cement Manufacturers Association (1965), Fifth Annual Report, 1965 (CMA: Bombay).

Communist Party of India, Central Party Education Department (1974), Guidelines of the History of the Communist Party of India (CPI: New Delhi).

Congress Socialist Forum (1957), Keep the Flame Alive: A Thesis by a Group of Congress Workers (CSF: New Delhi).

Federation of Indian Chambers of Commerce and Industry (1927-1966), Proceedings of the Executive Committee, Vol. I, 1927-1966 (FICCI: New Delhi).

FICCI (1927-1966), Correspondence and Relevant Documents for the Year, Vol. II, 1927-1966 (FICCI: New Delhi).

FICCI (1927-1966), Proceedings of Annual Meetings, Vol. III, 1927-1966 (FICCI: New Delhi).

FICCI (1930), Representation Submitted to H.E. the Viceroy of the Committee of the Federation on the Present Political Situation in India in 1930, (FICCI: New Delhi).

FICCI (1951), Silver Jubilee Souvenir, 1927-1951 (FICCI: New Delhi).

FICCI (1954), Imports and Industrial Development (FICCI: New Delhi).

FICCI (1955), The Second Five Year Plans (FICCI: New Delhi).

FICCI (1958), Industrial Progress – Who Gains (FICCI: New Delhi).

FICCI (1960), Draft of the Third Plan (FICCI: New Delhi).

FICCI (1963), Seminar on Problems of Private and Public Industrial Undertakings (FICCI: New Delhi).

FICCI (1965), The Constitution of the Private Sector Industries During the Plans (FICCI: New Delhi).
FICCI (1966), 'Men of FICCI' (FICCI: New Delhi).
FICCI (1966), Draft of the Fourth Plan: An Appraisal (FICCI: New Delhi).
FICCI (1966), Fourth Plan: Better Performance or Bigger Size (FICCI: New Delhi).
FICCI (1966), Procedures of Industrial Licensing (FICCI: New Delhi).
FICCI (1966), Whither Rupee (FICCI: New Delhi).
FICCI (1969), Foreign Collaborations (FICCI: New Delhi).
FICCI (1969), Private Industry for National Development (FICCI: New Delhi).
FICCI (1969), Procedures For Industrial Licensing Since 1960 (FICCI: New Delhi).
FICCI (1976), Five Decades of Progress (FICCI: New Delhi).
FICCI (1976), Memorandum of Articles of Association of the Federation of Chambers of Commerce and Industry (FICCI: New Delhi).
Forum of Free Enterprise (1966), Basic Documents (FFE: Bombay).
Forum of Free Enterprise (n.d.), The Forum of Free Enterprises (FFE: Bombay).
Indian Chamber of Commerce (1965), Government and Business (Text of Speeches at the Indian Chamber of Commerce, Calcutta, 11 April 1965, by G.L. Tanda, Satyanaraian Sinha and G.D. Birla) (ICC: Calcutta).
Indian Industrial and Commercial Congress (1927), Report of the Fourth Session of the IICC (IICC: Calcutta).
Indian National Congress (1956), Report of the General Secretaries, from January 1955 to February 1956 (Indian National Congress: Amritsar).
Indian National Congress, All India Congress Committee (n.d.), Resolutions on Economic Policy and Programme, 1924-1954 (AICC: New Delhi).
Swatantra Party (1959), Swatantra Party Preparatory Convention (Swatantra Party: Bombay).

4. Unpublished or Restricted Documents and Papers

Kaur, Jitender (1976), *Role of Pressure Groups in the Process of Decision-Making: A Study of FICCI*, M.Phil. Dissertation, Centre for Political Studies, School of Social Sciences, Jawaharlal Nehru University, New Delhi, mimeo.
Kaviraj, Nilanjana (1978), *India's Policy of Nonalignment: A Study in its Origins and Evolution, 1947-1964*, Ph.D. Thesis, School of

International Studies, Jawaharlal Nehru University, New Delhi, mimeo.

Markovits, Claude (1978), *Indian Business and Nationalist Politics from 1931 to 1939: The Political Attitude of the Indigenous Capitalist Class in Relation to the Crisis of the Colonial Economy and to the Rise of the Congress Party*, Ph.D. Thesis, University of Cambridge, mimeo.

Purshotamdas Thakurdas Papers, Nehru Memorial Museum and Library, New Delhi.

(B) SECONDARY SOURCES

(1) (a) *Newspapers and Periodicals*

- *AICC Economic Review* (New Delhi).
- *Capital* (Calcutta).
- *Commerce* (Bombay).
- *Company News and Notes* (New Delhi).
- *Congress Bulletin* (New Delhi).
- *Eastern Economist* (New Delhi).
- *Economic and Political Weekly* (Bombay).
- *Economic Times* (Bombay).
- *Economic Weekly* (Bombay).
- *FICCI Fortnightly Review* (New Delhi).
- *FICCI News and Notes* (New Delhi).
- *FICCI Newsletter* (New Delhi).
- *Hindustan Times* (New Delhi).
- *New Age (Weekly)* (New Delhi).
- *New Age (Monthly)* (New Delhi).
- *Times of India* (New Delhi).
- *Young Indian* (New Delhi).

(b) Who's Who and Yearbooks

- *Times of India Who's Who and Yearbook*, Various Issues
- *Lok Sabha Who's Who*, Various Issues
- *Rajya Sabha Who's Who*, Various Issues

(2) Books

Aiyar, S. P. and P. Srinivasan (1965), *Studies in Indian Democracy* (Allied Publishers: New Delhi).

Almond, G.A. and G.B. Powell Jr. (1966), *Comparative Politics: Developmental Approaches* (Amerind: New Delhi).

Antonova, K. et al. (1978), *A History of India*, Vol. II (Progress Publishers: Moscow).

Bagchi, Amiya K. (1975), *Private Investment in India: 1900-1939* (Orient Longman: Madras).

Baldwin, George B. (1959), *Industrial Growth in South India* (Free Press: New York).

Basu, S.K. (1958), *The Managing Agency System in Prospect and Retrospect* (Word Press: Calcutta).

Berna, James (1960), *Industrial Entrepreneurship in Madras State* (Asia: Bombay).

Bettelheim, Charles (1977), *India Independent* (Khosla: New Delhi).

Bhagwati, Jagdish N. and Padma Desai (1970), *India, Planning for Industrialisation and Trade Policies Since 1951* (National Bureau of Economic Research: New York).

Bhagwati, Jagdish N. and T.N. Srinivasan (1976), *Foreign Trade Regimes and Economic Development: India* (National Bureau of Economic Research: New York).

Birla, G.D. (1950), *The Path to Prosperity* (The Leader Press: Allahabad).

Birla, G.D. (1953), *In the Shadow of the Mahatma* (Orient Longman: Calcutta).

Birla, G.D. (1980), *Towards Swadeshi: Wide-ranging Correspondence with Gandhiji* (Bharatiya Vidya Bhavan: Bombay).

Birla, L.N. (1969), *Struggle for Growth* (World Press: Calcutta).

Brady, Robert (1943), *Business as a System of Power* (Columbia University Press: New York).

Braunthal, Gerald (1965), *The Federation of German Industry in Politics* (Cornell University Press: Ithaca).

Brecher, Michael (1966), *Nehru: A Political Biography* (Cambridge University Press: London).

Brecher, Michael (1966), *Succession in India* (Oxford University Press: London).

Brown, Judith M. (1972), *Gandhi's Rise to Power: Indian Politics, 1915-1922* (Cambridge University Press: Cambridge).

Buchanan, Daniel M. (1966), *The Development of Capitalistic Enterprises in India* (Frank Cass: London).

Bukharin, Nikolai (1973), *Imperialism and World Economy* (Monthly Review Press: New York and London).

Burman, Debajyoti (1950), *Mystery of Birla House,* Vol. I-II, (Udayana Press: Calcutta).

Chandra, Bipan (1969), *The Rise and Growth of Economic Nationalism in India* (People's Publishing House: New Delhi).

Chandra, Bipan (1979), *Nationalism and Colonialism in Modern India* (Orient Longman: New Delhi).

Chaube, Shibani Kinkar (1973), *Constituent Assembly of India: Springboard of Revolution* (People's Publishing House: New Delhi).

Chaudhuri, Asim (1975), *Private Economic Power in India – A Study in Genesis and Concentration* (People's Publishing House: New Delhi).

Chinai, Babubhai M. (1972), *India's March Towards Democratic Socialism: A Businessman's Perspective* (Shri Bhirhad Bharatiya Samaj: Bombay).

Das, Durga (ed.) (1973), *Sardar Patel's Correspondence, 1945-1950,* Vol. I-X, (Navjivan Publishing House: Ahmedabad).

Dasgupta, A. and Nitish Sengupta (1978), *Government and Business in India* (Allied Publishers: Calcutta).

Dasgupta, L.R. (1946), *Indian Chamber of Commerce and Commercial Associations* (Eastern Chamber of Commerce: Calcutta).

Dasgupta, Ranajit (1970), *Problems of Economic Transition: Indian Case Study* (National Press: Calcutta).

Desai, A.R. (1976), *Social Background of Indian Nationalism* (Popular Prakashan: Bombay).

Deshmukh, C.D. (1957), *Economic Development in India: 1946-1956* (Asia: Bombay).

Deshmukh, C.D. (1974), *The Course of My Life* (Orient Longman: New Delhi).

Dhekney, M.R. (1971), *Chambers of Commerce and Business Associations in India* (Popular Prakashan: New Delhi).

Dutt, R. Palme (1970), *India Today* (Manisha: Calcutta).

Duverger, Maurice (1972), *Party Politics and Pressure Groups* (Thomas Nelson: London).

Eckstein, Harry (1960), *Pressure Group Politics: The Case of the British Medical Association* (Stanford University Press: Stanford).

Ehrmann, Henry W. (ed.) (1958), *Interest Groups on Four Continents* (University of Pittsburg Press: Pittsburg).

Ehrmann, Henry W. (ed.) (1958), *Organised Business in France* (Princeton University Press: Princeton).

Erdman, Howard L. (1967), *The Swatantra Party and Indian Conservatism* (Cambridge University Press; Cambridge).

Erdman, Howard L. (1971), *Political Attitudes of Indian Industry: A Case Study of the Baroda Business Elite* (Oxford University Press: New York).

Fadia, Babulal (1980), *Pressure Groups in Indian Politics* (Radiant: New Delhi).

Frankel, Francine R. (1978), *India's Political Economy, 1947-1977: The Gradual Revolution* (Princeton University Press: Princeton).

Gadgil, D.R. (1962), *Planning and Economic Policy in India* (Gokhale Institute: Poona).

Gadgil, D.R. and M.V. Namjoshi (1959), *Origin of the Modern Indian Business Class: An Interim Report* (Institute of Pacific Relations: New York).

Gopal, Sarvepalli (1976 and 1979), *Jawaharlal Nehru: A Biography*, Vol. I-II, (Oxford University Press: New Delhi).

Gordon, A.D.D. (1978), *Businessmen and Politics: Rising Nationalism and a Modernising Economy in Bombay, 1918-1933* (Manohar Publishers: New Delhi).

Gough, Kathleen and Hari P. Sharma (1973), *Imperialism and Revolution in South Asia* (Monthly Review Press: New York and London).

Goyal, S.K. (1971), *Industrial Regulation by Government*, (Indian Institute of Public Administration: New Delhi).

Goyal, S.K. (1979), *Monopoly Capital and Public Policy* (Allied Publishers: New Delhi).

Goyal, S.K. et al. (1967), *Banking Institutions and Indian Economy: A Critical Review* (United India Press: New Delhi).

Gupta, Sobhanlal Datta (1979), *Justice and the Political Order in India* (K.P. Bagchi: Calcutta).

Hanson, A.H. (1966), *The Process of Planning* (Oxford University Press: London).

Harris, F.R. (1968), *Jamsetji Nusserwanji Tata: A Chronicle of Life* (Blackie: Bombay).

Hazari, R.K. (1961), *Big Business in India: A Study of Ownership and Control* (All India Trade Union Congress: New Delhi).

Hazari, R.K. (1966), *The Structure of the Corporate Private Sector* (Asia: Bombay).

Husain, Zakir (1967), *Capitalism: Essays in Understanding* (Asia: Bombay).

India International Centre (IIC), (1966), *Social Responsibility of Business* (Manaktalas: Bombay).

Jayakar, M.R. (1958 and 1959), *The Story of My Life*, Vol. I-II (Asia: Bombay).

Jog, N.G. (1969) *Saga of Scindia* (A Golden Jubilee Volume) (Scindia Steam Navigation Company: Bombay).

Joshi, Arun (1975), *Lala Sri Ram: A Study in Entrepreneurship and Industrial Management* (Orient Longman: New Delhi).

Joshi, L.A. (1965), *Control of Industry in India: A Study in Aspects of Combination and Concentration* (Vora: Bombay).

Kalelkar, Kaka (ed.) (1951), *To a Gandhian Capitalist: Correspondence Between Mahatma Gandhi and Jamnalal Bajaj and Members of His Family* (Hind Kitabs: Bombay).

Kanoria, S.S. (1972), *New Horizons for Business* (New India Printing Company: Calcutta).

Karanjia, R.K. (1960), *The Mind of Mr. Nehru: An Interview* (George Allen & Unwin: London).

Karnik, V.B. (1980), *M. N. Roy* (National Book Trust: New Delhi).

Key, V.O. Jr. (1959), *Politics, Parties and Pressure Groups*, 4th edition (Crowell: New York).

Khanolkar, G.P. (1969), *Walchand Hirachand: Man, His Time and Achievements*, (n.d.: Bombay).

Kidron, Michael (1965), *Foreign Investments in India*, (Oxford University Press: London).

Kochanek, Stanley A. (1968), *The Congress Party of India*, (Princeton University Press: Princeton).

Kochanek, Stanley A. (1974), *Business and Politics in India*, (University of California Press: California).

Kothari, Rajni (1970), *Politics in India* (Orient Longman: New Delhi).

Kothari, Rajni (1976), *Democratic Polity and Social Change in India* (Allied Publishers: New Delhi).

Krishnan, T.V. Kunhi (1971), *Chavan and the Troubled Decade* (New Delhi).

Kulkarni, V. (1951), *A Family of Patriots: The Bajaj Family* (Bombay).

Kurein, K. Matthew (ed.) (1975), *India: State and Society* (Orient Longman: Madras).

Kust, Matthew J. (1964), *Foreign Enterprises in India* (University of North Carolina Press: Chapel Hill).

Levkovsky, A.I. (1964), *Capitalism in India: Basic Trends in its Development* (People's Publishing House: New Delhi).

Lokanathan, P.S. (1935), *Industrial Organisation in India* (Allen & Unwin: London).

Low, D.A. (1968), *Soundings in Modern South Asian History* (nd.: London).

Macpherson, C.B. (1977), *The Life and Times of Liberal Democracy*, (Oxford University Press: Oxford).

Malaviya, H.D. (1965) *The Danger of Right Reaction*, (New Delhi).

Malenbaum, Wilfred (1962), *Prospects for Indian Development* (Allen & Unwin: London).

Mandel, Ernest (1971), *Marxist Economic Theory* (Rupa: New Delhi and Calcutta).

Mankekar, D.R. (1968), *Homi Mody: A Many Splendoured Life* (Popular Prakashan: Bombay).

Martinussen, John (1980), *The Public Industrial Sector in India* (Institute of Political Science: University of Aarhus, Denmark).

Marx, Karl (n.d.), *Capital*, Vol. I (Progress Publishers: Moscow).

Mehta, Asoka (1950), *Who Owns India?* (Chetna Prakashan:

Hyderabad).

Mehta, M.M. (1952), *Combination Movement in Indian Industry* (Friends Book Depot: Allahabad).

Mehta, M.M. (1961), *Structure of Indian Industries* (Popular Book Depot: Bombay).

Misra, B.B. (1961), *The Indian Middle Classes* (Oxford University Press: Oxford).

Mohnot, S.K. (1962), *Concentration of Economic Power in India* (Chaitanya Publishing House: Allahabad).

Moraes, Frank (1957), *Sir Purshotamdas Thakurdas* (Asia: Bombay).

Morris-Jones W.H. (1978), *The Government and Politics of India* (B.I. Publications: New Delhi).

Mukharji, P.B. (1967), *Social Responsibilities of Business* (Conference on Social Responsibility of Business: Calcutta).

Munshi, K.M. (1967), *The Indian Constitutional Documents,* Vol. I (Bharatiya Vidya Bhavan: Bombay).

Myrdal, Gunnar (1968), *Asian Drama: An Inquiry into the Poverty of Nations,* Vol. I-III (Allen Lane: London).

Namboodiripad, E.M.S. (1958), *The Mahatma and the Ism* (People's Publishing House: New Delhi).

Natarajan, L. (1956), *American Shadow over India* (People's Publishing House: New Delhi).

National Council of Applied Economic Research (NCAER) (1959), *The Managing Agency System* (Asia: New Delhi).

Nayar, Baldev Raj (1972), *The Modernization Imperative and Indian Planning* (Vikas Publishing House: New Delhi).

Nehru, Jawaharlal (1956), *The Discovery of India* (Signet Press: Calcutta).

Nehru, Jawaharlal (1958), *A Bunch of Old Letters* (Asia: Bombay).

Nehru, Jawaharlal (1962), *An Autobiography* (Allied Publishers: New Delhi).

Nehru, Jawaharlal (1971), *Selected Works* (Orient Longman: New Delhi).

Nigam, R.K. and N.C. Chowdhury (1961), *The Corporate Sector in India: A Factual Representation of Long and Short-term Trends* (Manager of Publications: New Delhi).

Nigam, R.K. and N.O. Joshi (1961), *The Pattern of Company Directorships in India* (Manager of Publications: New Delhi).

Ornstein, Norman J. and Shirley Elder (1978), *The Interests Groups, Lobbying and Policy-making,* (Congressional Quarterly Press: Washington, D.C.).

Pandey, B.N. (1979), *The Indian Nationalist Movement, 1885-1947: Selected Documents* (Macmillan: New Delhi).

Paranjape, H.K. (1964), *The Planning Commission: A Descriptive Account* (Indian Institute of Public Administrative: New Delhi).

Paranjape, H.K. (1974), *India's Strategy for Industrial Growth: An Appraisal* (n.d.: Bombay).

Paranjape, H.K. (1976), *The Poverty of Policy and Essays in Economic Policy and Administration* (Somaiya: Bombay).

Park, Richard L. and Irene Tinker (1959), *Leadership and Political Institutions in India* (Princeton University Press: Princeton).

Parvate, T.V. (1962), *Jamnalal Bajaj*, (Navjivan Prakashan: Allahabad).

Pavlov, V.I. (1964), *The Indian Capitalist Class: A Historical Study* (People's Publishing House: Bombay).

Pavlov, V.I. et. al. (1975), *India: Social and Economic Development (18th-20th Centuries)* (Progress Publishers: Moscow).

Payer, Cheryl (1974), *The Debt Trap* (Monthly Review Press: New York and London).

Preobrazensksky, E. (1965), *The New Economics* (Oxford University Press: London).

Raj, K.N. (n.d.), *The Politics and Economics of "Intermediate Regimes"* (Gokhale Institute: Poona).

Ranadive, B.T. (1953), *India's Five Year Plan* (Current Book House: Bombay).

Ranadive, B. T. (1954), *The Crisis of Indian Economy* (People's Publishing House: Bombay).

Rao, B. Shiva (ed.) (1967), *The Framing of India's Constitution: Select Documents*, Vol. I-V (Indian Institute of Public Administration: New Delhi).

Rao, P. Chentsal (1966), *Private Enterprise in Indian Economy* (Vora: Bombay).

Rao, V.K.R.V. (ed.) (1971), *Values and Economic Development – Report of Social Responsibility in Business* (Vikas Publishers: New Delhi).

Ray, Rajat (1979), *Industrialisation in India: Growth and Conflict in the Private Corporate Sector, 1914-47* (Oxford University Press: New Delhi).

Rosen, George (1951), *Industrial Change in India* (Asia: Bombay).

Rosen, George (1962), *Some Aspects of Industrial Finance in India* (Asia: Bombay).

Rosen, George (1970), *Democracy and Economic Change in India* (University of California: Berkeley).

Roy, Ajit (1965), *Planning in India: Achievements and Problems* (National Press: Calcutta).

Roy, Ajit (n.d.), *Monopoly Capitalism in India* (Naya Prokash: Calcutta).

Roy, N. C. (1972), *Mystery of Bajoria-Jalan House* (The Author: Calcutta).

Rungta, Radhe Shyam (1979), *The Rise of Business Corporation in India, 1851-1900* (Cambridge University Press: Cambridge).

Sabade, B.R. and M.V. Namjoshi (1967), *Chambers of Commerce in India*, (Asia Publishers: Poona).

Sabade, B.R. and M.V. Namjoshi (1977), *Chambers of Commerce and Trade Associations in India* (Shubhada Saraswat: Poona).

Sarkar, Sumit (1973), *The Swadeshi Movement in Bengal, 1903-1908*, (People's Publishing House: New Delhi).

Sen, Mohit (1977), *Revolution in India: Path and Problems* (People's Publishing House: New Delhi).

Sen, Sunil Kumar (1975), *The House of Tata (1839-1939)*, (Progressive Publishers: Calcutta).

Shah, K.T. (1947), *National Planning: Principles and Administration* (National Planning Committee Series) (Vora: Bombay).

Sharma, R.C. et al. (1977), *Modern India: Heritage and Achievement* (G.D. Birla 80th Birthday Commemoration Volume Committee: New Delhi).

Shroff, A.D. (1964), *Finance and Industry in India* (Forum of Free Enterprise: Bombay).

Singh, Khushwant and Arun Joshi (1968), *Shri Ram: A Biography* (Asia: Bombay).

Singh, Tarlok (1969), *Towards an Integrated Society* (Orient Longman: New Delhi).

Singh, Tarlok (1974), *Indian Development Experience* (Macmillan: New Delhi).

Singh, V.B. (ed.) (1965), *Economic History of India, 1857-1956* (Allied Publishers: New Delhi).

Sitaramayya, Pattabhi (1947), *The History of the Indian National Congress*, Vol. I-II (Padma Publishers: Bombay).

Society for Democracy (1972), *Monopolies and Public Policy* (People's Publishing House: New Delhi).

Subramaniam, C. (1972), *India of My Dreams* (Orient Longman: New Delhi).

Sweezy, Paul M. (1968), *The Theory of Capitalist Development*, (Monthly Review Press: New York and London).

Thakurdas, Purshotamdas, J.R.D. Tata, G.D. Birla et al. (1944), *A Plan of Economic Development for India*, Part I-II (The Commercial Printing Press: Bombay).

Timberg, Thomas A. (1978), *The Marwaris* (Vikas Publishing House: New Delhi).

Tomlinson, B.R. (1976), *The Indian National Congress and the Raj, 1929-1942* (Macmillan: London).

Tomlinson, B.R. (1979), *The Political Economy of the Raj, 1914-1947* (Macmillan: London).

Truman, David (1957), *The Governmental Process* (Knopf: New York).

Tyson, Geoffrey (1961), *Managing Agency: A System of Business Organisation* (Hoogly: Calcutta).

Ulyanovsky, R. and V. Pavlov (1975), *Asian Dilemma: The Essence of Social Progress in Transitional Period* (Progress Publishers: Moscow).

Venkatasubbiah, H. (1977), *Enterprise and Economic Growth: 50 Years of FICCI* (Vikas Publishing House: New Delhi).

Wadhva, Charan D. (ed.) (1977), *Some Problems of India's Economic Policy* (Tata McGraw-Hill: New Delhi).

Weiner, Myron (1957), *Party Politics in India: The Development of a Multi-Party System* (Princeton University Press: Princeton).

Weiner, Myron (1962), *The Politics of Scarcity: Public Pressure and Political Response in India* (University of Chicago Press: Chicago).

Weiner, Myron (1967), *Congress Party Elites* (Department of Government, Indiana University: Bloomington).

Zaidi A.M. and S.G. Zaidi (1979), *The Foundations of Indian Economic Planning* (S. Chand: New Delhi).

(3) Articles

Anonymous (1969), "Growth of Business Houses: Tatas, Birlas, Mafatlals", *Company News and Notes*, Annual No. 1, January 1969.

Arora, Dolly (1981), "Big Business, Influence-Generation and Decision-making in India", *Economic and Political Weekly*, 28 February, Review of Management.

Bhambhri, C.P. (1974), "Industrial Bourgeoisie and the Indian Political System", *Indian Journal of Public Administration*, July-September, pp. 576-593.

Finer, S.E. (1956), "The Federation of British Industries", *Political Studies*, Vol. IV, No. I, pp. 61-84.

Finer, S.E. (1958), "Review of V.O. Key Jr.'s, Politics, Parties and Pressure Groups", *Political Studies*, Vol. VI, pp. 265-266.

Gadgil, D.R. (1955), "Indian Economic Organisation", in Kuznets, Simon et. al. (eds.), *Economic Growth: Brazil, India, Japan* (Duke University Press: Durham), pp. 448-463.

Gadgil, D.R. (1977), "Planning without A Policy Frame", in Wadhva, C. D. (ed.), *Problems of India's Economic Policy* (Tata McGraw Hill: Bombay).

Garson, G. David (1974), "On the Origins of Interest Group Theory: A Critique of A Process", *American Political Science Review*, Vol. LXVIII, No. 4, 1505-1519.

Ghosh, Arabinda (1974), "Role of Large Industrial Houses in Indian Industries, 1946-68", *Indian Economic Journal*, May-June, pp. 313-345.

Ghosh, Arabinda (1975), "Concentration and Growth of Indian Industries, 1948-68, *The Journal of Industrial Economics*, Vol. XXIII, No. 3, pp. 203-222.

Goyal, S.K. (1971), "Joint Industrial Sector", Paper Presented at Seminar on, Industry and the Fourth Plan, University of Bombay, 29-31 March, mimeo.

Goyal, S.K. (9 May 1964) "Mahalanobis Report: A Critique", *Mainstream*.

Guha, Amalendu (1970), "The Comprador Role of Parsi Seths, 1750-1850", *Economic and Political Weekly*, 28 November, pp. 1933-1936.

Guha, Amalendu (1970), "Parsi Seths as Entrepreneurs, 1750-1850", *Economic and Political Weekly*, 29 August, M107-M115.

Hazari, R.K. (1958), "Inter-Corporate Investment: The Birla Group of Companies", *The Economic Weekly*, 6 November.

Hazari, R.K. (1960), "Ownership and Control", *The Economic Weekly*, 26 November, 3 December, 10 December.

Hazari, R.K. (1965), "The Great Escape: Concentration Good, Monopoly Justiciable", *The Economic Weekly*, 18 December.

Kannangara, A.P. (1968), "Indian Millowners and Indian Nationalism before 1914", *Past and Present*, No. 40, July, pp. 147-164.

Kochanek, Stanley A. (1970), Interest Groups and Interest Aggregation: Changing Patterns of Oligarchy in the FICCI", *Economic and Political Weekly*, Special No. July, pp. 1291-1308.

Kochanek, Stanley A. (1971), "The FICCI and Indian Politics", *Asian Survey*, Vol. XI, No. 9, September, pp. 866-885.

Krishna, Gopal (1966), "The Development of the Indian National Congress as a Mass Organization, 1918-1923", *Journal of Asian Studies*, Vol. XXVI, No. 3, May, pp. 413-430.

Lamb, Helen (1951), "Business Organisation and Leadership in India Today", in Park, Richard L. and Irene Tinker (eds.), *Leadership and Political Institutions in India* (Princeton University Press: Princeton), pp. 251-267.

Lamb, Helen (1955), "The Indian Business Communities and the Evolution of an Industrial Class", *Pacific Affairs*, Vol. XXVII, No. 2, June, pp. 101-116.

Malenbaum, Wilfred (1971), "Politics and Indian Business: The Economic Setting", *Asian Survey*, Vol. XI, No. 9, September, pp. 841-849.

Milbraith, Lester W. (1968), "Lobbying", *International Encyclopedia of*

Social Sciences, Vol. IX (Free Press: New York), pp. 441-442.

Mukherjee, Aditya (1976), "Indian Capitalist Class and the Public Sector", *Economic and Political Weekly*, 17 January.

Mukherjee, Aditya (1978), "Indian Capitalist Class and the Congress on National Planning and Public Sector, 1930-47", *Economic and Political Weekly*, 2 September.

Murti, B.V. Krishna (1960), "The Plan and the U Sector", *The Economic Weekly*, 24 September, pp. 1439-1440.

Namboodiripad, E. M. S. (1973), "On Intermediate Regimes", *Economic and Political Weekly*, 1st December, pp. 2133-2140.

Nayar, Baldev Raj (1971), "Business Attitudes towards Economic Planning in India", *Asian Survey*, Vol. XI, No. 9, September, pp. 850-865.

Paranjape, H.K. (1977), "Industrial Growth with Justice – India's Strategy", in Wadhva, Charan D. (ed.), *Some Problems of India's Economic Policy*, (Tata McGraw Hill: Bombay), pp. 325-355.

Prakash, V. (1966), "Industrial Concentration and Countervailing Powers", *Indian Economic Journal*, January-March, pp. 538-544.

Prakash, V. (1966), "Production Concentration and the Consumer – Comments on a Point Touched by the Monopolies Inquiry Commission", *Artha Vijnana*, June, pp. 172-185.

Ram, Bharat (1963), "Government and Private Sector", *Indian Journal of Public Administration*, July-September.

Sandesara, J.C. (1966), "A Critique of the Monopolies Commission's Report", *Indian Economic Journal*, April-June, pp. 688-708.

Shenoy, S.R. (1967), "A Note on Mr. Sandesara's Critique", *Indian Economic Journal*, April-June, pp. 657-661.

Index